Davidson
1995

DRAMA

IN EARLY TUDOR BRITAIN

1485–1558

DRAMA

in Early Tudor Britain

1485–1558

Howard B. Norland

University of Nebraska Press

Lincoln and London

Publication of this book was assisted
by a grant from
The Andrew W. Mellon Foundation.
Acknowledgments for the use of previously
published material appear on pages xiii–xv.
© 1995 by the University of Nebraska Press
All rights reserved
Manufactured in the United States of America
∞ The paper in this book meets
the minimum requirements of American National
Standard for Information
Sciences — Permanence of Paper for Printed Library
Materials, ANSI Z39.48-1984.
Library of Congress Cataloging in Publication Data
Norland, Howard B.
Drama in early Tudor Britain, 1485–1558 / Howard B. Norland.
p. cm.
Includes bibliographical references and index.
ISBN 0-8032-3337-X (cl)
1. English drama — Early modern and Elizabethan, 1500–1600 — History
and criticism. 2. English drama — Middle English, 1100–1500 — History
and criticism. I. Title.
PR646.N67 1995
822'.209 — dc20
94-12253
CIP

For Brenda

CONTENTS

Preface ix
Acknowledgments xiii
Introduction xvii
Abbreviations xxix

PART ONE: POPULAR DRAMATIC TRADITIONS

1. The Saints' Plays 3
2. The Civic Drama 16
3. The Morality Play before the Reformation 37
4. Folk Drama 48

PART TWO: CONTEMPORARY VIEWS OF DRAMA

5. The Terentian Commentaries 65
6. Erasmus 84
7. Vives 95
8. More 111
9. Attitudes of Reformers and Humanists 128

CONTENTS

PART THREE: THE SECULARIZATION OF THE MORALITY

10. The Prodigal Plays — 149
11. Redford's *Wit and Science* — 161
12. Skelton's *Magnificence* — 175
13. Bale's *King John* — 188
14. *Respublica* — 199
15. Lindsay's *Satire of the Three Estates* — 210

PART FOUR: THE DEVELOPMENT OF COMEDY

16. Medwall's *Fulgens and Lucres* — 233
17. *Calisto and Melebea* — 244
18. *Johan Johan* — 255
19. Udall's *Roister Doister* — 267
20. *Gammer Gurton's Needle* — 280

PART FIVE: THE EMERGENCE OF TRAGEDY

21. Watson's *Absalom* — 295
22. Christopherson's *Jephthah* — 307
23. Grimald's *Archipropheta* — 319

Conclusion — 335
Notes — 343
Works Cited — 359
Index — 383

PREFACE

*T*HIS book focuses on the major dramatic traditions that prevailed in Britain between the reigns of Richard III and Elizabeth I. A time of great social, economic, and intellectual change, after nearly a century of foreign wars and civil strife, the Tudor era also marked a significant transition in drama as the medieval traditions either adapted or gave way to a changing cultural context and a renewed interest in classical models. In accordance with the dominant critical theory of the period, represented by Horace, the late classical and Renaissance commentators on Terence, and the contemporary views of Erasmus and Vives, I examine the drama performed between 1485 and 1558 in relation to the genres that give the individual plays form and perspective. As Rosalie Colie points out, "literary invention — both 'finding' and 'making' — in the Renaissance was largely generic, and that transfer of ancient values was largely in generic terms, accompanied by generic instruments or helps" (17). Colie goes on to demonstrate that the most distinguished Renaissance poets exploited and adapted motifs and materials of several kinds of poetry in a single work while using a particular literary type as a guide.

Playwrights of early Tudor Britain seem to have operated in a similar manner, but because the older, native traditions of drama were being challenged by humanism, the new learning, and by Protestantism, the new religion, the system of modeling upon which generic traditions depend, as Bakhtin notes (Todorov 82–83), became particularly complex. A growing number of volumes in the *Records of Early English Drama*

(*REED*) series are providing detailed evidence of the extensiveness and durability of native drama as well as the ubiquity of itinerant professional players, but the new developments in dramatic production and composition in early Tudor Britain occurred in response to academic and political demands. In this context old forms were adapted to new ends as the morality play framework was accommodated to secular subjects and the ancient forms of comedy and tragedy were redefined for contemporary society.

The following chapters attempt to demonstrate this transition from essentially a local, popular, religious context to a more extensive and more varied secular orientation. The discussion of popular drama in part 1 is not meant to be an exhaustive analysis of individual works but rather is intended to characterize the nature and form of the native dramatic traditions in order to better understand how they affect the plays being composed and performed from Henry VII's reign through Mary's. Contemporary views of drama considered in part 2 should make clearer the assumptions and interpretations of drama instilled in students by their masters, but also the perceptions of the role of drama in education and in society by the most influential leaders of early Tudor Britain. The last three parts of this study concentrate on the plays created during this period. Part 3, dealing with the secularizing of the morality play, examines adaptations of moral allegory to educational concerns, political satire, and religious propaganda. The development of comedy traced in part 4 features key experiments in comic form as elements from both native and foreign models are adjusted to contemporary interests and expectations. The emergence of tragedy considered in part 5 demonstrates the integration of classical form with biblical content in three overlooked academic dramas of the 1540s.

Rather than offering a comprehensive survey of early Tudor drama, this study examines individual plays that represent variations in the principal dramatic traditions in early Tudor Britain. Heywood's debate plays, for example, are not included because they appear to be more literary than dramatic; and school dialogues such as *Thersites*, as well as court and civic pageants are outside the purview of this study because of their

PREFACE

quasi-dramatic nature. Though the plays that are examined in detail are considered in relation to their particular traditions, they are recognized as individual artistic efforts presented at a particular place and time. The context of the dramatic performance is regarded as especially important in evaluating the significance and effectiveness of the play.

Finally, the chapters of this book were written to be read in sequence or as individual units. Each chapter is designed to stand independently, though each is also a segment of a larger division. Cross-references to related material are included in order to facilitate readers' particular lines of inquiry. Quotations in foreign languages are translated for the sake of continuity except where the original foreign language is an issue, as, for example, in *Johan Johan*. Published translations are used when they are available; otherwise I have provided my own.

ACKNOWLEDGMENTS

*I*WISH especially to thank the publishers of journals and collections of papers for permission to include here revised versions of my previously published essays. Also to the following organizations I am indebted for providing a forum for oral presentation of aspects of this study as my research progressed: the International Association of Neo-Latin Studies; the Rocky Mountain Medieval and Renaissance Association; the Central Renaissance Conference; the International Congress on Medieval Studies at Kalamazoo; La Société internationale pour l'étude du Théâtre Médiéval; the International Congress on Patristic, Medieval, and Renaissance Studies; the Sixteenth Century Studies Conference; the Renaissance Conference of Southern California; the Pacific Northwest Renaissance Conference; and Le Colloque international d'études humanistes, Université François-Rabelais, Tours.

To the staffs of the following libraries I express my appreciation for their assistance in making my research pleasant and fruitful: the British Library, the University of London libraries, the Bodleian Library at Oxford, the Bibliothèque nationale, the Strahof and Charles University libraries in Prague, the Folger Shakespeare Library, the Huntington Library, the Newberry Library, the Beineke Library at Yale University, and the University of Toronto, McGill University, Université de Montréal, and University of Nebraska libraries. For financial support of my research, I thank the Folger Shakespeare Library for a fellowship that helped me launch my research on Tudor drama and dramatic theory several years ago, the University of Nebraska Research Council for con-

ACKNOWLEDGMENTS

tinuing support of my research through summer fellowships and grants, and the College of Arts and Sciences and the Department of English at the University of Nebraska for providing released time from teaching and travel funds to pursue my research.

Finally, I thank those who provided the inspiration, moral support, and assistance to bring this study to a conclusion. To Mark Eccles and Madeleine Doran, who at the University of Wisconsin first inspired my interest in Renaissance drama and whose published works continue to guide my critical judgment, I shall always be indebted. To the many scholars who have walked this way before me and whose ideas have informed my perceptions, I owe more than I can document. To Clifford Davidson and Thomas Berger for their invaluable advice on various points in my manuscript, I extend particular thanks. To Roma Rector, LeAnn Messing, and Linda Rossiter I offer thanks for their skill, endurance, and good humor in typing and correcting my manuscript in its various stages. To Genevieve, Timothy, Jean-Paul, and Caroline I express my appreciation for the moral support and understanding that allowed me to complete this work. Last of all, to my wife, Brenda Hosington, for her continuing inspiration, gentle criticism, and infinite patience, I owe the deepest gratitude.

Earlier versions of some chapters have been previously published:

Chapter 4, as "Folk Drama in Fifteenth- and Sixteenth-Century England," in *Le Thêâtre et la Cité dans l'Europe médiévale*, *Fifteenth Century Studies* 13 (1988): 321–34.

Chapter 6, as "The Role of Drama in Erasmus' Literary Thought," in *Acta Conventus Neo-Latini Bononiensis, Proceedings of the Fourth International Congress on Neo-Latin Studies* (Binghamton, New York: Medieval and Renaissance Texts and Studies, 1985), pp. 549–57. Reprinted with permission of the publisher.

Chapter 7, as "Vives' Critical View of Drama," in *Humanistica Lovaniensia, Journal of Neo-Latin Studies* 30 (1981): 93–107.

Chapter 8, as "The Role of Drama in More's Literary Career," in *The Sixteenth Century Journal* 13.4 (1982): 93–107.

ACKNOWLEDGMENTS

Chapter 11, as "The Dramatic Spectacle of Wit's Progress," in *Spectacle et Image dans l'Europe de la Renaissance*, ed. André Lascombes (Leiden: E. J. Brill, 1993).

Chapter 18, as "Formalizing English Farce: *Johan Johan* and Its French Connection," *Comparative Drama* 17 (1983): 141–52, and reprinted in *Drama in the Middle Ages, Comparative and Critical Essays*, Second Series, ed. Clifford Davidson and John H. Stroupe (New York: AMS Press, 1991), pp. 356–67.

Chapter 19, as "*Roister Doister* and the 'Regularizing' of English Comedy," in *Genre* 18 (1985): 323–34. Reprinted by permission of the University of Oklahoma.

Chapter 23, as "Grimald's *Archipropheta:* A Saint's Tragedy," in *The Journal of Medieval and Renaissance Studies* 14 (1984): 63–76. Reprinted by permission of the publisher. © 1984, Howard B. Norland.

INTRODUCTION

When Henry VII became king of England and Wales in August 1485, drama extended to all corners of the commonwealth and to every level of society. Not only were the representations of the miracles and martyrdoms of saints regularly performed in local parishes, but also the commemorations of Corpus Christi and other religious holidays were produced by guilds of artisans and merchants in cities throughout the kingdom. In addition, the bold adventures of the folk heroes Robin Hood and St. George were enacted at manor houses and village greens to celebrate Christmas, Shrovetide, and other festive occasions; and civic records indicate a growing number of professional players offered at guildhalls and innyards lessons in morality laced with passion, pathos, and crude jests. It would have been as difficult for a citizen of late-fifteenth-century Britain to escape drama as for a late-twentieth-century European or North American to avoid television. For the majority of the population at the beginning of the Tudor reign, drama was accessible in many forms; in a single community it might be possible within a year to attend a saints' play at the local parish church, Corpus Christi pageants on the market square, a professional morality or interlude at the guildhall, and a folk play on the village green.

With drama playing such a large part in the lives of British subjects, it is no wonder that the new king was regularly entertained at court by theatrical offerings prepared by William Cornish and others. Royal progresses generated masques and pageants as well as plays, and within a year of gaining the throne Henry was welcomed on a visit to York with a play by four clerks. In 1487, on his second visit to the city, he saw York's famous Corpus Christi cycle, and he also attended in the same year the Coventry Corpus Christi play, as his predecessor, Richard III, had done shortly before losing the crown two years earlier (Lancashire, *Dramatic Texts* xxiii and passim). Henry VII's personal support of drama is further indicated by his patronage of a company of adult players who performed primarily at court from 1494 until his death in 1509. The Gentlemen and Children of the Royal Chapel also received his support from 1501 to 1509. Henry VII's patronage of drama both by his attendance and by financial remuneration was carried on by his son, Henry VIII, and by his grandchildren Edward VI and Mary.

Henry VIII's adoption of a company of players began officially in 1494–95, when the Players of Lord Warden of Cinque Ports came under his protection, and his support continued into his kingship. His players, who split into two troupes between 1515 and 1521, performed regularly at court and throughout the kingdom. Henry VIII also maintained the Gentlemen and Children of the Royal Chapel until 1544. Edward VI, following in the family tradition, was as an infant named royal patron of a troupe of players, and he continued his protection of his company, which performed widely, through his six-year reign. His successor, Mary, from 1525 onward was official patron to the Princess's Players, who became the Queen's Players after her accession in 1553. Like her brother, Edward, Mary also provided periodic support of the Gentlemen and Children of the Royal Chapel. In addition to this pattern of patronage by the ruling monarchs, Henry VII's queen, Elizabeth of York, was the named patron of a company of players from 1492 until 1501, and all of Henry VIII's wives served for varying periods of time as royal protectors of playing companies.

The support of drama by the court extended to princes, royal protectors, and illegitimate sons of kings. Prince Arthur, the eldest son of Henry VII, served as patron of a company from 1494 until his early death in 1501, as both Henry VIII and Edward VI did while still princes. Both of Edward's lord protectors, the Duke of Somerset and the Duke of Northumberland, had players performing under their names while they

INTRODUCTION

presided over Edward's government; and the natural son of Henry VIII, Henry Fitzroy, as well as the natural son of Edward IV, Arthur Plantagenet, were patrons of strolling players. Various members of the early Tudor governments also took under their protection groups of players, including Thomas Howard, Lord Treasurer and Duke of Norfolk (1529–44); Thomas Seymour, Lord Admiral (1547–49); and Thomas Cromwell, Chancellor to Henry VIII, whose company performed from 1536 to 1540. Further support of the players came from various members of the nobility, such as the Earls of Arundell, who sponsored troupes from 1477 to 1544, and the Earls of Oxford, from 1492 to 1558.[1] The highest-ranking men and women of the kingdom provided moral and financial support of dramatic performance, though after the Reformation the plays became increasingly subject to censorship and governmental restrictions.

At the beginning of the Tudor era the only restraints to dramatic activity appear to have come from local authorities. City fathers might worry about drunkenness and immorality among the crowds attending Corpus Christi plays, and bishops might complain about gatherings for Robin Hood (see chapters 2 and 4), but for the most part the festive spirit associated with these dramatic performances was tolerated. As the "proclamation for whitsone plays" at Chester indicates, the plays were performed to increase the faith and devotion of the people, "but also for the comonwealth *and* prosperity of this Citty."[2] The commercial profit from the holiday gatherings was clearly recognized, though the justification was religious. The Lollard critic's charge in his *Tretise of Miraclis Pleyinge* that the saints' and scriptural plays were performed more "to plesyn the world" than to please God (43) may be true in some instances, but his argument that the plays were heretical and blasphemous in portraying sacred events was not widely endorsed by community or religious leaders, for the saints' plays flourished until the Reformation and the civic drama continued to be performed in many places into the late sixteenth century. Though it has been recently argued that their ultimate demise may have resulted more from aesthetic and commercial reasons than from governmental interference, censorship and declining local support brought the cycles to an end at Chester and York (see Woolf 312–23). Because the saints' and biblical civic plays were acted largely by amateurs, they provided opportunities for local citizens to participate in the drama, and the folk plays or mummings that survived in many places as late as the nineteenth and twentieth centuries afforded a more intimate dramatic experience for both performers and audience.

While folk, saints', and civic drama plays were being produced by amateurs in individual communities in early Tudor Britain, the tradition of traveling companies was evolving. Protected for the most part by aristocratic patrons, companies of actors consisting generally of four to six men and a boy or two proliferated in the late fifteenth and early sixteenth centuries. Mainly dependent on the money collected before or during performance, these wandering players offered drama that would meet the moral standards of the town councillors, who typically vetted the performances before presentation to the community, and still attract an audience willing to pay the price of admission. Although most of the entertainments offered by these touring companies have not survived, those that have indicate a compromise between didactic instruction and the perennial ingredients of popular entertainment: pathos and humor.

Morality plays, which in some instances may have been written for religious communities or schools, offered an adaptable vehicle for these professionals, because realistic and emotional dimensions could be elaborated, and jests could be readily inserted into the action. The late-fifteenth-century morality *Mankind* offers an early example of the type. As the sixteenth century proceeded, these popular moralities reflected change in audience taste and religious beliefs as the pre-Reformation youth-oriented moralities like *Hickscorner* gave way to prodigal plays and more secular entertainments in the mid-century (see chapters 3 and 10). As Craik in *The Tudor Interlude* and Bevington in *From "Mankind" to Marlowe* indicate in their earlier studies of the stagecraft and repertoires of these professional companies, the troupes offered a significant alternative to the amateur productions staged by the local citizens.

A new dimension to drama was introduced into early Tudor Britain by humanists who brought from the Continent an enthusiasm for classical languages and learning. With the adoption of the Roman playwright Terence in the grammar school curriculum as a model of Latin style came an intensive study of dramatic dialogue. Using the commentaries of the fourth-century grammarians—Donatus, Evanthius, and Diomedes—as guides, Renaissance scholars and schoolmasters published additional annotations about rhetorical, moral, and dramaturgical aspects of the Terentian texts used in the schools. Terence remained in most places an obligatory author and the favorite dramatist in the school curriculum through the sixteenth century, though selected comedies of Plautus and tragedies of Seneca were added in both schools and universities (see chapter 5). Drama thus became a major means of teaching Latin in Renaissance Britain as on the Continent.

Significantly the leading humanist, Erasmus, was not only personally fond of drama, especially Terence, but he also argued that Terence's comedies, which he interpreted in Donatian terms, were particularly attractive to and beneficial for students (see chapter 6). When Erasmus himself embarked on the study of Greek, he chose the work of the playwright Euripides as his master text and translated the tragedies *Hecuba* and *Iphigenia at Aulis* into Latin to perfect his knowledge of the Greek language. Erasmus's influence on Colet's refounded St. Paul's School and on other humanist programs in early-sixteenth-century Britain, as well as on such leading English humanists as Thomas More, is well known, but also important was the more cautious and critical view of drama expressed by the famous Spanish humanist Vives, who in the late 1520s was an influential adviser to Queen Catherine of Aragon and the Princess Mary as well as a respected scholar in university circles (see chapter 7). For the most part, humanists in England, including Thomas Elyot and Thomas Wilson, followed More in promoting classical drama as an especially effective means of teaching rhetorical skills and sound moral values, though detractors like the German critic of humanism Cornelius Agrippa struck a sympathetic chord among English reformers who worried about the Terentian examples of sexual license and rebellion against parental authority (see chapters 8 and 9). Concerns about the immorality of classical drama led to the creation of dramatic alternatives first to Terence and later to Seneca that were designed to reflect the Christian values of sixteenth-century society (see chapters 10 and 21). The model could be altered, but the method of using plays to teach language, rhetoric, and morality remained the same.

An important part of this instruction involved the performance of plays. Erasmus, representing humanist pedagogy, advocated dramatic performance as a means of developing oratorical skills not only by training the memory but also by practicing pronunciation of the Latin. To supplement the plays, both Erasmus and Vives wrote dialogues as exercises to improve schoolboys' mastery of colloquial Latin. In addition to classroom practices, dramatic performance may have become a regular feature in the study of Latin in the schools as it was at the universities. At Cambridge, classical comedies were performed from the first decade of the sixteenth century onward, and several of the colleges there formalized the practice. A comedy of Terence was staged at King's Hall, Cambridge, in 1510–11, according to college records, though undefined "ludi" were performed earlier, in 1503–4, 1507–8, and 1508–9 (*REED: Cambridge* 2: 711–12 and passim). Another Terentian comedy was acted at King's Hall in 1516–17; Queens' College, Cambridge, presented a comedy by Plautus in 1522–23; and other Cambridge colleges followed the pattern. Christ's College performed plays annually beginning in 1530–31, and St. John's followed the same practice from 1534–35, though occasional performances at St. John's had begun as early as 1524–25. Some colleges, including Queens', later mandated two plays a year, while others designated a distribution of tragedies and comedies and required as many as five or six plays annually, as at Trinity and St. John's in the middle of the sixteenth century.

The majority of the plays staged were classical, though both Latin and Greek plays by contemporary authors were also performed. Only a few plays in English were presented. The pedagogical purpose of the performances appears to have been dominant in the selection of the plays, but the direct involvement of both masters and students in the presentation of ancient and modern drama enhanced their practical

INTRODUCTION

knowledge of dramaturgy as well as their rhetorical skills. In addition to observing the amateur and professional drama in their local communities, the playwrights who emerged in the sixteenth century in Britain received obligatory classroom instruction in classical drama, as well as the opportunity in school or university to participate in dramatic performance.

Humanist instruction in classical drama began to affect the form of plays composed in Britain only in the second quarter of the sixteenth century, though at the beginning of the century humanist educational and social values began to be reflected. However, for the first forty years of Tudor rule the popular traditions afforded the major dramatic models, if not the content. The foremost model was the morality play, the last of the religious dramatic genres to evolve, and because of its adoption by the professional touring companies perhaps the most ubiquitous in the early sixteenth century. It was also the most flexible, for not only could it readily accommodate the elaboration of dramatic pathos and improvisational humor, but its subject matter could also be adapted to changing dramatic contexts and religious beliefs. Medwall's *Nature* and Rastell's *Nature of the Four Elements* at the turn of the century indicate a shift away from the conventional allegorical instruction of the Christian to seek salvation before death overtakes him. Medwall and Rastell, demonstrating the humanist emphasis on learning as the basis for a rewarding and virtuous life in this world, put new wine in the old morality bottle (see chapter 3); and as the sixteenth century proceeded, education became an increasingly important subject of plays written for schoolboys but also for those performed in the court and in the innyards and guildhalls by the professional actors, as versions of *Wit and Science* demonstrate (see chapter 11).

This concern with education secularized the morality framework and, incorporated with the prodigal son pattern, provided a moral alternative to Terence, as, for example, in the play *Acolastus* (see chapter 10). Another type of secularization of the morality is represented by the political allegories intended to instruct ruling monarchs and their counselors. Beginning with Skelton's *Magnificence* and continuing with Bale's *King John*, the anonymous *Respublica*, and Lindsay's *Satire of the Three Estates*, this adaptation of the morality also incorporated elements from other popular traditions and from classical drama as the plays commented on contemporary political and religious issues. Though retaining the framework of the morality, the allegory serves as a vehicle for social satire and religious reform. In spite of its essential paradigm of temptation-fall-redemption, the very looseness of morality play structure made possible an endless number of variations (see chapters 12–15).

The study of the comedies of Terence and Plautus in the schools and universities only gradually influenced dramatic composition. Rather, the native tradition, exemplified by comic incidents in civic drama and by the coarse humor of the popular moralities, dominated plays composed in the early sixteenth century. However, elements that later distinguished Renaissance English comedy became apparent in the first purely secular English play to survive intact, Medwall's *Fulgens and Lucres* (ca. 1497). Anticipating the romantic comedy of Lyly and Shakespeare, Medwall integrated *controversia*, a form adapted from classical rhetoric, with the wooing motif of folk drama, the *débat* of medieval poetry, and elements of the morality play (see chapter 16). *Calisto and Melebea*, a dramatic adaptation of Rojas's novel in dialogue popularly known as *Celestina*, which Rojas had himself linked to classical comedy, represents another experiment in early English comedy. Imposing a moral tone and moral ending on the Spanish original, the unknown English adapter averted the tragic conclusion of Rojas's novel but also reduced the comic dimensions of the roguish central character, Celestina (see chapter 17). The anonymous *Johan Johan*, an Anglicized version of a French farce, demonstrates great skill in accommodating another foreign model to an English audience. Though this play, published by Rastell in 1533, cannot truly be counted an English comedy, it served as a precedent for the incorporation of French farce in later Renaissance English drama (see chapter 18).

Only in the middle of the century did the classical models and the Terentian commentaries become truly formative influences in the composition of English comedy. In *Roister Doister* (1551–53), the schoolmaster Udall blended Terentian form with Aristophanic satiric motifs, but like his predecessors, he grounded his action in an English context and extended the satire through burlesque (see chapter 19). *Gammer Gurton's Needle*, written at about the same time for performance at Christ's College, Cambridge, adapted the conventions of classical Latin drama to contemporary English village life by blending elements of the French farce, the jestbook, and the morality play (see chapter 20). These mid-century academic dramas, traditionally considered to be the first "regular" English comedies (see, e.g., Baldwin, *Shakspere's Five-Act Structure* 380), demonstrate the early Tudor penchant for adapting foreign models to the native cultural context by integrating elements from popular traditions.

Like comedy, formal tragedy arose in early Tudor Britain out of the humanist education that promoted the study of classical drama as a means of inculcating virtue and cultivating eloquence (see chapter 21). The first reference to the performance of a tragedy appears in the accounts for Christ's College, Cambridge, in 1537–38 (Moore Smith 50), nearly thirty years later than the first allusion to the performance of a Terentian comedy; but within a half-dozen years of this date, the composition of formal tragedies in England began. Watson's Latin *Absalom* and Christopherson's Greek *Jephthah*, which was also translated by its author into Latin, were written by members of St. John's College, Cambridge, apparently for performance by students. Though their colleague Roger Ascham indicated an interest in Aristotelian theory at St. John's during this period (50), neither Watson nor Christopherson was guided by Aristotle's conception of tragedy; Watson in fact used principles of the Terentian commentator Donatus in structuring his tragedy. Both Watson and Christopherson depended primarily on classical models in transforming biblical narrative to tragic form; Watson followed Seneca in style and characterization as well as in focusing on the motifs of ambition and revenge, but he Christianized Seneca's stoicism. Christopherson imitated Euripides's *Iphigenia at Aulis* in dramatizing the daughter's sacrifice but transformed the characters into moral exemplars (see chapters 21–22). Nicholas Grimald at Oxford a few years later provided an alternative image of biblical tragedy. Representing John the Baptist as an archetypal reformer, Grimald fused elements of the Corpus Christi and saints' play traditions with the language and form of classical tragedy to create in his Latin *Archipropheta* a drama that anticipated the tragedies of Marlowe and Shakespeare (see chapter 23). Grimald's Reformation tragedy was published in Cologne in 1548, while the academic dramas of Watson and Christopherson remained in manuscript until the twentieth century, perhaps in part because of their authors' staunch Catholicism. These three plays, largely overlooked by modern critics and historians of British drama, offer three distinct and remarkably skillful experiments in formulating tragedy in England some twenty years before Britain's "first" English tragedy, *Gorboduc*, was composed by Sackville and Norton.

As this sketch of drama in Tudor Britain between Henry VII's acquisition of the crown in 1485 and Elizabeth's accession in 1558 indicates, and as subsequent chapters will demonstrate, the number and variety of dramatic performances that were available to the populace are amazing. The popular medieval traditions of the saints' and biblical civic plays flourishing at the beginning of the Tudor era continued to offer inspiration to new playwrights long after the number and frequency of performance began to wane. Folk plays remained a vital influence on both popular and learned drama through the period as their performance continued unabated. Morality drama proved to be the most adaptable and provided a form for secular as well as religious issues, but it also offered motifs and character types to be incorporated into the rediscovered and reshaped comedy and tragedy before being subsumed by the renewed ancient forms. The plays composed in early Tudor Britain integrated elements from several traditions, and even when a single classical or contemporary play or playwright provides a model, the sixteenth-century British author adapted, selected, and invented material gathered from a variety of sources in order to create a distinctive work. This kind of innovation illustrates the Renaissance concept of imitation in its best sense, but the final result appears to have been determined more by the context of performance and intuitive art than by

INTRODUCTION

inherited critical theory. The study of Terence and Seneca with the guidance of classical and contemporary commentators made the Renaissance schoolboy more aware of the details of dramaturgy, but when he later came to write his own comedy or tragedy, he also remembered the popular drama that had surrounded him from his birth.

ABBREVIATIONS

CompD	*Comparative Drama*
DNB	*Dictionary of National Biography*
fol.	folio sheet
JEGP	*Journal of English and Germanic Philology*
JMRS	*Journal of Medieval and Renaissance Studies*
MLN	*Modern Language Notes*
MLR	*Modern Language Review*
MP	*Modern Philology*
N&Q	*Notes and Queries*
n.s.	new series
OED	*Oxford English Dictionary*
PMLA	*Publications of the Modern Language Association*
PQ	*Philological Quarterly*
REED	*Records of Early English Drama*
RenD	*Renaissance Drama*
RES	*Review of English Studies*
s.d.	stage direction (line numbers are from editions in list of cited works)
sig.	signature (a gathering of pages in printed text)
SP	*Studies in Philology*
TLS	*Times Literary Supplement*

PART ONE

POPULAR DRAMATIC TRADITIONS

CHAPTER ONE

THE SAINTS' PLAYS

*E*XTENDING from at least the early twelfth century until well into the sixteenth, saints' plays appear to be among the oldest and most widely known drama in Britain. Performed in London and provincial towns throughout England, Scotland, and Wales, lives of saints as diverse as Catherine, Clotilda, Swithin, Laurence, Eustace, Denys, Susannah, Thomas Becket, George, and Mary Magdalene provided entertainment and edification on the days the church had designated the saints should be honored.[1] References to thirty-eight different saints, of which only six (Mary Magdalene, Paul, Andrew, James, the Blessed Virgin Mary, and Thomas the Apostle) are biblical, and sixty-six different plays have so far been discovered in extant records (Wasson, "Secular Saint Plays" 241). For the period from 1485 to 1558, at least twenty-two different plays involving fourteen saints have been identified.[2] Unfortunately, however, because the veneration of saints was one of the targets of reformist legislation under Henry VIII and Edward VI, the texts of all but a few of the plays have disappeared.

Only three complete texts of saints' plays have survived in Britain: two in the Digby manuscript dating from the early sixteenth century—*Mary Magdalene* and *The Conversion of St. Paul*—and the third, *Beaunans Meriasek*, in a Cornish manuscript dated 1504. *Mary Magdalene* and *The Conversion of St. Paul* probably owe their survival to their atypicality, which made them palatable to the English reformers (Bevington, *Medieval Drama* 662), in that Mary Magdalene and Paul were traditional examples of the redeemed sinner. The extant play of Mary Magdalene may in fact have been altered to fit the reformist perspective, with the morality-play conversion of Mary being grafted onto her biblical role and her subsequent career as a missionary saint, drawn from *The Golden Legend*, a traditional source for the saints' plays.[3] More typical of the saints' plays, as we can formulate the type from dramatic records in Britain and from an examination of contemporary French examples, is the less well known Cornish play, *Beaunans Meriasek*. This text, like the Digby saints' plays, represents a late development of the form, but considered along with the Digby texts and extant dramatic records, *Beaunans Meriasek* should help us to clarify the nature of the genre and its influence on later drama.

Saints' legends were, of course, popular for hundreds of years before they were given dramatic form.[4] The lives of those who witnessed their faith in the face of physical danger and death in the early years of the church had long provided models for godliness as well as spellbinding narratives of fabulous action. Caxton, in the preface to his translation of *The Golden Legend* in 1483, expresses the traditional didactic import of the saints' legends; he explains that he has made the work available "that it prouffyte to alle them that shal rede or here it redde / and may encreace in them vertue / and expelle vyce and synne / that by the ensaumple of the holy sayntes amende theyr lyvyng here in this shorte lyf / that by their merytes / they and I may come to everlastyng lyf & blysee in heuen."

The transformation of the legends from narrative to dramatic form may have developed out of the "farced epistle" in the church liturgy, as E. Catherine Dunn argues, because the speaker chanting the tropes in a celebration of a saint's feast assumes "a role in a fictive impersonation" as the martyrdom of the saint is evoked (9). However, the dramatic prototype of the saints' play existed at least as early as the tenth century in the nun Hroswitha's alternative to the classical Terence. Though her expressed object, "to glorify . . . the laudable chastity of Christian virgins" (*Plays* xxvi) for girlish charges, concentrates on a single virtue and represents fictional characters rather than legendary saints, the triumph of virtue in the most perilous circumstances, often through miraculous

4

means, is the customary pattern of her plays. Also the violence of the persecution, characteristic of the saints' legends and of medieval French saints' plays, is given a prominent place as well as "the dreadful frenzy of those possessed by unlawful love, and the insidious sweetness of passion" that brought "a blush to the cheek" of the chaste Hroswitha (*Plays* xxvii). A major difference, of course, between Hroswitha's plays and the saints' plays is the absence of ministering in imitation of Christ, an essential element of the saints' play, as we shall see. Most important, however, Hroswitha's "Christianized Terence" exploits man's and woman's perennial fascination for the marvelous and the perilous as it instructs its audience in the power of God, just as the saints' plays do.

How effectively the saints' plays accomplished these ends is indicated by a Wycliffite reformer's *Tretise of Miraclis Pleyinge* written near the end of the fourteenth century. Objecting to "miraclis of Crist and of hise seintis" being used "in bourde and pleye," the reformer describes "men and wymmen, seinge the passioun of Crist and of hise seinties, . . . movyd to compassion and devocion, wepinge bitere teris" (35–39). He decries such emotion as false because it is evoked by a mere illusion and because it arises more out of "compassion of peine" than out of the audience's realization of their own sins (43). Throughout this discussion, Christ and "hise seintis" are linked, which not only emphasizes the saints' imitation of Christ but also suggests that the indictment of religious drama under the general heading of miracle plays includes both saints' plays and plays depicting the ministry and passion of Christ usually associated with the biblical civic drama. This eyewitness account of a contemporary audience's response to martyrdom in performance implies a realistic portrayal of the sufferings and violent deaths of the saints, like the crucifixion of Christ in the York cycle and the hanging of faithful Christians in *Beaunans Meriasek*. Contemporary French drama, such as the *Mystère des trois doms* or *Mystère de Saint Denys*, may provide comparable examples. The fascination with torture and painful death must have contributed greatly to the audience appeal of the plays.

Although none of the surviving British texts represents the martyrdom of a saint, contemporary allusions and dramatic records indicate martyrdom to be a standard element of the saints' plays. In a preface to his *Life of St. Thomas à Becket* (ca. 1170–82), which includes the first allusion to saints' plays in England, William Fitzstephen identifies their subject matter as miracles and martyrdom.[5] The large number of plays about the English patron saint, St. George, which appear in some places to have degenerated into mummings, and about England's most famous martyr, St. Thomas Becket, attest to patriotic sentiments but also to an appetite for the marvelous and perilous. Interest in the spectacular moment of the miracle or of the agony of persecution is further demonstrated, of course, in the medieval and early Renaissance art depicting the ministry and passion of Christ and the miracles and martyrdom of saints in English as well as continental churches.[6] The Wycliffite critic of miracle plays, calling painting a "deed bok" and drama a "quick" one, expresses the greater capacity of the dramatized image to move the audience (*Tretise* 40), which in his view enhances its danger in distracting man from the true value of the works and word of God.

Whether the remarkable feats represented on the stage are miracles or martyrdoms, they are superhuman events enacted in a human context with which the audience can readily identify. Mary Magdalene's first miracle, for example, is set in homely circumstances. The appearance of the ship that is to carry Mary to Marseilles is accompanied by a "mery song" (*Digby Plays*, s.d. 1394),[7] which is followed by a comic beating of the shipman's boy for refusing to get dinner. When Mary moments later is challenged by a boasting King of Marseilles to demonstrate her God's might in the pagan temple, she causes an idol to "trembyll and quake," and a cloud to "comme . . . from heven, *and* set þe tempyl on afyer" (s.d. 1552–61). This miracle is made more striking by the realistic comic scene and vaunting dialogue that precede it. Similarly in *Beaunans Meriasek*, Meriasek's first demonstration of his special calling, the curing of a blind man and a cripple, follows the playing of a melody and a lengthy and prosaic attempt by his father and King Conan to persuade young Meriasek to marry. Again ordinary human concerns provide a context for the superhuman event.

The special calling of the saint sets him or her apart from ordinary men and women and their mundane concerns. The saints' play, therefore, represents an exemplary pattern of action that is essentially different from the morality drama. Unlike the morality, which offers a cautionary exemplum of generic man, the saints' play extends and repeats the example of Christ as it attests to the faith of individual men and women and their consequent investment with God's power. The morality play seeks an identification with the audience, who witness the universal pattern of temptation and sin followed by penitence and redemption, though with the grim warning of damnation for those who do not repent. The conflict waged over the soul of man is conceived in the realm of spirits who manifest themselves as vices and virtues, archetypal forms of motivation and behavior. The morality is thus essentially a play staged in the mind and encompasses all of mankind. It is, as a result, both symbolical and ahistorical. The saints' play, on the other hand, is grounded in history in that it focuses on particular persons who, it is supposed, lived at a particular time; but because each saint exemplifies the role of Christ in this world, he or she repeats the pattern of Christ. Therefore, in spite of individual variations, the repetition or reenactment of Christ's ministry on earth creates a recurrent pattern.[8]

This tends to soften the contours of the lives of individual saints and at the same time to invite the accretion of events that appear to have no historical basis. This tendency is frankly acknowledged by Reginald of Canterbury in his preface to his *Life of St. Malchus*: "If I ran across a good story anywhere," says Reginald, "I included it; for *all things are common in the communion of saints*. Since Malchus was just, saintly, loved by Christ and full of the very essence of righteousness, I do not deviate from the truth, no matter what miracles I ascribe to Malchus, even though they were manifested only in some other saint" (quoted in Charles Jones 61). Every saint is like Christ and every other saint in that each witnesses his faith in God and is invested with God's power. The similarities in the miracles performed prove their communion. This is evident in *The Golden Legend* and in *Mary Magdalene* and *Beaunans Meriasek*.

The commonality of legendary material as well as the absence of biblical authority for details in the lives of many of the saints created fewer restrictions for the authors of saints' plays than for the writers of biblically based civic drama. At the same time, the saint lore provided a wealth of examples of the marvelous and the perilous that could be readily turned into drama. Still, the informing principle of the saints as symbols of God's ministry in the fallen world focuses on faith as manifested in works in contrast to the reformist emphasis on the grace of God. Consequently what emerges is a chronological pattern of action replete with conflict, spectacle, and triumph. Apparently a number of the saints' plays, following the pattern of the narrative legends, began with the portrayal of the saint before his dedication to God. Both *The Conversion of St. Paul* and *Mary Magdalene* represent their protagonists in a pre-Christian state and then show their conversion. In the case of Mary Magdalene, her earlier condition is elaborated by the imposition of the morality pattern of temptation and sin; repentance then occurs through the direct ministry of Christ. Her conversion is made especially spectacular by Christ's exorcism of her seven devils (identified with the seven deadly sins) at the house of Simon the Leper.

Conversion offered an obvious opportunity for high drama, as evidenced also in *The Conversion of St. Paul*, but it was clearly not an essential part of the pattern of the saints' play. *Beaunans Meriasek* suggests the early life of St. Meriasek in a conversation with his parents about schooling, but from the beginning Meriasek's piety is indicated by his determination on Fridays to pray and to eat and drink little. A short time later he vows never to marry; instead he will become a knight of God in spite of family pressure to take a wife. At the conclusion of this scene the stage direction notes that "her meriasek weryth a prest ys govn" (s.d. 510).[9] What this suggests is that the crucial step for the saint is not conversion but dedication to the ministry of Christ, and it is dramatically marked. Rather than being histrionically portrayed, it is symbolized here by a change in costume.

It is the representation of the ministry that particularly distinguishes the saints' play from other religious drama, and it is this stage that offered the most spectacular opportunities for the marvelous and the perilous. The ministry of St. Paul is suggested at the third (and last) station in *The Conversion of St. Paul* by Paul's sermon on pride and the other deadly sins, but unlike most saints' plays that survived in Britain and France, the ministry of Paul is not manifested by his performance of miracles. However, Paul's life is threatened as a result of his belief, a frequent motif in saints' legends in anticipation of the martyrdom that many suffer.

In *Mary Magdalene*, the ministry of Mary is much more fully developed. After her biblical role has been completed, she in typical saintly fashion is sent as a missionary to Marseilles, where in spite of mockery and threats to her safety she preaches the wonders of God's creation and performs her first miracle, noted above, causing an idol to shake and the heathen temple to catch fire. Her second miracle is less dramatically spectacular but even more significant, for she causes the sterile queen to conceive. The effect of these miracles is the conversion of the king and his queen to Christianity. This traditional demonstration of God's power in the saints' plays often convinces even the most sinful unbeliever to accept Christ and serves as a paradigm to the audience for a reaffirmation of their faith. The conversion is often symbolized on stage by baptism, though it may be simply expressed by a verbal commitment. This pattern is complicated in *Mary Magdalene* by the king's determination to be baptised by St. Peter. The baptism is shown a short time later, but not before the queen dies in childbirth after insisting on accompanying her husband to the Holy Land. This event provides another opportunity for the miraculous, as the queen and her child are later restored to life through the intervention of Mary Magdalene. Curiously this miracle is not represented on stage but is narrated by the queen, who also describes her subsequent visit to Christ's sepulchre and other sites, as well as her baptism by St. Peter. Not designed to promote conversion, this miracle, imitating Christ's raising of Lazarus (Mary's brother in this play and in medieval legend), manifests God's concern for the faithful. The effect on the king is to strengthen his faith, which he demonstrates by building churches. Mary's ministry, though occupying only about one-third of the drama, conveys the essential pattern of the saints' play.

The ministry of St. Meriasek is even more fully elaborated in *Beau-*

nans Meriasek. Almost immediately after Meriasek puts on the priest's gown, he proves his special calling by restoring sight to a blind man and curing a cripple. Meriasek then proceeds from Brittany to Cornwall, where he performs more miracles, which in turn prompts a confrontation with Teudar, the ruling heathen lord. Like Paul and Mary Magdalene, Meriasek preaches a sermon centering on Christ's birth and death; but the Christian message falls on deaf ears, and Meriasek is threatened with torture if he will not deny Christ and worship "Mahond." After hiding under a rock, which thenceforward would be known as Meriasek's rock, Meriasek escapes to Britanny, where he miraculously tames a wolf that has been ravaging the countryside. Meriasek's peril is mirrored by the treatment of an earl and a doctor who refuse to deny Christ when threatened by the emperor Constantine and are hanged and then viciously run through with swords. After the archangels Michael and Gabriel bring the souls of these martyrs to Jesus in heaven, the ministry of Silvester comes into the foreground. Miraculously healing the leprous Constantine at the instruction of Jesus, Silvester baptises Constantine as a "splendor lucis" appears (s.d. 1835).

St. Silvester thus converts a heathen tyrant after St. Meriasek had failed, but Meriasek, having adopted a hermit's life, demonstrates his divine power by performing many miracles. He symbolically formalizes his ministry by accepting a bishopric after conventionally refusing it twice. Most of Meriasek's miracles are of a healing nature, and additional miracles are accomplished in the play by St. Silvester and the Blessed Virgin Mary in sequences of action that do not involve St. Meriasek. Most of this 4,600-line play, performed in two parts on successive days, is in fact devoted to the ministry of the saints as manifested in miracles, many of which are spectacularly represented. St. Silvester, for example, overcomes a fire-breathing dragon, after two magicians fall to the ground in fear, in an action that recalls St. George; and the Virgin Mary, responding to a grieving mother's prayer, descends with two angels in a blinding radiance and frees a young man from prison, which she sets on fire. What proves sainthood is the performance of miracles. As the Agnate in the play says of Meriasek, "If he were not a true saint / So many miracles clearly / He would never work" (2051–53).

The saints' investment with divine power entails a special relationship with God and the communion of saints and is often visibly portrayed in production. This may take the form of direct commerce with the divinity (usually in the form of Christ), angels, apostles, and the Virgin Mary, as the saints are given instruction or their prayers are answered. This special relationship is elaborated in *Mary Magdalene* after Mary goes into the wilderness to live free from sin; she is described in a stage direction as being taken up into the clouds and given heavenly food (s.d. 2018). This special treatment continues until Mary's death, when her soul is received by angels as her body is reverently buried. At St. Meriasek's death, Jesus dispatches angels to fetch Meriasek's soul, and Meriasek also receives a public tribute when those who have benefitted by his ministry gather to praise him. They emphasize his piety by pointing to his mortification of the flesh, as evidenced by his hair shirt, and to his abstemiousness; and they declare that he, like Mary Magdalene, has been nourished with angels' food. In addition, at his death he promises aid to those who pray to him. A house is to be established to honor him in Cornwall, even though his body will lie in another place, and the first Friday in June is designated his annual feast day. These details at the end of the play clearly indicate the occasion and purpose of the play's performance as the Cornish community celebrates its patron saint, but the extension of the saint's ministry after death is also stressed. The deaths of both Mary Magdalene and Meriasek are perceived as rewards for their faith as manifested by their works, and they join permanently the communion of saints.

The deaths of martyrs, such as St. George and Thomas Becket, were probably represented with their souls being brought to heaven as the souls of Mary Magdalene, St. Meriasek, and the Christian martyrs are represented in the first part of *Beaunans Meriasek*. However, the martyrdom would have made the ends of St. George and St. Thomas Becket even more spectacular as good triumphs over evil. Whether the saints die peacefully among friends or violently among enemies, their deaths are conceived as occasions for celebration.

The celebratory nature of the plays does not encourage individual characterization of the saints or the figures with which they have contact. The conventionality and commonality of the action make the saints appear to be very similar in spite of differences in historical place and time. More symbolic than real, they manifest the same virtues and values that set them apart from the world, but the worlds from which they are set apart are also remarkably similar. Stock figures of the tyrant and infidel, whether in biblical Damascus or medieval Cornwall, are boastful and threatening. Caesar, Herod, Pilate, and the King of Marseilles (initially) in *Mary Magdalene* share a high regard for their personal power and a hatred of Christians with Teudar of Cornwall, Constantine in Rome, and the tyrant whose prisoner is freed by the Virgin Mary in *Beaunans Meriasek*. The evil adversaries are as like to one another as the saints are to each other. Generic types fill out the human context, but they are conceived in functional terms. Cripples, blind men, mothers, magicians, or bishops owe their existence in a play to their interaction with a saint, and they are only most cursorily sketched. Historical figures such as Lazarus and Martha are no more clearly distinguished than generic types. Angels, apostolic saints, demons, and devils complete the context, and as in other religious drama of the time, they freely intermingle with the human characters. These allegorical figures, by nature one-dimensional, fetch and carry or complain and rejoice according to the orders of their masters and the demands of the saints. The world of the saints' play is peopled by shadows whose presence is necessary to reflect the glory of God in the heirs of his Son.

The cast of characters and the episodes selected for performance apparently depended upon the inherited lore and the invention of the authors, but in *Mary Magdalene* and *Beaunans Meriasek*, characters and episodes are introduced from diverse sources, giving the plays a patchwork effect. *Mary Magdalene* has long been regarded as a hybrid play, combining elements of the three major forms of medieval drama — the cycle, the morality, and the saints' play. The first part includes several scenes that resemble cycle drama, such as scenes 4, 5, 15, 18, 25, and 28, dealing with figures and incidents related to Christ's ministry, his crucifixion and resurrection, and the continuing ministry of the apostles.

Glynne Wickham argues that "an extensive stock of existing scenic units" have been adapted to "a new purpose" ("Staging of Saint Plays" 112–13), and Hardin Craig notes the difference in style between the parts that resemble cycle drama and the romantic parts drawn from *The Golden Legend* (*English Religious Drama* 316). In addition, Mary Magdalene's temptation, her fall into sin, and her redemption, as well as some scenes involving the devils, appear to be inspired by the morality play.

Beaunans Meriasek also contains elements from three distinct sources: the legend of St. Meriasek, the legend of St. Silvester, and the legendary story of the Virgin Mary's rescue of a youth imprisoned by a tyrant. These three narratives may be "unskilfully pieced together," as the translator Stokes notes (*Beaunans Meriasek* viii), but the method of composition appears to be similar to the one underlying *Mary Magdalene*. The saints' plays, like the legends, appear to be eclectic; when the particular legend of a saint did not provide sufficient opportunities for dramatic representation, other sources were readily utilized.

The structure invited variety and theatricality, yet it provided a kind of unity through the informing presence of the saint. In *Mary Magdalene*, the author rather ingeniously weaves together those biblical incidents that became associated with Mary Magdalene during the medieval period (see Garth 19) and thus provides a context for her relationship with Christ, which is extended in Mary's ministry in the latter part of the play. One might object on the grounds of organic unity to the inclusion of the vaunting speeches of Caesar, Herod, and Pilate, but as one critic has noted, they relate to the theme of sovereignty, which he believes pervades the play (Velz, "Sovereignty" 32–43). Another modern scholar finds "verbal and scenic coherence" established in the play through the recurrent motifs of "banqueting and nourishment and clothing" (Coletti, "Design" 313–33), and a third scholar suggests that the play is unified by the recurring movement from darkness to light, which is further strengthened by light imagery (Maltman 1:257–80). Whether or not the author of *Mary Magdalene* consciously sought to unify the play by any of these means, there is no doubt that he or she rather ingeniously integrated the morality pattern into the biblical context, which introduces a realistic element into the sacred story and humanizes the prospective saint. As a result, Mary becomes an identifiable model of the penitent who later becomes invested with the power of God.

Beaunans Meriasek, also, can be faulted for not fusing the diverse stories into a unified whole. The action involving St. Silvester is dropped into the story of St. Meriasek without warning and occupies our attention for a considerable period of time. Much later a connection is made between the saints: When Meriasek is appointed bishop, a message is anachronistically sent to Pope Silvester, who lived several centuries earlier. Otherwise the lines of action are quite independent of each other. The connection with the Virgin Mary's miraculous rescue of the imprisoned youth is also very tangential. Meriasek prays to Mary to cure some lepers, and his prayer is answered. The scene then shifts to a mother who prays to the Virgin to release her son from the clutches of a tyrant, and her prayers, too, are answered, even more extravagantly than Meriasek's. This incident is said in the text to be found in "miraculis de beato mereadoco" (the miracles of the blessed Mereadoc; 3,170), but the origin of the story has not been discovered.

Transitions between the separate actions may be lacking, but they are thematically linked. The Virgin Mary, Silvester, and Meriasek are all members of the community of saints, and all attest to the power of God.[10] Like the author of *Mary Magdalene*, the unknown author of *Beaunans Meriasek* is less concerned with causal relationships between characters and episodes than with providing dramatic variety while accomplishing his devotional purpose.

The saints' play, with its episodic yet patterned action, features the marvelous and the perilous, but it ultimately celebrates a superhuman hero in a fallen world. This dramatic model was subject to extension and adaptation. In France, the form was extended to cycle proportions as several days were devoted to the performance of plays dealing with the lives of several saints, as in the *Mystère des trois doms*, or focusing on a single saint, as in the *Mystère de Saint Martin*. In England the dramatic model survived long after the times demanded a change in the substance. The religious hero gave way to the secular, and worldly values replaced the spiritual as the form evolved in a variety of ways. An important influence in the emergence of tragedy in England in the middle of the sixteenth century, as Grimald's *Archipropheta* demonstrates (see chapter 23), the saints' play also contributed to Bale's portrayal of King John (see chapter 13) and to later "history plays" as diverse as *Tamburlaine* and *Henry V*. Further manifestations of the form are dramatic romances depicting the perilous and marvelous trials of virtue, such as *The Most Virtuous and Godly Susanna* and *The Winter's Tale*.[11] The Reformation may have caused the demise of the saints' play in Britain, but its progeny flourished for another century and longer.

CHAPTER TWO

THE CIVIC DRAMA

D RAMA representing biblical events became a popular tradition in Britain by the end of the fourteenth century. Performed in market towns particularly on summer holidays, such as St. Anne's Day, Whitsun, and Corpus Christi Day, these plays celebrated Christ's role in the redemption of man. Records indicate performances of single plays, groups of plays, and cycles lasting from several hours to three days. In York as early as 1376 a cycle of scriptural plays was produced, and cycles had also developed at Coventry by 1392, at Ipswich by about 1400, and at Exeter by 1413 (Lancashire, *Dramatic Texts* xvi and passim). Although at several provincial centers the cycles represented human history from the creation to doomsday, some appear to have concentrated on the New Testament, notably the cycle at Coventry. Perhaps most common were individual plays representing favorite biblical subjects, such as the sacrifice of Isaac, or a cluster of plays on the creation, as in the Cornish cycle, *Gwreans an Bys*, or on the nativity or the passion of Christ. Usually sponsored by craft guilds, the plays most likely were composed by clerks drawing upon biblical commentary as well as narrative versions of scriptural subjects, such as *The Northern Passion*, the *Meditationes*, or *Speculum Vitae Christi*. Dates of performance, lengths of production, and local arrangements varied considerably, but the extensiveness of this popular dramatic tradition is attested by records from Durham to Exeter and Norwich to Dundee.

Only a few individual texts and fragments survive in addition to four nearly complete cycles. Together they represent a very small percentage of scriptural plays produced in Britain during some two hundred years beginning in the late fourteenth century; and extant texts may not be as characteristic of the type as earlier scholars implied, for most come from the four extended cycles. A continuous performance of plays from dawn to dusk as is said to have occurred at York, and a series of plays presented over three days developed in Chester in the later years of production. They appear to be exceptional; most towns were probably unwilling or unable to mount such ambitious undertakings and settled for less expensive annual or periodic productions involving fewer participants and presenting a reduced scope.

The York and N-Town manuscripts, dating from the last third of the fifteenth century, represent the plays as they were performed in the last years of the War of the Roses and the early years of Tudor rule; the Towneley manuscript appears to derive from the first half of the sixteenth century, while the Chester manuscripts date from the end of the sixteenth and early seventeenth centuries, after the performance of the plays had ceased.[1] Manuscript evidence and civic records suggest continual revision of the plays, dictated by changes in sponsorship by the guilds as well as by governmental and religious authorities, particularly from the late 1530s onward. In addition, attempts to improve the plays or to increase audience appeal may have led the Wakefield Master, the York Realist, and the N-Town compiler to rewrite old plays and introduce new ones into the cycles. The cycle texts that have survived appear to be master or control copies that reveal several stages of revision and varying degrees of integration of individual plays. How closely a script represents an actual performance we will never know, but it appears that the written texts were subject to constant adaptation depending upon the exigencies of particular performances. It is also quite possible that individual plays from the master copy were selected for performance on different occasions, which would account for two shepherds' plays in the Towneley cycle and two series of passion plays in the N-Town cycle. Everything seems to point toward considerable fluidity in the textual basis for performance.

The surviving manuscripts represent cycles that had been developing over many years, perhaps in the case of York and Chester at least a hundred years, though the Towneley and N-Town manuscripts may indicate more recent development because of their dependence on later contemporary sources.[2] The late fifteenth and early sixteenth centuries, from which most surviving texts of plays and fragments date, appear also to have been the period of greatest activity for civic drama. In addition to the dozen or so provincial centers identified as supporting scriptural plays before 1460, more than a score of new sites of performance emerge over the next seventy-five years, including Salisbury (1461), Stamford (1465), Lincoln (1472), Great Yarmouth (1473), Plymouth (1479), Ashburton (1492), Canterbury (before 1494), Bristol (1499), Glastonbury (1500), as well as about ten other places before 1535 (Lancashire, *Dramatic Texts* xxvi).

Interest in biblical civic drama appears to peak in the early sixteenth century; in Chester, for example, the one-day cycle was expanded to three days as its time of performance was shifted from Corpus Christi Day to Whitsun; but after Henry VIII's reign ended in 1547, a clear decline in performances is evident. Whether reformers' acrimony and governmental interference were the major factors, as Harold C. Gardiner argues (47–62), or whether they had become a moribund dramatic form, as Rosemary Woolf claims (312–23), by the middle of the sixteenth century the scriptural civic drama had lost its popular support in many places; and efforts during Queen Mary's reign to revive the old tradition at New Romney, Southwark, and a few other sites largely failed (Lancashire, *Dramatic Texts* xxix–xxx). Yet performances continued in several towns well into the reign of Queen Elizabeth. Scriptural plays were presented at Salisbury until 1569, at Sherborne until 1574, at St. Ives and Chester until 1575, at Tewkesbury until 1578, at Boston until 1579, and at Coventry and York until 1580 (Lancashire, *Dramatic Texts* xxx). Strong commercial and religious centers some distance from London appear to have maintained the popular civic tradition longest.

The civic dramas, more than any other contemporary dramatic form, were community endeavors, for not only did the plays depend on the commercial support of the sponsoring guilds, they also drew upon educated clerics for the texts and upon local citizens for the acting talent.

The number of people involved and the amount of time and money expended are indicated by the texts and account books, but the degree of cooperation required at all levels of production from the preparation of the staging apparatus to the memorizing of lines no doubt served to unify the community, which also provided the majority of the audience, though the announcement of banns in neighboring towns and villages indicate attempts to expand the audience. Glynne Wickham believes that "no other occasion in the life of the community could compare with [the civic drama] in promoting unity of purpose, self-fulfillment, and egalitarianism in the sight of the Almighty, notwithstanding the obvious distinctions of birth, wealth, education, and skill dividing each member of that community from his fellows" (*Medieval Theatre* 76). This, according to Wickham, accounts for the plays' popularity for more than two centuries.

The requirements of the presentation may be a major factor in the tradition's longevity, but equally important must have been the nature of the message conveyed, for as Northrop Frye points out, "The scriptural plays . . . present to the audience a myth already familiar to and significant for that audience, and they are designed to remind the audience of their communal possession of that myth" (282). The shared experience of the Christian myth is celebrated in a community effort designed to promote religious devotion and commercial profit. As the "proclamation for whitsone plays" included in one manuscript of the Chester cycle expresses, the plays are performed "not only for the augmentation *and* Increase of the holy *and* Catholick faith of our Savior Iesu Christ *and* to Exort the minds of comon people to good deuotion *and* holsome doctrine therof, but also for the comonwelth *and* prosperity of this City."[3] The spiritual gains of the citizens are given primary place, but the scribe also recognizes the commercial profit brought to the city by the performances.

The devotional purpose of the plays is, of course, their traditional justification, and though the Lollard critic in his *Tretise of Miraclis Pleyinge* recognizes the representation of religious events in dramatic form as superior to religious painting as a "layman's book"—"betere thei [plays] ben holden in mennus minde and oftere rehersid by the pleyinge of hem than by the peintynge, for this is a deed bok, the tother a qu[i]ck on" (*Tretise* 40) — he seeks to refute this defense of plays by suggesting they are performed more "to plesyn to the world" than to please God. In answer to those who say " 'Pley we a pley of Antichrist and of the Day of Dome that sum man may be convertid therby,' " he declares that this is an example of the heresy that Paul condemns in Romans 3:8 of doing " 'yvel thingis, that ther comyn gode thingis' " (43).

This Lollard attack not only reveals the conventional defense of biblical and miracle or saints' plays, it also links the representation of scripture in drama to painting or visual art. Contemporary visual art in the churches and cathedrals can perhaps help us to imagine the dramatic presentation of certain scriptural events, as M. D. Anderson in *Drama and Imagery in English Medieval Churches* and Clifford Davidson in *Drama and Art* have suggested, but especially significant in the comparison is the view that the dramatic portrayal is the more powerful and, therefore, from the perspective of the Lollard critic, the more dangerous. The weeping he describes at the portrayal of Christ's passion attests to the emotional effect on the audience, even though he believes the emotion is misplaced: The audience should rather weep for their own sins and those of their children (43). Audience response was clearly a primary consideration in the performance, as the proclamation introducing the N-Town cycle frankly expresses: "we purpose us pertly stylle in þis prese / þe pepyl to plese with pleys ful glad" (*Ludus Coventriae* 1).[4] Whether the plays provoked conversion, tears, or aesthetic enjoyment, their success must have depended upon their ability to please audiences, and that must have been a major concern in the continuing revision of the cycles.

To ensure that the devotional message was not missed, a presenter often spelled out the significance of the action. For example, the expositor at the end of the Chester "Sacrifice of Isaac" explains that the sacrifice "in example of Jesus done yt was" (465). The Doctor in the York cycle and Contemplacio in the N-Town cycle perform similar instructive functions, but by doing so they stress the presentational nature of the drama. They serve as an extradramatic device to narrate what is not dramatized and to link the separate segments. Whether the individual plays are presented in procession at designated stations, as at York and Chester, or on scaffolds erected in one location, as in N-Town, the presenter emphasizes the chronological exposition of the dramatic action. He stands in for the authors, and given his interpretive role he may have been played by a cleric or at least the part may have been acted in a clergyman's gown. A spokesman of the church, he carries on the function of the priest in liturgical drama as he provides a context for a scene and explains its meaning. The explicator at times disappears from the stage, and his part is assumed by God, Noah, the prophets, John the Baptist, or other principal characters in the scenes. As with the removal of the formal chorus in classical drama, the expository function is transferred to characters more directly involved in the drama.

The reduction of the role of formal presenter signals a more representational mode of drama seen as well in the plays of the Wakefield Master, where the contemporary social context becomes more fully ingrained in the drama. The York Realist and the N-Town compiler also make their plays more lifelike by adding realistic details and colloquial speech. The vulgar and violent Cain and the sheep-stealing Mak with his southern tooth in the Towneley plays, the sadistic torturers of Christ in York, and the foul-mouthed accusers of Mary in N-Town amplify biblical narrative in a contemporary idiom that must have engaged the audience, but making Joseph a comic old cuckold borders on blasphemy, as we shall see later. Representing divine mysteries in human form the Lollard critic found reprehensible; he declares: "Whoever so doth, he errith in the byleve, reversith Crist, and scornyth God . . . for in that he takith the most precious werkis of God in pley and bourde, and so takith his name in idil and so misusith oure byleve" (*Tretise* 35).

This sweeping indictment of scriptural and miracle plays apparently did not find much support among fifteenth- and sixteenth-century audiences. Rather they must have been moved by the humanizing pathos of Isaac and Abraham as they prepare for the sacrifice and have been entertained by the comic parody of the nativity in *The Second Shepherds' Play*, but the coarse insults and innuendoes surrounding the virgin birth, especially in N-Town, may have been more problematic. To present scriptural truths in a context with which the audience could identify and in a manner that would engage and entertain them was the challenge facing the writers, producers, and actors of the civic drama, but the desire to entertain may have taken them occasionally beyond what the church or civic authorities regarded as good taste.

The common identification of this drama with Corpus Christi goes beyond the popularity of Corpus Christi Day as the time of performance, for the plays essentially celebrate Christ's sacrifice to redeem mankind. Regardless of the length of the performance or the number of episodes presented, the central role is Christ's. The birth, crucifixion, and resurrection of Christ, the focal events of Christianity that inspired liturgical drama, serve as the foundation of scriptural civic drama. The cycle may begin with the creation and fall of man, but these events are perceived in terms of man's corruptibility and his dependence on Christ for his redemption.

Other Old Testament narratives confirm the pattern of the fall and the promise of redemption. The plays of Cain and Abel and of Noah and the flood re-enact the fall but also look toward Christ's sacrifice, which is prefigured by Isaac, and the plays of the prophets emphasize the coming of the redeemer. Even if only a single episode is depicted, as in the Brome "Sacrifice of Isaac," or if a series of related events is represented as in the Cornish cycles, they inevitably imply Christ's redemption of man. If Christ's instruction of the elders or His ministry is portrayed by the performance of miracles and the conversion of the woman taken in adultery, the action depicts a caring Christ fulfilling His destiny, which He both symbolically and realistically confirms in the passion sequence, the essential subject of both the cycle and the noncycle civic drama. The episodes of the harrowing of hell and Christ's appearance to the Marys and His disciples exemplify the climax of His relationship to man as man prepares for the final judgment, the traditional conclusion of the cycles. When plays are devoted to Mary's conception, her education of the elders, and her assumption, as in the N-Town cycle, her role is basically an extension of Christ's. Whether these plays, especially associated with Corpus Christi Day, present the scope of human history as perceived from the Christian perspective or focus on only a part, they celebrate the body of Christ as the key to salvation.

The telescoping of time and space as biblical events are presented on a series of pageant carts or on a multiple stage may appear naive to a modern audience, but the medieval and early Renaissance viewer, conditioned by the iconographical rendering of sacred narrative in painting or stained glass and by processions in which events and characters of the Old and New Testaments are often juxtaposed, would have accepted without difficulty Moses moving from Pharoah's court to Mount Sinai and back and then to the Red Sea in some 400 lines of dialogue, as in the York cycle, or the prophets assembling all in one place to prepare the audience for the birth of Christ, as in the N-Town group of plays. Whether the contemporary spectator believed in the Augustinian view of time and history, as Kolve (120) and Kahrl (129) have argued, is not as important as his belief in a providential universe. That God directed the course of human history was manifested in the cycles, and those incidents chosen by the clerics and the guilds to exemplify God's design need not be presented in a continuous or realistic mode to convey the message. The individual events dramatized were like beads on a string; new ones could be added and others removed at any point, as was frequently done, provided a general chronological order was maintained. The time or space between actions was not important; what was important was that the image conveyed the scriptural truth.

The scriptural truth, as established by narrative and visual traditions as well as by biblical commentary, determined the general outlines of the events and offered some details for embodying them on the stage, but the choice of the tradition or commentary to follow remained the playwright's, and the authors and actors were together responsible for interpretive emphasis and details of performance. A comparison of extant versions of obligatory scenes relating, for example, to the sacrifice of Isaac, the nativity, or the passion indicates considerable freedom in the rendering in spite of a general adherence to the biblical text.

Typically in the amplification of scriptural narrative for a contemporary audience, events are fleshed out with humorous, pathetic, or justifying actions. The most obvious examples of the addition of humor are found in the Wakefield Master's rendering of Noah's shrewish wife, the vulgar Cain with his saucy boy, and the conniving Mak in the sheep-stealing episode that dwarfs the celebration of Christ's birth. The pathetic is developed in varying degrees in versions of the sacrifice of Isaac by emphasizing the love between father and son, or by developing the son's fear and courage in addition to the father's divided obligations at the moment of the sacrifice. The pathos of Christ's suffering is extended by the realistic details of the torture, particularly in the Towneley and York versions. Also action may be added to the biblical account out of a sense of justice, as in the case of Herod, who after ordering the slaughter of innocents is shown grieving over the loss of his own son or dying himself as a kind of divine retribution for his criminal act. However, one of the most curious and complex examples of amplification is the representation of the conception of Christ. A comparison of the cycles' rendering of this central Christian mystery illustrates the traditional details associated with the conception as well as individual variations in emphasis and details.

Though the biblical accounts of the conception of Christ are quite straightforward, the annunciation, Joseph's relationship with Mary, and the nativity are elaborated in the Apocrypha and later in narrative poems. In addition, the annunciation and the nativity had been favorite subjects of visual art for centuries, so the cycle playwrights had many precedents upon which to draw. The general pattern of the action had been set, but there were many differences in detail and emphasis. All four extant cycles as well as the "Pageant of the Shearmen and Taylors" from Coventry emphasize a great difference in age between Joseph and Mary in accordance with the apocryphal, narrative, and visual art traditions, but the manifestations and implications of an old man marrying a young wife are variously perceived. Joseph is described in Matthew 1:18–19 as a "just man," who upon finding Mary pregnant "before they came together," "not willing to make her a publick example, was minded to put her away privily" (King James version). However, in the cycle versions he is cast in the role of an old cuckold who believes himself deceived by his child-bride. The biblical Joseph's sensitivity is redirected from shielding Mary from public shame to a primary concern for his own personal honor or fear of becoming a comic butt. The Chester Joseph, after declaring that he is old and impotent, laments his lot as a cuckold: "lett never [an] ould man / take to wife a yonge woman" (*Chester Mystery Cycle* VI, 145–46); and the Joseph of the Coventry "Pageant of the Shearmen and Taylors," after accusing Mary of lying about the conception, turns to the audience:

> All olde man, insampull take be me, —
> How I am be-gylid here may you see! —
> To wed soo yong a chyld. (133–35)[5]

Later in the Chester cycle Joseph narrates Gabriel's confirmation of Mary's sinless state (VII, 524–47), but in the Coventry "Pageant of the Weavers" Joseph continues to complain about the demands of a young wife.

In the Towneley cycle Joseph announces that he is "passed . . . all preuay play," and though he does not blame Mary for her "woman maners" (X, 210), he refuses to be a father to her child.[6] More kindly toward Mary than his Chester and Coventry counterparts, the Towneley Joseph is the focus as he narrates the earlier betrothal ceremony and reacts to Mary's condition. The York Joseph also believes his plight results from the great difference between his and Mary's ages, and though he recounts the prophecy of a "maiden clene" bearing a child (XIII, 61–62), he is convinced that he is beguiled.[7] Joseph here is more plaintive and mournful than angry. Yet the pattern for each of these Josephs remains essentially the same: All perceive themselves suffering the inevitable fate of a January-May marriage, and each, though concerned with how he will be regarded by others, is reconciled to his role as surrogate father after the angel confirms Mary's innocence. Yet the variations in reaction individualize the images of Christ's earthly father as they represent how an unimaginative and suspicious mortal responds to the mystery of Christ's Incarnation. The awesomeness of God's design is emphasized by the portrayal of a common man's involvement in the sacred mystery, but the realistic rendition of a comic old cuckold reacting to his young wife's apparent infidelity skirts the borders of blasphemy.

The most complex and most ambiguous treatment of this central episode in the cycles occurs in the N-Town group. Compared to the other cycles, which devote one or two plays to the annunciation of and reaction to the conception of Christ, N-Town explores the conception in four plays. Mary, whose role is much greater in this series, is introduced in "The Conception of Mary" as a holy child destined to bear the baby Jesus when an angel announces Mary's impending birth to her mother, Anne, who like Sarah and Rachel has previously been barren. Mary's divine purpose is reiterated in the following play in her identification as "God's wife" when the three-year-old Mary instructs her elders in the temple, which the bishop perceives as "An hey meracle" (*Ludus Coventriae* IV, 148). After this representation of a divine Mary, she is betrothed to the aged and lame Joseph. The unnaturalness of her marriage is emphasized by Mary's youth, Joseph's shame, and their mutual reluctance to marry. Joseph says, "it is a straunge thynge An old man to take a yonge wyff" (X. 182), and both vow to remain chaste after marriage. Three maids are assigned to protect Mary's good name as Joseph prepares to labor in a far country for nine months. Most of the details regarding Mary's early life and betrothal can be found in the apocryphal *Pseudo-Matthew* and in the medieval narrative poems *The Life of Saint Anne* and Lydgate's *Life of Our Lady*, but the contrast between the heavenly childlike Mary and the doddering old Joseph is more fully emphasized in the play.[8] Joseph and Mary appear to be fulfilling a most unpleasant and unnatural task against their will.

A parliament in heaven intervenes between the betrothal and the annunciation as the prophecies of a messiah are recounted and the Daughters of God (Truth, Mercy, Justice, and Peace) plead for man's redemption through Christ. Though the annunciation scene appears to be an obligatory scene in all of the cycles, N-Town is the only cycle that represents the moment of Christ's conception. After Mary declares her willingness to bear God's son, "þe holy gost discendit with iii bemys to our lady... And *so entre All thre to here bosom*" (*Ludus Coventriae* s.d. XI, 292).⁹ Whether the beams were represented by cloth streamers, by fireworks as at a portrayal of the annunciation at Florence, or by some other means, the visual staging may have reminded the audience of the well-known myth of Jupiter wooing Danae in a shower of gold, commented upon by St. Augustine, Vives, and other critics of drama (see chapters 5, 7, and 9).¹⁰ The sensual nature of the conception is emphasized by Mary's response:

> A now I ffele in my body be
> parfyte god *and* parfyte man
> havying Al schappe. of chyldly carnalyte
> Evyn Al at onys. þus god be-gan. (XI, 293–96)

A mating is suggested also by Gabriel's identification of Mary as God's "turtyl" and "his pleynge fere" — terms of endearment — as well as "goddys chawmere and his bowre." In the same speech Mary is called God's "dowtere," "modyr," and "sustyr" (XI,313–16) as secular images and language provide a human dimension in the conception.

When Joseph returns from a nine-month absence, he pounds on the door to gain admittance in a situation that recalls the fabliaux.¹¹ Finding his wife obviously pregnant, he, like the other Josephs, interprets this as a warning to old men not to take a "ʒonge wench" as a wife and worries about his reputation:

> Alas Alas my name is shent
> all men may me now dyspyse
> *and* seyn olde cokwold . . . (XII, 53–55)

Joseph's selfish concerns and his coarseness in his accusations contrast with Mary's patience and holiness, and unlike the other cycles, the angel appears to both Joseph and Mary to resolve the quarrel rather than to Joseph alone in his sleep, as in the biblical account. Responding more emotionally to the angel's words than his counterparts in the other cycles, Joseph weeps and then "ffor joy" does "qwedyr & qwake" (XII, 180). Begging forgiveness, he offers to kiss Mary's feet, but in a moment of wry humour, Mary answers:

> Nay lett be my fete not þo ȝe take
> my mowthe ȝe may kys i-wys
> *and* welcom on to me. (XII, 186–88)

This account of the mundane Joseph's reaction to the mystery of the conception offers greater variety and intensity in the dramatic portrayal than the other extant cycles, but what especially distinguishes N-Town is the unique representation of the trial of Joseph and Mary.[12]

A scurrilous summoner pushes his way through the crowd and, establishing a homely context for the trial, he addresses the locals, "Thom tynkere and betrys belle / peyrs pottere *and* whatt at þe welle" (Prologue 13–14). Mocking Joseph as an impotent old cuckold and Mary as a fresh young wench, two vulgar detractors accuse the holy couple of immorality as they scorn the divine conception of Christ. One comments:

> in Ffeyth I suppose þat þis woman slepte
> With-owtyn all coverte whyll þat it dede snowe
> And a flake þer of in to hyre mowthe crepte
> *and* þer of þe chylde in hyre womb doth growe. (XIV, 273–76)

This shocking application of a folk jest to the central Christian mystery leads to the comic punishment of the blasphemer after Joseph and Mary prove their innocence. Although the apocryphal *Pseudo-Matthew* and Lydgate's *Life of Our Lady* offer many of the details of the trial, the N-Town play appears to revel in its vulgarity and bawdy comedy, but it ends with the bishop and all others on stage kneeling to Mary as they beg her forgiveness.

This devotional mood is abruptly shattered when Joseph, a tired and irritable old man, complains that Octavian has commanded all to register at their native cities; and when Mary asks Joseph to pick cherries for her, he grumpily responds that the tree is too high, and then adds, "lete hym pluk ȝow cheryes be-gatt ȝow with childe" (XV, 38). The tree then bears fruit and bows to Mary, causing Joseph to fear he has offended God. Again the human dimension in the Incarnation borders on blasphemy.

Perhaps the most awesome challenge to the miraculous conception, however, occurs after the birth of Christ, when the midwives examine Mary. This sequence, portrayed also in the Chester cycle but not so dramatically, derives from apocryphal tradition and offers tangible proof of Christ's divinity. In the N-Town play, the midwife Zelomye perceives that the Christ child, who has been born before her arrival, "nedyth no waschynge as other don" (XV, 229) and expresses belief in Mary's virginity even though her breasts are full of milk; but the other midwife, Salomee, is not convinced and in probing Mary to test her virginity, Salomee's hand withers as punishment for her lack of faith.[13] The pattern of doubt begun with Joseph's doubt of his child-bride's fidelity, which is extended to society in the trial before the bishop, reaches its climax in the doubting midwife's physical test of Mary's virginity after Christ's birth. This mundane response to the mysterious workings of God is placed in a context that the audience would recognize and appreciate as the biblical account is amplified by sensational and humorous elements borrowed from literary precedents and contemporary conventions.

A unifying factor in the amplification of biblical accounts for the civic playwrights was the repetition of themes, motifs, and character types. Salomee's doubt repeats Joseph's doubt, but the physical probing also anticipates doubting Thomas, who thrusts his hand in Christ's side after the resurrection (Kolve 139). The sacrifice of Isaac as a foreshadowing of Christ's crucifixion may have been emphasized by Isaac carrying wood to the altar in a manner to suggest Christ bearing the cross, and the binding of Isaac's hands and feet may also have resembled the preparation of Christ for His crucifixion (Rendall 221–32). As the moral commentators in the cycles and modern scholars have pointed out, biblical history was perceived by the medieval mind as rich in typological significance, and the plays emphasize these connections. The fall of Lucifer in the Chester cycle establishes the theme of the fall that is demonstrated by Eve, Adam, and Cain, who becomes a type of Satan. Noah's flood, intended to purge the fallen, introduces the motif of baptism, but it also is a precursor of Doomsday, when the evil are punished and the good rewarded. The pharaoh's subjection of the Jews foreshadows Herod's slaughter of the innocents and the persecution of Christ by Pilate, Herod, and the Roman soldiers. Just as Moses led the Israelites to the Promised Land, Christ offers salvation to the penitent sinner.

The conventional links between Old and New Testament events may have been made in the cycles by the repetition of blocking and stage business as well as by costumes, and in some instances the pattern is extended to nonbiblical actions drawn from apocryphal and other narrative sources. For example, in the N-Town series, in which Mary has a major role, plays devoted to the annunciation of Mary's birth and Mary's instruction of the elders follow the paradigm of the life of Christ, and as a result they emphasize the divinity of Mary, which is confirmed by Mary's assumption in imitation of Christ's ascension. The typological association of events unifies the plays, but it also demonstrates the central role of Christ in the history of man.

The typological association of events identifies such characters as Abel, Isaac, and Moses as types of Christ, while Cain, the Pharaoh, Herod, and Pilate become types of Satan; but characterization often also involves assigning language and character traits that humanize and localize the biblical figures. The major exceptions to this process are the sacred personae: God, Jesus, and Mary. God, primarily characterized as an authoritarian voice, was usually presented in regal robes with a mask or gilded face, as in the Chester "Purification, and Christ with the Doctors" (Salter, *Medieval Drama* 76). His position, traditionally above the main playing area, precludes His direct involvement in the actions of men. Because His character is determined by His dramatic function, He is vengeful or merciful depending upon the biblical event presented. The Holy Spirit and angels, attired in accordance with iconographical tradition, have no identity beyond being instruments of God's will.

Jesus, though represented in human dimension, appears more symbolic than real. The play texts emphasize His divinity from the annunciation to His final ascension; whether appearing as a child to the elders in the temple or as a minister instructing His disciples and performing miracles, He is distinguished by his superhuman knowledge and power.

His sympathy toward man is climaxed in the Passion, but even here, where His human dimension is most developed, His silence, calm, and endurance contrast with the emotional responses of His followers, His accusers, and His torturers. Christ maintains His dignity in spite of the physical and mental abuse to which He is subjected.

Mary is represented in a similar fashion. The Blessed Virgin commands respect throughout the accusations of Joseph and the vulgar innuendoes of the summoner, detractors, and others who suspect her morals in the N-Town cycle. The expansion of her role in that cycle extends the divine aspects of her character as she anticipates the twelve-year-old Christ's scene with the elders by instructing priests on the meaning of the psalms at the age of three; her sinless character is further emphasized, following her ascension to heaven, by her coronation. However, Mary demonstrates the human emotions of fear before finding her lost child in the temple with the elders, of grief when witnessing her son's crucifixion, and of joy upon being reunited with Him. Her function as Christ's mother determines her role, and though her human nature is evident, her divine nature places her above reproach even when her virtue is questioned.

This is not the case for her husband, Joseph. As we noticed above, his character is all too human, for he suspects the divine conception and initially rejects his role as Christ's earthly father. Responding first like an aging cuckold, Joseph after being enlightened becomes a paradigm of the repentant sinner. Joseph's character does not develop; rather his role shifts from one contemporary type to another. Most of the other biblical characters are similarly identified with recognized types. The pharaoh and Herod are tyrants who manifest pride and willfulness reminiscent of Satan, for like the fallen angel they seek to thwart God's divine plan. Herod is memorable as a character because of his extreme pride and rage. Ranting and raving both on the pageant wagon and in the crowd in the Coventry "Pageant of the Shearmen and Taylors" make him an archetypal tyrant and an example of bombastic acting that had grown old-fashioned by the end of the sixteenth century, when Hamlet warns the player not "to out-Herod Herod" (*Hamlet* III.ii).

Noah's wife is characterized as a shrew, Cain as a rustic bully, and Mak in *The Second Shepherds' Play* as a cunning thief by the Wakefield Master. They are effective comic characters because of the realistic details and colloquial speech they exhibit. The shrewish wife who defies and abuses her husband provokes laughter as her disobedience of God's command is passed over, but when Cain's obscenities lead to blasphemy and murder, the comic mode becomes tragic. Based on traditional types, they become vivid through the exaggeration of recognized traits. Mak, having no biblical counterpart, plays a more complex role, and more individualizing details are included in his character, such as the southern accent he adopts when trying to hide his true identity from the shepherds; but his character is that of the trickster in the oral folk tradition. The Wakefield Master uses Mak to infuse comedy into a biblical event, but again he forms a functional character; the plot determines Mak's role, which is memorable because of the realistic details used to flesh out his character type.

The characters are typical as well as being typological, but they are also essentially tropological, designed to convey the didactic meaning of the plays (see Vinter 120 and Clopper 6). Whether exemplifying man's penchant for evil through lying and stealing like Mak, through blasphemy and murder like Cain, through willfulness like Noah's wife, or through pride and rage like Herod; whether demonstrating man's lack of faith like Joseph and Thomas; or whether manifesting models of religious devotion like Abel, Isaac, and John the Baptist, the characters of the cycle plays offer instructive examples of scriptural truths as they direct the audience to shun vice and embrace virtue. Given the relationship of character to moral purpose, it is no wonder that allegorical characters associated with literary, visual, and morality play traditions found their way into biblical civic drama. The N-Town cycle employs Contemplacio as a moral commentator and represents Truth, Justice, Mercy, and Peace discussing the fate of man in a parliament in heaven, but perhaps its most striking adoption of an allegorical element is the introduction of Death to strike down proud Herod as he banquets after the slaughter of the innocents. The allegorical figures are but a more obvious manifestation of the functional nature of the characterization designed to elaborate the scriptural message.

Performed essentially by amateurs, the roles must have been played with varying degrees of effectiveness.[14] When the plays were performed on pageant wagons at several locations, as in the York and Chester cycles, scores of actors would have been needed. David Mills counts 320 speaking parts in the York cycle and 270 in the Chester, and in the two extant Coventry plays 38 characters appear (59).[15] In addition, walk-ons and extras are required in a number of scenes, such as the slaughter of the innocents and Noah's flood. Even allowing for some doubling of roles, with actors in early plays returning after their plays were finished to take parts in the later plays, local talent must have been stretched rather thin. The number of Christs required in the York cycle would alone have been a major requirement; unevenness in performance must have been inevitable, and judging by the drink supplied, as indicated by records, the unevenness may have increased as the day wore on. Fines were levied in some instances on actors who forgot their lines, and good performances may have earned increased stipends in the following year, but the amateurism portrayed by the Worthies in *Love's Labour's Lost* and by Bottom and his fellows in *A Midsummer Night's Dream* must have been common. Annual performances would not have been sufficient to season the actors, though the repetition of the same play at several locations on the same day may have improved performance. Perhaps one reason for the frequent revision of the cycles was dissatisfaction in the playing of particular segments. Parts such as Herod's or Christ's in the passion sequence may have been crowd-pleasers that encouraged Herod's rantings or elaboration of the stage business in the crucifixion. In the N-Town cycle, with its fixed location, a greater professionalism could emerge (see Bevington, "Discontinuity of Medieval Acting Traditions" 13) as the casting requirements would be reduced and star roles developed for such figures as Herod, Christ, and the Blessed Virgin Mary, who appear in several plays.

The professionalism encouraged among the actors in the N-Town cycle is complemented by its staging, which is the most sophisticated among the cycles. The single location with a large open area and a number of scaffolds allowed for more complexity, including processions of as many as twenty-seven figures in the prophets play, flying devices for the ascents and descents of angels, Christ, and Mary, as well as simultaneous staging. In the second passion play sequence, simultaneity enhances the drama as Jesus is brought before Herod, Pilate, and Annas and Caiaphas, who occupy separate scaffolds, Peter denies Christ, Judas commits suicide, and Jesus is abused by the soldiers. Multiple acting areas not only made possible a larger cast at one place at the same time, thus providing a larger context for the focal action, but also it must have quickened the pace as the action could shift from one scaffold to another or to the platea, or place between the scaffolds, without the delays that would occur as pageant wagons were moved into and out of the stations in the processional staging of the York and Chester cycles.

When the action is performed on a succession of carts, it is bound to seriatim presentation, and the acting areas are constricted. Even when an upper platform may have been used to represent heaven, a mountain, or some other particular place, most of the action appears confined to one level. Herod may have left his pageant wagon to frighten the crowd at Coventry, but the stage remained essentially a one-dimensional and relatively small space. Its exact size is not clear, but it appears to have comfortably accommodated five or six people. Many of the scenes involve only two or three characters at one time, though others, such as the shepherds' plays or the adoration of the magi, require five actors to be on stage at the same time. Crowd scenes — the slaughter of the innocents, the harrowing of hell, the last judgment in the York and Chester cycles — employ token soldiers, mothers, or departed souls, and no more than a half-dozen people appear on stage at one time. The constricted area on the pageant wagon entailed a flexible though symbolic use of place, but the size of the pageant wagon and its necessary portability allowed for fewer options in staging than the platea-scaffold arrangement used for the Towneley and N-Town cycles.[16]

The symbolic indication of place implicit in the presentational mode of production takes different forms in the various scriptural plays, and so do other aspects of the staging. All of the extant plays depend upon stage properties that are more symbolic than real. Though live horses and sheep may appear in some plays, the animals that board Noah's ark were probably represented pictorially. Much attention is given to realistic details of the cross on which Christ is crucified, particularly in the York cycle, but the grave in which He is buried is only suggested as the body is wrapped in a winding sheet and anointed. The Red Sea that engulfed the Pharaoh's forces as they pursued the Israelites was probably represented by moving cloth, and the beams that pierce Mary's bosom at the moment of conception in the N-Town cycle may have been cloth streamers or fireworks, but they spark the audience's imagination to flesh out the illusion. Similarly, costumes are used to suggest social position by contemporary equivalents: Herod and Pilate appear in the Chester cycle in the guise of French lords, and Annas and Caiaphas wear bishops' robes. Anachronisms abound, but they are the natural result of the design to present scriptural truths in a context that an unlettered audience would understand.

Biblical plays served as laymen's books just as surely as the stained glass windows, wall paintings, and sculptures instructed worshipers in cathedrals. As a Warwickshire priest in *A C Mery Tales*, published in 1526, is reported to have told his parishoners after reciting the twelve articles of the creed, "yf you beleue not me, then for a more suerte & suffycyent auctoryte, go your way to Coventre, & there ye shall se them all playd in Corpus Christi playe" (quoted in Alan Nelson 138). Though this quip may satirize contemporary religious instruction, it probably reflects a common view of religious drama. The message of Christ expressed in lively action provoking pathos, fear, horror, and humor must have been more memorable than listening to the reading of Latin texts or even preachings in the vernacular, for the plays brought the sacred mysteries to the level of ordinary people. Watching Yorkshire shepherds complain about the weather and shrewish wives or hearing an aged husband accuse his pregnant young wife of infidelity establishes a homely context for the birth of Christ that entertains as it instructs. Though the entertainment may have occasionally gotten out of hand and the instruction may not have suited everyone's taste, particularly that of the Wycliffites and Protestant reformers, local communities maintained the periodic dramatic event perhaps as much for personal enjoyment as for moral duty. When the financial and spiritual support of the guilds waned and the harassment of the government and the reformed church increased in the second third of the sixteenth century, the cycles appear to have been reduced in length, in frequency of performance, and in the number of sites where they were produced. They remained longest in provincial cities least affected by the growing number of professional troupes and the expanding repertoire of secular entertainment emerging in London and the university centers of Oxford and Cambridge.

CHAPTER THREE

THE MORALITY PLAY
BEFORE THE REFORMATION

*T*HE morality play is traditionally said to have flourished from the fourteenth to the seventeenth centuries.[1] Yet as John Wasson points out, no record of dramatic performance of a morality before 1500 has been discovered ("The Morality Play" 214), and only three complete dramatic texts of moralities composed before 1500 are extant: *The Castle of Perseverance, Wisdom,* and *Mankind,* all preserved in the Macro manuscripts. A fourth play, *The Pride of Life,* believed to date from the latter part of the fourteenth century, exists only in fragmentary form. If we add Medwall's *Nature* and the anonymous *Everyman* (apparently an English translation of a Dutch original), both of which may date from the 1490s, moralities account for less than 5 percent of the drama identified as written or performed in the fifteenth century.

In the first thirty years of the sixteenth century, moralities increase to 15 percent of recorded drama. Of the twelve possible moralities written or performed in this period, four are labeled in the *Annals of English Drama* as political, and only six of the twelve are now extant. From 1531 to 1558, or from the English Reformation to Elizabeth's accession, the total number of identified dramatic compositions grows considerably, and the number of moralities doubles; but of twenty-seven plays identified as moralities, fourteen are considered to be political or are related to the Catholic-Protestant controversy. Moralities in this period account for nearly 20 percent of identified dramas.[2] Through the sixties, seventies, and early eighties, probable moralities continue to account for 20 to 25 percent of the drama, but after 1583 the proportion drops to less than

10 percent, and "it dwindles to almost nothing (three out of nearly two hundred) in the nineties" (Weld 56).³

What these figures suggest is that the morality play in England is essentially a sixteenth-century phenomenon that grows in popularity as the century progresses until it peaks in the early years of Elizabeth's reign; but it never accounts for more than one-fourth of the plays being written and produced, and by the mid-eighties the form was passing out of fashion. When compared with the saints' plays, which flourished for some four hundred years, or biblical civic drama, which was performed over a period of more than two hundred years, the morality had a relatively short life.

Several scholars have suggested that the morality play arose from the medieval sermon.⁴ Arnold Williams reasons: "Preaching was the method used to popularize religion, and one can view the moral play as the furthest extension of popular preaching." He connects this phenomenon with the development of the mendicant orders in the thirteenth century and sees Wycliff at the end of the fourteenth century in the popular preaching tradition ("English Moral Play" 13). The paternoster play, performed at intervals from at least the late fourteenth century until 1572 at York, apparently linked the seven petitions of the Lord's Prayer to the seven deadly sins and to key episodes in biblical history for the purpose of moral instruction.⁵ With its emphasis on confession and penitence, the paternoster play is also thought to be, if not the direct ancestor of the morality, at least an important influence on its development (Williams, "English Moral Play" 13, and Potter 16–29). Other perceived influences include the *psychomachia*, or conflict between the soul and body, deriving from St. Paul, Tertullian, St. Cyprian, Lactantius, and Prudentius (Thompson 320–33), and the popular medieval dance of death theme. The first extant example of the morality, the fragmentary *Pride of Life*, concentrates on the King of Life's ignorant and prideful refusal to accept death, which comes to all regardless of social station. The three Macro moralities, though they share some qualities, are sufficiently different to make a common ancestor unlikely. However, all are expressly designed to convey an ethical concept.

The didactic purpose of the morality is shared by the saints' plays and biblical civic drama, but differences in the mimetic basis and in didactic perspective clearly distinguish the morality from its dramatic predecessors. Addressed to each member of the audience individually, the lesson of the early morality focuses on man's relationship to God and on the fate of his soul after death. In contrast, the saints' and scriptural plays are oriented toward a congregation or community gathered to commemorate a saint or a major holy day. Like liturgical drama, biblical civic plays re-enact sacred events for communal effect. The atmosphere is one of devotion or celebration, and even though particular performances may have evoked something other than a religious response, worship is an essential element as shepherds and wise men gather around the baby Jesus in a stable or as Mary Magdalene demonstrates her holiness by performing miracles. The morality, not tied to the church calendar or religious festival, does not offer an occasion for worship but rather one for self-examination. Not dependent on biblical or historical models, like the scriptural or saints' plays, the morality more freely adapts traditional allegorical symbols and invents characters to visualize its didactic purpose.[6]

Because the didactic purpose in the early moralities is to lead man to repentance, the emphasis is on warning man of sin, which is demonstrated by a negative exemplum. Whereas the saints' plays present particular men and women imitating Christ in overcoming evil through miracles and martyrdoms, the moralities convey an image of weak man readily falling into sin and ultimately being saved less through his own good deeds than through the mercy of God. Because the central figure is typically a generic figure of mankind, the view of man is even bleaker. Rather than depicting man's potential for good in an evil world, as in the saints' play, the morality shows Mankind with a propensity for evil in spite of baptism; his hope for salvation rests primarily upon humbling himself before God in order to avoid damnation. Perhaps this emphasis on Everyman's corruptibility and his dependence on God's grace made the morality play more acceptable to the reformers than the civic religious drama or saints' plays, for it is the evangelistic nature of the morality that most clearly distinguishes its didactic perspective from those of its dramatic predecessors.

The morality was also more adaptable to changes in religious thought. Unlike the scriptural and saints' plays, which depict events originating in the Bible and saints' legends, the early moralities present interpretations of Christian doctrine without the restrictions of inherited "historical" actions. Consequently the morality became a ready vehicle for directly presenting new religious views as they emerged, while the saints' play and later the religious civic drama, linked to Catholic tradition, were suppressed. The adaptability of the morality form inevitably led to its secularization, for it could as readily express views on education or politics as on religion. Essentially ideological, the morality's appeal is more to the intellect than to the emotions, and as a consequence its most receptive audience consisted of the educated and the aristocratic, for after the Reformation in England the morality becomes increasingly a vehicle of political and sectarian interests as well as a more explicit means of instructing schoolboys in the importance of study (see chapters 10–15).

The didactic perspective of the morality is reflected in its mimetic form. With a greater concern for ideas than for historical figures or events, the morality portrays an abstract pattern of action extrapolated from Christian doctrine and observed human behavior rather than a received sacred story adapted to a familiar and often contemporary context. As a result, the morality is more presentational than the scriptural and saints' plays, which depend on the visual imitation of events like the sacrifice of Isaac or the healing of a cripple. The morality often simply illustrates the meaning by symbolic rather than realistic action. For example, in *Mundus and Infans*, generic mankind's progression through seven stages of his life is indicated by changes in his name. Called Dalliance by his mother, Infans is christened Wanton by Mundus, and then in succession is named Love-Lust and Liking, Manhood Mighty, Shame, Age, and finally Repentance. Changes in his character as he passes from birth to death are signified by the names he bears rather than by actions, though in performance very likely each phase in his life was reinforced by changes in costume.

Dress was used extensively in the moralities to symbolize a character's nature, as is evident in the elaborate costumes worn by the figures in *Wisdom*. Wisdom (Christ) is dressed in regal purple and ermine, while Anima (Soul) appears as a maid in rich attire, and Lucifer enters "in a dewylls array wythout and withyn as a prowde galonte" (1.325).[7] Mind, Will, and Understanding when they fall into sin are each accompanied by six appropriate attendants intended to signify the facets of sin that they have entered. As in *Mundus and Infans*, symbol is substituted for action. In *Mankind*, Mankind's acceptance of the sinful life by swearing to perform the seven deadly sins is symbolized by his coat being shortened by his misleaders. This alteration may satirize a contemporary new fashion in dress, but its main intent is to emphasize the altered condition of Mankind's soul. Occasionally realistic touches make the symbolic more concrete, as when the tavern is depicted as a place of sinful resort in *Nature* and *Youth*. Whether the tempters are called Sensuality and Pride or Risk and Lechery, drunkenness and whoring are presented as real temptations to which man readily succumbs, even if the scenes depend more on narration than representation to convey their meaning.

When the contemporary world is suggested in the moralities, the image is usually highly simplified. Dichotomized into forces of good and evil, the world is perceived as a treacherous abode for mutable man. Surrounded by sober virtues and lively vices, man is readily swayed by forces more powerful than he, and he appears often to be essentially a pawn in a game whose rules he learns by his errors. Though man is the most important figure in the morality in being the object of the *psychomachia*, he is little developed as a dramatic character. That he represents all mankind militates against individualism, and he often emerges as quite formless. However, it is significant that the King of Life, the central figure of the first extant morality, is presented as a strong if misguided character. By contrast Humanum Genus of *The Castle of Perseverance* is little more than a cipher who conventionally succumbs to sins of the flesh as a youth and to avarice as an old man. He exhibits no distinguishing marks of temperament, occupation, or class as he illustrates the perils of sin in the fallen world. Mankind, the title character in the later Macro manuscript, is distinguished by his vocation as a farmer and by his frustration at Titivillus's trick of placing a board where Mankind is digging, yet the dramatic emphasis remains more on the tempter than the tempted. Later, when Mankind is led to despair by Mischief and accompanying vices, Mankind is the focus of the action; but the vices have most of the lines as the tragic prospect of suicide is dispelled by comedy when the vice New Guise nearly hangs himself. Even at this climactic moment when Mercy raises Mankind from despair, Mankind is acted upon rather than acting. Everyman, by whose name the most famous morality of the period is known, is a more fully realized dramatic character and truly dominates his play both by his almost constant presence on stage and by the majority of lines being assigned to him. He invites empathy when he is forsaken by companions upon whom he had relied, and he demonstrates at length the pattern of contrition that leads to his salvation. The wages of sin and the achievement of salvation are expressed in a human dimension that is rare in the morality and probably accounts for this play's fame and continued dramatic success.

Moralities written both before and after *Everyman* typically subordinate man to the major actors in the *psychomachia*, the virtues and the vices. An interesting variation on this procedure is *Wisdom*, which pits Christ against Lucifer and divides man's soul into its component parts — Mind, Will, and Understanding — who succumb to the temptations of Lucifer but are later led to repentance by Wisdom. This play dissects the central generic figure as it focuses on the primary antagonists — Lucifer and Christ — in the temptation and redemption scenes, and it represents the fallen Mind, Will, and Understanding by three groups of six characters each, who signify the facets of sin through their costumes and their dance. More a pageant than a drama, *Wisdom* depends on spectacle rather than emotion to illustrate theological doctrine, as the emphasis remains more on the forces of good and evil than on man himself.

These forces sometimes exhibit realistic details and can be linked to contemporary types, like the vices in *Mankind* — Nought, New Guise, and Nowadays — whose names suggest their contemporaneity. Pride and Riot in *Youth* also offer an image of early Tudor bullyboys. Stage directions occasionally specify the dress of contemporary types for vices. In *Wisdom*, for example, the vices representing the corruption of Understanding are described as "six Jorours, gownyde, wyth hodys abowt her nekys" (*Macro Plays* s.d. 725), and depicting the sins of Will are "six women in sut, thre dysgysyde as galontys and thre as matrones" (s.d. 753). Yet in spite of attempts to suggest contemporary society, these figures remain abstract concepts parading in modern dress, as their names — Wronge and Sleyght, Dobulness and Falsenes, Rekleshede and Idyllnes — indicate. This moral pageant illustrates most obviously the pervasive morality technique of ideas determining the characters. As Michael Kelley explains, actors in a morality do not "impersonate" human beings; they "present . . . abstract concepts" (23–25).

The presentation of abstract concepts of virtue is less effective dramatically and didactically than the presentation of vices. Whether called Mercy, Pity, Contemplation, or Charity, the virtues exhibit a colorless sameness. They are more instructive voices than embodied characters, and their seriousness makes them easy targets for comedy. Mercy's tedious and pretentious address to the audience at the beginning of *Mankind* is interrupted by Mischief, who mocks the Latinate style — "Corn seruit bredibus, chaffe horsibus, straw fyrybusque" (*Macro Plays* 57) — and explains that he has "cumme hedyr to make . . . game" (69). Billington argues that this is a Shrovetide play and Mercy is to be perceived as a fool (46–54), but this is not consistent with his role at the end of the play as Mankind's redeemer. Mischief, as we should expect, scorns goodness, but the effectiveness of moral instruction may be undercut if the audience welcomes the irreverent intrusion of vice. The initial ineffectuality of virtue is a common theme in the morality, as generic man disregards virtue's warnings and turns to the livelier company of the vices. The failure of virtue is emphasized by his being bound, as Charity is in *Youth* and Pity in *Hickscorner*; each is ultimately freed by other virtues, which triumph in the end not because of their dramatic strengths but because in the providential universe of the English morality play good must prevail.

The vices create most of the dramatic interest in the moralities before the English Reformation. Both livelier and more individualized than the virtues, the vices provide suspense and comic diversion. They are the initiators of the action and typically direct the plot up to its climax, man's repentance. The vices in *The Castle of Perseverance* are rather wooden, but as the morality develops in the later fifteenth and early sixteenth centuries, they become more fully embodied dramatic characters. The burlesque and scatological humor of Mischief, Nought, New Guise, and Nowadays in *Mankind* may largely explain the play's contemporary popularity as well as its interest to the modern student of early English drama, but another dimension of the vices' appeal for a fifteenth-century audience is indicated by the spectacular appearance of Titivillus. The collection of money from the audience, occurring in *Mankind* between Titivillus's anticipated appearance and his actual appearance, exploits his attraction.

Pride and Sensuality in Medwall's *Nature* and Pride and Riot in *Youth* provide diverting wit and comedy as they offer serious threats to the generic figures of naive man in the two plays. However, it is in *Hickscorner* (or *Hick Scorner*), the only extant pre-Reformation morality that is titled for one of the vices, that the vices offer the most striking image. Hickscorner has a minor if impressive role in the corruption of Imagination and Freewill, attributes of generic man; they have through their license become vices. Their accounts of their exploits as well as their altercation and their binding of Pity provide the dramatic interest in the play. In the absence of a central generic man they fulfill his role, and in the end they are unconvincingly converted by Perseverance and Contemplation. The formula of repentance and amendment prevails only after an exploitation of sinful revels. The attractiveness of vice enhances its danger, but if it is not countered by equally powerful forces of good, one remembers the images of sin rather than the sermons of the virtues.

The drama of the morality derives from generic man's association with the vices. Following the pattern of the prodigal son, man readily falls prey to the attractions of sin. Traditionally youthful characters succumb to sensual desire in the anonymous *Youth*, Medwall's *Nature*, and Rastell's *Four Elements*, while the old fall to covetousness in *The Castle of*

Perseverance and *Nature*. The interaction between the young man and the vices who lead him to a tavern are usually more concrete and more memorable than the temptations of the old man or the scenes in which the sober virtues appear. Often hiding their true natures by changes in name or costume, the vices demonstrate their wiliness. In Medwall's *Nature*, Pride poses as Worship, Wrath as Manhood, Gluttony as Good Fellowship, and Covetise as Worldly Policy. This warning of the deceptiveness of evil becomes a convention of the sixteenth-century morality, but it takes on another dimension in the political allegories. In Skelton's *Magnificence*, the only extant play of this type before the Reformation, the youthful Magnificence, misled by such figures as Cloaked Collusion posing as a priest named Sober Sadness, puts aside Measure and makes Liberty his guide. The far-reaching consequences of this action emphasize the warning of the evil influences in the king's court in the form of churchmen and courtiers. The interaction of the archetypal prodigal with his misleaders offers opportunities for great variation, but it also provides the occasion for political and satiric comment (see chapter 12).

The fall into sin may occupy the majority of the playing time, but repentance is pervasively the climax of the plot of the morality. Every man who falls into sin inevitably falls out again because he is finally made aware of his error. Like temptation, repentance is often presented in only the barest outline. A sermon by Reason or Charity or Contemplation may be enough to lead to repentance and reformation, as in *Nature*, *Youth*, and *Hickscorner*, but if the fear of damnation is enhanced by the threat of imminent death, as in *The Castle of Perseverance* or *Everyman*, repentance obviously offers a more effective dramatic climax. Development of the emotions of fear and despair as a prelude to repentance creates the most memorable moments in morality drama. Potential tragedy is dispelled by the comic hanging of New Guise in *Mankind* and by the instruction of Knowledge in *Everyman*. If the primary purpose of the early moralities is to lead individual members of the audience to repentance, the portrayal of the climactic repentance ultimately determines the play's effectiveness both as an evangelistic device and as drama.

Repentance in the Christian paradigm leads to reformation and ultimately to salvation, but in the early moralities the suspense of impending death and final judgment heightens the drama. Both *The Pride of Life* and *Everyman* focus on death from the beginning, while *The Castle of Perseverance* presents death only at the end; but all three conceive of life in terms of the judgment at its end. The debate in heaven at the conclusion of *The Castle of Perseverance* makes the final judgment particularly important, and as in *Everyman*, man's unworthiness is overcome only by God's mercy.

Mankind signals the pattern of the early-sixteenth-century moralities as death fades into the background and amendment is perceived as the beginning of a new life. Though both *Nature* and *Mundus and Infans* portray aging man, neither makes death imminent. *Youth*, *Four Elements*, and *Hickscorner* emphasize the correction of the young and end with reformation. *Youth* includes much theological instruction and many allusions to Christ's sacrifice for man, but the play remains oriented toward *this* world rather than the world *to come*. The ending of Rastell's *Four Elements* is apparently lost, but Nature's final speech leaves us with a very secular and pragmatic view of man. Nature says that it is "full necessary . . . somtyme to satisfy / Thy sensuall appetyte," though one should not overdo it. "Sciens" or knowledge is perceived as the way to advance (R. Axton, ed., *Three Rastell Plays* 1432–43). *Hickscorner* ends with the promise of Imagination to "forsake . . . sin forever" and of Freewill to "dwell with Contemplation" (Lancashire, ed., *Two Tudor Interludes* 1005–8). The tragicomic ending of the early moralities, which demonstrates the feared death as the beginning of everlasting life, has given way to moralizing about leading a better life on earth.

The morality play, which emerged in the medieval period, is adapted in the early sixteenth century to a new perspective. Its flexibility may have allowed it to escape the fate of the saints' plays and later the civic religious drama as the Reformation gathered force in England, but the morality never gained the popularity or survived as long as its dramatic predecessors. Lacking both the historical context and the human dimension of the scriptural and saints' plays, the morality appealed more to the intellect than to the emotions. Though pathos fleshes out the abstract pattern in *Everyman*, and farce and social satire offer diversion and topical interest in *Mankind* and *Hickscorner*, the morality ultimately failed as a popular form because of its mimetic limitations. The morality play became increasingly secularized as the sixteenth century proceeded, but only when its motifs were incorporated into the rediscovered forms of tragedy and comedy or combined with the popular saints' play to create a new dramatic form, the history play, did the morality find its most significant role in the development of English drama. As it became assimilated with the more mimetic genres, it began to wane as an independent entity, and by the end of the sixteenth century it had virtually passed out of existence as an independent dramatic form.

CHAPTER FOUR

FOLK DRAMA

Civic and guild records, letters, and diaries attest to a flourishing tradition of folk drama in England and Scotland in the fifteenth and sixteenth centuries. A play celebrating the victory of the English over the Danes appears to have been regularly performed at Coventry on Hock Tuesdays from 1416 to 1561, when it was temporarily suspended. Later revived, it was performed before Queen Elizabeth in 1575, and according to Robert Laneham's account, it was a lively performance, involving a large number of actors and featuring the role of women (*REED: Coventry* x–xxi and 272–76). How many other communities commemorated a secular historical event in pageant or play it is impossible to know. More common were local plays presenting the exploits of the mythical Robin Hood and St. George. By the fifteenth century Robin Hood plays were performed from Devon to Dundee (Wiles 64–67), and St. George, a favorite subject of saints' plays, had before the sixteenth century become a central character in popular entertainments across England (Ordish, "Folk-Drama" 314–35). In some areas plays featuring both Robin Hood and St. George were performed, as is indicated in Sir John Paston's letter to his brother John dated April 16, 1473, complaining about the loss of a servant who was "to pleye Seynt Jorge and Robynhod *and* the Shryff off Notyngham" at Norfolk (quoted in *Revels* 1:134). Yet in spite of the many references to the folk drama, only a few fragmentary texts have survived from the period. Dramatic episodes involving Robin Hood and the Friar and Robin Hood and the Potter were printed as "the playe of Robyn Hoode, verye proper to be played in Maye games" in an appendix to William Copland's edition of the *Gest of Robin Hood* (ca. 1562).[1] The two episodes may be from different plays, for they appear to be dramatically unrelated except for the appearance of Robin Hood in both. Another twenty-line fragment of a Robin Hood play from about 1475 has survived, but no text of a St. George play from the fifteenth or sixteenth century is extant.

Folk drama texts that are available were collected largely in the nineteenth and twentieth centuries and represent a tradition that had evolved over some three hundred years after the end of the Tudor period. However, because motifs and characters from late medieval and early Renaissance folk plays appear in scriptural and morality plays as well as in sixteenth-century dramatic interludes, we have some historical basis for interpreting the later texts. Ballads and folk tales from Plantagenet and Tudor England can also offer some guidance in interpreting nineteenth- and twentieth-century mummers' plays. In addition, comparison with extant folk drama in other cultures may prove useful, but ultimately we must realize that the conclusions we reach can be only conjectural. Reexamination of historical evidence has led recent scholars such as Richard Axton and Thomas Pettit to challenge the interpretation, developed by Ordish, Baskervill, Dean-Smith, Helm, and Brody, that folk drama is a degeneration of the death-rebirth ritual described by James Frazer in *The Golden Bough* as the "Killing of the Tree-Spirit."[2]

Whether or not it originated in primitive ritual, the dramatic activity in which the folk participated in the fifteenth and sixteenth centuries was closely linked to seasonal celebrations, especially Hock Tuesday, Christmas, Plough Monday, Shrovetide, St. George's Day, and May Day. Occasional and festive like the saints' and biblical civic plays, folk drama most resembles the saints' play in its use of legendary materials, though the guiding spirit of the folk performance is more heroic or patriotic than religious and is entertaining rather than didactic. The mythical story of St. George rescuing an Egyptian princess from a Moroccan prince and slaying a dragon forms the basis of the action, but, as with the saints' play, accretions from various historical, legendary, and popular sources are easily accommodated in the dramatic structure. As a result anachronisms abound in the extant texts. Lord Nelson or Oliver Cromwell can readily rub shoulders or cross swords with St. George, or King George as he is called in some places after the eighteenth century. The skeletal plot was fixed, but the essential elements allowed for much individual variation in detail.

Because folk drama was an oral tradition like the early epic and the folk tale, it probably combined memorized formulaic passages with improvisation. Commedia dell'arte with its set scenarios and improvisational dialogue may offer the closest dramatic parallel. Like the actors playing the Pantalone or Zanni, the performers in the folk play must have relied on memorized patterns in both speech and action, though imperfect recall and the exigencies of the occasion must have led to some spontaneity and adjustment in the dramatic interaction. In the extant texts of the folk plays, which apparently record the dialogue of particular performances or reconstruct performance as remembered by participants, we note many lines and phrases that reappear with some variation in versions from widely scattered areas. Even given the publication of chapbooks of mummers' plays in the nineteenth century, the repetition of stock lines in particular dramatic situations suggests that they are relics of memorized formulaic passages. One of the most repeated patterns is the vaunt of a challenger. Slasher in the Syresham, Northamptonshire, play, "written down by a baker's man in 1887," declares when he encounters King George:

> Since my head is made of iron, my body's made of steel,
> My hands and feet and knuckle bones,
> I challenge thee to feel.[3]

Some 110 lines later, Hector repeats the pattern with a slight variation:

> Since my head is made of iron, my body made of steel,
> My feet and hands and knucklebones I challenge thee to feel.
> (Helm 3)

The Sergeant, who challenges King George in the Branston, Lincolnshire, "Plough Play," last performed about 1913, varies the refrain:

my head is made of iron
My body is guarded with steel
My legs and arms are made of the best beaten brass
And no man can make me feel. (Helm 12)

Even Old Dame Jane in the Plumtree, Nottinghamshire, text follows the formula, when confronting Beelzebub:

My head is made of iron;
My body's made of steel;
My hands and shins are knuckle bone,
And you can't make me feel. (Helm 15)

This vaunt of the armored knight is hardly appropriate to an old crone, but it seems to have stuck in the memory of the performer or the observer who recorded the play. The wide currency of these bold lines attests to more than free borrowing among local communities; it suggests the tradition of formulaic memorizing of lines to fit particular situations regardless of their appropriateness to the speakers.

Another widespread example of the memorized pattern that incorporates individual improvisation is the role of the doctor. He is usually "called on" to the stage after a challenger has been struck down; then after some haggling over the fee, the doctor talks of his travels and his cures. The Greenodd, Lancashire, Pace-Egg play illustrates the pattern. When asked how far he traveled, Dr. Brown responds:

From Hip-tip-to, Tallyantic Ocean,
Ninety degrees below bottom,
Where I saw houses built of rounds of beef, slated with
    pancakes; . . . (Helm 67)

Later he claims he can cure

Ipsy-pipsy, palsy and the gout,
The plague within and the plague without.
If there's nineteen devils in that man
I'm sure to drive one-and-twenty out. (Helm 68)

Variations on this pattern of comic bragging appear in a host of other plays, and often the lines are reduced to nonsense as the ludicrous claims are extended or the performer misremembers his lines.

Successive performances at different locations on a festive occasion as well as annual repetitions of the play fixed the pattern of action and the major characters in the drama, but as with oral tales, new details must have been introduced as other elements were forgotten. In examining extant texts of mummers' plays representing performances from the late eighteenth to the early twentieth century, we must realize much has changed even though the skeletal action and central characters may remain. Just as in the childhood game of passing a secret around a circle, alteration occurs as the tellers of the secret supplement memory with imagination. We would expect some energetic performers to elaborate their parts and others to abbreviate theirs as a result of faulty memory or weariness. If a comic routine proved popular, the performer might extend it as the celebrated comic actor Tarlton had the reputation of doing. Comic improvisation, a common practice among professional actors as indicated by Hamlet's directions to the players to let the clowns "speak no more than is set down for them" (III.ii), probably also reflects contemporary folk practice. This may account for the elaboration of the quack doctor's boasts and the addition of other comic routines, such as the cure of a horse, as well as new comic characters. If a planned or unplanned addition were well received, it would, no doubt, be retained in successive performances while less popular parts might be cut. The lengths of the plays and the proportionate parts related to the pattern of action were thus probably determined by the success of the performers.

Though the performers may have been drawn from different groups within the communities, the casts must have remained relatively stable with only a small number of new actors being added over a period of years. Whether the performers were apprentices, gangs of farm-workers (Helm 18), tenant farmers as in the eighteenth-century *Revesby Sword Play* (Pettit, "English Folk Drama" 5–6), or members of families traditionally involved in performance, as recent mummers in Ireland have indicated (Glassie 45–48), they were well known to each other and their audience. By repetition they would have developed a standard presentation that could exploit the particular talents of a participant as a swordsman, female impersonator, or comic doctor. Except for the sword dance the dramatic personae typically interact in twos or threes; as a result a sword fight or a cure focuses on individual performance. A new actor could be initiated into the group with relatively little rehearsal, and a continuity of performance would be maintained.

The auspices of performance as indicated by contemporary references and surviving texts appear to have varied with the nature of the entertainment and local traditions. Robin Hood plays and Hock Tuesday celebrations of local history were apparently performed outdoors before a community audience, and records suggest the collections were to support religious or civic organizations. On the other hand, the *Revesby Sword Play* and other texts featuring ploughboys appear to have been performed at the manor house for the lord's household. The surviving St. George plays seem generally to have been performed indoors at major houses in the community and later at public houses. Whatever the location, the performance appears to have been inevitably followed by a collection of money, food, or drink. Though the Robin Hood dramatic episodes printed in the sixteenth century do not include a *quête*, records indicate "gaderyngs" of money were a part of the Robin Hood entertainments if not their motivation.[4] Clearly the audience was expected to pay for the privilege of watching a performance, and in the case of at least the later plough plays, failure to pay could result in the performers "ploughing" the ground around the house of the stingy host (Ordish, "English Folk-Drama" 169).

The obligation to pay for a performance imposed on a household must have occasionally caused annoyance, and by the mid-sixteenth century mummings were being regarded as a public nuisance. In 1549 Bishop Latimer complained about the gatherings for Robin Hood (Dobson and Taylor 39), and in 1555–56 the civic authorities in Chester prohibited "mummying in any place" within the city and threatened imprisonment and fines for anyone allowing "any person or personees to play at any vnlawfull gaymees within his or ther house" (quoted in *REED*:

Chester 56). The Merchant Adventurers at Newcastle upon Tyne, in a statute in 1554 directed at their apprentices, link mumming with dicing, card-playing, "typlinge; daunseng and brasenge of harlotes" (quoted in *REED: Newcastle upon Tyne* 25). This association of folk entertainment with revelry is developed later by Phillip Stubbes in his *Anatomie of Abuses* (1583), where he decries the immoral activities promoted by stage plays and interludes, lords of misrule, and May games (sigs. Lv–M4). It appears to have been this kind of moral concern that led the Scottish Parliament in 1555 to ban Robin Hood festivities (Dobson and Taylor 40). Moralists after the Reformation perceived in folk entertainment a license to be curbed, but attempts to suppress the mummings proved unsuccessful in spite of the fact that their celebratory nature may have gotten occasionally out of hand.

The playing area, established in an impromptu manner by the presenter calling on the audience to "make room" as in the Tudor interlude, was probably small and enclosed by spectators, who very likely interacted with the performers, as in the French *sottie* tradition and the interludes performed in households of the aristocracy — Medwall's *Fulgens and Lucres* (ca. 1497), for example, or the anonymous *Johan Johan* (1533) attributed to Heywood (see chapters 16 and 18). However, because the folk performers would have been better known to the audience than the actors of the interlude, the intimacy between actor and spectator would probably have been even greater.

In comparison with the interlude, the folk dramas were short. The two dramatic episodes of Robin Hood published in the sixteenth century extend only to 250 lines, and if they were played consecutively would require about fifteen minutes to perform. Texts collected in the last two centuries range from less than 100 lines to nearly 600 lines with the majority not exceeding 300 lines. The oldest text of this group, the *Revesby Sword Play*, is also the longest at 569 lines, though among the later texts the *Minehead Mummers Play*, last performed in 1880, is unusually long at 452 lines. The performance time appears to have ranged from ten to thirty minutes, depending upon the length and number of combats as well as on the elaboration of the comic routines. Only one-quarter to half the length of the typical interlude, the folk play featured lively action and humorous entertainment followed by communal fellowship as the audience shared food and drink with the players.

The brevity of the performance as well as the festive mood of both the audience and the players did not foster subtlety in character development. Either the stock characters are simply identified as they are "called on," or they introduce themselves. The hero, whether St. George or Robin Hood, is distinguished by his martial prowess. Though Robin Hood depends upon his men to aid him in his conflicts with the friar and the potter, St. George alone usually dispatches his foreign and domestic adversaries, the Black or Moroccan Prince, the Turkish Knight, the Noble Captain of France, and the Bold Slasher. The combatants vaunt their physical skills before they demonstrate them, and the doctor likewise brags of his healing powers before administering the cure. Because the characters were well known to the audience from previous performances, the dramatic focus would have been more on the actor's rendition of the role than on the character himself. The players' skills as swordsmen in the parts of St. George and his adversaries, as portrayers of evil menace in the Black Prince and Bold Slasher, or as comic improvisers in the role of the doctor, would have been judged rather than the meaning of the character in the dramatic context. As in Kabuki drama, the Chinese opera, and other traditions that repeat stock characters and well known plots, emotional and comic exaggeration in the folk drama roles would have been encouraged, as would, perhaps, physical dexterity.

The traditional mumming costumes that survived into the nineteenth and twentieth centuries suggest the characters presented: the combatants are attired in uniforms of an earlier period in a photograph of the Minehead Mummers (Helm 44), or in tunics and gowns in a photograph of the Leeds Mummers from about 1880 (Helm 64). Female impersonators appear in contemporary women's dress, while Father Christmas, who by the nineteenth century was a popular presenter of the other dramatic characters, wears a white-trimmed robe and long beard in the Minehead Mummers photograph. Stock roles are indicated by costume, but individual distinctions among characters of a specific type, such as St. George's adversaries, appear to have been less clearly maintained, though the Black or Moroccan Prince must have been represented by a black costume or blackened face. The big head that is struck off in combat traditionally distinguishes one adversary, and particular props also help to characterize other roles, such as Beelzebub with his frying pan, which conventionally served in the collection at the end of the performance. If, as has been argued, the Green Knight who is decapitated by Sir Gawain in the medieval romance represents a motif of folk drama (R. Axton, "Folk play" 5), the adversary with a false head must have been a conventional feature from at least the fourteenth century. Beelzebub with his frying pan may be a later variation of the folk-play figure represented in Titivillus, the spectacular devil with a net whose appearance prompts the collection in the late-fifteenth-century morality play *Mankind* (Smart 21–25).

In any case, costumes clearly contributed to the characterization of the performers. Though their personal identities may have been hidden by elaborate headgear or a blackened face, their costumes heightened the unreality of their roles. This is especially emphasized by the morris dancers who became characterized by feathers, strips of cloth or paper, and frequently a blackened face. The effect is to accentuate the impersonation and the sense of fantasy or illusion. Again the exaggerated attire and grotesque makeup of the Kabuki and Peking opera performers might serve as a modern dramatic parallel in spite of the obvious difference in amateur and professional performance.

The separation of dramatic performance from real life is essential to the presentation of the action in the plays. The characters are called on by a presenter or by other performers, but they are barely identified before they engage in combat. The challenge serves as motivation for the combat, but the motivation for the challenge is only hinted at or ignored altogether. The context for the combat remains vague as neither time nor place of the dramatic action is indicated. The focus is on the action, which invariably includes two elements, as Margaret Dean-Smith points out: "the *agon* or contest and the 'cure' or resurrection" ("Life-

Cycle Play" 245). In the hero-combat plays collected in the last two centuries featuring St. George, the contest is simply a sword fight usually followed by the resuscitation of St. George's adversary. However, in the fifteenth and sixteenth centuries, St. George's prowess may have also involved victory over the dragon, the traditional climax to the legend as indicated both by Spenser's *Faerie Queene* and Richard Johnson's *History of the Seven Champions of Christendom*, a prose romance first published in 1596 and adapted for the stage by John Kirke in 1638.

That the Tudor St. George folk plays may have included overcoming a monster or dragon is suggested also by the recurrence of the motif in the interludes *Wit and Science* (ca. 1539), *The Marriage of Wit and Science* (1569), and *The Marriage Between Wit and Wisdom* (1579), where Wit must overcome the monster Tediousness in order to win the bride (see chapter 11). The big head that is struck off in several folk plays collected in the nineteenth and twentieth centuries may be a remnant of St. George's killing of the dragon. The combat is extended in some of these later folk plays by the introduction of the father or father-in-law, usually identified as the King of Egypt, who seeks revenge after the "death" of the Moroccan Prince; but the result is little more than a repetition of the first combat as a second adversary is defeated. Further adversaries may appear, but the outcome remains essentially the same. A number of variations occur in the extant folk drama texts, which appear to draw ultimately on the St. George legend that includes the rescue of the Egyptian princess, the intended bride of the Prince of Morocco.

The wooing featured in several nineteenth- and twentieth-century folk drama texts offers another variation on the pattern of the contest. In these plays the lady typically rejects her lover, who joins the army, and after considering the offers of other suitors, she accepts the Fool. Though in the extant texts the contest is usually determined by the superior wit of the Fool, a physical combat may occur, as in the Branston, Lincolnshire, play, where a ridiculous King George is easily overcome by the Sergeant, yet the combat has no effect on the wooing contest. The competition is complicated when Old Jane claims the Fool has fathered her child, but her threat to the impending marriage is quickly dispersed. The pattern is similar to Duessa's attempt to thwart the marriage of Una and the Red Cross Knight in Book I of *The Faerie Queene*. The wooing play may be a type of folk drama that extends as far back as the medieval period (Baskervill, "Mummers' Wooing Plays" 225–72), though it is not clearly identified in any records of the time. However, if the episode in the proclamation of the banns of David Lindsay's *Satire of the Three Estates* (1552), featuring the Fool's wooing of the cotter's shrewish wife, incorporates a motif from folk drama, as Richard Axton claims ("Folk play" 9–10), the wooing play may have been a more popular genre than extant evidence indicates. Certainly the wooing contest between servants A and B for the maid Jone in Medwall's *Fulgens and Lucres* smacks of folk entertainment (Baskervill, "Conventional Features" 424–25); the contest involves singing, wrestling, and a "just at farte pryke in cule" — and ends in scatological insult with neither gaining the girl because she has already chosen a husband (see chapter 16). This parodic counterpoint to the rivalry for the hand of Lucres in the serious plot may reflect a type of folk drama that is only dimly glimpsed in the extant wooing play texts.

Whether the resurrection of the fallen adversary in folk drama was also an archetypal pattern reflecting the death-rebirth cycle of pagan ritual, as post-Frazerian folklorists believe, or whether this part of the sequence derives from the *Herberie* in the jongleur tradition, as argued by Thomas Pettit ("Ritual and Vaudeville" 12–13), the cure offered by the doctor in folk drama texts of the last two centuries inevitably is the occasion for comedy following the violent or suspenseful contest. The doctor, called on to treat the "dead" combatant, brags of his travels and his miraculous cures and often continues the comic exaggeration and incongruity in his diagnosis. In the Branston, Lincolnshire, play the doctor says King George, who has been struck down by the Sergeant, is not dead but in a trance:

> He's been living nineteen days out of a fortnight
> By mistake: He swallowed our donkey and cart
> And choked himself with a pillow, poor fellow. (Helm 13)

The cure can also be comic, as in the Islip, Oxfordshire, play performed in 1894, in which Molly falls down with the toothache and a nail is extracted from her mouth (Helm 73). The comic cure is extended to a horse, who has air blown into him in the Dorchester (Dorset) Mummer's Play recorded by the British Broadcasting Company in 1936. The comedy involving the doctor was also occasionally extended by a comic servant, such as Fat Jack in the Islip, Oxfordshire, play (Helm 70). Whether the revival of the fallen was comic in the folk drama of early Renaissance England is not clear, though if the revival of Wit by Honest Recreation after he had been overcome by Idleness and Ignorance in *Wit and Science* reflects the cure motif of contemporary folk drama, as Baskervill suggests ("Conventional Features" 426), the comic tone may have been a regular part of the resuscitation then as well as later. A comic servant mocks his physician master in the fifteenth-century Croxton *Play of the Sacrament*, but a more comparable image of the comic doctor is represented in *Misogonus* (ca. 1550–1577), where the vice-parasite Cacurgus impersonates a quack doctor who brags of his travels and his cures in the manner of the folk type (III.iii). His blackened face further links him to the mumming tradition (see chapter 10). Dr. Caius in *The Merry Wives of Windsor* may owe something to the folk drama doctor, and the claims for miraculous cures parodied by Jonson in *Volpone* and *The Alchemist* also recall the folk motif.

Extant texts of folk drama collected in the last two centuries demonstrate that the comic spirit dominated a number of the plays, and additional comic characters and actions were included to enhance the entertainment even if they contributed nothing to the central action. Clowns and fools serve as presenters, and a comic Beelzebub or Hobby Horse is sometimes introduced as a diversion before or during the *quête*. In the Antrobus, Cheshire, "Soul-Caking Play," for example, Letter In, Derry Doubt, and Wild Horse and Driver enter with Beelzebub after the traditional combat and comic cure to provide additional entertainment before the final collection (Helm 70–71). This inclusion of unrelated elements takes various forms, as the number of adversaries in the St. George plays is increased or a hero-combat sequence is introduced into a wooing pattern in the Branston, Lincolnshire, text (Helm 11–13). The most extended example of the introduction of unrelated elements is the *Minehead Mummers Play,* which includes comic beatings, sword fights, dances, comic dialogues, and a wooing sequence, all of which required eighteen performers according to a photograph of the cast (Helm 44), an unusually large number for surviving folk drama texts. This is an extreme instance of the desire to entertain prevailing over any other concern. If nineteenth- and twentieth-century texts are exemplary of the values of the earlier folk drama, unity of action or theme appears not to have been a consideration as motifs and characters were added to heighten the entertainment.

The humor and lively action that provided the entertainment in the fifteenth- and sixteenth-century folk drama may have been similar to that in the texts collected in the last two centuries. Though the burlesque element implied in some of the physical combats and wooing episodes could be a later development, *Roister Doister* (ca. 1553) draws upon folk drama in its burlesque of heroic and romantic traditions (see chapter 19). Just as the melodramas of the nineteenth century were parodied in the twentieth, or as the euphuistic style and pastoral conventions of the previous generation were burlesqued at the end of the sixteenth century, Bold Slasher and Old Dame Jane may be satiric thrusts at old-fashioned taste. However, in the absence of a corpus of fifteenth- and sixteenth-century folk drama texts, the burlesque element cannot be finally determined. Likewise many of the nonsense lines that contribute humor in modern texts of folk plays may result from the garbling of lines through misremembering and misunderstanding. As in such folk variations as "sparrow grass" for asparagus, performers depending on an oral tradition no doubt covered their mental lapses with invention, so that the doctor's diagnosis of a patient's condition resulting from the swallowing of a "donkey and cart" in the Branston, Lincolnshire, play may be a substitution for a more logical explanation. Still, in spite of some changes in the comic material, the desire to entertain without conscious didactic intent probably distinguished the folk drama of Plantagenet and Tudor England from the religious drama of the saints', scriptural, and morality plays.

Because the folk play was probably the most pervasive form of drama in medieval and early Renaissance England, its influence on the development of both dramatic components and audience response as professional theater emerged is probably far greater than we realize today. Folk plays provided the opportunity of close observation of the dramatic process in performance for a large proportion of the population, and for a significant number of men in local communities it offered participation in the production of drama. Though E. K. Chambers perceived folk drama to have "contributed but the tiniest rill to the mighty stream of modern drama" (*Medieval Stage* 1:182), Baskervill, Axton, and Pettit have made us increasingly aware of the characters and motifs from folk plays that appear in the civic drama, moralities, interludes, and later Renaissance comedies and tragedies. Perhaps even more important to the development of drama in Tudor England, folk plays epitomized the dramatic license that reformers and moralists after 1536 sought unsuccessfully to curb.

PART TWO

CONTEMPORARY VIEWS OF DRAMA

CHAPTER FIVE

THE TERENTIAN COMMENTARIES

*T*HE comedies of Terence provided the first and probably most extensive study of drama for the Renaissance schoolboy. Introduced as early as the second form at Eton, Terence was generally studied in the lower forms in England in the early sixteenth century, though later he was shifted to the upper forms as Cicero gained dominance (Baldwin, *Shakspere's Small Latine* 1:641 and 749–51). A standard school author on the continent, Terence was studied as well in universities throughout Europe. Records of a leading English university bookseller for 1520 indicate that more copies of Terence and Cicero were sold than any other classical authors (*Cambridge History of English Literature* 3:19–20), and a professorship in Terence was established by Frederick the Wise, Duke of Saxony, at the University of Wittenberg, where Terence's plays held preeminence in the curriculum (Robbins 24). This extensive study of Terence spawned more than five hundred editions of his plays between 1470 and 1600, according to H. W. Lawton (267–71), though T. W. Baldwin estimates that there "were from seven hundred to a thousand complete editions of Terence before 1600" (*Shakspere's Five-Act Structure* 172).

Beginning with Calphurnius's edition in 1476, most of the texts included the commentary of the fourth-century grammarian Donatus on five of Terence's six plays, as well as essays on comedy by Evanthius and Donatus; apparently no commentary by Donatus on *Heautontimorumenos* survived, and Calphurnius, emulating Donatus's format, supplied his own. In 1492 at Lyons an edition of Terence was published with

65

annotations by Guido Juvenalis, introducing a vogue of supplementary commentary that continued for seventy years, as more than twenty-five scholars added notes and corrected the inherited medieval text of the plays. Though many of these annotations appear to be redundant, they often elaborate aspects of the Donatian-Calphurnian commentary, and they occasionally offer new perspectives on the text as well as new information. The supplementary notes generally reflect the scholarship of the regions where the editions were printed; however, the de Roigny edition of the plays published in Paris in 1552 and the triplex edition in Lyons in 1560 incorporate comments by Italian, German, and Dutch as well as French scholars, which attests to the international nature of Terentian studies.

Three editions of Terence were published in England near the end of the fifteenth century (1483?, 1497, and 1504), but all were based on continental editions, and no further editions were printed in England until 1583. The English demand appears to have been met by continental presses; as a result no English scholars are represented in the Renaissance commentaries. A translation of *Andria*, the earliest English version of a classical play to be printed, was published by Rastell in the third decade of the sixteenth century; [1] and *Flovres for Latine Spekynge*, quotations selected and translated by Nicholas Udall, first appeared in 1533. Fifty years later a complete Terence was printed in London from an edition published in Lyons in 1569. Another edition was printed in Cambridge in 1589, and two more editions were published in London before 1600. Translations of Terence into English by Kyffin in 1588 and Bernard in 1598 reflect the influence of the continental commentaries to the end of the century in England, though Terence's preeminence in the schools had begun to fade throughout Europe in the latter part of the century, as is indicated by a diminution of texts after 1580 (Lawton 560). For more than a century, however, the premiere playwright of the Renaissance, as measured by formal study and printed editions, was Terence. Plautus, Seneca, Euripides, and Aristophanes were occasionally taught and editions of the works were published, but Terence held the position as a dramatist in sixteenth-century Europe that Shakespeare holds in the English-speaking world today.

Terence occupied the same position in the study of Latin that Menander held in the study of Greek for Quintilian (*Institutio oratoria* 1.8.7–9), but the interest in Terence goes far beyond a means to learn a language. Paul Theiner finds that Terence, whose popularity as a school text in the Middle Ages was attested by a large number of illustrated copies of his works,[2] was perceived in the medieval period as "an authority to be cited on the subject of human nature and the mores of men" as well as a source of "rhetorical and personal ornament" (244–45), but Renaissance writers extend Terence's significance by emphasizing his literary craftsmanship and by recognizing his special appeal to youth. Erasmus, who, it is claimed, "memorized all of Terence" while still a child, expresses a common Renaissance view of Terence in a letter to a friend: "the style of his comedies is wonderfully pure, choice, and elegant . . . you will be able to learn from him, if from anyone, how those ancient writers of Latin actually spoke" (*Collected Works* 1:58). The quality of Terence's colloquial Latin was particularly admired in the sixteenth century, and his moral perspective was explained and defended. Erasmus in his preface to his edition of Terence in 1532 sums up the reasons for Terence's status as a major school author: "No other author can teach one better the purity of Roman speech, nor is any pleasanter to read or more suited to young minds" (*Opus Epistolarum* 9:402).

How Terence was taught to the schoolboys is indicated by contemporary editions that incorporate the commentaries of Donatus and supplementary notes by Renaissance scholars. Erasmus in *De ratione studii* (1511) advises his friend John Colet, who was developing the curriculum for the newly reconstituted St. Paul's School, that the schoolmaster teaching literature should begin with a "brief appreciation of the writer"; comment on his "circumstances, his talent, the elegance of his language"; distinguish the nature of the comic genre—"its origins, the number of types of comedy and its laws"; explain "the gist of the plot"; identify the meter; consider various aspects of style, including archaisms, neologisms, and figures of speech; compare parallel passages with their Greek sources; and finally "bring out the moral implication" (*Collected Works* 24:682–83; see chapter 6). Following the essential pattern of the

Terentian commentaries, this advice appears to reflect the general way that Terence was taught.

Vives supports this method by recommending in his *De institutione feminae Christianae*, addressed to Princess Mary Tudor, that Donatus be used for the study of Terence "as well as some more recent commentators," for as he notes, "expositors explain everything, with a minimum of time and work, which leads to usefulness and advancement of knowledge" (*Vives and the Renascence Education of Women* 247). That the format of the Terentian commentaries was followed by schoolmasters is confirmed by Cardinal Wolsey's mandate to his teachers at Ipswich on September 1, 1528. Wolsey declares that in the reading of Terence:

> We particularly recommend to you to endeavor to make yourselves Masters of every Passage requiring immediate Explanation. As for Instance, supposing you are to give the plan of one of *Terence's* comedies, you are to preface it with a short Account of the Author's Life, his Genius, and his Manner of Writing. You are next to explain both the Pleasure and profit that attends the reading of Comedies. You are next, in a clear, but succinct Manner, to explain the Signification, and Etymology of the Word, to give a Summary of the Fable, and an exact Description of the Nature of the Verse. You are then to construe it in its Natural Order. *Lastly*, You are carefully to mark out to your Pupils every striking Elegance of Stile, every antiquated Expression, every thing that is new, every grecicised Turn, every thing that is obscure, every Etymology, derivation, or Composition, that may arise; whatever is harsh or confused in the Arrangement of the Sentence. You are to mark every Orthography, every Figure, every graceful Ornament of Style, every rhetorical Flourish, whatever is proverbial, all Passages that ought to be imitated, and all that ought not. (Quoted in Baldwin, *Shakspere's Five-Act Structure* 169)

All the tasks that Wolsey demands of his teachers — the account of Terence's life and special genius, the summary of the fable, the pleasure and profit to be gained, as well as a close examination of the language and style — are exactly what the Terentian commentaries provide. This insistence on the methods of the commentators appears to give the standard practice official authority and as a result perhaps to extend the practice to more remote areas of the kingdom.

Donatus and subsequent commentators, being schoolmasters, printers, and clerics, treat the comedies as academic texts, not as scripts to be acted, though Donatus sometimes alludes to performance. The medieval belief that Terence's plays had "originally been mimed by masked actors while the dialogue was read by the poet or by his friend Calliopus" (*Revels* 2:147; see Marshall 1–39 and 366–89) appears not to have been endorsed by Renaissance scholars, and as the sixteenth century wore on, performances of the plays in the schools and universities increased. The practice of reading Latin aloud in the schools no doubt included the plays of Terence as well as the colloquies of Erasmus and the *Linguae latinae exercitatio* of Vives, and this may have led to the enactment of scenes if not entire plays in the classroom, as is hinted at by Vives (*Opera* 6:307; see chapter 7).

Official recognition of the performance of classical plays begins to appear in 1510–11, when Terence was presented at King's Hall, Cambridge. In 1516–17 Terence was again produced, and in 1519 Plautus was performed at Greenwich for Henry VIII, possibly by the boys at St. Paul's. Plautus's *Miles Gloriosus* was produced in Cambridge about 1522, as Stephen Gardiner recalled (F. P. Wilson 103), and in 1528 Terence's *Phormio* was presented at a banquet hosted by Cardinal Wolsey (Anglo 41–42). In 1545 St. John's and Queens' College, Cambridge, mandated production of two classical plays per year; and in 1560 Trinity College, Cambridge, ordered the performance of five plays a year. Meanwhile at Oxford, Christ Church established in 1554 that the Christmas festivities would henceforth include two comedies and two tragedies (one of each in Greek and in Latin) (Boas, *University Drama* 16–17). By the middle of the century, production of Terence as well as other classical authors had become standard practice at least for some students at the universities. How extensive performances in the schools became it is impossible to tell, but the university productions may reflect dramatic activity in the grammar schools.

Although Donatus and his Renaissance successors appear to concentrate more on the rhetorical aspects of the plays than on their dramatic nature, their literary merit was not ignored. Commentators' imposition of the oratorical structure of *exordium, narratio, confirmatio, refutatio,* and *peroratio* on the plays—Willichius in the middle of the sixteenth century imposed it on individual scenes as well—and their consideration of natural and artificial proofs in the dialogue as though the characters were engaged in a series of debates may distort the drama from a modern critical perspective; but the effect is to call attention to Terence's craftsmanship.[3] Their identification of the figures and tropes that Terence employed so naturally in his characters' conversations prompts the reader to admire the grace and eloquence of a master stylist. Terence's plays were clearly regarded as models of rhetoric, but a student guided by the commentaries would also learn a good deal about dramatic theory.

Providing the central critical perspective on the comedies, Donatus focuses on the positive features of Terence's art by explaining and justifying it in terms of contemporary critical doctrine and common sense. Though augmented by Aristotle and Cicero, Donatus's critical perspective is essentially Horatian; his views of dramatic structure, decorum, moral utility, and artistic unity owe more to Horace than to any other critical authority. However, for his discussion of the development of comedy and its historic types, Donatus draws upon various classical accounts. What is significant is the conception of comedy that he conveys.

He begins his essay "De comoedia," which prefaced virtually all of the editions of Terence published in the sixteenth century, with a definition: "Comedy is a play (*fabula*) containing diverse practices of public and private manners by which one learns what is useful in life, and what, on the contrary, ought to be avoided" (Hilger 14).[4] Donatus defines comedy in terms of its substance and its purpose, which is perceived to be a guide for behavior. He also provides a Greek definition: "Comedy is a concise view of personal affairs, without risk" (14). Limiting comedy to personal affairs, not public and private as he said earlier, this definition adds that comedy avoids danger. His final definition he attributes to Cicero: "Comedy is an imitation of life, a mirror of custom, an image of truth"

(14–15). Frequently quoted throughout the sixteenth century, this statement is reputed to have come from *De re publica*, but since the portion of the work from which it allegedly came was lost before the Renaissance, Donatus's essay is responsible for its later currency. Among those who later drew upon this definition in England were Thomas Lodge, in his defense of drama in 1579, and Ben Jonson, in his choral commentary in *Every Man out of His Humour* in 1599 and his prologue to his revised *Every Man in His Humour*, published in 1616. Donatus goes on to consider the historical source of comedy, and taking up again the idea of comedy as "a mirror of daily life," he notes the pleasure taken in perceiving "the imitation of life and custom" (Hilger 15). He also suggests that for the ancient Greeks comedy publicly exposed the vices of guilty individuals. Echoing Horace's perspective of *utile et dulce*, Donatus emphasizes both the pleasure and the profit inherent in comedy from its beginnings. He then proceeds to a discussion of the nature of comedy by considering its historical development, its types, its structure, its occasions for production, its staging, and its music.

Donatus's preface on comedy was supplemented in the commentaries by an essay on drama attributed to Donatus but written by the grammarian Evanthius. Part of an essay on Greek comedy by Diomedes, a later classical grammarian, was added to the prefatory material published with the commentaries by Ioannes Theodoricus, identified as "Spicilegium." Although repeating much of the historical information found in Donatus, Evanthius and Diomedes compare comedy with tragedy in terms of their origins, their subject matter, and their dramatic structures. They also comment on satire, the satyr play, the use of the chorus, and the use of masks, as well as supplying additional information on the types of comedy. Providing the bases for much of the later commentary about the plays, these three essays were regarded as the most authoritative consideration of comedy for the Renaissance. Echoes from these essays coupled with critical views from Horace's *Ars poetica* and Aristotle pervade the comments of the Renaissance scholars on Terence's plays.

Remembering the prefatory essays ascribed to Donatus, Erasmus in his advice on the teaching of Terence in *De ratione studii* stresses that the nature of the comic genre, including "its origins, the number of types of comedy and its laws," should be explained to the student (*Collected Works* 24:682–83). Willichius some forty years later in his foreword to Terence's *Eunuchus* combines the view of comedy found in the commentaries with Aristotle's distinction between comedy and tragedy; he draws this conclusion about the place of the ridiculous:

> It is sufficiently clear in the commentaries of many that comedy is chiefly a pattern of civil life. Also, Aristotle has very wisely called it *mimesis*, because it is a kind of imitation or representation of the manners and actions of domestic life. Aristotle separates comedy from tragedy by means of persons and manners, in so far as comedy is an imitation of humbler persons and leaner fortunes. Then it is clear that comedy is not subject to just any vices, but needs jokes, witticisms and the ridiculous, which nevertheless is not altogether averse to ugliness. For the ridiculous is a kind of fault, but this ugliness, it is supposed, is without pain, harm, or misfortune. (Quoted in Herrick 77)[5]

This emphasis on the need for laughter in comedy but without pain, which subtly elaborates inherited theory, is indicative of the positive contributions of the Renaissance commentators. The more astute scholars build on the foundations of their critical predecessors; the less astute simply repeat them.

Even more important than the concept of comedy for the Renaissance scholars' and schoolboys' perception of Terence was Donatus's analytical method. Though many of his notes are glossarial and rhetorical, he frequently explains the functions of individual scenes and characters as well as particular speeches and lines. Beginning with the first scene of *Andria*, which was Terence's first comedy and the first to appear in the standard editions, as well as the most extensively annotated and the most widely taught of his plays, Donatus points out that the function of the scene is exposition, or, as he puts it, the narration of the argument is presented here because it is not expressed in a prologue. He notes that

Terence provides the narrative naturally in conversation rather than in a long speech. Donatus adds that Sosia is a protatic character — appearing only in the *protasis*, or first part of the play, for the purpose of exposition — and his role is compared to Davus's in *Phormio* and Philotidis's and Syrae's in *Hecyra*, Terence's later comedies.

Other commentators frequently repeat and elaborate Donatus's notes. For example, Petrus Marsus, after recognizing that the first scene of *Andria* is necessary because the information is not conveyed in a prologue, adds that the scene shows the decorum of the servant Sosia and the anxiety of Simo over his son's life as well as Simo's loquacious nature. Marsus notes further that the scene comments on the nature of virtue, a proper education, and social custom. He concludes that Sosia, having served his purpose in the narration, is no longer needed, while old Simo remains to participate in further actions (*Andria* I.i.1). Donatus later points out that Crito is introduced only at the end of the play to reveal the true identity of Glycerium and thus resolve the action. Donatus implies that everything Terence includes in his drama has a purpose that should be recognized. Donatus's functional analysis as supplemented by later commentators emphasizes the conscious artistry of Terence and suggests a controlling design in his plays; and it was this view of Terence that was very likely conveyed by the Renaissance schoolmasters.

For Donatus the key to the controlling design is the plot; like Aristotle, he regards the plot as the most important element in drama. In both his prefatory summaries of the plays and his comments on individual lines, Donatus focuses on the relationship of characters and actions to the plot. The central factor in the Terentian plot for Donatus is error, which creates the complication; when error is exposed and the truth revealed, the resolution occurs. The primacy of the plot and its dependence on error are illustrated by Donatus's summary of *Adelphi*. After indicating that Aeschinus, raised indulgently by his uncle Micio, had promised to marry the Athenian virgin whom he had violated, Donatus explains the action that occurs in the play:

> While [Aeschinus] was repeatedly about to bring the affair to the knowledge of the father by whom he had been adopted, he was

> induced through the requests of his brother, Ctesipho, who was confined to a more moderate and strict life with Demea, his stern and rustic father, to seize a prostitute from a pimp for his brother. When this is accomplished, the play becomes filled with a manifold error: for Demea was quarreling with Micio as if he was the one who misled the adopted youth into corrupt morals, not knowing that he had misled his own son, Ctesipho; and he is deceived by Syrus and Micio through the entire play.... The mother of the girl believes that Aeschinus has taken the prostitute for himself. This perturbation is soon brought back into tranquillity. For, when the matter is explained about the violation of the virgin, Micio gives the loving Aeschinus the girl that he had longed for, and takes the mother for himself. Demea, when Ctesipho is in fact found to be in love with the prostitute, is angry at first, but afterwards he becomes calm and gives Ctesipho permission to have her. (Hilger 45–46)

This blow-by-blow account of the action avoids value judgments as it indicates the centrality of error to the complication and resolution of the plot. In his comments on the individual scenes and lines of the play, Donatus points out how and why the errors occur as he relates the prejudices and character traits of the fathers to their misjudgments. He particularly notes how easily in IV.ii the harsh Demea is led into error by Syrus, who describes Ctesipho as moral and upright as a result of his strict upbringing, while Ctesipho is at that very moment enjoying the prostitute who had been captured for him.

Donatus's concept of the division of comedy into the *protasis*, *epitasis*, and *catastrophe* is often compared by rhetoricians to the conventional structure of an oration, with its *narratio*, *confirmatio*, and *peroratio*; but again in the Donatian scheme the emphasis is on the plot, as Donatus makes clear in his definition of the individual parts in his prefatory essay on comedy. He writes:

> The *protasis* is the first action of the play in which part of the plot is made known and part is concealed so that the audience may be held in suspense. The *epitasis* is the complication of the plot and by

the refinement of this complication the plot is woven together. The *catastrophe* is the resolution of the play through which the outcome of the action is made clear. (Hilger 19)[6]

Corresponding to Aristotle's "beginning, middle, and end," Donatus's division became the conventional conception of dramatic structure for Renaissance scholars. Though the *protasis* came to be associated with the introduction of the major characters of the play, and the latter part of the *epitasis* was designated as the *summa epitasis* or *catastasis* by sixteenth-century critics to indicate the climax of the action or a counterturn, Donatus's three-part division in terms of plot remained intact well into the seventeenth century.[7] Ben Jonson uses this terminology in *The New Inn* and *The Magnetic Lady*, written near the end of his career. Donatus usually identifies in his commentary exactly where the *epitasis* and *catastrophe* begin, and subsequent commentators accept his designations though occasionally with modification. Barlandus notes that Donatus divides every play into three parts and adds his own perception of what they represent. He says: "We call the first growing tumult the *protasis*, the warmest bustle the *epitasis*, the sudden change of events the *catastrophe*" (*Andria* IV.v.796). Latomus especially comments on Donatus's division and occasionally distinguishes the *summa epitasis*, as in *Andria* IV.v (in de Roigny's ed.), the scene that immediately precedes Crito's entrance and the *catastrophe*, or resolution of the plot.

Donatus is thought to have preserved the original act-division of Terence's plays accredited to Varro (Baldwin, *Shakspere's Five-Act Structure* 29), though the practice of dividing plays into five acts, Donatus says in his preface to *Adelphi*, derives from Greek drama, where the acts are distinguished by the chorus (Hilger 43). Evanthius specifically links the five-act structure to Old Comedy. Recognizing the difficulty in distinguishing the acts in Latin plays, apparently because a chorus is no longer used to mark them, Donatus in his preface to *Andria* says the end of an act occurs "when the stage is vacated by all the characters so that the chorus or musicians can be heard" (Hilger 35). His acceptance of the conventional view is linked with his endorsement of the Horatian dictum that no play should be shorter or longer than five acts. The five-act division was accommodated to the three-part structure by Donatus and his critical successors as acts 1 and 2 were linked with the *protasis*, acts 3 and 4 with the *epitasis*, and act 5 with the *catastrophe*. As T. W. Baldwin explains, this division became the basis of dramatic structure for Shakespeare and his contemporaries.[8]

Donatus accepts the conventional division of Terence's comedies into five acts, but he appears much less concerned about the formal partitioning than with the internal structure. The three-part development of *protasis, epitasis,* and *catastrophe* provides a skeletal form, but Donatus and later commentators also note Terence's skill in the creation and integration of the details of the play. Usually called *oeconomia*, Terence's artistic control in building a scene or pattern of action as well as in relating conversations or scenes to one another was particularly admired. Incorporating continuity, manipulation of details for dramatic impact, and conciseness, *oeconomia* was perceived as a key to effectiveness in conveying dramatic situations and relationships. When Terence fulfilled a number of functions in a single speech or scene, he was particularly commended. For example, Donatus notes the *oeconomia* in *Andria* III.i, a scene of only twenty-two lines, where Simo is deceived by Davus as a result of his own suspicious nature at the same time that the hidden birth of Pamphilus's child is revealed. The scene also raises questions about Pamphilus's character, expresses Simo's suspicious nature, and further complicates the error that pervades the play. Terence's integration of two plots in each of his surviving plays but one provided many opportunities for *oeconomia* and for the commentators' admiration of Terence's skill.

Latomus among the later commentators is perhaps most concerned with *oeconomia*, and he points out several variations of it. In *Heutontimorumenos* Chremes says that he can afford to give no more than two talents in dowry for his daughter if he is to prevent his estate and his son Clitipho from being ruined (V.i.941). Latomus notes this reference to Clitipho is an example of *oeconomia* because it relates to Clitipho's difficulties with money, considered in the following scene. *Oeconomia* here is perceived in terms of continuity, but this example is also preparation for what is to follow. Terence's skill in preparing the audience for future action or revelation — identified in the commentaries as *praeparatio, praestructio,* or *paraskeue,* a manifestation of *oeconomia* — is frequently noted. Donatus points to three occasions in *Andria* (I.i.71ff, I.i.119ff, and I.iv.274ff) where Glycerium's virtue is mentioned as preparation for her later recognition as Chremes's daughter and her future status as an Athenian matron. A more subtle example of foreshadowing that Donatus notes in *Andria* is Davus's recounting of the "wild story" he has heard that Glycerium, cast ashore after her father was lost in a shipwreck, was taken in by Chrysis's father (I.iii.220ff). Davus discounts the story as improbable, though it is later proved to be true. This kind of *oeconomia* is particularly characteristic of Terence, as Philip Harsh demonstrates in his monograph *Studies in Dramatic "Preparation" in Roman Comedy.* Donatus, noticing the frequency of the device in his commentary, calls attention to Terence's artistic control.

Another manifestation of Terence's artistry noted by Donatus and later commentators was Terence's use of decorum. This principle, considered by Aristotle and Cicero in their rhetorical theory and applied to literature by Horace in his *Ars poetica,* was an important critical criterion for the late classical grammarians. First noting Terence's preservation of the laws of character, Evanthius then justifies Terence's departure from decorum: "No one preserved the laws of character concerning condition, age, rank in society, and part to be played more diligently than Terence. Indeed, he alone dared — when he was trying for verisimilitude in a fictional plot — to bring onto the stage prostitutes who were not evil women, even though this was contrary to the rules of comedy" (Hilger 28). This is generally the view also of Donatus in his commentary; he notes Terence's observance of decorum in creating traditional comic types of fathers, sons, slaves, and prostitutes. But Donatus in his preface to *Adelphi* especially commends Terence's skill in individualizing the types, often through contrast, as with the fathers, the harsh Demea and the lenient Micio (Hilger 45). He also notes that the good prostitutes in such plays as *Eunuchus* and *Hecyra* are justifiable variations from the stock portrayals of comedy (*Hecyra*, V.i.727 and V.iii.836). Later commentators generally follow Donatus and Evanthius in complimenting Terence for joining invention with decorum to create lifelike but individualized characters.[9]

The other major aspect of decorum for the grammarians, as for Horace, was the artist's inclusion of matters appropriate to the genre adopted. As Horace expresses at the beginning of *Ars poetica*, it is ludicrous for a painter to join a human head to a horse's neck, so is it ridiculous to treat a comic subject in a tragic style. Generic conventions dictated a sense of propriety, and Terence was regarded as a model of decorum for the comic genre. Again Evanthius expresses the grammarians' perspective:

> Although Terence did everything with the greatest skill, he should be especially admired because he kept the manners of men in mind so that he might write comedy; and he tempered passion lest he might leap over into tragedy. We have found that his propriety, along with some other things, is little observed by Plautus, Afranius, Appius, and many other of the great comic writers. Also admirable among Terence's virtues is that his plays are composed with such moderation that they neither swell up to the loftiness of tragedy nor are they cast down to the baseness of the mime. (Hilger 28–29)

Admiration for Terence's propriety in avoiding the pathos of tragedy and "the baseness of the mime" in comparison with Plautus and other classical writers underlies many of Donatus's comments about generic decorum. For example, in his preface to *Phormio*, Donatus notes that "the play is constituted in almost greater emotions than the comic style demands, although everything is tempered by the art of the playwright" (Hilger 52). As in his justification of Terence's departure from the conventions in character portrayal, Donatus here judges Terence's straining of comic decorum acceptable because of his art.

Though later commentators generally endorse Horace's and the grammarians' concept of decorum without elaboration, Badius in his

Prenotamenta to his 1504 edition of Terence's plays discusses decorum in its various aspects. Elaborating particularly on Horace, Badius, as Robbins notes, "presents the most systematic treatment of decorum among the sixteenth-century editions of Terence" (46). Badius considers decorum in relation to character types, such as the *senex*, to fortune, status, or occupation, and to passions or emotions, which are perceived as individualizing factors in characterization. In his next chapter, entitled "De rerum decoro," Badius discusses decorum in connection with genre and relates this concept to consistency of character and *oeconomia*. He then proceeds to "the decorum of words" and considers their appropriateness in terms of subject matter, persons, and genre. Finally in discussing the decorum of the whole work (*decoro totius operis*), he judges Terence to be always perceptive and consistent in his observance of decorum, unlike Plautus, who is described as more obscure. Badius, elaborating and extending classical doctrine, makes decorum a cardinal principle of dramatic theory. Reprinted in several later editions of Terence, Badius's essay became one of the most influential treatments of decorum in the sixteenth century. His views are echoed by a number of later writers, including Thomas Lodge in his defense of drama in 1579 (Ringler 164–71).

Another Horatian concept adopted by Donatus and elaborated in Renaissance commentaries was the moral perceived in comedy. As noted above, Donatus's first definition includes the statement that in comedy "one learns what is useful in life and what, on the contrary, ought to be avoided," and Cicero's definition quoted by Donatus also implies a moral purpose in the description of comedy as "a mirror of custom, an image of truth," as Renaissance critics interpreted it. The didactic was bolstered by the pseudo-Servius commentary, dating from the eighth century but less widely circulated than the Donatian, which stresses the influences of comedy on behavior: "It is . . . the intention of the author to describe characters; its utility that we might know how to fashion good character for ourselves" (quoted in Baldwin, *Shakspere's Five-Act Structure* 69). Donatus, playing the role of schoolmaster, usually notes the *sententiae* embedded in the dialogue and sometimes elaborates on their meaning, but he also comments on the moral implications of particular characters and actions. He frequently notes the impulsiveness of youth and their concern with pleasure; he registers the moral responsibility of a young man to a woman he has impregnated, as in *Andria* and *Adelphi*; and he indicates the duty of sons to their fathers. The moral message is thus pitched to schoolboys, though he also recognizes the harshness and impatience of fathers like Demea and the follies of such characters as Thraso, the boastful coward in *Eunuchus*. Overall Donatus's moral perspective is rather moderate and urbane. The many sexual adventures upon which Terence's plots depend are tolerantly regarded as manifestations of youthful passions, and when they are judged, they are perceived more in terms of foolishness than immorality.

Later commentators, particularly those in northern Europe, where the Reformation affected the moral perspective, took a harder line on the moral lessons to be gained from Terence's plays. Melanchthon, who was deeply involved in the Lutheran movement, particularly emphasizes the didactic element in his edition of 1527. Commenting on *Andria*, he expresses his general view of the moral dimension: "Authors of comedies wish to show examples of familiar manners and events by which we may be admonished and so the more prudently judge of human affairs and enrich our manner of speaking. . . . In recounting the argument of the plays, the chief care of the poet should be to set forth counsel. . . . Nor, indeed, is comedy anything other than an image of human counsels and events" (quoted in Herrick 73). Melanchthon then proceeds to summarize the action of *Andria* in terms of "counsel and events" as they are represented in the conventional division of *protasis*, *epitasis*, and *catastrophe*. Melanchthon's didactic *argumenta* for each of Terence's plays became almost as standard in northern European editions of Terence as Donatus's commentary.

Other commentators also elaborate the moral import of Terence's plays. Responding to Pamphilus's confession to his father that he loves Glycerium but will give her up or do anything that his father wishes (*Andria* V.iii.896), Rivius comments on what the speech reveals about Pamphilus' character and the relationship between father and son. Then after directing the reader to consider Solomon and Christian morality in his judgment of the young man, Rivius recalls Cicero's view of comedy, which he reduces to "a mirror of human life" (*speculum vitae humanae*), and then recounts the voluptuousness and other moral errors represented in comedy that youth should avoid.

This perception of the utility of comedy in terms of its negative examples led moralists as early as St. Augustine to suspect Terence's influence. The scene that was singled out by St. Augustine and later moralists as a paradigm of art inducing immorality was Chaerea's narration of his rape of Pamphila in *Eunuchus* (III.v.581). Chaerea describes how looking at a picture of Jove "sending down a shower of gold into Danaë's bosom" led him to imitate the god's example by forcing himself on the sleeping girl. Vives too found such scenes reprehensible and suggested that such flagrant images of immorality should be removed from Latin comedy texts to be used by students (*Vives: On Education* 51–52; see chapter 7). Significantly, Donatus, moralizing on this scene, points out the imprudence of Thais in leaving Chaerea as a "custodian" for the girl, while Latomus and other later critics comment on Chaerea's immorality.

Erasmus, responding to those who claim Terence's plays "contain nothing but lechery and immoral love-affairs between young people," answers that comedy was "invented for the purpose of showing up men's vices":

> For what are comedies but the artful slave, the love-crazed youth, the suave and wanton harlot, the cross-grained, peevish, avaricious old man? These characters are depicted for us in plays, just as in a painting, so that we may first see what is seemly or unseemly in human behaviour and then distribute affection or rebuke accordingly. (*Collected Works* 1:59)

This is not simply a defense of Terence but a defense of comedy, whose function is didactic. It is part of the responsibility of the schoolmaster, as Erasmus notes in *De ratione studii*, to bring out the "moral implications" of Terence's plays, and the Renaissance commentators sought to make the schoolmasters' task easier. Though the negative images receive most of the attention in the commentaries, a more positive aspect of the didactic is perceived by Wagnerus in his letter of 1550 to his nephew, Willichius Junior, which was reprinted in later editions of Terence's plays. Wagnerus says that comedy "commends virtues and censures vices, and exhibits the manner of virtue in whatever age, sex, or condition you please. Here may be perceived the image and lively type of nearly all domestic actions. Thereto let one consider that of Demea in *Adelphi*. I bid him view the lives of men as it were in a mirror and take from others an example for himself" (quoted in Herrick 132).

Wagnerus's contribution to Terentian scholarship was brief but perceptive, for it is also he who most cogently expresses what the commentators most prize in Terence: his art in ordering and arranging his materials. Wagnerus writes:

> An architect, when he erects a building, would be ridiculous if he put together stones, timbers, cement, and other things necessary for the construction, without making use of art in ordering and arranging these materials. So an orator or a writer would be judged no expert, even though he had goodly words, grave sentiments, and strong arguments impromptu, if he did not dispose every part in its place and the whole course of the discourse "in an orderly fashion." (Quoted in Herrick 98)

The parts of a composition arranged in a relationship like the parts of a building, with each part fitting with the others to form a whole, is the conception underlying the functional analysis of Donatus and his successors, in which each element is considered in terms of its relationship to the overall design of the play. This Aristotelian and Horatian principle of artistic unity is best expressed by Evanthius in his praise of Terence's dramatic skill: "Terence is so attentively aware of plot and style that he always either guarded against or attended to those things which would be detrimental to the play; also he joined the middles with the beginnings and ends so skillfully that no part seems to be added to one another, but the whole seems to have been composed coherently and as a single body" (Hilger 29). This representation of Terence as a model of organic unity complements his image as a master of rhetoric. For the students being introduced to drama in the Renaissance classrooms, what Donatus and his successors most importantly convey is the controlled artistry of Terence as revealed in the details of his plays. This appreciation of artistic merit along with practical criticism fostered the popularity of Terence's plays in the schools of the sixteenth century. Finally, Donatus and his humanist followers provided an alternative to native drama and inspired new generations of writers to imitate and adapt classical comedy.

CHAPTER SIX

ERASMUS

*A*LTHOUGH Erasmus, so far as we know, never wrote a play and never commented on contemporary stage productions, drama held a special place in his life from his childhood to his old age. Beatus Rhenanus, Erasmus's devoted assistant and first biographer, reports that as a child Erasmus "memorized all of Terence" (Olin 53); and Erasmus himself writes that at school he "used secretly to go through a whole comedy of Terence with [a friend] sometimes in a single night" (*Collected Works* 4:18).[1] In 1489 Erasmus sent a copy of Terence's plays, which he had "written out with [his] own hand," to a friend with this message: "Please bestow on this my little gift, . . . the same affection as you have shown me. I shall finally be sure you have given it such affection when you show that you have studied it diligently and when I hear that it is always on your person and in your hands and on your lap." (*Collected Works* 1:58). Erasmus goes on to express why he prizes Terence so highly:

> The style of his comedies is wonderfully pure, choice, and elegant, with very little roughness. . . . There is also a polished and witty charm; . . . you will be able to learn from him, if from anyone, how those ancient writers of Latin actually spoke, who nowadays are made to stammer even worse than ourselves; and this is why I am of the opinion that you ought not merely to read him again and again, but even learn him by heart. (1:58)

Erasmus's admiration of Terence's style for its purity, elegance, and "polished and witty charm" reflects the typical justification for Terence's place in the school curricula of the period, but Erasmus's enthusiasm goes far beyond the educationist's cliché. In answer to those who claim that Terence's plays "contain nothing but lechery and immoral love-affairs between young people," Erasmus declares:

> These fools, these goats, who grasp only at wickedness since wickedness alone is native to them, for they are at once ignorant and malicious, fail to perceive how much moral goodness exists in Terence's plays, how much implicit exhortation to shape one's life.... Nor do they understand that this kind of literature is entirely suitable — nay, was invented — for the purpose of showing up men's vices. For what are comedies but the artful slave, the love-crazed youth, the suave and wanton harlot, the cross-grained, peevish, avaricious old man? These characters are depicted for us in plays, just as in a painting, so that we may first see what is seemly or unseemly in human behaviour and then distribute affection or rebuke accordingly. (1:59)

Erasmus takes the opportunity not only to defend Terence from charges of immorality but also to express the salutary effects of literature in general and comedy in particular.

Erasmus concludes by pointing to both classical and Christian authorities who learned from Terence and who loved him: "He who wishes to speak must choose Terence, whom Cicero and Quintilian and Jerome and Augustine and Ambrose learned in youth and frequented in old age; whom, lastly, no one but a barbarian has ever failed to love" (1:60). This enthusiasm for Terence may betray Erasmus's youth; yet in his preface to his edition of Terence published more than forty years later, in 1532, though his tone is more restrained his conception of Terence's special qualities seems little changed. The aging Erasmus declares, "No other author can teach one better the purity of Roman speech, nor is any pleasanter to read or more suited to young minds" (*Opus Epistolarum* 9:402). Erasmus recognizes Terence's special appeal to youth, perhaps remembering his own experience; but as we shall see, Terence remained one of Erasmus's favorite authors throughout his life.

Though he regarded Plautus as a lesser literary craftsman than Terence, in a letter addressed to William Blount prefacing the first edition of the *Adagia* (1500), Erasmus praises Plautus for overflowing with adages: "It is this faculty above all that has given him title to be compared with the Muses themselves for eloquence" (*Collected Works* 1:258). In Erasmus's final edition of the *Adagia* in 1533, references to Plautus are equal in number to Horace and exceeded only by Cicero among Roman writers (Phillips, *The "Adages"* 393–404). Erasmus's interest in Plautus is further indicated by his edition of Plautus's twenty comedies with notes in 1530. Classical writers of comedy appear to have provided especially fertile ground for Erasmus in collecting adages; Aristophanes runs a close second to Homer as a source among the Greek writers included in the 1533 edition of *Adagia* (Phillips, *The "Adages"* 393–404). Erasmus's easy familiarity with classical comedy is also evident in the many allusions to Terence, Plautus, and Aristophanes in his correspondence as well as in his other works.

Erasmus's concern for classical tragedy may not be as pervasive as his interest in comedy, though on both Seneca and Euripides he expended much scholarly effort. He apparently proposed an edition of Seneca's tragedies in 1512, but this was rejected by Josse Badius (*Collected Works* 2:231). However, Badius did publish an edition of the tragedies in 1514 that included Erasmus's notes. During this period, Erasmus was more concerned with the errors and false attributions in the Senecan canon than with the tragedies as drama. Questioning whether the tragedies were written by the same man who wrote the philosophical and rhetorical works, Erasmus suggests that the tragedies may have been written by a son or brother of the rhetorician (*Opus Epistolarum* 8:37). Later Erasmus expresses some bitterness about his scholarship on Seneca. In describing how his own works might be divided in a collected edition, Erasmus writes: "In Seneca I can claim nothing for myself, except that in that field I lost much labour by trusting to the promises of my friends" (*Collected Works* 24:697).

His work on Euripides was more rewarding as well as more influential. When Erasmus determined to learn Greek, he chose the works of

Euripides as his text, and in 1506 his translations of *Hecuba* and *Iphigenia at Aulis* were published by Badius. Erasmus's translations went through twenty-two printings between 1506 and 1567 (Vander Haeghen 25–26), and his text of *Hecuba* was acted on at least one occasion (*Collected Works* 4:134). The two tragedies that Erasmus translated are among the best-known of Euripides's works in the sixteenth century and may have inspired other translations of Greek tragedy at the beginning of the Elizabethan period (E. Jones, *Origins of Shakespeare* 117–18). How famous Erasmus's translations of Euripides were is indicated by Thomas Lodge in his defense of poetry in 1579. Lodge writes: "What made Erasmus labor in Euripides tragedies? Did he endeuour by painting them out of Greeke into Latine to manifest sinne vnto vs? or to confirme vs in goodness?" (*Elizabethan Critical Essays* 1:68). Lodge's interpretation of Erasmus's motivation appears to have been prompted by Lodge's desire to strengthen his defense of drama, but it is in keeping with Erasmus's view of the moral instruction of literature in general and drama in particular.

Erasmus expanded his defense of classical literature in his *Antibarbari*, begun probably in the 1490s though not published until 1520 (*Collected Works* 23:2–6). Finding ignorance, arrogance, and misplaced religiosity to be the chief enemies of humanist learning, Erasmus takes issue with those who object to instruction in "heathen" literature, especially comedy. Parents are said to complain: "Are we sending our children to school ... or to the brothel? For those three letters which the old man in Plautus was so proud of knowing [A-M-O: I love you], we can easily learn at home" (*Collected Works* 23:38). When Batt, Erasmus's spokesman, is finally prompted to respond, he launches into a lengthy declamation ridiculing such obtuse opinions and declaring the benefits gained from a study of literature. Most importantly, literature is said to "mould our character, quiet our passions, check our uncontrolled impulses, give mildness to our minds in place of savagery" (*Collected Works* 23:64).

Erasmus is not so positive about pagan literature in his handbook on the Christian life, *Enchiridion militis christiani* (1503), where he warns the reader to choose his works carefully and read rapidly, "like someone just traveling through rather than taking up residence there," though Erasmus also explains that this literature "shapes and invigorates the youthful character and prepares one marvelously well for understanding Holy Scripture" (*Enchiridion* 51). He especially emphasizes the allegorical reading of classical myths and of the epics of Homer and Virgil, but he also alludes to the moral instruction in Euripides and points out the power of drama to move an audience to action (134–35).

In his *De ratione studii*, first published in 1511 though probably drafted several years earlier, Erasmus outlines a program of study that places drama at the forefront of imaginative literature. He gives priority to playwrights in his selection of both Greek and Roman authors; he explains his choice as follows: "A true ability to speak correctly is best fostered both by conversing and consorting with those who speak correctly and by the habitual reading of the best stylists. Among the latter the first to be imbibed should be those whose diction, apart from its refinement, will also entice learners by a certain charm of subject-matter" (*Collected Works* 24:669). After naming Lucian, Demosthenes, and Herodotus, he declares that among the Greek poets he assigns "first place to Aristophanes, second to Homer, third to Euripides" (*Collected Works* 24:669). Erasmus says Menander would have been given first place, apparently by Quintilian's precedent, if his comedies were extant. Erasmus continues:

> Among Latin writers who is more valuable as a standard of language than Terence? He is pure, concise, and closest to everyday speech and then by the very nature of his subject-matter, is also congenial to the young. Should someone think that a few, selected comedies of Plautus, free from impropriety, should be added to the above, I would personally not demur. Second place will go to Virgil, third to Horace, fourth to Cicero and fifth to Caesar. (*Collected Works* 24:669)

Erasmus says Sallust might also be added. Though he does not ignore the great epical poets and orators, Erasmus places his favorite authors first — Lucian, Aristophanes, and Terence, and he also includes Euripides and Plautus. These are, except for Aristophanes, the same writers that he chose to translate and edit, as we have already noted, and they are also among those that are most often quoted in the *Adagia* (Phillips, *The "Adages"* 393–404). Erasmus expresses his fondness for classical drama in his selection of authors, and he illustrates his recommended method of instruction with a dramatic text.

Using his beloved Terence as a model, Erasmus suggests that the schoolmaster begin with a "brief appreciation of the writer"; comment on his "circumstances, his talent, the elegance of his language"; distinguish the nature of the comic genre, "its origins, the number of types of comedy and its laws"; explain "the gist of the plot"; identify the meter; consider various aspects of style, including archaisms, neologisms, and figures of speech; compare parallel passages with their Greek sources; and finally "bring out the moral implication" (*Collected Works* 24:682–83). Erasmus's advice follows the general pattern of the fourth-century commentary on Terence by Donatus, which includes a life of Terence, an essay on comedy, short summaries or "arguments" of each part of the plays, as well as notes identifying figures of speech, glossing difficult passages, and comparing Terence's lines with those of other writers (see chapter 5). Erasmus's later edition of Terence, like many other contemporary editions, includes the Donatian commentary and prefatory material and adds Melanchthon's *argumenta* as well.

Though following an established procedure, Erasmus significantly emphasizes genre. He explains in *De ratione studii* that "in approaching each work the teacher should indicate the nature of the argument in the particular genre, and what should be most closely observed in it" (*Collected Works* 24:687). He then distinguishes comedy and tragedy in terms of the emotions aroused and the decorum to be followed. Erasmus's reference to the "varieties of Comedy" reflects Donatus's discussion of the kinds of comedy that flourished in the ancient world — *palliata, togata*, and *Atellana* (*Commentum Terenti* 1:22–31) — but Erasmus also seeks to differentiate individual qualities of each play. He recommends that the schoolmaster "deal with the arguments of the speakers as if they were set pieces of rhetoric" (*Collected Works* 24:687). The consideration of dramatic dialogue in rhetorical terms is, of course, common in the Renaissance, but Erasmus in suggesting an analysis of the arguments of individual speeches emphasizes issues as well as form. This concern with meaning leads naturally to the moral implications. Moral aspects of an action, occasionally noted by Donatus, are often elaborated by Renaissance commentators, and Erasmus endorses this practice. However, after using Terence to illustrate the method of teaching an author, Erasmus cites as moral examples Orestes, Pylades, and Tantalus, which come not from the comedies of Terence but from the tragedies of Euripides and Seneca. The didactic element is here not simply a justification of literature; rather it is regarded as complementing the rhetorical instruction.

Erasmus made ancient Greek and Roman playwrights the cornerstone of his program of study, which he sent to Colet for his newly established St. Paul's School and which became a model for grammar school education in sixteenth-century England (see Baldwin, *Shakspere's Small Latine* 1:123–30). Drama also heavily influenced his most famous work, *Moriae encomium* (*The Praise of Folly*) published in 1511, the same year as *De ratione studii*. In a letter to Sir Thomas More prefacing the printed edition, Erasmus, attempting to forestall his critics, writes: "They will loudly accuse me of imitating the Old Comedy or some kind of Lucianic satire, and of attacking the whole world with my teeth" (*Collected Works* 2:163). The relationship of this work to Lucian and the appropriateness of its dedication to More, who joined Erasmus in the translation of some of Lucian's dialogues, have been given much critical attention. More's appreciation of the satire might be expected not simply because of its Lucianic quality but because of More's special interest in drama, of which Erasmus was well aware.

Though Erasmus's mock encomium may convey the flavor of an academic lecture hall, the concept is dramatic. Folly's cockeyed but meaningful perspective on the world recalls an Aristophanic *agon*, and the irony operates in a truly dramatic way. Leonard Dean explains:

> Erasmian irony . . . produces a meaning comparable to that derived from a play or from any piece of literature conceived as drama.

The irony is composed of the simultaneous expression of several points of view, just as a play is composed of speeches by many different characters; and the meaning of the irony and of the play is not that of any one point of view or of any one character, but of all of them interacting upon each other. The result is not paralysis or abject relativism, but a larger truth than that presented by any one of the elements alone. ("*The Praise of Folly*" 53–54)

Folly may be confined to monologue, but her changes in tone and point of view as she catalogs the variety of folly in the world create a dramatic effect.

When Erasmus adopts the dialogue form, he moves even closer to drama. From the dialogues of Plato, Cicero, and Jerome as well as Lucian and more contemporary examples, Erasmus had many models to imitate, and it appears, as Margaret Mann Phillips notes, that the dialogue particularly "satisfied his taste for acute observation and the analysis of real experience. It was a form which allowed for epigrammatic conciseness, a special excellence of his own style" ("Erasmus and the Classics" 27). His use of dialogue in his early *Antibarbari* does not exploit the dramatic potential of the form; rather the opinions of the ignorant establish a context for a declamation attacking their prejudices and defending the classical heritage. In addition, a number of the dialogues included in the first edition of *Colloquia* in 1518 are rather wooden, and some are essentially narratives with one character describing an action or situation to another. However, many of the colloquies added in 1522 and later are much more fully developed in terms of plot and characterization. Craig Thompson calls them "incipient dramas or novels" (*Colloquies* xxvi).

A number of names and idioms in the colloquies are drawn from Terence, but more important are the dramatic elements Erasmus created. A few memorable characters emerge, such as the bluff, hard-living soldier Polyphemus and the shrewish servant Margaret, modeled on Erasmus's own housekeeper; and some dialogues give a vivid sense of place and interaction, though they may at times become overburdened with ideas or erudition. Some are remarkable for their natural ease, wit, and exchange of ideas. One such example is the colloquy that goes by the title "Proci et puellae" (1523); it represents an insistent young man seeking to win the favors of a witty and wise maiden. The characters of the young lovers are subtly revealed by their dialogue, and their words so aptly convey their emotions that all that is lacking is a stage. It is no wonder that some of the colloquies were in fact acted out by students (see *Opus Epistolarum* 7:508 n.4). When the Sorbonne in 1526 censured *Colloquia*, citing sixty-nine passages as erroneous or as tending to corrupt the morals of youth, Erasmus in the next edition responded that the book is not corruptive but instructive; and he claims that it will lead students "to many more useful studies: to poetry, rhetoric, physics, ethics, and finally to matters of Christian piety" (*Colloquies* 633). Erasmus may have been right; he may indeed have inspired students to take up poetry and perhaps drama as well. In any case the work became "the uncontested publishing success of the sixteenth century"; it went through some 120 printings before 1600.[2]

Erasmus recommends that classical drama be given a prominent place in the school curriculum; he proposes the way it should be taught; and he even provides some instructive examples of dramatic dialogue. In addition, he makes a number of comments on literature and on the creative process that are especially relevant to drama. Like most rhetoricians and educational theorists of his time, Erasmus advocates the imitation of carefully selected models as the basis for composition. A primary principle in his pedagogical theory, imitation is the method underlying *De copia* and the other manuals he provided the young scholars of his time. He was very much aware, however, that the process could stifle the imagination and reduce creativity. In his *Ciceronianus* (1528), a dialogue that is said to reveal the gifts of a "budding playwright" (Telle 211), Erasmus repudiates the imitators of Cicero who follow their model so slavishly that they disallow any word in their discourse not found in Cicero. Bulephorus, speaking for Erasmus in the dialogue, approves of imitation "that aids rather than hinders nature; that corrects rather than destroys nature's gifts." He declares that successful imitation "culls from all authors, and especially the most famous, what in each excels and accords with your own genius, ... digesting them and making them your own" (*Ciceronianus* 123).

Erasmus argues that not only must the models be chosen carefully, they must also be used discriminatingly. Further, one must be eclectic as well as selective in order to create something worthy of attention. Erasmus is in his *Ciceronianus* speaking particularly about style, but this perspective can apply more generally to artistic creation. Erasmus practiced what he preached most notably in the *Colloquia* and *Moriae encomium*, which, though inspired by Lucian and classical drama, adapt characteristics of their models so skillfully as to make the results appear new. Erasmus did not, so far as we know, write plays or directly advise others in dramatic composition, but if he had done either, he would undoubtedly have looked to Terence and perhaps Aristophanes as models for comedy and to Euripides and perhaps Seneca for tragedy.[3]

A second principle underlying Erasmus's critical theory is the concept of decorum most fully elaborated in classical criticism by Horace and conventionally adopted by Renaissance rhetoricians. Erasmus discusses decorum briefly in *De ratione studii* and implies its relevance to both literary form and to the creation of character. Significantly, his examples are drawn from Terence. He links decorum in comedy with "the portrayal of our common life" and with milder emotions than those of tragedy (*Collected Works* 24:687). After expressing the importance of decorum to genre, Erasmus applies decorum more specifically to the characters of comedy: "Youths should fall in love, ... pimps should perjure themselves, ... the prostitute should allure, the old man scold, the slave deceive, the soldier boast" (24:687). This is the general decorum of character that is to be observed in the "portrayal of our common life." But Erasmus points out that the poet must by his own judgement distinguish characters from one another. To illustrate, Erasmus describes Terence's individualization of characters of the same type, such as pairs of old men — the violent and morose Simo in contrast to the civil and calm Chremes in *Andria* or the chiding and merry Micio in contrast to the spiteful Demea in *Adelphi*. Erasmus notes that the pairs of young men and the pairs of slaves in the two plays are also well differentiated.

Marvin Herrick calls this individualization within a class "artistic decorum" (140–41), though it is not so identified by Erasmus. Erasmus may be implying that there is room for art within the concept of decorum, but, more importantly, he is emphasizing the necessity of individualization and its compatibility with decorum. In *De copia* Erasmus discusses the weight of precedent in portraying mythical and historical figures, and following the line of Cicero and later rhetoricians he explains that in creating character one must consider nationality or country, sex, age, fortune, disposition, and common affections as well as peculiar differences. Again, Erasmus emphasizes distinguishing the individual within the class, and again he uses Terence as a model of this practice, and he alludes to Plautus as well (*Collected Works* 24:582–87).

Erasmus's deep interest in drama is reflected in the theory, the models, and the tools that he provided and that shaped the educational program in England and elsewhere.[4] A boy growing up in the sixteenth or seventeenth century would probably have been introduced to formal drama in the way that Erasmus advised, just as he would have learned to write from textbooks that Erasmus authored. Erasmus's influence on the development of drama in the Renaissance extends beyond his perspective on classical dramatists and the proper method for teaching Terence, to the creative process itself. It may well be, as has been said, that without Erasmus, we would not have had Shakespeare (Baldwin, *Shakspere's Small Latine* 1:116, and E. Jones, *Origins of Shakespeare* 13).

CHAPTER SEVEN

VIVES

*J*UAN Luis Vives, sometime protégé of Erasmus, tutor of Princess Mary, confidant of Queen Catherine, friend of More, and enemy of Wolsey, has received remarkably little attention from scholars of the English Renaissance. In the context of the ubiquitous reputation of Erasmus and the martyrdom of More, the less colorful Spaniard has been overlooked, yet his association with Oxford University and the Court of Henry VIII during the critical period of 1523 to 1528 makes his relationship with the humanist movement in England especially important. Several of Vives's most significant works on education — including his plans of study for girls and boys as well as *De institutione feminae Christianae, De officio mariti,* and *Introductio ad sapientiam* — were written during his "English period"; and his major book on educational theory, *De disciplinis,* followed within three years of his departure from London. When the body of his work, spanning a period of more than twenty years, is considered, Vives must be regarded as one of the principal figures in the northern Renaissance, along with Erasmus, More, Budé, and Melanchthon, yet except for Foster Watson's effort to make some of Vives's principal educational works accessible in English in the early years of this century, Vives's writings, most of which are available only in their original Latin or in Lorenzo Riber's Spanish translation (Madrid, 1947), have been largely ignored by scholars writing in English. Scholars of Spanish intellectual history and literature have fortunately been more active in studying Vives; especially notable are the works of Bonilla and Bataillon, and the more recent monograph in English, *Juan Luis Vives*

(1970), by Carlos Noreña, examining the thought of Vives.[1] The standard edition of Vives's works remains Mayáns's eighteenth-century edition, which was reprinted in facsimile in 1964.[2]

As a result of Vives's relative neglect, his attitude toward literature in general and drama in particular has received only scattered comment. J. W. H. Atkins in *English Literary Criticism: The Renascence* discusses Vives's literary theory, but regarding Vives and Erasmus as complementary spokesmen of humanism, Atkins fails to develop important differences between their views of literature and especially of drama (35–65). T. W. Baldwin, on the other hand, contrasts their attitudes toward literature in education, and while championing Erasmus's literary humanism, which produced a Shakespeare, Baldwin declares that for Vives, "Literature, as such, is merely tolerated, if that. . . . The old conventional trivium, with its literary objective, does not play any fundamental part in his thinking. The Renaissance, as such, has hardly touched him" (*Shakspere's Small Latine* 1:192).

Even more extreme is Noreña's declaration that Vives "despised the world of poetry and fiction" because he considered it "full of evil and lust" (296). Neither Baldwin nor Noreña examines Vives's view of drama. Both Bonilla and Bataillon comment briefly on his negative criticism of literature and drama in *De disciplinis* and *De ratione dicendi*, though both also note the exception he makes of *Celestina* as well as his qualified approval of allegory in the theater (Bonilla 2:129; Bataillon 2:216–22). However, neither of these scholars examines Vives's literary theory in detail, and their observations on his view of drama are brief. An analysis of Vives's attitude toward drama and its place in his pedagogical programs reveals a deep suspicion of the power of drama to corrupt at the same time that it recognizes its perennial appeal.

Vives first indicates his attitude toward drama in 1518, in his *Fabula de homine*, where he creates a fable of the theater to express the nature of man. Drawing upon Pico's conception of man as having both animal and divine parts, Vives represents man as an actor who so impresses the audience of gods that they invite him to become a spectator with them. Vives describes the event this way: "When the gods saw man and embraced their brother, they deemed it unworthy of him to appear on a stage and practice the disreputable art of the theater, and they could not find enough praise for their own likeness and that of their father" (*Fabula* 391). The allegory is clear enough in terms of man's being invited to join the heavenly host almost as an equal, but the conventional metaphor of the world as a stage takes on an element of reprobation as the stage is viewed as unworthy of man and the art of the theater as disreputable. Thirteen years later, in his *De tradendis disciplinis*, Vives again uses the theater metaphor to register his disapproval of dramatic performance. In explaining why professors in an academy should not teach the same subject at the same hour, Vives writes, "There is a pandering to the audience, as it were to the public in the theatre, who are pleased not with the best man, but with the best actor" (*Vives: On Education* 61). In this comparison Vives appears to question audience taste as well as to imply a lack of principle on the part of the playwright and/or actors. No redeeming value in the performance is indicated.

In his commentary on Saint Augustine's *City of God*, published in 1521 and dedicated to Henry VIII, Vives expresses his view of drama more directly. Generally sympathetic with Augustine's negative attitude toward the theater, Vives often elaborates on Augustine's criticism. Following Augustine's reference to plays as "those spectacles of vncleannesse, those licentious vanities," Vives adds the note, "There was both most beastly shewes presented and most filthy words spoken" (*Of the Citie of God* 48). After Augustine's discussion of the Greeks honoring their actors while the Romans withheld citizenship from theirs, Vives comments: "It must of force be granted that the *Players* were the most pernicious men of conditions that could be, and the vilest in their villanies: because they could not be allowed for Citizens of that Cittie, which harboured so many thousands of wicked and vngratious fellowes, all as Cittizens" (72).

When Vives gives an account of the development of drama in the classical world, he provides a rather conventional summary drawn largely from Donatus and Diomedes, fourth-century grammarians whose comments were traditionally published in Renaissance editions of Terence;

however, in describing the kinds of drama that existed in ancient times, Vives emphasizes their immorality:

> The *Tragedie* discourseth of *Lamentable* fortunes, extreame affects, and horrible villanies, but farre from turpitude. The *Comedie* treates of the *Knaueries and trickes of loue*. . . . The *Satyre* containeth the looser *Faunes*, and *Siluanes* whose rusticall iestes delighted much, and sometimes they would lament. But as they were vncleanely and slouenly goddes, so were their speeches often times foule, and dishonest to heare. But the *Mimikes* forebore no beastlinesse, but vsed extreame licentiousnesse. (*Of the Citie of God* 65)

Given this perspective, we might expect Vives to moralize at length on Augustine's example of art provoking immorality in Terence's *Eunuchus*, where the lustful Chaerea, gazing upon a picture of Jove sending a shower of gold into the lap of Danaë, declares he will follow Jove's example in satisfying his desire. Instead, Vives explains the context of the action in Terence's play and provides a more detailed account of the myth of Danaë; then he merely adds that there is no lock strong enough to keep out corruption bought with "golden guifts" (63). Yet this image of art stimulating or justifying immoral actions, especially among youth, later became a central concern in Vives's attitude toward literature in general and drama in particular. In the first part of *De disciplinis*, entitled *De causis corruptarum artium* (1531), Vives returns specifically to this incident in Terence's *Eunuchus*, and interprets it as an example of drama inciting youth to pursue vice (*Opera* 6:94–95).

When Vives published his commentaries on *The City of God* in 1521, however, he was not prepared to ban all imaginative literature because it could provoke immorality. When Augustine speaks of Plato expelling the poet from his republic, Vives carefully qualifies Plato's words. Vives explains that Plato excludes from his ideal state only poets who represent wickedness of the gods and who evoke "vnmanly affections." Plato is said not only to allow poetry that is manly and honest but also to point out the poet's positive guidance and his inducement to moral action (II.14, p.74). Vives here seems to be expressing his own perception of poetry as a powerful force for good although it can also be used for wrongful purposes. Like Plato, Vives believes one must choose literary works with the aim of promoting virtue.

Vives illustrates this aim in the readings he recommends in *De ratione studii puerilis* (1523) for the education of the seven-year-old Mary Tudor. Seneca is the only dramatist listed among the approved authors, though Cicero, Plutarch, Plato, Horace, and Lucan are perceived to meet Vives's criteria of cultivating "right language and right living" (*Vives and the Renascence Education of Women* 146–47). Vives does not include the standard school text of Terence, but promotes instead Christian poets as well as Jerome, Augustine, Erasmus's *Enchiridion*, and More's *Utopia*. In his parallel plan of study for boys, written in the same year and addressed to Charles, the young son of Lord Mountjoy, Vives does include Terence but apparently feels the need to justify his choice. He says, "For daily conversation Terence is of great importance. Cicero made considerable use of him. Indeed, on account of the charm and gaiety of speech in his plays many thought they were written by nobles of the highest families" (*Vives and the Renascence Education of Women* 245). Earlier, in his commentary on *The City of God*, Vives notes that Terence knew Scipio and Laelius, and, apparently following Quintilian (*Institutio oratoria* X.i.99), Vives says that "many thinke that they helped him in writing of his commedies" (71). Vives points to the prologue of *Adelphi* as evidence.

In his plan of studies for boys, his invocation of Cicero, the master of rhetoric and moral philosophy, and his identification of Terentian style with aristocratic demeanor appear to give Terence an aura of respectability. Vives goes on to recommend Latin historians, agricultural writers, and poets, but he ignores Plautus and merely alludes to Seneca as the only Latin tragedian to survive. Lucan is singled out for special praise, and again his standard list of Christian poets—Prudentius, Prosper, Paulinus, Servilius, Juvencus, and Aratus—is suggested. For the study of Greek, Vives advises that the orators and philosophers be read first and then Aristophanes (because he's easy to translate) and Homer; after that Euripides and Sophocles might be read.

The reasons for Vives's negative view of drama become more evident as his career proceeds. He declares his moral orientation most explicitly in his *Introductio ad sapientiam* in 1524: Learning is "syncere and fruitefull" only if it is applied to the end of "Vertue and well doinge" (*Introduction to Wysedome* sig. C4v). As Sister Marian Tobriner points out in her edition of *Introduction to Wisdom,* Vives conceives of virtue in the sense of *pietas* "wherein personal godliness and social righteousness become synonymous" (66). The promotion of virtue is, of course, a humanist creed throughout the Renaissance; both Erasmus and More would heartily agree that education should lead students to the practice of virtue, but neither perceived virtue in so narrow or so emphatic a sense as Vives. Later, in *De tradendis disciplinis* (1531), Vives clarifies the significance of piety in life and, by implication, in education: "Since piety is the only way of perfecting man, and accomplishing the end for which he was formed, . . . piety is of all things the one thing necessary" (*Vives: On Education* 18). His paramount concern for piety leads Vives to reject any works that do not obviously reinforce the practice.

In his *Introductio ad sapientiam,* Vives sets down the principle that "Authours that wryte wantonlye, wherby may spring occasion of hurt, must not be touched, leste any filthines remain in the mynde throughe the redyng of them" (*Introduction to Wysedome* sig. C4v).[3] The fear that the depiction of wantonness will lead readers to practice it is expressed in his warnings that women not be allowed to read bawdry, particularly the works of Ovid, and they should also be dissuaded from chivalric romances because of their deleterious effect on personal values (*De institutione feminae Christianae* I.v).[4] Believing that the minds of men and particularly women are very susceptible to any outside influence, he considered the written word to have the power of promoting good or evil. In his *De officio mariti* (1528), he explains:

> Ther be some kind of letters & writynges yat pertayne only to adourne & increase eloquence withall. Some to delite and please. Some that make a man subtile and craftye. Some to know naturall thynges, and to instruct and informe the mynde of ma*n* withall. The workes of Poetes, the fables of *Milesij,* as that of the golden

asse, and in a maner all *Lucianes* workes, and manye other whiche are written in the vulgar tonge, as of Trystram, Launcelote, Ogier, Amasus [Amadis] and of Artur, the whiche were written and made by suche as were ydle & knew nothinge. These workes do hurt both man & woman, for they make them wylye & craftye, they kyndle and styr vp couetousnes, inflame angre & all beastly and filthy desyre. (*The office & dutie of an husband* sig. o)

This image of the effects of literature emphasizes the evil rather than the good, and since this is directed at men of marriageable age, not the seven- to fifteen-year-olds in the schools, it does little credit to the intelligence or judgment of adult society. It was this corrupting effect of literature that Stephen Gosson and Philip Stubbes seized upon fifty years later in their crusade to ban poetry.

Vives's counsel to husbands and his advice on the teaching of girls and boys express his view of the role of literature in the education process, and this view leaves little room for drama. In his *De tradendis disciplinis* in 1531, he develops his pedagogical theory and elaborates his critical views of literature as he reveals more clearly his negative attitude toward drama. He establishes his perspective in the preface. Though recognizing the authority of the ancients, he declares that their heathen errors must not be allowed to contaminate our religion or to stifle our search for knowledge. He states, "It is far more profitable to learning to form a critical judgment on the writings of the great authors, than to merely acquiesce in their authority" (*Vives: On Education* 8). Quoting Seneca's words, "Qui ante nos ista moverunt, non domini nostri, sed duces sunt" (*Opera* 6:7)—Those who have gone before us are not our masters but our leaders"—Vives stresses: "Truth stands open to all. It is not as yet taken possession of. Much of truth has been left for future generations to discover" (*Vives: On Education* 9). This view of ancient authors as leaders rather than masters provides the key to Vives's treatment of the Greek and Roman classics throughout his work. He is critical in his judgment and selective in his use of his classical heritage, and he is not timid in rejecting or adapting their words.

Vives first addresses the causes of corruption in the arts, and in poetry he finds "accounts of war, parricides, adulteries, . . . frauds, [and] impieties" (*Opera* 6:94) it is in this context that he cites Chaerea's justification of lust in Terence's *Eunuchus* that Augustine had earlier decried. He also alludes to Plato's expulsion of the poet from the state as a bad influence on the citizens. Vives declares Homer's hero Achilles to be a brutal savage, and Ulysses, though purported to be a model of prudence, to be in fact "a cheat and a liar" (*Opera* 6:96). When he turns to drama, his animus toward the theater that he had revealed in his commentary on *The City of God* becomes more emphatic. Plays are said to consist of the intrigues of love, "the wiles of prostitutes, the perjuries of bawds, and the roughness and vainglory of soldiers" (*Opera* 6:99).[5] These representations are viewed as especially harmful for boys, girls, and wives. Love and vice, Vives says, always triumph in comedy, and the result is to encourage immorality. He does, however, exclude the tragicomedy *Celestina* from this indictment because the illicit love is punished by death.[6] Vives goes on to consider the language and decorum of Plautus and Terence, but the tone of moral disapproval continues to the end of the discussion.

After considering the causes of the corruption of the arts in seven books, Vives becomes more constructive when he turns to the transmission of knowledge through education. As in his earlier pedagogical works, Vives emphasizes moral philosophy, history, and rhetoric. His continuing first priority of piety or the practice of virtue accounts for his high regard for moral philosophy, but he now articulates that a complementary purpose of education is practical usefulness (*Vives: On Education* 33, 284), which explains his placement of history and rhetoric in the first rank of academic subjects. Literature is perceived as serving the purposes primarily of moral philosophy and rhetoric and to a lesser extent of history. Cicero, Quintilian, and Plutarch are Vives's guides in expressing both educational goals and methods.

Plutarch provides the rationale for the study of literature as well as a precedent for the advice Vives had earlier expounded in his plans of study for both girls and boys. Altering Plutarch's metaphor of the bee finding honey "amid the most pungent flowers and the roughest thorns"

(*Moralia* 1:170–71), Vives compares heathen literature to a great field in which "useful herbs spring up in one place, and noxious weeds in another; whilst in a third part the field is planted with flowers, which serve for pleasure and adornment" (*Vives: On Education* 48–49). Worthy sentiments, warnings against vice, and praise of virtue, as well as models of eloquence, can be found in pagan works, though the writings must be chosen carefully (*Vives: On Education* 49). Some authors, including Martial and Catullus, should be avoided because of their scurrilous subject matter, and even the nobler works can be made more beneficial by adaptation into a form consistent with the Christian faith. An example Vives cites is St. Ambrose's pious adaptation of Cicero's *De officiis* (*Vives: On Education* 51). Anything that runs counter to Christian teachings should be eliminated, even if it means sacrificing the most prestigious works of the past. As Vives puts it, "It is better to accept the Christian teaching handed down through Christian tradition from Christ than to learn from monumental works of the impious, even if we cut out those things which might injure the integrity of good morals" (*Vives: On Education* 52). Christian piety is the determining factor in selecting educational texts, not aesthetic judgment.

Vives recognizes the delight and usefulness of non-Christian literature, but he believes it is the responsibility of teachers and educational leaders to excise obscene or offending passages. He declares that "whoever will undertake this expurgation will do a great service not only to his contemporaries and to posterity, but also to poetry itself and to poets" (*Vives: On Education* 128). It is in this context that he considers Latin comedy. He first mentions Caesar's approval of Terence as "a lover of a pure style" and then disparages Plautus for an "antiquarian" style and for allowing "his slave-characters great license, while he sought to gain the laughter and applause of the theatre by frowardness of speech and by not too much purity in his ideas." Vives concludes, "I should like to see cut out of both of these writers all those parts which could taint the minds of boys with vices, to which our natures approach by the encouragement, as it were, of a nod" (*Vives: On Education* 136). In *Th'overthrow of Stage-Playes* (1599), after citing Augustine's illustration of Chaerea justifying his lust by Jove's precedent in Terence's *Eunuchus*, John Rainolds points to Vives's advice on expurgating Terence and perceives Plutarch as Vives's source. Rainolds declares:

> Sundry men of note in our memorie also, not onely among professors of purer religion, but even among the Papists, haue advised Scholemasters & instructors of youth either not to read *Terence* to their Scholers, or if they will read him, not to read him all. *Ludovicus Vives*, having declared in generall out of *Plutarch* touching the reading of *Poëts*, that, vnlesse you vse it most warily, it hurteth; and therefore, if a *childe* may be allowed to meddle with it, *their writings would be purged first, & filthy matters be wholly cut out of them*: Doth wish the same concerning *Terence* in speciall *for those thinges which might defile the mindes of children with such faultes and vices, as naturally wee are prone to*. (123)

In contrast to Erasmus and other contemporary humanists who recommend Roman comedy in general and Terence in particular for instruction in colloquial Latin, Vives warns against using both Terence and Plautus, not only because of their questionable morality but also because they represent the language of dramatic characters with little education and low social position who do not use correct Latin (*Vives: On Education* 137). Vives appears to qualify his earlier recommendation of Terence "for daily conversation" in his plan of study for boys. Vives also dismisses Terence's most honored interpreter, the fourth-century grammarian Donatus, as often misguided in his explanations (*Vives: On Education* 160–61), though earlier Vives had recommended Donatus as an aid to understanding Terence.[7] The pedagogical tradition of making Terence one of the major Latin texts in the schools, which spawned the numerous Renaissance commentaries that elaborated upon Donatus, gives way to pious and practical moral training.

Vives contends that poetry should be "relegated 'to the leisure hours of life.' It is not to be consumed as if it were nourishment, but is to be treated as a spice" (*Vives: On Education* 138). With this view he naturally finds Roman comedy unworthy of serious study. His emphasis on historians and orators as well as moral philosophers elevates Sallust, Tacitus, and Lucan to the company of Cicero and Plutarch and determines his preferences in poetry for Virgil, Horace, and Seneca. When Vives alludes to Senecan drama, he refers to the moral instruction to be gained. Vives declares, "To encourage to right manners and morals, Cicero is good; to ward off from what is morally bad, read Seneca. Seneca has elegant, sharp and brief sentences which he hurls like thonged darts" (*Vives: On Education* 193). The negative *exempla* and *sententiae* are what Vives notices as he ignores the sensationalism and emphasis on fate so apparent to a modern reader of Seneca.

In developing his theory of imitation, Vives identifies the models for tragedy as Seneca and Euripides (*Vives: On Education* 193). Vives recognizes that Sophocles has been highly regarded in the past, but like most of his contemporaries, Vives prefers Euripides. The basis for his preference he finds in Quintilian, who places Euripides "on a level with the greatest philosophers on account of the deep seriousness of his maxims" (*Vives: On Education* 145). Again moral rather than aesthetic reasons determine Vives's judgment. It is no wonder that he found "little good fruit" in Aristotle's *Poetics*, which Vives describes as "occupied entirely with the consideration of old poems and with those niceties in which the Greeks are so tiresome, but which one may, with their kind permission, call inept" (*Vives: On Education* 158). The aesthetic considerations of drama in the *Poetics*, which were made accessible by the Latin translation of 1498, held little interest for Vives, probably because of his negative attitude toward drama as well as his preoccupation with the moral.[8] Later, in *De ratione dicendi* (1532), Vives refers to Aristotle's theory of imitation expressed in the *Poetics* to explain the appeal of drama to man, who delights in imitation because he is by nature imitative. Rather than considering the aesthetic implications, however, Vives once again stresses the moral dangers of drama (*Opera* 2:220).

Vives identifies Terence and Aristophanes as the models for comedy (*Vives: On Education* 193), but he does not develop this thought. He seems merely to be registering contemporary opinion. We have already noticed his rather guarded comments on Terence in other contexts, and his allusions to Aristophanes are always perfunctory. He describes Aristophanes as "gay" or merry on one occasion (*Vives: On Education* 145), but he demonstrates little familiarity with his plays. His earlier recommendation that Aristophanes be read because he is easy is a little surprising given his squeamishness about scurrility in Martial and Plautus. Perhaps Vives is depending on a very limited or secondhand knowledge of Aristophanes. His interest in Greek drama was clearly subordinate to his interest in Greek orators and historians or to Homer, whom he discusses at length in terms of the good and bad elements in his works. Vives's perfunctory treatment of Greek drama in his proposed curriculum is further indicated by his suggestion at the end of his extended discussion of Homer: "If the reader likes he may add for reading what is left us of Aristophanes and Euripides, then ... Hesiod and a few Greek epigrams which are witty without being immoral" (*Vives: On Education* 147). This is hardly an endorsement for his models of comedy and tragedy.

Vives's negative attitude toward drama is further expressed in his advice on the teaching of *elocutio*, or oral delivery. Recognizing the value of declamation in his *De causis corruptarum artium*, he urges voice training and believes that students should learn gesture "as a constituent part of the oration" (*Opera* 6:171–80), but, as Foster Watson points out, he does not advocate acting in stage plays as Francis Bacon later does (*Vives: On Education* cix–cx). In the sixteenth century in England and on the Continent it became a growing practice in the schools for students to perform plays in Latin and even occasionally in Greek as part of their training in rhetoric (Boas, *University Drama* 15–16), and in some instances Erasmus's *Colloquies* were acted out (*Opus Epistolarum* 7:508 n.4). Vives, however, recommends restraint in oral readings in class. His animus toward the theater is reflected in his choice of words. He says that the Latin should be "distincta pronuntiatione, et gestu intelligentiam adjuvante, dummodo ne ad histrionicum deveniat" — "pronounced distinctly and with gestures which may help understanding, so long as it does not degenerate into the theatrical" (*Opera* 6:307).

Underlying this distrust of the dramatic is Vives's fear of corruption of one's morals through the imagination, which is indicated many times in his pedagogical works but which is expressed perhaps most clearly in *De tradendis disciplinis*. He states:

> Poems contain subjects of extraordinary effectiveness, and they display human passions in a wonderful and vivid manner. This is called *energia*. There breathes in them a certain great and lofty spirit so that the readers are themselves caught into it, and seem to rise above their own intellect, and even above their own nature. But amongst all these, so charming virtues, very fatal faults are mixed, disgraceful subjects are partly described and expressed and partly even commended. Faults of this kind can do great harm, if the reader has confidence in the writer, and if his verses gain a lodgment in the listener's mind, unconsciously through the sweetness of the verse. (*Vives: On Education* 126)

It is after expressing this power of poetry on the minds of readers that Vives again notes Plato's banishment of Homer from his ideal republic, and this leads Vives to Plutarch's advice that boys be reminded "that poetry is not real life but a kind of painting" (*Vives: On Education* 127). Vives's concern is that readers will become so caught up in the fiction that they will no longer distinguish between fantasy and fact, between the imitation of life and reality. Because drama imitates life even more realistically than poetry, it is even more dangerous in its power to corrupt.

A year after *De tradendis disciplinis*, in *De ratione dicendi*, Vives returns to the subject of drama, and he explains more specifically the potential of drama to corrupt. He declares that actions expressing both good and evil are indiscriminately mixed in the theater, and an audience cannot sort out the beneficial from the harmful. He quotes Horace's famous dictum, "Omne tulit punctum, qui miscuit utile dulce" — "he who has mixed profit with pleasure has won all the votes" — but he does not trust the spectators to make the proper moral judgment. Vives approves of the more recent allegorical drama that through the portrayal of virtues and vices admonishes the audience to moral action, provided these plays are not so obscure as to be misunderstood by the common people (*Opera* 2:

220–21). However, because man's vulnerability to corruption is magnified by the dramatic illusion, the potential for evil, in Vives's view, may outweigh the benefits to be gained.

Vives made no significant statements about drama after 1532, but in 1538 he published what became his most popular work, *Linguae latinae exercitatio*, a series of dialogues dealing primarily with schoolboys' manners and activities. Unlike Eramus's *Colloquia*, which included learned topical discussions and diverting tales that appealed at least as much to an adult audience as the students to whom they were directed, Vives's dialogues are oriented toward the interests of the seven- to fourteen-year-olds who would be using them as classroom exercises. Though heavily weighted with moral instruction, in keeping with Vives's educational priorities, some of the exchanges are quite witty and occasionally humorous. The dialogue entitled "Garrientes" represents the chatter of schoolboys that ranges over many subjects; the tone is light and the conversation lively. The dramatic interplay is at least as effective as a number of contemporary interludes. Foster Watson, who translated the *Exercitatio* into English in 1908, notes Vives's aptitude in his dialogues for adapting the discourse of his characters to their diverse personalities (*Les relacions* 220; Vives, *Tudor School-Boy Life* xxxvii–xxxviii). Vives does indeed demonstrate a talent for drama, and perhaps it was the dramatic qualities that made his dialogues popular in the schools of the sixteenth century and later. After Erasmus's colloquies were judged to be dangerous, Vives's *Exercitatio* replaced them in Spain (Bataillon, *Erasmo y España* 2:250–51), but the popularity of Vives's dialogues went far beyond his native land. Juan Estelrich notes that the *Exercitatio* went through more than 200 editions before 1941 (90). Ironically the most widely diffused of Vives's works is the one that approaches the mode of drama. In the *Exercitatio*, Vives develops the imitation of life that he recognizes would delight an audience, but he laced his imitation with moral precepts to direct young minds to pursue virtue.

How much influence Vives had on the education of young minds in England and on the continent has been variously assessed; Estelrich counts nearly 500 editions and translations of Vives's works and regards his influence to be very significant in Europe and elsewhere (119–20). Jacques Parmentier begins his study of English education with Vives and considers his effect on the educational theory of Thomas Elyot, Roger Ascham, and Richard Mulcaster, as well as on the thinking of Milton and Locke (9–23); and Foster Watson discusses Vives's influence on the intellectuals of the early Tudor period, including Sir Richard Morison, John Skelton, John Palsgrave, John Leland, John Ritwise, and Nicholas Udall (*Les relacions* 193–206, 218–21). However, T. W. Baldwin calls Vives's ideas about education "cloistered" and declares that "Grammar school masters faced a situation so different that Vives . . . could . . . have had but little if any influence upon them. . . . Erasmus and men of his mind had already determined the fundamental curriculum and the pedagogical processes and attitudes of the grammar schools" (*Shakspere's Small Latine* 1:199). In contrast, Pearl Hogrefe believes that Vives had "a large influence on studies at Oxford" and that his friends, including Linacre, Tunstal, Fisher, Latimer, Mountjoy, and More, diffused his ideas. Hogrefe also points out that Hyrde's English translation of *De institutione feminae Christianae* went through eight editions and Morison's English translation of *Introductio ad sapientiam* five printings in the sixteenth century (238). Noreña claims that along with Erasmus, Ramus, and Melanchthon, Vives was "the most read Humanist of northern Europe in the second half of the sixteenth century" (1).

Vives's effect on the development of drama in the English Renaissance is even more difficult to assess. On the one hand, his concern with the power of drama to promote immoral actions provided arguments for Rainolds and his fellow moralists who sought to close the theaters. Vives's thoughtful wariness was probably more anticipatory than formative, but he clearly alerted the pious to the dangers of the imagination when prompted by "a local habitation and a name." On the other hand, his healthy attitude toward the classics as leaders rather than masters, as models to be adapted rather than slavishly imitated, may have influenced his student at Oxford, Nicholas Udall, to transform the structure and motifs of Roman comedy into a native context (see chapter 19).

How many other budding playwrights may have encountered Vives's view of the classics we shall never know, though even Shakespeare began his career by altering Plautian and Senecan models. Perhaps Ben Jonson best shows the dramatic legacy of Vives. We do not know when Jonson discovered Vives, but in his commonplace book entitled *Timber, or Discoveries*, published after his death, he left translated portions of *De disciplinis*, including the part of Vives's preface that sums up his view of the ancients (see Simpson 208–10). It is, however, in his dramatic practice that Jonson illustrates "the proper use of the classics," as expressed by Vives (see Mason 289). Drawing upon classical themes as well as classical sources, Jonson seeks to "translate" ancient models of tragedy and comedy into the contemporary idiom. He was not always successful, but it is Vives's principle of classical adaptation that informs Jonson's best work. As John Donne says in a Latin verse on Jonson's comic masterpiece, *Volpone*, Jonson is "segui aemularierq[ue]" — "following and yet rivalling" — the ancients as he makes new art out of the old (Jonson 11:318).[9] Though Ben may not be a "son" of Vives, Jonson highlights Vives's dramatic connection, one which has been too long overlooked.

CHAPTER EIGHT

MORE

*F*REDERICK S. Boas called Thomas More the "presiding" spirit of the "new drama" in the early sixteenth century (*Tudor Drama* 3). That More was a brother-in-law of John Rastell, printer and author of interludes, and the uncle of John Heywood, the most talented playwright of the Henrician period, perhaps prompted this designation, but a number of modern scholars have also perceived More's influence on the drama, in a variety of ways. Gustav Ungerer speculates that the anonymous *Calisto and Melebea* was commissioned for performance in celebration of the marriage of More's son John in 1529 (25–26); Gibson and Patrick and Hogrefe suggest that Rastell's *Nature of the Four Elements* was written under More's influence because of its "allusions to contemporary learning" and "the enthusiasm of More's circle for education" (Gibson and Patrick 256–57; Hogrefe 143–44); and A. W. Reed conjectures that Heywood's *Pardoner and the Friar* drew upon More's youthful poem about a sergeant pretending to be a friar (*Early Tudor Drama* 137–38). It has even been suggested that the *Four P.P.* and *Johan Johan*, traditionally ascribed to Heywood, may in fact have been written by the young Thomas More (Boas, *Tudor Drama* 15–16). However, none of these claims for More's role in the development of early Tudor drama has been convincingly demonstrated. More may have known intimately several of the early authors of interludes and may have encouraged their efforts by introducing their work to other members of the court circle or even commissioning performances himself; but William Roper, More's son-in-law and first biographer, and other contemporaries make no mention of More's involvement in dramatic activity after his youth. Yet it is evident from his works that More's early interest in drama continued and in fact informed his writings, from his juvenilia to his last words penned in the tower.

More may have been introduced to drama by his father, who served as Master of the Revels at Lincoln's Inn in 1488–89, when Thomas was about ten years old (Schoeck 426–27), but it was in the household of Cardinal Morton a year or two later that More first participated in dramatic activity. Roper reports that More, "thoughe he was younge of yeares, yeat wold he at Christmas tyde sodenly sometimes steppe in among the players, *and* neuer studyeng for the matter, make a *par*te of his owne there presently among them, *whi*ch made the lookers on more sporte then all the plaiers beside" (7). Later sixteenth-century biographers, Harpsfield and the unidentified Ro: Ba:, elaborate on More's popularity with the audience and especially with the Cardinal, who is said to have often remarked to the nobles present, "Whosoeuer liueth to trie it, shall see this Childe proue a notable and rare man" (Ro: Ba: 21; see also Harpsfield 10–11).

Whether Cardinal Morton's chaplain, Henry Medwall, composed the plays in which More performed, as some scholars have speculated, is not known (see Reed, *Early Tudor Drama* 100–101, Schoeck 426–27, and R. W. Chambers, *Thomas More* 56–57). However, the improvisational quality of youths A and B who "step in among the players" in Medwall's *Fulgens and Lucres*, even though their parts may have been played by professional actors, suggests the kind of role More may have acted. Certainly the comic wit and the parody would be most easily performed by household pages, of which More was one; and in the context of the lengthy arguments of the principal characters in the play, the boys offer a change of pace and humor that appeal to a banquet audience (see chapter 16).

More's early interest in drama is further suggested by his youthful composition "A mery jest how a sergeant would learne to playe the frere," a humorous narrative in doggerel rhyme that describes how a sergeant, masquerading as a friar in order to outwit a merchant, is beaten up by the merchant, his wife, and his maid. As is customary in jests, the emphasis remains on the action, and the characters are not developed; but the situation is vividly presented, the climax involves dialogue, and the fight is rendered in dramatic detail (*The Workes* 1: sig. Ciiv). The form and style suggest oral delivery, and the poem ends with the following direction:

> Play not the frere,
> Now make good chere,
>   And welcome euery chone.

These words imply a social occasion like those in which interludes were performed (*The English Works* 1:15; see also Gordon, "Dramatic Elements" 24–25).

Young More is also said to have devised a series of pageants on painted cloth with accompanying verses representing various stages in the life of man as well as allegorical figures of Death, Fame, Time, and Eternity. The pageants, related by the progression of time, demonstrate the triumph of the love of God over mutability, which is at the end celebrated by the poet in Latin verse. The conception smacks of contemporary court and civic entertainments and ends with the image of the poet expressing a didactic message.

Erasmus reports that as a youth More wrote "comoediolas"—"little comedies"—and acted in them (*Opus Epistolarum* 4:16); and in one of his earliest extant letters, written to John Holt about November 1501, More refers to a comedy about Solomon to which he apparently contributed some parts (*Correspondence* 3). Since Holt was a distinguished schoolmaster and the author of *Lac Puerorum*, a Latin grammar in English, it may be, as William Nelson suggests, that More wrote his "little comedies" for performance in the schools (xxix; see also Hogrefe 143–44). Neither Roper nor his other sixteenth-century biographers mention More's authorship of plays; however, John Bale in 1557, in his catalog of More's writings, begins with "Comoedias iuueniles, Lib.1" (*Scriptorum Illustrium* 655). This note corroborates Erasmus's allusion to More's authorship of several comedies, even though More in his letter to Holt refers only to one.

More's youthful interest in drama appears to have taken a new turn when he and Erasmus in late 1505 began translating Lucian, who profoundly influenced the later work of both. Though More translated only four dialogues to Erasmus's twenty-eight, More's four are among the fourteen longer ones included. Perhaps the most important in relation to More's view of drama is *Menippus*, which provided the metaphor of the stage that More used later in his history of Richard III and in *The Four Last Things*. Menippus, describing his view of the figures in Hades, says:

> As I looked at them it seemed to me that human life is like a long pageant, and that all its trappings are supplied and distributed by Fortune, who arrays the participants in various costumes of many colours. Taking one person, . . . she attires him royally, placing a tiara upon his head, . . . but upon another she puts the costume of a slave. . . . And often, in the very middle of the pageant, she exchanges the costumes of several players; . . . forcing Croesus to assume the dress of a slave and a captive, . . . when the time of the pageant is over, each gives back the properties and lays off the costume along with his body, becoming what he was before his birth, no different from his neighbour. (*Complete Works* 3-1:36–37, 176–77)

The comparison of drama to life, which became a cliché in the sixteenth century and which Shakespeare adapted so ingeniously, was not the only fruit More plucked from *Menippus*. He also encountered the moral dilemma of Menippus in his response to literature. Menippus says that as a boy he felt an "uncommon impulsion" toward "amours and assaults" after reading about them in Homer and Hesiod, but he learned as he grew older that "the laws contradicted the poets and forbade adultery, quarrelling, and theft" (*Complete Works* 3-1:26–27, 171). Menippus describes the attraction of poetry to the naive mind, against which Plato, Plutarch, Saint Augustine, and later More's friend Juan Luis Vives warned; and his answer to the problem comes not from the philosophers who disagree in their advice but in the perspective gained from a visit to the dead.

Menippus provokes the reader to question both the "silly fictions of the poets" and the "fruitless contentions of philosophers," as More explains in the dedicatory letter to Thomas Ruthall prefacing his translation of Lucian's dialogues (*Complete Works* 3-1:5). While appreciating Lucian's avoidance of easy moralizing, More recognizes the power of his instruction. More says:

> If, most learned Sir, there was ever anyone who fulfilled the Horatian maxim and combined delight with instruction, I think Lucian certainly ranked among the foremost in this respect. Refraining from the arrogant pronouncements of the philosophers as well as from the wanton wiles of the poets, he everywhere reprimands and censures, with very honest and at the same time very entertaining wit, our human frailties. And this he does so cleverly and effectively that although no one pricks more deeply, nobody resents his stinging words. (*Complete Works* 3-1:3)

Here More finds a model of literary merit; Erasmus in his prefatory letter states a similar view of Lucian's value as a subtle moral exemplar. More's and Erasmus's translations may have contributed to a Lucianic vogue in the first half of the sixteenth century (*Complete Works* 3-1:xviii), but for both More and Erasmus, Lucian represented the integration of dramatic comedy with prose dialogue, as Lucian himself claimed (6:425–27), for the purpose of instruction and entertainment.[1]

More's prose has long been recognized as having a dramatic quality; whether derived from his translation of Lucian, from fourteenth- and fifteenth-century devotional tracts, as R. W. Chambers claims ("Continuity of English Prose" cxxi–xxxiv), from the "dramatic *vulgaria*" More would have encountered in school, as William Nelson suggests (xxvii), or from his own youthful comedies, the dramatic element remains a consistent characteristic of More's style throughout his career. This is especially evident in his first major work, the fragmentary history of Richard III, written about 1513. This intriguing biography that provided the basis for Shakespeare's popular play has often been compared to drama in style as well as conception. A. F. Pollard declares that More's history "has all the requisite stage-properties: it begins with the *dramatis personae*, and a third of the text consists of their speeches; dates are almost as rare in More as they are impertinent to any legitimate drama, and his Richard III possesses all the qualities for a villain of the piece. All other elements except the dramatic are eschewed" (230).

A. R. Myers questions "whether More regarded himself as writing history; his story is much more like a drama." Myers goes on to identify Richard as "a personified Vice in a Renaissance equivalent of a morality play" (515). These assessments have led one recent scholar to consider the work a "satirical drama" (Hanham 152–90), and another to argue that the structure of More's *Richard III* is "similar to a morality play, using an *exemplum* to show how the violation of natural order ... brings consternation and woe upon the land, and God's punishment on the offender" (Kincaid 231). However, More does not bring Richard's career to the retributive conclusion that Shakespeare does; More breaks off after the murder of the young princes, when Richard becomes troubled with fearful dreams. Perhaps it is Shakespeare's successful adaptation that underlies these attempts to make More a dramatist, for it is unlikely that More viewed his work as a play or that the model for his structure was a morality.

More's technique may be dramatic, but his models can be found in classical prose. Like Lucian, More brings elements from the stage to a genre noted for its high seriousness. Seeking to make recent events both interesting and instructive to his contemporaries, More looked beyond the native chroniclers to historians of the ancient world. As Richard Sylvester has pointed out, More may have found in Sallust "a model for fictionalized speeches" and in Suetonius the character and atmosphere of dissimulation and deceit that mark his Richard; but it was Tacitus who provided the most fully developed example of the interrelationship between men and events presented in an atmosphere of dissimulation. Tacitus's portrayal of Tiberius is the precedent for More's Richard. Noting the parallel motifs in the two works, Sylvester also identifies the method as "essentially dramatic" in both (*Complete Works* 2: lxxxvi–xciii).

One of the most dramatic scenes in More's *Richard III* is Richard's accusation that Queen Elizabeth and Shore's wife disfigured him with witchcraft, which is a pretext to condemn Hastings, Mistress Shore's new "protector," of treason. More presents the scene in dialogue that demonstrates the histrionic character of Richard III and emphasizes the response of his audience. Richard begins by asking,

> What were they worthy to haue, that compasse & ymagine the distruccion of me, being so nere of blood vnto the king and protectour of his riall person & his realme. At this question, al the lordes sat sore astonied. . . . Then the lord chamberlen, as he that for the loue betwene them thoughte he might be boldest with him, aunswered and sayd, that thei wer worthye to bee punished as heighnous traitors whatsoeuer they were. And al the other affirmed the same. That is (quod he) yonder sorceres my brothers wife & other with her meaning the quene. At these wordes many of the other Lordes were gretly abashed that fauoured her. . . . Then said the protectour: ye shal al se in what wise that sorceres and that other witch of her counsel shoris wife with their affynitie, haue by their sorcery & witchcraft wasted my body. And therwith he plucked vp hys doublet sleue to his elbow vpon his left arme, where he shewed a werish withered arme and small, as it was neuer other. And thereupon euery mannes mind sore misgaue them, well perceiuing that this matter was but a quarel. (*Complete Works* 2:47–48)[2]

The proof of the dramatic value of More's rendering is Shakespeare's memorable expansion of this scene, though in conception it is unchanged. Richard's delight in his role-playing, which Shakespeare makes the salient feature of his character, is in More Richard's most distinctive quality. It is this aspect of Richard's character, which More created apparently without any help from Machiavelli, that led More to recast Lucian's metaphor of the theater.

Likening Richard's initial refusal of the kingship to the consecration of a bishop who ritualistically refuses the office the first two times it is offered but on the third offer accepts, More then goes on to adapt from *Menippus* the extended comparison of the theater to life, but in More's version the illusion takes on a new dimension since it involves a king. More writes:

> And in a stage play all the people know right wel, that he that playeth the sowdayne [sultan] is percase a sowter [shoemaker]. Yet if one should can so lyttle good, to shewe out of seasonne what acquaintance he hath with him, and calle him by his owne name whyle he standeth in his magestie, one of his tormentors might hap to breake his head, and worthy for marring of the play. And so they said that these matters bee Kynges games, as it were stage playes, and for the more part plaied vpon scafoldes. In which pore men be but the lokers on. And thei that wise be, wil medle no farther. For they that sometyme step vp and playe with them, when they cannot play their partes, they disorder the play & do themself no good. (*Complete Works* 2: 80–82)

More extends the metaphor of an actor performing in a Corpus Christi play[3] being thrust out of his role by a naive acquaintance to a warning not to discountenance a king, adapting the Lucianic original to the specific context, and ironically portending his own fate. When he refused to continue playing his part in Henry VIII's scenario of divorce, More did indeed "disorder the play," and he caused his last scene to be played on a scaffold. His evocation of the tyrant Richard's strategy in dramatic terms reveals More's sensitivity to role-playing in life as it warns his readers of the deadly designs of those who wield power.[4] Perhaps it was More's awareness of his own potential for angering a king that led him to break off this biography of a tyrant a few pages after this warning. When he returned to literary instruction some three years later in the *Utopia*, he protected his position by creating a persona to present potentially dangerous ideas and by constructing a dialogue to express different perspectives on the issues considered.

If More wrote the discourse on Utopian society and government (Book II) before composing the dialogue (Book I) that introduces it, as appears to be the case (*Complete Works* 4:xv–xxiii), he must have felt the need not only to present an image of the European world against which the Utopian world was to be measured, but also to establish a fictional context for the narration. Plato, whose *Republic* is the most obvious model for More's subject, uses the dialogue form to present his ideal commonwealth. However, many other classical and Renaissance examples of the form were also available to More, including dialogues by Cicero, Augustine, and Italian humanists of the Quattrocento, as David Marsh demonstrates in *The Quattrocento Dialogue*.

The dialogue became a favorite instrument of contemporary controversialists such as Hutten, Manuel, Murner, and Filfelo, but More in *Utopia* adopts a method that comes closest to the dialogues of Lucian (Pineas, "More's Use of the Dialogue Form" 193–206).[5] Like Lucian, More creates a major persona to convey his ideas in a dialogue that he dominates not simply by controlling its direction but by relying on narrative to express his view. In the manner of Menippus, who relates his journey to the underworld, and Tychiades, who describes his visit to Eucrates in *Philopseudes*, Hythloday is essentially *Utopia's* narrator, yet the action evolves in a dramatic way. Though briefly described when he is introduced, Hythloday reveals his perspective and his character through his own words. A spokesman for a radical alternative to contemporary Western society, he first discusses the social injustices that pervade the nominally Christian world before depicting the virtues in action in Utopian society. More reserves for himself the role of the skeptical observer and reporter. He may share qualities with the Socratic *eiron*, but he does not carry out a philosophical investigation, nor is it his purpose to draw out the *alazon*-like Hythloday for repudiation, as in the Socratic method. Rather, More's persona is a political realist, who counsels accommodation to the situation at hand rather than withdrawal from a king's court and who wishes for a greater reformation of society than he believes possible. More thus moderates the zealous view of Hythloday.

Underlying the work, as Edward Surtz indicates, is the conflict between the protagonist Hythloday and "the entire Christian West in its present state — degenerate, deformed, and unreformed" (*Complete Works* 4: cxxxvii). Hythloday's antagonists take various forms in the first book as the social ills created by human greed are considered; the presence of the corrupt Western society is maintained through the second book by periodic references to contemporary attitudes and by an implicit contrast between the Utopian society and the Christian West. The opposition is most dramatically portrayed in the first book as the group in Peter Giles's garden are made aware of the misplacement of values in their society. Though not hostile to Hythloday, More and his friends feel obliged to defend their society against Hythloday's attack. Pervading this conversation is a dramatic tension between Hythloday and his audience that continues through the second book.

Another dimension of the drama is brought out in Hythloday's description of a conversation that took place at Cardinal Morton's residence. Hythloday's opponents there are much more outspoken in their defense of contemporary society than the group of friends assembled in Giles's garden, and Cardinal Morton intervenes on more than one occasion to keep the peace. This dialogue-within-a-dialogue takes a comic turn when it is proposed that male beggars be made "lay-brothers" and female beggars nuns (*Complete Works* 4:81–85). The recalled conversation vividly evokes the kind of scene More may have observed as a page to the Cardinal. Surtz, who discusses the dramatic technique of the *Utopia* at length and even finds the work to be divided into three acts, suggests that the reader has "the sensation of witnessing a drama" (*Complete Works* 4:cxxxiv). Perhaps Surtz goes a bit too far in making the *Utopia* a play, but the dramatic nature of the work is clearly evident, for More's method, like Lucian's, is to blend elements from the theater with the traditional form of dialogue.

Given his dramatic bent, it is rather surprising that in the Utopian world More created there appears to be no drama. The Utopians, when not working or studying, divert themselves with music, conversation, and a few well-chosen games. In addition to chess, they play a game that has a remarkable resemblance to the pattern of the morality play. Hythloday describes the game as a battle between the virtues and the vices in which are "exhibited very cleverly, to begin with, both the strife of the vices with one another and their concerted opposition to the virtues; then, what vices are opposed to what virtues, by what forces they assail them openly, by what stratagems they attack them indirectly, by what safeguards the virtues check the power of the vices, by what arts they frustrate their designs; and, finally, by what means the one side gains the victory" (*Complete Works* 4:129). Hythloday does not indicate whether the game involves two or several players and whether the battle is fought symbolically on a board like chess or individuals impersonate the vices and virtues, but the game offers instruction of the sort we find in the morality play.

The Utopians are introduced to Greek drama by Hythloday on his fourth voyage, but their response to Aristophanes, Euripides, and Sophocles is not recorded. They are described as "very fond of the works of Plutarch and captivated by the wit and pleasantry of Lucian" (*Complete Works* 4:183). Their fondness for Plutarch, in particular the *Moralia*, is to be expected in light of their concern for ethics, though why these rather humorless folk appreciate Lucian is not so obvious. More's own fondness for Lucian may explain the comment, or perhaps it is to their undeveloped sense of humor that his "wit and pleasantry" appeal. No mention is made of Latin works being offered to the Utopians; this is not surprising given Hythloday's devotion to Greek and to philosophy as well as his judgment that in philosophy "there is nothing valuable in Latin except certain treatises of Seneca and Cicero" (*Complete Works* 4:51). More allows the predilections of his narrator to determine the choice of books, and as with a number of other views of Hythloday, they do not necessarily reflect the opinion of More. In accordance with the recommendations of his fellow humanists, Erasmus and Vives, More mentions specifically Homer, the recognized master of the epic; Aristophanes, the model for comedy; and Euripides, the model for tragedy. What is surprising is the inclusion of Sophocles among the dramatic poets. Sophocles is not included in Erasmus's first list of Greek authors in *De ratione studii*, though he is mentioned later in the same work; and Sophocles is also largely ignored by Vives. Plutarch is not included in Erasmus's plan of study; he does, however, occupy a central position in Vives's educational works. Lucian, as we would expect, is given a prime place by Erasmus (*Collected Works* 24:669), though Vives warns that Lucian should not be read (*Opera* 4:363). Surtz suggests that Hythloday's list of books can be "filled out" by Erasmus's recommendations (136), but since More placed artistic consistency in the character of Hythloday before his own personal judgment, one must be wary of Hythloday's preferences.

We are on somewhat safer ground in interpreting the words More assigns the persona of himself in *Utopia*, and it is this persona who not only expresses an interest in drama but reveals a critical perception of dramatic decorum. In response to Hythloday's cynicism about the intellectual's influence on kings, which is meant to justify Hythloday's refusal to be a king's counselor, More explains "another philosophy, more practical for statesmen, which knows its stage, adapts itself to the play in hand, and performs its role neatly and appropriately" (*Complete Works* 4:99). Comparing the king's court to the theater, More indicates that the effective counselor must accommodate his words of advice to the circumstances in which he finds himself. Illustrating the matter of appropriateness with examples from Roman drama (not the Greek preferred by Hythloday), More suggests that Hythloday adjust to the conditions at hand:

> We have the situation in which a comedy of Plautus is being performed and the household slaves are making trivial jokes at one another and then you come on the stage in a philosopher's attire and recite the passage from the *Octavia* where Seneca is disputing with Nero. Would it not have been preferable to take a part without words than by reciting something inappropriate to make a hodgepodge of comedy and tragedy? You would have spoiled and upset the actual play by bringing in irrelevant matter — even if your contribution would have been superior in itself. Whatever play is being performed, perform it as best you can, and do not upset it all simply because you think of another which has more interest. (*Complete Works* 4:99)

This perceptive application of decorum, the cardinal principle of Horace's *Ars poetica*, demonstrates more than the subtle understanding of a politician; it also suggests a direct knowledge of dramatic form.

Whether More can be credited with expressing a theory of the unities before Castelvetro, Vida, and Sidney, as George Williamson claims (294–96), may be questionable, but More speaks with the authority of experience both as a king's counselor and as an involved spectator, if not as an active participant in drama. It is also significant, as John Crossett explains, that More apparently drew upon the "Senecan" *Octavia* for the controversy he represented between Hythloday and the More persona that provoked the illustration (577–80). The character of Seneca in *Octavia* takes up many of the same points made by Hythloday, a curious irony for the Greek enthusiast.

Even though More became increasingly involved in political and religious issues after writing *Utopia* in 1516, his interest in literature and drama continued. In a letter to Oxford University in 1518, More responds to the academics and clerics who inveighed against the study of Greek and found imaginative literature a waste of time. After explaining the contribution of Greek letters to biblical scholarship of the past and present, More writes, "A knowledge of human affairs, too, is sensible, a thing so useful to the theologian, that without it he may perhaps sing pleasantly to himself, but he will certainly sing foolishly to the people. And this knowledge can nowhere be drawn more abundantly than from the poets, orators, and historians" (*Correspondence* 116). This placement of poetry alongside the more utilitarian subjects of oratory and history gives literature a primary position in education in More's view. Later, in his *Dialogue Concerning Heresies* (1529), he defends the study of poetry against Tyndale and Lutherans who "would now haue al lernyng save scripture only clene cast away." More declares, "Albeit poetes ben with many men taken but for paynted wordes, yet do thei much helpe the iudgement, and make a man among other thynges well furnyshed of one speciall thynge, without which all lernynge is halfe lame . . . a good mother wyt" (*The Workes* 1:153). This high priority given poetry in personal development is in keeping with the humanist creed More shared with Erasmus and Vives.

More's position on drama in the education of his children is more difficult to assess. Erasmus's famous comparison of More's household to

Plato's academy emphasizes the instruction in Christian religion and indicates study of the "liberal sciences," but the primary concern is said to be with piety and virtue (*Opus Epistolarum* 10:139). It is no wonder that Vives was so admiring of More's household, since piety and virtue are the explicit aims of education in his view (*Opera* 1:12).[6] Erasmus also mentions that in More's household there is "always alacrity, nor is sober mirth lacking" (*Opus Epistolarum* 10:139). However, he does not indicate what in the "liberal sciences" are studied or how the studies carry out the aim of virtue and piety. Erasmus's praise may imply general conformity with his *De ratione studii*, which he offered their mutual friend, Dean Colet, upon the refounding of St. Paul's School. In Erasmus's pedagogical scheme drama has a primary place; he names Terence first in the study of Latin and lists Euripides and Aristophanes among the Greek authors to be read (see chapter 6).

Whether the students in More's "academy" participated in dramatic performance is not indicated, but if his daughters "desputyd in philosophie afore the Kyng*is* Grace," as Palsgrave notes in a letter to More (*Correspondence* 405), their skill in declamation that gained them a royal audience may have been aided by acting out plays of Terence and Plautus, as was done in a number of the formal schools of the time. We have no warrant for designating More as "Head of the Drama Department" in his academy, as H. A. Mason calls him (48), but given his reputation for performance as a youth, expressed by Roper, who married Margaret More, the star pupil of the school, we might expect some dramatic activity beyond the classroom exercise of translating Terence. Perhaps this activity was one of the manifestations of alacrity and sober mirth that Erasmus noticed in More's school.

Whatever instruction in drama More advocated, he draws upon drama repeatedly in his devotional and polemical writings. In his discussion of pride in *The Last Four Things* (1522), More varies the Menippean metaphor of role-playing in life, used earlier in his history of Richard III, to prove the folly of pride. More says of the "lorel" proud of wearing a golden gown while playing "the lord in a stage playe": "Woldest thou not laugh at his foly, considering that thou art very sure, that whan the play is done, he shal go walke a knaue in his old cote: Now thou thinkest thy selfe wyse ynough whyle thou art proude in thy players garment, & forgettest that whan thy play is done, thou shalt go forth as pore as he. Nor thou remembrest not that thy pageant may happen to be done as sone as hys" (*The Workes* 1:84). This comparison of the ephemerality of life to a dramatic performance may not be as poetic as Macbeth's discourse on life as "a poor player, / That struts and frets his hour upon the stage," but it is nearly as poignant; and it demonstrates again More's sensitivity to dramatic illusion.

Another example of his use of drama to clarify and emphasize is his explanation, in *A Treatise upon the Passion*, of the Holy Eucharist containing Christ's true presence as well as representing His dying body on the cross. More compares this holy mystery to a prince deciding to play his own part in an interlude, and then asks, "dyd he not there his owne persone vnder the fourme of a player, represent his owne persone in fourme of his own estate?" (*Complete Works* 13:157).[7] This rather surprising explanation, which recalls More himself stepping in among the players as a youth, appeals to audience familiarity with contemporary court entertainments that occasionally represent the monarch on stage.

In his *Responsio ad Lutherum* (1523), More associates Luther with ridiculous and unsavory figures from Roman comedy; the tone is set in the first sentence of the work as More refers to Luther's "Thrasonic vainglory" (*Complete Works* 5-1:41). Terence's braggart Thraso, commonly used by controversialists in the period to insult their opponents, is compared to Luther again a few pages later and periodically throughout the work. Two other Terentian characters—Phormio, the parasitic blackmailer in the play bearing his name, and Parmeno from the *Eunuchus*—are also invoked to repudiate Luther. However, as J. M. Headley demonstrates, More's indebtedness to Roman comedy in *Responsio ad Lutherum* appears to go beyond his allusions to characters: More uses a colloquial style comparable to that of Plautus and Terence as well as devices such as pleonasm, diminutives, anaphora, alliteration, assonance, and etymological wordplay that abound in these comic playwrights. Headley says, "In Roman comedy, . . . More found a world where language, tone and characters were eminently suitable for his polemical needs" (*Complete Works* 5-2:816).

That More conceived of the controversy he had entered in dramatic terms is suggested by his comment on Luther's invitation to his opponents to confront him in Wittenberg:

> He [who accepts Luther's invitation] will contend with the scoundrel in his own theater, where the seats have been packed with scoundrels who, as their heresiarch twists the words of scripture to an adulterated meaning, as he jeers at the authority of all the learned men of antiquity, as he hisses at the public faith of so many ages, and as he curses all that is holy, at each blasphemy will applaud and repeat, 'Bravo!' But at each word of the one who would come to dispute with Luther, with shouting, grimacing, stomping, pounding, they will interrupt him, hoot at him, hiss him off the stage. If he will persist in the face of all this and overcome their shouts with reason, they will finally kill him on his departure. (*Complete Works*, 5-1:43–45)

More prefers to play his role in the religious controversy from afar as he creates his drama on the printed page. His part as a spokesman for the orthodox position increased as he disputed with Tyndale and other reformers who emerged in the ten years following *Responsio ad Lutherum*. Several of these works adopt the dialogue form, and most manifest the dramatic qualities we expect in More's colloquial prose, but none matches the comic spirit of his response to Luther.

After the termination of his official position in Henry VIII's government, More turned away from polemics to more ascetical concerns, but he continued to use the dialogue form. His last dialogue, *A Dialogue of Comfort Against Tribulation*, written in the tower during his imprisonment, is in some respects his most remarkable. Purporting to have been "made by an hungaryen in laten, & translatyd out of laten into french, & out of french into Englysh," *A Dialogue of Comfort* represents conversations between Anthony, a prisoner, and his nephew Vincent, who seeks comfort against tribulation, for "the world is here waxen such / & so gret perilles appere here to fall at hand" (*Complete Works* 12:3). Anthony, who is described by his nephew as a man who has "so long lyvid vertuously" and as "lernyd in the law of god" (*Complete Works* 12:3), is More's chief spokesman in the work, and his similarity to More in situation and temperament gives his words added significance. That the man suffering the discomforts of confinement and threatened with greater peril should provide solace to a youthful, free man is ironic, but it mirrors More's position in relation to his family and to the young men who had viewed More as their mentor, as Roper makes clear (97–102). By distancing the discussion of his concerns as he prepares to depart the world, More reduces the emotional quality as he concentrates on a reasoned assessment of the contemporary state of affairs.[8] This integration of serious matter with the techniques of drama, which he had learned from Lucian, is the final manifestation of More's lifelong interest in the theater. From his boyhood to his death, drama played a major role in More's literary career.

CHAPTER NINE

ATTITUDES OF REFORMERS AND HUMANISTS

*D*RAMA became an increasingly important concern in educational, religious, and political circles in the early sixteenth century. The views of More and the Continental humanists, especially Erasmus and Vives, significantly influenced the ways in which the English thought about drama, and a few native authors express their aims, apologize for their efforts, or explain their intentions in prologues, epilogues, or prefaces to their plays. With the growing moral concerns about poetry in general and drama in particular in the second quarter of the sixteenth century, courtiers, clerics, scholars, and rhetoricians address the role of drama in education and social behavior. Many of the remarks are not very perceptive or original, but they reflect the views of public leaders who articulated and shaped the thoughts of groups in their society. What becomes increasingly apparent as the decades pass is the schism between moralistic reformers and humanists in their judgments of the effects of plays and imaginative literature on the youth and other impressionable members of society. The power of poetry, enhanced in dramatic performance, to move its audience to good or evil action becomes the central issue of the conflict.

Growing interest in the influence of drama on individual thought and behavior is reflected in various attempts to regulate dramatic activity and to promulgate political and religious positions through drama. Although a few discussions of the negative aspects of dramatic performance before the English Reformation, such as the Wycliffite *Tretise of Miraclis Pleyinge*, are extant, and occasional efforts by the church and local governments to regulate dramatic performances are evident, after 1530 groups within the church and the state become increasingly involved in both promoting and censuring dramatic productions. Miracle and saints' plays may have been the first casualties of the Reformation as monasteries were dissolved and their libraries destroyed. Texts of saints' plays, once widely performed throughout Britain, disappeared along with the icons identified with Catholicism. Plays related to the Virgin Mary may have particularly fallen victim to anti-Roman zeal (Gardiner 54–57). The religious civic drama was subjected to governmental regulation, beginning in Henry VIII's reign and continuing in Edward's; and though in Mary's reign a brief revival of religious drama occurred in some places, the cycles died out altogether under Elizabeth (Wickham, *Early English Stages* 2.1:54–75). Religious drama was not the only subject of external interference; folk drama too was suspect, and attempts were made in Chester, Newcastle, and other places to curb the mummers' plays. While folk and religious traditions were being restricted, new plays promoting the reformist and Catholic perspectives carried the factional battle onto the stage. Bale, Lindsay, and others who made the morality play into a vehicle for political and religious propaganda demonstrate the potential for drama to persuade and incite to action (see chapters 13–15).

It was this atmosphere that provoked the state and local governments to attempt to exercise control over dramatic offerings. In 1543, the Act for the Advancement of true Religion and for the Abolishment of the Contrary, forbidding "interpretacions of scripture, contrary to the doctryne set forth or to be set forth by the kynges maiestie," was passed, apparently to stifle the use of scriptures in drama for polemical purposes (E. K. Chambers, *Medieval Stage* 2:221–22; Kahrl 132). In 1545 the city of London proclaimed "the Abolyshm(en)t of Interludes" specifically on Sunday and holidays during Evensong or other divine services and restricted performance to approved premises. The justification for this action is made on moral grounds: "a greate p(ar)te of the youthe ... & manye other light Idle and evyll disposed p(er)sones daylye and Contynuallye frequentynge hauntynge & followynge ... playes haue ... bene ... moved & provoked therebye to all provytye p(ro)clyvytye & Redynes of dyvers & sondrye kyndes of vyce & synne" (quoted in Wickham, *Early English Stages* 2.1:327). In 1549 all plays were banned by state order for two months in the purported interest of civil order (Wickham, *Early English Stages* 2.1:67–68), and in 1551 Edward's government sought to regulate dramatic performance with the indirect result of suppressing the older religious drama (Gardiner 57–62). Miracle plays were revived by Mary in 1557, but her government also sought to control dramatic performance by censorship (Wickham, *Early English Stages* 2.1:71–72). The increasing regulation of dramatic activity on religious, moral, and political grounds was climaxed by Elizabeth's Act of Uniformity, passed in 1559, which effectively brought an end to the polemical interludes, as well as the religious cycles and Catholic moralities (Wickham, *Early English Stages* 1:240). Increasing awareness of the power of drama to change minds and provoke action appears to have led to restrictions on dramatic activity in order to protect the positions of the ruling group in both the church and the state.

This climate of fear about the effects of drama, which culminated in the closing of the theaters in 1642 by the Puritan Commonwealth, began to develop in the early sixteenth century. Erasmus and Vives address the moral concerns of churchmen and scholars regarding the teaching of classical drama in England and Europe (see chapters 6–7), and Renaissance commentators on Terence especially emphasize the moral instruction in his comedies (see chapter 5). The moral issue of drama is often incorporated in more general concerns about literature or poetry in relation to education or public morality, though frequently drama is singled out for special comment. In England at the beginning of the sixteenth century, no particular doubts about the morality of drama appear to have surfaced, though by 1509 Stephen Hawes felt compelled to defend poetry in his *Passetyme of Pleasure*. An avowed follower of Lydgate, Hawes explains in his representation of the education of an ideal knight the allegorical method of poetry. He declares that "vnder a fayre fayned fable / A trouth appereth gretely profytable" (Hawes, 713–14); and in answer to "rude people / oppresst with blindess" (791) who do not understand the meaning of poetry, who think "poetes / but depaynt and lye / Deceyuynge them / by tongues of flattery" (811–12), Hawes claims poets "fayned / no fable without reason / For reasonable is / all theyr moralyte" (953–54).[1] Hawes interprets the myths of classical poetry, including the stories of Atlas, Pluto, Cerberus, and Hydra, moralistically, and then delineates the didactic message of poetry:

> Thus the poetes / conclude full closely
> Theyr fruytfull problemes / for reformacyon
> To make vs lerne to lyue dyrectly
> Theyr good entent / and trewe construccyon
> Shewynge to vs / the hole affecyon
> Of the waye of vertue / welthe and stablenes
> And to shyt the gate / of myscheuous entres. (1114–20)

The charge that poets are liars is thus answered by claiming that they promote virtue by expressing a higher truth through feigning.

Leonard Cox, in *The Arte or Crafte of Rhethoryke* (1529), suspects the credence of poets because, he says, "it is the nature of poetes to fayn and lye / as bothe Homere and Virgile / which are the princes and heddes of al poetes do witnesse the*m* selfe." To illustrate his point he alludes to the lies poets have written about Pluto's underworld kingdom, and then adds the examples of Erasmus's *Praise of Folly* and Plato's commonwealth, where no man should have his own wife but "euery woman shalbe commune to euery man" (53–54). These superficial examples of lies and the advocacy of immorality demonstrate that literature must be read with care, for not all is what it may appear to be. Nevertheless Cox makes many references to classical authors to explain and illustrate the principles of rhetoric; for instance, he paraphrases Simo's description in Terence's *Andria* of the delights of youth in horses, hunting, and books to indicate the nature of adolescence as an example of the decorum involved in characterizing persons in an oration (55). Cox is clearly not opposed to literature; rather he implies that the nature of imitation demands a sophisticated judgment on the part of the reader and the orator, who draws on the examples of poetry and drama for guidance.

Henry Cornelius Agrippa, the German critic of humanism, ignored the subtleties of poetic creation and appreciation; denouncing poetry as wanton and deceptive, he claimed it to be the preserver of idle and foolish opinions. In a work published in 1530 entitled *De incertitudine et vanitate scientiarum et artium*, he condemned both poetry and drama as well as other "arts and sciences" that mislead society. Though not translated into English until 1569, Agrippa's diatribe appears to have been influential in its original Latin version in providing ammunition for the moralistic attack on poetry and the theater in England after the Reformation. In a chapter devoted to poetry, Agrippa charges that it is "an Arte, that was deuised to no other ende, but to please the eares of foolishe men, with wanton Rithmes, with measures, and weightinesse of sillables, and with a vaine iarringe of wordes, and to deceiue mens mindes with the delectation of fables, and with fardels of lies. Wherefore, she dothe deserue to be called the principall Authoure of lies, and the maintainer of peruerse opinions" (Agrippa fol. 11).[2]

The falseness of poetry derives from its end to give man pleasure, but in Agrippa's view it is especially dangerous because poetry's "lies are fained with so greate skill, that oftentimes they hinder true histories," as in the case of Dido's adultery with Aeneas and the fall of Troy (fol. 12). Agrippa perceives this power of poetry to mislead and provoke error as the major reason for poetry's condemnation by learned men of the past: "*Augustine* willeth that it shoulde be banished out of the Citie of God: *Plato* the Pagane driueth it out of the Common Weale. *Cicero* forbiddeth it to be admitted" (fol. 12). Claiming that the ancient Romans held poetry in dishonor, as witnessed by Gellius and Cato, and that the Athenians condemned Homer "as a madde man," Agrippa concludes that "all vertuouse men haue dispised Poetrie, as the mother of lies" (fol. 12–13). To further reinforce his point, he declares that Democritus termed poetry "no Arte, but a madnesse"; Augustine called it "the Wine of errour, ministred by drunken Doctours"; and Hiero named it "the meate of Devils" (fol. 13). This venomous attack on poetry provided both argument and evidence for moralistic critics in England for more than a hundred years.

Agrippa's attack on the performance of plays is both shorter and less shrill, but it significantly condemns both the actors and the audience. After noting that the city of Marseilles would not admit players "because their argumentes for the most parte contained the actes, and dooinges of Harlottes, to the ende that the custome of beholdinge suche thinges, mighte not also cause a license of folowinge it," Agrippa expands on the public immorality provoked by the immoral plays. He says, "This Arte, is not onely a dishonest and wicked occupation, but also to behold it, and therein to delite is a shameful thinge, because that the delite of a wanton minde is an offence" (fol. 32). Later, in a discussion of bawdry, Agrippa lists comedies among the "wanton rithmes, fables, and pastorical songes, Epigrams, . . . and dishonest verses, taken out of the most secrete armarie of Venus" that "turneth al chastitie upset downe, and corrupteth the good disposition & manners of youth" (fol. 97–98). Then after identifying the "chiefest bawds . . . emonge the auncientes" as Callimachus, Pindar, Sappho, Catullus, Vergil, Ovid, Juvenal, and Martial, Agrippa denounces the "histories of love" involving Lancelot and Tristram, which "corrupt the chastity of maidens and wives," and warns that Dante, Petrarch, Boccaccio, and Peter Bembo induce readers to immorality through their writings (fol. 98). It is in this context that Agrippa offers as proof of art provoking immoral action the example from Terence's *Eunuchus* of Chaerea's justification of his rape of Pamphila as a result of gazing at an image of Jove sending a shower of gold into Danaë's bosom. This incident from Terence, upon which Augustine, Vives, and several Renaissance critics commented (see chapters 5 and 7), later became favorite evidence for the antitheater movement that gained momentum in the last quarter of the century. Drama was only one target in Agrippa's war on the arts and sciences, but his attack found sympathy among clerics, scholars, and moralists who feared the power of the word and image to corrupt and mislead.

Among those to whom the spirit of Agrippa appealed was John Jewel, bishop of Salisbury and a major spokesman for the reformist position in the church. In "Oratio Contra Rhetoricam," composed about 1548, Jewel attacks rhetoric as perpetrating fraud and lying, and he denigrates Cicero and Demosthenes as false models for the orator. Though this essay may be particularly directed against the Ciceronians, whose slavish imitation of their master also aroused Erasmus's spleen twenty years earlier (see chapter 6), Jewel appears to distrust imaginative composition and eloquent style. Focusing on the potential of language to deceive, he advocates plain speech as the ideal (*Works* 4:1284–90).

Thomas Becon, a reformer propagandist, was more explicit in his warnings about the dangers of the written word. In *A New Catechisme sette forth dialoge-wise in familiar talke betwene the father and the son*, published in 1550, Becon in the spirit of Agrippa charges that such "wanton and unhonest" writers as Martial, Catullus, Tibullus, Propertius, Cornelius Gallus, and the "wicked and ungodly" Lucian should be kept away from youth "lest by the reading of them they make shipwreck both of their faith and manners, and in their tender years drink in such corruption as shall be noisome unto them all their life after" (282–83). Becon, like Agrippa, notes historical precedents for dealing with poets: he points out that the Lacedaemonians threw out the books of the poet Archilochus; Plato expelled poets from his republic; and Augustus Caesar banished Ovid. However, Becon qualifies his sweeping condemnation of filthy pagan writers by saying, "To interlace godliness in the lessons of profane writers maketh greatly unto the advancement of virtue; and heathen authors so read profit very much" (283). Altering the texts for moral instruction makes them acceptable, but Becon's emphasis is on the dangers of literature for the unwary.

Pietro Martire Vermigli, called Peter Martyr in England, was named Professor of Divinity at Oxford in 1549. In his *Commentaries upon Judges*, completed by the end of 1560, he elaborates the reformers' distrust of imaginative literature and finds fables, which in his view include comedies and tragedies, particularly suspect. Noting that Plato excluded from his republic poets who "spake of gods, as though they should speake of men" and represented both gods and men committing the same sins, Martyr demonstrates the evil effect of fables with the classic example of Chaerea in *Eunuchus*, who "(beholding a wanton table in the harlotes house, wherein was printed Iupiter persyng into Danae by a showre) began to haue a pleasure in himself, bicause he beyng a vile man did those thinges, which he knew by that table the chief God in the olde time committed. I did it (sayth he) and I dyd it with a good will" (fol. 159). This depiction of Chaerea being erotically aroused by an image of Jupiter and Danaë is more explicit than most of the moralists' allusions to this Terentian incident as an example of art inducing immorality.

As further proof of the immoral examples of the gods in the fable, Martyr cites Augustine's response, described in his *Confessions*, to learning as a child about Jupiter's adultery. Martyr concludes, "The mindes and affections of men are prone inough vnto vices: wherfore it is wickedlye done, that children and younge men should in that age be by vyle and filthye fables stirred vp unto sins" (fol. 159). Again concern about the impressionable minds of youth provides the rationale for banning certain classical works. Martyr does not single out drama for comment, though in *A briefe Tretise, Concerning the vse and abuse of Dauncing*, drawn from his *Commentaries upon Judges* and published in an English translation some twenty years later, Martyr enigmatically warns, "Let not Clarkes approche the Theatre" (sig. D.ii), by which he indicates the inappropriateness of clerics to participate in or attend plays. Though reasons for this statement are not developed, presumably it is based on moral grounds.

In response to these critical characterizations of literature as a source of moral corruption and drama as an activity to be avoided, a second generation of humanists, following in the wake of Erasmus and More, defended poetry and drama on pedagogical, rhetorical, and moral grounds. Foremost among these post-Reformation defenders was Thomas Elyot, a courtier who also served the cause of learning. In his *Book named The governor* (1531), in which he explains the preparation of gentlemen for their natural roles of leadership and delineates the personal qualities they should manifest, Elyot gives imaginative literature a prominent place in the educational process.

Focusing on classical authors, Elyot defends both the poetic art and its practices against contemporary attack. He writes: "The name of a poet, whereat now (specially in this realm) men have such indignation that they use only poets and poetry in the contempt of eloquence, was in ancient time in high estimation: insomuch that all wisdom was supposed to be therein included, and poetry was the first philosophy that ever was known: whereby men from their childhood were brought to the reason how to live well, learning thereby not only manners and natural affections, but also the wonderful works of nature" (46). Elyot directs his readers to Plato, Aristotle, and Cicero to prove the high estimation in which poetry was held, and alludes to the Latin term *Vates*, meaning "prophets," that was applied to poets in Roman society to confirm their special place.

Elyot then sets out "to show what profit may be taken by the diligent reading of ancient poets, contrary to the false opinion, that now reigneth, of them that suppose that in the works of poets is contained nothing but bawdry . . . and unprofitable leasing," or lying (47). Addressing the charges of the "ignorant . . . that in Terence and other that were writers of comedies," nothing is "contained but incitation to lechery" (47), Elyot first defines comedy and then explains its moral instruction in the terms of Erasmus and the Terentian commentators (see chapters 5–6). Elyot declares: "Comedies, which they [the ignorant] suppose to be a doctrinal of ribaldry, . . . be undoubtedly a picture or as it were a mirror of man's life, wherein evil is not taught but discovered; to the intent that men beholding the promptness of youth unto vice, the snares of harlots and bawds laid for young minds, the deceit of servants, the chances of fortune contrary to men's expectation, they being thereof warned may prepare themself to resist or prevent occasion" (47–48).

After adapting the Ciceronian definition of comedy as a mirror of life and an image of truth, made famous by Donatus (see chapter 5), Elyot emphasizes the negative examples that warn youth to shun vice. Then after alluding to the positive instruction of the wise, moral statements, or *sententiae*, as well as the examples of eloquence to be emulated, Elyot concludes: "If the vices in them [comedies] expressed should be cause that minds of the readers should be corrupted, then by the same argument not only interludes in English, but also sermons, wherein some vice is declared, should be to the beholders and hearers like occasion to increase sinners" (48). That Elyot regards comedy as another form of moral instruction like sermons and "interludes in English," which in 1531 would mean primarily the obviously didactic morality plays, may result from his defensive posture, though it also indicates that the moral quotient is the major consideration in his literary judgment.

Elyot quotes passages from Terence and Plautus to illustrate their instruction to shun vice and embrace virtue, but he admits that some poems include "light matter." Following Plutarch, Elyot declares that is not sufficient cause for abandoning "all their works, no more than it were to forbear or prohibit a man to come into a fair garden lest the redolent savours of sweet herbs and flowers shall move him to wanton courage, or lest in gathering good and wholesome herbs he may happen to be stung with a nettle" (49). A man must distinguish the good from the evil, and apparently he learns to do this by the guidance of his schoolmaster and by experience. It is significant that Elyot regards comedies to be the proper study of youth but considers tragedies to be appropriate for a mature man. Elyot remarks, "When a man is come to mature years, and that reason in him is confirmed with serious learning and long experience, then shall he, in reading tragedies, execrate and abhor the intolerable life of tyrants, and shall contemn the folly and dotage expressed by poets lascivious" (33).[3] Again the moral element is paramount, but the older, experienced man can more readily understand and appreciate the lessons of tragedy as well as the errors of misguided poets.

Elyot's eloquent defense of poetry and drama in *The Governor* carries on the humanist spirit of Erasmus and More and anticipates the argument of Sidney, but near the end of his career he presents what appears to be a different view of poetry. In the dialogue called *The Defence of Good Women*, published by Elyot in 1545, Caninus claims that the poets confirm his argument that women are inconstant; however, Candidus, questioning the authority of poets, declares they were never held "but in smal reputacion" and neither Plato nor Cicero would admit them to the "publike weale." Candidus explains:

> The cause why they were soo litell estemed was, for as muche as the more part of their inuencions consisted in leasinges, or in

steryng vp of wanton appetities, or in pouryng out, in railynge their poison of malice. For with their owne goddes and goddesses were they so malaperte, that with their aduoutris they filled great volumes. Jupiter, whom thei cal kyng of goddes and of men, they bryng hym out of heauen to his harlottes transfourmed sometime into a bull, an other tyme lyke a ramme, a stinkyng gote or a serpent. (sig. Bv)

Appearing to have taken his text from Agrippa, Candidus charges poets with perpetuating lies and immorality as the defence of women prevails over his defense of poetry. However, we must remember that this is a dialogue in which both disputants take extreme positions. The exaggeration in the fictionalizing becomes more apparent near the end of Candidus's speech, in his description of other poets humbling themselves to their mistresses "as thei wold licke the dust from their slippers," and then after "the flame of carnalitie is quenched" or the "women . . . constantly refuse their unhonest desires, " these poets maliciously denigrate women for inconstancy. Elyot here may be mocking contemporary sonneteers imitating Petrarch, though classical poets, especially Catullus, would also fit the description.

What Candidus objects to is the abuse of poetry for dishonest or immoral ends. He decries the raillery of malice as vehemently as the arousal of wanton appetites, but he explains that if poets "make verses, conteynyng quicke sentences, void of rebauldry, or in the commendacion of vertue some pratie allegory, or do set forth any notable story, that do I set by the*m* as they be well worthy" (sig. Bv). Elyot is distinguishing between poets who misuse their calling and those who fulfill it properly. His position here is generally consistent with his position in *The Governor*, as Partee notes (330–35), though his emphasis is changed in keeping with the context. Elyot is calling attention to the nettles to be avoided, but he is not ignoring the "good and wholsome herbs" to be gathered in the garden of poetry. His judgment of poetry continues to be a moral one, and though he may appear to give aid and comfort to its detractors, he remains a believer in the power of poetry to promote virtue.

Another believer in the moral value of literature was Thomas Lupset, a follower of Erasmus, a scholar at Oxford, a friend of Reginald Pole, and a tutor to Cardinal Wolsey's natural son. In *An Exhortation to Young men*, published in 1535, five years after his death, Lupset declares that reading the "olde substanciall workes" of literature "shal besyde the perfection of knowledge, gender a certayne iudgement in you, that you shal neuer take delite nor pleasure in the trifles and vayne inuentions that men nowe a daies write." This discerning judgment, he believes, "can not be gotten but by a longe exercysynge of our wittes with the best sorte of writers" (262). He particularly recommends the holy fathers and philosophers, including Aristotle, Plato, and Cicero; and he adds, "Specially rede with diligence the workes of Seneca: of whom ye shall lerne as moche of vertue as mans wit can teche you" (245). Agreeing with Elyot that the inculcation of virtue is the primary reason for the study of literature, Lupset also sees that reading the best writers develops intellectual and moral judgment.

Learning from the best minds of the past, a cardinal principle of humanism, is more fully expressed by Thomas Wilson, a former student of the translator of Terence and playwright Nicholas Udall. At the beginning of his practical *Arte of Rhetorique* (1553), Wilson explains that "before we use either to write, or speake eloquently we must dedicate our myndes wholly, to folowe the moste wise and learned menne, and seke to fashion, aswell their speache and gesturyng, as their wit or endyting. The whiche when we earnestly mynde to do, we cannot but in time appere somewhat like theim" (fol. 3). Wilson is describing the method of imitation advocated by Erasmus and generally used in rhetorical training in the schools: studying the best examples and imitating them improves one's skills in composition and declamation.

Also in the humanist tradition Wilson emphasizes the moral wisdom to be gained. Regarding poets among "the moste wise and learned menne" to be studied and imitated, Wilson explains that they express their meanings through tales: "These tales were not fayned of suche wise menne without cause, neither yet continued vntyll this tyme, and kepte in memorie without good consideration. . . . For undoubtedlye there is no one tale emonge al the Poetes, but vnder the same is comprehended some thing that perteyneth eyther to the amendement of maners, to the knowledge of trueth, to the settynge forthe of Natures woorcke, or elles to the vnderstandinge of some notable thynge done" (fol. 104). Wilson illustrates this method of poetic instruction by pointing to the *Iliad*, which describes "strengthe and valeantenes of the bodye," and the *Odyssey*, which sets "forthe a lyuelye Paterne of the minde," as both Plutarch and Basilius Magnus indicate.

Poets used fables to express their instruction, says Wilson, because they were "wise men" and "durst not openlye rebuke" but instead "tolde menne by shadowes what they shoulde do in good south" or else "that none myght vnderstande, but those vnto whom they pleased to vtter their meaninge" (fol. 104). Providing many examples of fables from both the classical and Christian traditions, Wilson interprets their meanings in moral terms. Danaë illustrates virtue being overcome by money, and Isis shows how beauty may overcome the beast. More complex are Hercules's labors which, according to Wilson, demonstrate "that reason should withstande affection, and the spirite should fight, against the fleshe" (fol. 105). Perhaps most interesting is Wilson's interpretation of St. George killing the dragon that would have devoured the virgin: "Whereby is none other thyng me*n*t but that a Kyng and euery man vnto whom the execution of iustice is committed, should defende the innocent against the ungodly attemptes of the wicked, and rather kill such deuilles by marcial law, than suffer the innocentes to take any wrong" (fol. 105). This extension of the saint's tale to the political realm may have surprised the mummers who performed St. George, but it indicates how Wilson responded to literature and how he believed it should be read.

He implies that the poet fulfills the functions of the orator, who teaches, delights, and persuades (fol. 1), a view of the poet that is later expressed by Sidney (34–38). In fact much of the advice that Wilson gives students of rhetoric about preparing orations applies as well to imaginative writers, and since his *Arte of Rhetorique* proved to be such a popular success, going through eight editions in thirty-two years,[4] its influence on the poets and playwrights who emerged in the last half of the sixteenth century and later was inevitable. Not only does Wilson endorse the humanist doctrine of imitation of the best models, but also he emphasizes that "arte [is] a surer guide, then nature." As he explains, "Those that haue good wittes, by nature, shall better encrease theim by arte, and the blunte also shalbe whetted through art, that want nature to help them forward" (fol. 3).

What Wilson means by art is the method of rhetoric which he advocates, as is indicated by the title of his book. Concentrating on the first three processes of rhetoric—invention, disposition, and elocution—Wilson explains the aspects of composition that an effective writer must master. His advice on finding material to make an argument and arranging the parts for greatest effectiveness is quite conventional, but in his comments on style he takes a more emphatic position. He says that the writer should be "shorte," "plaine," and reasonable (fol. 58), rather than affected or "ouer fine"; avoiding "straunge ynkehorne termes," he should "speake as is commonly receiued" (fol. 86). Wilson explains that "Composicion . . . is an apte ioynyng together of wordes in suche order, that neither the eare shal espie any ierre, nor yet any man shalbe dulled with ouerlong drawing out of a sentence, nor yet muche confounded with myngelyng of clauses, suche as are nedelesse, beyng heaped together without reason, and vsed without number" (fol. 88). Wilson's rejection of the elaborate Ciceronian style for a plainer one emphasizes a colloquialness that is both apt and clear, exactly the features prized in the Latin style of Terence (see chapter 5).

Though much of his theory of composition may have implications for dramatic writers, Wilson says nothing directly about drama. He does, however, comment on "the occasion of laughter," which relates to comedy. He perceives laughter to derive from "the fondnes, the filthines, the deformitee, and all suche evill behauior, as we se to bee in other" (fol. 74–75). His association of laughter with ugliness, foolishness, and "evill behauior" links classical theory with Christian morality, for in his view the representation of folly or vice provokes scorn manifested in laughter. The provocation of laughter thus becomes a technique of the satirist or moral instructor to inculcate virtue, as Ben Jonson later describes, in the prologues to his revised *Every Man in His Humour* and to *The Alchemist*, and demonstrates in his comedies. Laughter becomes a moral corrective as it dissuades the audience from pursuing the foolish or evil behavior that is scorned.

One other comment by Wilson that may be particularly relevant to drama is his advice on oral delivery. He suggests that those who "haue no good voices by nature" will find that "Exercise of the bodie, fastyng, moderacion in meate, and drynke, gaping wyde, or singyng plaine song, & counterfaityng those that do speake distinctly, helpe muche to haue a good deliveraunce" (fol. 119). Physical fitness and exercise of the voice are as appropriate for the actor as for the orator, and again imitation is recommended as a principal method of personal development.

Wilson's influence on dramatic performance in the years that followed may not be significant, but his instruction in rhetoric, his defense of poetry, and his view of the meaning of literature had ramifications for schoolmasters and their students, who became the authors and audiences of succeeding generations. Wilson incorporates the humanist's appreciation of the best of the classical heritage with the moralist's concern for inculcation of virtue in his practical guide for the orator, poet, or playwright.

Less enthusiastic about the classical heritage is Martin Bucer, who became a professor of divinity at Cambridge in 1549. In his *De Regno Christi*, which he presented to Edward VI at Christmas 1551, Bucer included a section titled "De honestis ludis," in which he advocates the development of Christian drama to promote piety and the "amendment of character." Bucer acknowledges the wit, charm, and "grace of language" in Aristophanes, Terence, and Plautus as well as "the dignity, the subtlety and the polished style of Sophocles, Euripides and Seneca" (quoted in Wickham, *Early English Stages* 2.1:330).[5] But he argues that the Bible offers more directly instructive stories for the Christian audience. He recommends, therefore, that "religious men" compose plays that represent "human thoughts, actions and fortunes, both those of everyday, ordinary people, as happens in comedies, and of unusual characters such as excite greater wonder, which is the mark of tragedy, likely to unite the principles of a religious life to a sure amendment of character" (329). Making the conventional distinction between comedy as the affairs of ordinary people and tragedy as the unusual that inspires wonder, Bucer orients the action to specifically religious ends.

To illustrate his conception of scriptural drama, Bucer suggests that appropriate subjects for comedy would be the quarrel between Abraham's and Lot's shepherds or Isaac's winning of Rebecca as his bride, which could depict parents dutifully seeking "religious marriages for their children" and "the loyalty and the devotion of honest servants." Tragedies would be made of those stories "thickly packed with godlike and heroic people, with emotion, with character, with actions and with unforeseen events," which have the power "to strengthen faith in God, to arouse love and desire of God and to create and increase not only admiration of piety and justice, but also the horror of impiety and of the sowing and fostering of every kind of evil" (329). Drama is thus to further religious indoctrination, but apparently aware of contemporary biblical plays designed to promote both religious and political views, Bucer recommends censorship as the means of directing the religious instruction. Bucer's ambitious program of scriptural drama was not implemented, though the tradition of plays based on the Bible written by the reformers Bale and Grimald, as well as by the Catholic apologists Watson and Christopherson, continued (see chapters 21–23). Bucer's endorsement of censorship of drama may have been more eagerly received, for it confirmed a practice begun in the previous reign that became increasingly regarded as a means of controlling sedition and protecting the party in power.

Some eight years after Edward received *De regno Christii*, rather different advice was given to his sister, Elizabeth, shortly after her coronation, as the religious question intensified and the regulation of drama tightened. In *A Woorke of Ioannes Ferrarivs Montanus, touchynge the good orderynge of a Common weale*, translated by William Bavande in 1559, the moral issue of drama is again addressed. After declaring that students should be protected from filthy authors, Ferrarius says that "Prophane writers muste be so taught, that thei maie drawe as nigh as can bee to our religion, neither by any kind of construyng, swarve one iote from it" in order that "good education and godliness [be] ioyned together" (fol. 77–78). Likewise in the staging of plays care must be taken that they benefit rather than harm their audiences. Ferrarius notes that in the old days "the exercise of Stage plaiying . . . set forthe, partlie to delight, partlie to moue us to embrace ensamples of vertue and goodnesse, and to eschue vice and filthie livyng" (fol. 81–82). But man is easily corrupted by "naughtie ensamples and talke." The power of drama through gesturing and "the eloquence of the bodie" can "moue any manne" to good or evil (fol. 100–101). The exhibition of filthy matters "minister occasion of volupteousnesse," and "mockyng plaies . . . corrupte good manners, causyng the audience to departe worse from the*m*, then thei came to theim" (fol. 101–2).

On the other hand, Ferrarius finds that some plays provide effective instruction. *Andria*, the most popular of Terence's plays in the Renaissance, demonstrates "what a shamefull reproche it is to be tied with Venus ba*n*des, and to trouble your parentes" (fol. 102–3). Other instances of practical instruction from classical comedy and tragedy are cited, though no references are made to contemporary plays. Ferrarius concludes that "there shall be no Tragedie, no Comedie, nor any other kinde of plaie, but it maie encrease the discipline of good maners, if by the helpe of reason and zeale of honestie, it bee well emploied" (fol. 103). He endorses drama as a powerful force for good, yet he also recognizes that in the hands of the dishonest or malicious it can be a powerful force for evil. Bavande's translation of Ferrarius in 1559 thus endorses the humanist defense of poetry and drama, though it also serves as a warning to the new queen and her court of the potential social corruption if drama were not controlled.

Ferrarius's work emphasizes the role of drama in education and in social morality, which was reflected in the series of acts designed to regulate dramatic activity. The argument over whether or how drama should be taught or performed was essentially a moral one, but in the 1540s and '50s it became increasingly tied to religious and political issues. The attack of Agrippa and his spiritual brothers was ably met by the defense of Elyot and the second generation of humanists, and drama survived, though under tighter restrictions. But the war over the benefits and dangers of the proliferation of drama in Tudor society had only just begun.[6]

PART THREE

THE *SECULARIZATION* OF THE MORALITY

CHAPTER TEN

THE PRODIGAL PLAYS

*T*HE movement toward youth-oriented morality drama, beginning with Medwall's *Nature* (1490–1501) and continuing in *Youth* (1513–29), *Hickscorner* (1513–16), and Rastell's *Nature of the Four Elements* (1517–18), developed after the Reformation into a distinct dramatic type in which education of the adolescent became the central focus. The educational interludes adapted the traditional morality pattern of the fall and redemption to more specific and more secular purposes. Incorporating elements from romance, folk drama, classical comedy, and biblical parables, the pedagogical plays presented a variety of dramatic entertainment and instruction. Although originally designed for performance by children for children, educational interludes later were adapted for production by professional troupes for popular audiences.

The educational interlude that most closely retained the traditional morality form, though it incorporates the Reformation perspective, is R. Wever's *Lusty Juventus*, written between 1547 and 1553, during the reign of young Edward VI, and apparently performed by a small professional company. As the title page indicates, "Foure may play it easely," though all four actors must also sing "part-music," as David Bevington notes (*From "Mankind" to Marlowe* 21), for music is an important part of the spectacle. The prologue emphasizes the natural concupiscence of the young, but adds that "in youth men maye be best / Trayned to verture by godly mean" (Wever 15–16).[1]

Lusty Juventus becomes an object lesson of this message as he first celebrates in song the pleasure of youth, but then is instructed by Good Councell not to waste his time and by Knowledge not to be deceived by false teachers. As a sign of the Reformation, Juventus is presented with the New Testament as a guide, and he intends to go to a "preaching"; but as in the old morality, he is dissuaded from the virtuous path by a tempter, Hypocrisie, posing as Friendship. Hypocrisie, exploiting current religious controversy, discredits religion by directing Juventus "The old popish priestes [to] mocke and despyse" (683). Juventus then follows the traditional prodigal's route by joining Fellowship and Abhominable Living, a whore posing as Honesty, as he reverts to his original view that youth should pursue pleasure. Again the influence of the Reformation is evident when Juventus, made to realize his sinful ways, falls into despair but is restored by Gods Mercyfull Promyses, who, quoting Ezekiel, Paul, and St. Augustine, reminds Juventus of God's grace. In contrast to the Catholic *Everyman*, good works and penance are not demanded; repentance coupled with God's mercy achieves redemption, and the parable of the prodigal son is cited as the paradigm of God's love (1077) for sinful man. Unlike the earlier moralities, the vices play a relatively minor role as the emphasis falls more on redemption than on sin. *Lusty Juventus*, however, follows the traditional morality scheme except for its Reformation perspective, and it does not incorporate motifs from other literary and dramatic types, as other contemporary educational interludes do.

More complex and more secular than *Lusty Juventus* were the prodigal plays initially written and performed in the schools. Developed on the Continent by schoolmasters to supplement or "correct" the perspective of Roman comedy, the prodigal plays combine Terentian technique with morality form to create instructive entertainment for both children and their parents. Most influential of these plays written in Latin were *Asotus* and *Rebelles*, by Macropedius, and *Acolastus*, by Willem de Volder, known as Gnapheus.

Asotus, apparently written about 1510 for performance by schoolboys but not published until 1537, adapts the biblical story of the prodigal son to the contemporary world by expanding the nature of the prodigality and the relationships between the two sons and their father, who we are told in the prologue represents God. Justifying his disregard for the unity of time by citing Plautus's *Captives* as a precedent, Macropedius presents Asotus in the first four acts being misled by Colax, a parasite, and other evil companions to pursue hunting, drinking, and whoring, much in the manner of vices leading youth into sin in the morality plays. But here the negative exemplum is set off by the positive example of the elder son, who industriously tends the fields. When Asotus's partying leads to a confrontation with his father, Asotus demands his inheritance, and after much concern by his father and contempt by his brother, Asotus departs. A year elapses between acts 4 and 5, and Asotus's impoverished state, perceived first in a vision by his father, is recounted by a traveler before the destitute Asotus returns and is joyfully reunited with his father and begrudgingly greeted by his morose brother. The play fleshes out the biblical parable by presenting the provocation for the prodigal's departure and by elaborating the irritation of the elder brother. In its five-act structure it resembles Roman comedy.

More directly important as a model of the prodigal plays in England was the popular *Acolastus*, published in 1529 in Holland and reprinted forty-seven times by 1587 (Slim 3). It was translated into English in 1540 by Palsgrave, a friend of Cromwell and the king and the former schoolmaster to both Princess Mary and Henry VIII's illegitimate son, Henry Fitzroy. This version of the biblical parable, identified as *The Comedy of Acolastus*, self-consciously imitates Plautus and Terence as it seeks to offer a more Christian lesson for schoolboys than the pagan playwrights provide. The adaptation of Roman conventions for a moral purpose is particularly emphasized by Palsgrave in his translation and accompanying commentary. The prologue declares the intention of the play is not to displace Plautus and Terence as preeminent masters of comedy but to supplement their work. In his rendering of the prodigal son's story, de Volder adds a good counselor for the father, a bad counselor for the son, a parasite (Pamphagus), and a hungry victim of parasites (Pantolabus), as well as a pander and prostitutes. The characters are given allegorical or Roman names depending upon their dramatic origins.

THE SECULARIZATION OF THE MORALITY

The fusion of classical and morality elements is also apparent in the action, which represents the conventional fall of the prodigal into bad company and his subsequent drinking, whoring, and dicing, which in this version occupy most of acts 2 through 4. Like *Asotus*, the play *Acolastus* develops the relationship between father and son and indicates that the father has a vision of his son's trouble before the prodigal returns; but unlike Macropedius's play, *Acolastus* represents the course of the prodigal's destitution, his employment by a swineherd, and his complaints about his miserable condition and about women, whom he compares to wolves (IV.vi, p. 149).[2] Jack Wilton in Nashe's *Unfortunate Traveller*, describing a performance of *Acolastus* he claims to have seen at Wittenberg, says the play was "filthily acted"; the only thing done well "was the prodigal childs hunger," because most of the schoolboy actors were "hungerly kept" (Nashe 2:249–50). However, the singling out of this point in the play suggests that for Nashe it was the most memorable element. The translator Palsgrave particularly comments on the two laments of the destitute Acolastus (IV.vi and V.ii), which, Palsgrave says, bring the comedy to its "Ectasis" (Epitasis?) and "draweth shortlye after towards his *catastrophen*" (145–46). Palsgrave, noting the rhetorical schemes that are used in these speeches in imitation of Terence, Plautus, Vergil, and Seneca, follows the precedent of the commentaries on Terence by Donatus and Renaissance humanists, but Palsgrave's concern also suggests that these speeches received special attention when the play was studied in the schoolroom. *Acolastus* concludes with the prodigal returning to his father and gaining forgiveness, but no elder brother appears to question the feasting to follow, unlike the biblical source and Macropedius's rendition. The peroration emphasizes the Christian moral by noting God's mercy and the grace that is obtained through repentance. The religious message not to be found in Terence thus justifies the play's composition.

Another Dutch precedent for the English prodigal plays, but one that offers a different dramatic emphasis, is Macropedius's *Rebelles*, written in Latin about 1510 but not published until 1535. This play focuses more directly on child-rearing as a source of prodigality. Addressed particularly to students though with implications for their parents as well, *Rebelles* represents the consequences of two indulgent mothers' refusal to allow their sons to be physically punished for misbehaving. Lacking discipline, the boys develop contempt for education and authority; as a result they pursue the typical prodigal's path by going to a tavern, pursuing prostitutes, and losing their money in a game of dice. After also losing their clothes and being thrown into the street, the boys turn to stealing to pay for their pleasures and are arrested; though their pious old schoolmaster saves them from the gallows, they are to be whipped as punishment. Both boys, who repent their errors for the benefit of their fellow schoolboys, and their mothers, who realize the dangers of indulgence and praise God's benevolence, are held up as negative examples. The epilogue, after reminding the audience that this play is a "model of virtue," sums up the message: Mothers, don't spoil your children; and, boys, "Respect our rightful laws . . . and practice decent behaviour" (Macropedius 104–5). Described by C. H. Herford as "a graphic picture of school-boy adventure . . . and the *bizarre* blending of Plautus's genial worldliness and Hebraic solemnity" (88), *Rebelles*, with its emphasis on the dangers of sparing the rod, establishes the major theme of the English educational interludes written after 1540.

One of the most intriguing of these prodigal interludes is *Misogonus*, which survives in fragmentary form in a manuscript dated 1577 though there are several indications that the play was composed much earlier. Internal allusions push the date back at least to 1560, according to some critics, and if *Nice Wanton*, which was written before 1553, did in fact borrow from *Misogonus* as has been alleged, a version of the play may go back to Edward's or even to Henry VIII's reign (J. Farmer, *Six Anonymous Plays* 403–12).[3] The date remains a mystery, as does the author. Though the prologue is attributed to "Thomas Richards," modern scholars have not accepted him as the play's author. Laurence Johnson, who matriculated at Cambridge in 1570 and received his B.A. in 1573–74 and his M.A. in 1577, may be responsible for the extant version of the play, as has been argued, but he may have been simply the reviser of an earlier version, possibly written by Anthony Rudd.[4] Circumstances of composition remain unclear, as do the auspices of performance, though it is generally believed to have been designed for production by boys. In spite of the many questions regarding its creation and its fragmentary nature, *Misogonus* offers a unique combination of classical and contemporary elements.

Emphasizing at the beginning of the play that his child, Misogonus, was spoiled after his mother's death, the father, Philogonus, notes that a faulty education and too much liberty have led his son to disdain his parent, though Eupalus, resembling the good counselor Eubulus in *Acolastus*, reassures him that his son will reform. The play initially proves that the anxious father is right and the reassuring counselor is wrong, as Misogonus demonstrates his arrogance and his appetite for idleness and pleasure. Typical of the misled youth of the morality tradition, Misogonus demands a delectable wench, and he also learns dueling. His chief guide, combining the qualities of the vice and the Roman intriguing servant reminiscent of vice-parasites in the Continental prodigal plays, Cacurgus is called Will Summer, which indicates his added dimension as a fool who serves as both a comic chorus and a manipulator of the action. Cacurgus humors the father while laughing at him (Farmer, *Six Anonymous Plays* I.ii, p. 147), leads the prodigal to celebrate pleasure in song (II.ii, p. 163) and in person, and provides an ironic commentary in asides as the father laments Misogonus's waywardness (II.iii, p. 167).

Typical of the prodigal plays, the tavern scene features drinking, dicing, and whoring, but here the action is more realistic, and a satiric element is added by a drunken priest, famous for his lechery and gambling, who ignores his duties at the church service to join the prodigal in debauchery. The whores are significantly called Brown Bessie and Maid Marion, characters from contemporary folk drama. As in *Asotus*, the father interrupts the party, though here the interruption is instigated by Cacurgus "for good sport." The anticlerical element contributes to the atmosphere of debauchery, yet it is incidental to the major theme of prodigality resulting from indulgence of the child. Both before and after interrupting the drunken revels, Philogonus rues his failure to provide discipline. Quoting Solomon's maxim "He that spareth the rod hates the child" — the cliché of the disappointed parent — Philogonus wishes he had hired proper tutors, for "Education is the best thing that can be, of a truth" (II.iii, pp. 167–68). Lamenting his son's behavior and his own misery, Philogonus tells parents to learn from his example (II.v. pp. 191–92); then in a song addressed to mighty Jove but asking pity for "Christ's sake," he registers his own blame for not imposing discipline and remembers other fathers — Phoebus, Daedelus, and Priam — grieving over their sons. The pattern of the prodigal prevails through act 2, when suddenly an unexpected solution to Misogonus's contempt and Philogonus's grief is offered.

Stealing from Roman comedy the "romantic" motif of the lost child who is fortuitously discovered, as Madeleine Doran notes (162–63), the play provides the good son that Philogonus had failed through lack of discipline to develop. Act 3 is devoted to telling the tale of an elder son being sent to his maternal uncle in Apollonia at birth, but the comic dimension and suspense of the tale are enhanced by the rustics, who provide information about the secret son, and by the vice-parasite Cacurgus, who seeks to prevent the truth from becoming known by threatening the witnesses and discrediting their testimony. A domestic quarrel between the rustics Codrus and Alison, the malapropisms of Isbell, and the stammering of Madge are brought to a comic climax by Cacurgus, who in the manner of the quack doctor from contemporary folk drama brags of his travels and cures as he tries to intimidate the simple servants:

> I have been one and twenty mile beyond the moon.
> Four years together I touched the sun when it rose.
> ... There is no sickness, disease, or malady,
> But I can tell only by viewing of the hand.
> ... I can cure the ague, the measles and the French pock,
> The tetter, the morphew, the bile, blain, and weal,
> The megrim, the maidens, and the hitchcock,
> ... My head is so full of the supermundal science
> That I am faint to bind it, lest my brains should crow.
>   (III.iii, pp. 217–18)

Cacurgus' association with the mummers is further suggested by his claim that his father "was also a natural Ethiopian" (p. 217), indicating he is playing in the black face of the folk performers (see chapter 4).

Act 4 represents God's providence as the lost son, Eugonus, returns, but again a humorous context is provided by the servants' verification of the rightful heir, who is identified by an extra toe on his right foot. Crito, whose name indicates his Terentian origin, conducts the examination of the evidence, but the classical revelation of the truth takes a moralistic turn when the prodigal, after threatening the good elder brother, is disowned by the father, falls into despair, and contemplates suicide. However, in the tradition of the morality play hero, Misogonus repents and then addresses the schoolboy audience:

> O, all ye youthful race of gentle blood,
> >   take heed by this my fall;
> ... Take heed of ill company, fly cards, and dice,
> >   and pleasures bestial;
> Eschew a whore as ye would a scorpion,
> >   and beware of her enticements!
> Children! obey your parents with due reverence and fear:
> ... Beside godliness and learning all things
> >   in this world are but transitory.
> >   (IV.iv, p. 243)

Misogonus asks for his father's forgiveness, and it is assumed that he receives it, though the ending of the play is lost. The play apparently concludes in the conventional manner of the prodigal plot, though given the emphasis on the dangers of sparing the rod, we could expect Philogonus to reiterate that theme as he is reunited with his chastised son, Misogonus. Incorporating elements from Continental dramatic precedents of the prodigal, from classical models, from native morality plays, and from contemporary comic and folk conventions, *Misogonus* provides a remarkable fusion of disparate elements and offers a unique anticipation of the Elizabethan drama to follow.

Offering another example of a father indulging his son with disastrous results is *The Disobedient Child*, written before 1553 and perhaps as early as Henry VIII's reign by Thomas Ingelend, "late student in Cambridge," according to the title page of the edition published in the early 1560s. Based on Ravisius Textor's *Juvenis, Pater, Uxor, The Disobedient Child* appears to be a school play addressed to both boys and their parents, though the particular circumstances of production are not known. Focusing on the father-son relationship, this educational interlude portrays the waywardness of the son not in the prodigal pursuit of pleasure—drinking, whoring, and dicing—but rather in an imprudent marriage. Like Philogonus in the play *Misogonus*, the father here realizes too late that he has not been strict enough in disciplining his son, who ignores his advice to pursue an occupation or go to school: "A man without knowledge . . . May well be compared to one that is dead" (Farmer, *Dramatic Writings* 47).[5] While the ineffectual father laments that "now-a-days . . . Science and learning is so little regarded" (55), the wilful son marries without his father's consent. The son's prodigality is depicted by the extravagence of the wedding feast, and the folly of the marriage is demonstrated by the bride's shrewishness, anticipated by her pointed nose and shrill tongue. The destitution of the prodigal is manifested by his poverty and his subjection to his wife, who physically assaults him and forces him to perform the household chores. A morality-play Satan appears and explains to "my dear children" in the audience (80) that he is responsible for sowing strife between husband and wife as well as leading the young man to scorn learning, but Satan does not interact with any of the characters; rather he remains a choric voice warning the audience to resist temptation.

In contrast to the typical prodigal or youth-centered morality play, when the repentant son returns to his father and confesses "his naughtiness" (83), the father, instead of celebrating his son's homecoming or restoring him in the family, tells him that he would have avoided his fate if he had listened to his father. Then the father, identified as a rich man in the text, reminds his son of the archetypal shrew, Xantippe, and the long-suffering Socrates, as he sends the prodigal back to his wife with only the promise that a little help will be provided. The father's mercy is limited, and the son must live with his foolishness. The Perorator at the end offers a lengthy sermon elaborating Solomon's message for parents — *Qui parcit virgae, odit filium* (Who spares the rod, hates the child) — and warning the boys about the troubles that result from disobeying their parents, troubles that are compounded by a hasty marriage (88–91).

Unusual in that it ends on an unhappy note, *The Disobedient Child* also represents a negative view of women and a harsh view of marriage. The father warns his son at the beginning that a wife "is a burthen and yoke all thy life" (53), and after hearing that his son has married, quotes Hipponax:

> Who said with a wife are two days of pleasure;
> The first is the joy of the marriage-day and night,
> The second to be at the wife's sepulture. (69)

The implication at the end is that the son has enjoyed the first day of pleasure but must wait a very long time for the second. The emphasis on domestic relationships extended here to the wife offers a vibrant image of the sixteenth-century family as dramatic precedents appear to give way to contemporary observation.

Developing the familial relationship even further as it demonstrates the tragic results of sparing the rod is *Nice Wanton*, also attributed to Thomas Ingelend because of similarities with *The Disobedient Child*; however, no conclusive link to Ingelend has yet been discovered. Printed anonymously in 1560, *Nice Wanton* was apparently written between 1549 and 1553, during the reign of Edward VI, though it was revived for Queen Elizabeth. Directed more at parents and guardians than at schoolboys, the play very likely was performed at court by the Children of the Chapel, as is indicated by the extensive cast, including a jury of twelve, and by the many songs in the performance (Wickham, *English Moral Interludes* 143–44).[6] The play is short at 550 lines, and though it could be performed in little more than half an hour, an interval may occur in the middle of the play to represent a lapse of time in the action. The brevity of the play and its interruption after barely fifteen minutes may point to its performance during the course of a banquet, as Glynne Wickham suggests (*English Moral Interludes* 144), but whatever its auspices, *Nice Wanton* provides a significant variation on the pattern of the prodigal.

The prologue introduces the theme of the play by quoting Solomon — "He that spareth the rod, the child doth hate" — but rather than focusing on the indulgent father, *Nice Wanton*, like Macropedius's *Rebelles*, represents a pampering mother; and in addition to a prodigal son, a prodigal daughter is featured. To accentuate their prodigality and to offer a positive alternative, a good son is also introduced. Given biblical names suggestive of their characters, the good son is called Barnabas and the wayward children are named Ismael and Dalilah. Dalilah is identified as the "nice wanton," making this not only the first educational interlude to feature a feminine prodigal but perhaps also the first interlude to be named solely for a feminine character, if we exclude the morality-saints' play *Mary Magdalene*. The mother is given the name Xantippe, though she is characterized by foolishness rather than shrewishness. As in the typical prodigal play, the young desert education for pleasure except for the pious and conscientious Barnabas, and, encouraged by the vice Iniquity, Ismael and Dalilah demonstrate their prodigality by dicing, though Dalilah is also identified as a whore by Iniquity.

Following the intermission the wages of sin are manifested by the diseased and wretched Dalilah, who now, filled with shame, seeks death, and by Ismael, who is tried and sentenced to the gallows for burglary and murder. Not only do the prodigals pay for their sins by death — Dalilah dies of the pox and Ismael is hanged — but even more significantly, the indulgent mother is said by Worldly Shame to be "the cause of their death" (470). The climax of the play comes as Xantippe is prevented from suicide by her good son, Barnabas, who reminds her of her dereliction of duty and concludes that the evil children received God's justice. The small comfort he offers his mother is that Dalilah repented her sins before she died, and he urges his mother to seek God's grace. The epilogue reiterates the message of the prologue — not to spare the rod — as it exhorts all parents: "Be not negligent, / But chastise [children], before they be sore infect" (531–34). The perspective of the educational interlude has shifted almost completely from the child to the parents, who must bear responsibility for their children's actions, and the schoolboy audience has been replaced by adults.

The educational interludes featuring the prodigal became within a generation oriented toward adults. Even when they continued to be performed by boys, the special appeal to children's interests faded and the adapted form catered to their parents' concerns and tastes. Terentian technique gave way to popular motifs, and though morality play conventions continue, the pattern changes as the vision becomes more secular. Growing realism in domestic relationships and in the social context reinforce the increasingly pragmatic vision of the plays. Whether entertainment dominates or instruction is emphasized, the context of the school with its particular image of education has disappeared. Adult audiences and adult players continued to learn from the children's plays as later playwrights adapted the patterns and combinations of the educational interludes. In the merging of the diverse traditions of the morality play, Roman comedy, romance, and folk drama, the educational interlude provided the foundation for the unique comedy of the later Elizabethans.

CHAPTER ELEVEN

REDFORD'S *WIT AND SCIENCE*

*T*HE educational morality takes another form in a series of plays that allegorize the gaining of knowledge. The first of these plays, *Wit and Science*, written by John Redford during his tenure as Master of Choristers at St. Paul's Cathedral between 1531 and 1547, represents a remarkable fusion of literary and dramatic traditions. In substituting knowledge for salvation as the goal of human endeavor, Redford appears to be extending the pattern of such youth-oriented morality plays as Medwall's *Nature* and Rastell's *Four Elements*, which emphasize instruction as preparation for life in this world rather than in the world to come. Although *Wit and Science* retains the morality paradigm of temptation, fall, and redemption, the pattern here particularly recalls the young man in Proverbs, chapter 7, who is distracted from his pursuit of wisdom by a harlot. Enclosing this didactic exemplum is the framework of the romantic quest in which a knight proves his mettle and wins his bride by defeating her enemy, though in representing the confrontation between the youthful Wit and the giant Tediousness, Redford drew upon contemporary folk drama.

Informing Redford's portrayal of the romantic quest is the tradition of intellectual allegory, which may derive from a popular medieval and Renaissance textbook, Martianus Capella's fifth-century *De Nuptiis Philologiae et Mercurii*. The vogue of intellectual allegory in England in the fifteenth and early sixteenth centuries is evidenced by Lydgate's translations of Deguileville's *Pèlerinage de la vie humaine* (ca. 1330) and *Les Échecs amoreux* (ca. 1374) in the early fifteenth century, as well as four other compositions, *A Pageant of Knowledge* (ca. 1430), *The Court of Sapience* (ca. 1470), *The Castell of Labour* (1503), and Stephen Hawes's *The Passetyme of Pleasure*, printed in 1509 and reprinted four times by 1555 (Lennam 96–97). These courtly allegories representing instruction in the seven liberal arts and the acquisition of wisdom offered sophisticated literary models for Redford, while more immediate court pageants provided guidance in adapting the form for dramatic presentation.

That *Wit and Science* was designed to be performed before Henry VIII and his court is suggested by Reason's address at the end of the play "to our most noble kyng & quene in especiall / to ther honorable cowncell / & then to all the rest" (*Wit and Science* 1121–22).[1] The singling out of the king for special notice is not unusual, but the fact that the queen and council are also specifically mentioned points to their physical presence. Unfortunately no clue is given as to which of Henry's queens is addressed, and the particular date of performance remains unknown. In preparing this entertainment for a royal production, Redford utilized his boys' choral talents by including three songs, the last sung in parts, as well as instrumental music and a lively dance. With a larger number of actors than the typical companies of strolling players, Redford was less constrained by doubling of parts, and since his company was made up entirely of boys, he could offer a larger number of female parts; thus in *Wit and Science* he required a minimum of eleven actors and created four significant female roles.

In staging his play Redford appears to have had access to materials and techniques previously used in other court entertainments. As R. A. Duffy suggests, "'rock' settings . . . seemed to dominate many of the indoor entertainments and at least one important public pageant" performed earlier, and the "mount" is a prominent feature in royal pageants and allegorical tournaments from the celebration of Prince Arthur's marriage to Catherine of Aragon in 1501 to the coronation revels for Edward VI in 1547 (184–86). Whether Redford used part of a previously built set for his Mount Parnassus or developed the idea after observing contemporary pageants, his stage appears to have been considerably more elaborate than the raised platform of the conventional interlude. That a raised portion of the playing area or an upper level is used to represent Mount Parnassus is suggested by the exit of Wit, Study, and Diligence (s.d. 131) when they set out for Mount Parnassus and their reappearance when they reach the Mount, where Wit encounters Tediousness who prevents access to the Mount. Wit also exits the playing area and reappears before his second encounter with Tediousness (s.d. 953), which Confidence says was observed by Lady Science from Mount Parnassus: "vpon yonder mowntayne on hye / she saw ye strike that hed from the bodye" (1012–13). The stage direction that Wit "cumth in & bryngth in the hed vpon his swoorde" (s.d. 1001) after the combat suggests the beheading occurs offstage even though Tediousness may die on stage (999); no doubt the severing of the head and the placing of it on Wit's sword could be more quickly accomplished out of view of the general audience, but if Science is placed at a higher vantage point, she could presumably observe both the combat and the decollation.

Another indication of a multidimensional playing area for *Wit and Science* is the placement of Tediousness. When he makes his entrance, he delivers a thirty-line speech and then pushes his way through the audience as he warns, "Stand back ye wrechys . . . make roome I say" (175–80), before confronting Wit. He says he has been roused from his "nest" (150), and after defeating Wit, Tediousness declares, he will return to his "owne nest" (237). Tediousness apparently uses a different door for entering or leaving the playing area than do the other characters, and it would seem that if he is preventing Wit's access to Mount Parnassus, his "nest" must be below the main playing area where the combat occurs, and this necessitates his passing through a part of the audience before arriving on the stage. Again the multidimensional courtly pageants may offer a precedent, though the religious civic dramas often depend also on at least two levels for staging. The initial performance of *Wit and Science* on a stage oriented to court pageantry enhances the dramatic spectacle implicit in Wit's progress.

In making the allegorical concrete, Redford represents Wit's progress to knowledge through a series of vivid dramatic images. Like Graunde Amour striving to win the hand of La Bell Pucell in *The Passetyme of*

Pleasure, Wit is prepared by a group of instructors for his quest to overcome Tediousness and gain Science. Not having the leisure to be trained in all of the Seven Arts like Graunde Amour in Hawes's 5,816-line poem, Wit depends only on Study, Diligence, and Instruction, and because of his impatience he quickly abandons Instruction. However, his most important guide is said to be the glass given to him by Reason, the father of his prospective bride. This mirror, in which Wit is directed "beholde yee / youre sealfe to youre selfe," symbolizes self-knowledge as exemplified in Alciati's "Emblem of the Seven Sages," where a mirror is portrayed on the left of the figure and the verse explains that the "Spartan Chilon used to order each person to know (*nosco*) himself: / a mirror (*speculum*) in the hands / or a looking-glass will represent this" (*Emblemata* no. 187). The Glass of Reason is, however, ignored by the impetuous Wit when he is defeated by Tediousness and disgraced by Idleness. Only after he has been transformed into a fool does Wit remember the mirror and examine himself. By viewing the faces of members of the audience that are fair and clear, he becomes aware that the "shamefully blotted" image of himself is accurate (829–35). The Glass of Reason thus dramatizes the importance of self-examination to perceive truth; after this self-perception is realized, Wit moves toward redemption and his ultimate goal of knowledge.

The full-length portrait of Wit in his pre-lapsarian state that he sent to Science as a token of love at the beginning of the play further emphasizes his visual degradation as the portrait is compared by Science and her mother, Experience, with the disgraced Wit. The portrait and the mirror especially accentuate the visual change in Wit after succumbing to Idleness, but in the earlier challenge of Tediousness, Wit's failure to use the Glass of Reason, like his abandonment of Instruction, also contributes to his fall. What finally seals Wit's doom in his first encounter with Tediousness is his irrationality in challenging Tediousness before his page Confidence returns from Science with the Sword of Comfort. When he is accompanied by Confidence and armed with the Sword of Comfort in his second combat, Wit easily overcomes Tediousness. Redford's representation of his allegory depends on particular symbols as well as dramatic images.

In expressing the didactic message, Redford integrates both learned and popular traditions. Graunde Amour may be a model for Wit, but Hawes's intellectual knight far surpasses the prowess of the youthful Wit by overcoming two evil giants and a dragon in order to win his lady. A more immediate precedent for the combat between Wit and Tediousness is the legendary St. George as portrayed in contemporary folk plays. St. George's adversaries in the later versions of the folk play, collected in the nineteenth and early twentieth centuries, are usually exotic pagan knights or a monstrous creature called Big Head, who may be a remnant of the traditional dragon. Tediousness incorporates aspects of both types of adversary. When he enters he "cumth in w^t a vyser over hys hed," according to the stage direction (s.d. 145), and after downing Wit in the first combat, Tediousness warns the audience not to come near his "snowte" (230), thus suggesting a large beastlike head. It is this oversized head that Wit presents as a trophy on his sword after his victorious second encounter. Tediousness, like St. George's pagan adversaries, boasts of his power when he first appears, and he demeans Science as a "drab" and a "whore" (159–60); after he has overcome Wit, he swears "by mahownde bones" and "by mahownde nose" (225–27) in the typical manner of the Black Prince and other pagan challengers in the folk plays (see chapter 4). Craik (*Tudor Interlude* 53) and Duffy (185) compare Tediousness to the wild man who appears in some contemporary court pageants, while his costume may owe something to the wild man, his words and actions more closely resemble the St. George folk play.

The apparent death and revival of Wit in his first combat is also a regular feature in folk drama. The stage direction says, "Wyt fallyth downe & dyeth" (222), but rather than using the folk comic doctor who restores the fallen hero to life, Redford resumes the allegorical pattern and introduces a musical interlude through Honest Recreation, Comfort, Quickness, and Strength, who raise the stricken warrior. Like King Lear being restored to sanity by music and the loving mercy of Cordelia, Wit is healed by the therapeutic power of song and the tender concern of Honest Recreation. His revival offers him an opportunity to redeem himself in a second encounter, as in the folk play, and as if recalling his folk model Wit swears "by saynt george" (269). But before this return engagement Redford complicates the plot and extends the allegory by presenting his hero with a new test patterned after the contemporary morality play.

Reason blames Wit's defeat on his failure to obey Instruction, but the moral dimensions of his fall soon become apparent. Angering Reason by ignoring his advice, Wit manifests lechery in attempting to kiss Honest Recreation, and he denies his love for Science (270–90); his vulnerability is thus indicated before the temptation of Idleness. As expressed in Proverbs 1:7, "fools despise wisdom and instruction" (Geneva Bible), and in spite of warnings against Idleness, like the young man of Proverbs 7:5–27, Wit succumbs to the charms of the harlot and deserts his pursuit of knowledge.[2] In the dramatization of Wit's second fall, the allegory is clarified through a series of visual images. Wit puts off the garment previously given to him by Science before engaging in a galliard; at the conclusion of the dance, Wit demonstrates his physical and moral weakness by abandoning Honest Recreation and falling into the lap of Idleness. Honest Recreation's warnings are answered by Idleness who, claiming Honest Recreation to be the "roote of all vyce," catalogs the "abhominacions" brought in "vnder the name of honest recreacion . . . dawnsyng . . . syngyng/pypyng/& fydlyng" (whose performance we have just witnessed) as well as "maskyng" and "mummyng," which she lumps together with the idle pastimes of "cardyng" and "dycying" (369–85).

Wit's failure to perceive Idleness's faulty reasoning even after it is rebutted by Honest Recreation demonstrates his lack of knowledge, and he falls asleep "full of sloth" (429). The blackened face, Idleness's "marke" (435), which Wit receives while in her lap, is conventionally linked with the devil, as Wit later declares upon viewing his face in the Glass of Reason (839–40); but it is also characteristic of St. George's pagan adversaries in the folk drama. However, it is in the exchange of clothes with Ignorance that Wit graphically demonstrates his transformation while under the spell of Idleness. Putting the fool's long ears, hood, and coat on Wit while he sleeps is a variation on a popular morality play motif of using costume as a form of disguise, usually by vices masquerading as virtues. Here, by comparison, the fool's trappings complement the blackened face in establishing Wit's new identity, of which he is totally unaware. The fact that Science's garment, formerly worn by Wit, will not stay on Ignorance's back suggests its inappropriateness for the fool, while the fool's coat, on the other hand, fits the fallen Wit so well it appears to have "bene made evyn for [his] bodye" (586). Wit can readily become a fool, but a natural fool cannot become knowledgeable, as is demonstrated by Ignorance's burlesque attempt to learn his own name. Parodying Wit's loss of his identity because of his failure to heed Reason and to continue his pursuit of knowledge, Ignorance is instructed by Idleness to repeat the syllables of his name, but he is unable to tell at the end of the lesson who he is or what he has learned (555–56). Like the degraded Wit, he lacks knowledge and therefore is unable to wear the garment given by Science to Wit.[3]

It is Wit's recognition of himself as a fool by viewing himself in the Glass of Reason, after being identified as Ignorance by Science and her mother, Experience, that is Wit's first step toward redemption. Wit takes on the appearance of Ignorance, and his degraded condition is further evidenced by his lecherous attempt to kiss Science. As he had earlier mistaken the nature of Honest Recreation by asking for a kiss, here he misunderstands the nature of Science as he follows his physical desires rather than his mental capacity. The comparison of the full-length portrait of the earlier innocent Wit with the corrupted Wit who has assumed the image of Ignorance manifests Wit's internal transformation. His realization of his loss of his former identity as perceived by others prompts him to draw out the Glass of Reason and to measure the effects of his sojourn with Idleness against his former image. Emphasizing Wit's moral alteration with both a mirror and a full-length portrait enhances the dramatic spectacle as it clarifies the didactic message of the play.

While following the morality paradigm of temptation, fall, and redemption, Redford represents Wit's reformation as beginning with his recognition of his fallen condition. After his second fall Wit gains self-knowledge, but he also accepts Reason as his guide rather than rejecting him as he had done after his defeat by Tediousness. Reciting Wit's errors, his broken promises, and his abuse of himself in becoming "a verye stark foole" (876), Reason demands that Wit submit to the Whip of Shame. As in the pre-Reformation morality, repentance is succeeded by penance, graphically demonstrated here by physical punishment. This purging of the sinful self is symbolized by Wit casting off the dress and trappings of the fool and putting on new apparel. Reason then explains for the audience the moral illustrated by Wit's example:

> Who lyst to marke now this chance heere doon
> may se what wyt is wythout reson
> what was this wyt better than an asse
> being from reson strayde as he was
> but let pas now / synce he is well poonyshyd
> And therby I trust meetely well monyshed. (908–13)

Concluding the pattern of the morality play with redemption, Redford returns to Wit's original mission to overcome the giant Tediousness, who blocks Wit's ascent up Mount Parnassus and his marriage with the Lady Science.

The renewed Wit is this time fully prepared for his adversary. Having learned his lesson from his two previous failures, he now heeds Reason and obeys Instruction, but he is also now armed with the Sword of Comfort, a token from Lady Science for which Wit has given her his Heart of Gold, and he is accompanied by Confidence. Wit's victory is easy because he uses his knowledge effectively; as Instruction explains, "where strength lackth policye supplieth" (1001). As his reward, Wit receives from Science the gown of knowledge, apparently an academic gown worn by graduates, as distinguished from the garment of knowledge, suggesting a student uniform, that Wit wears at the beginning of the play and discards before dancing the galliard and falling into the lap of Idleness.[4] Wit has now passed his final examination, and Science descends from Mount Parnassus to receive the severed head of her enemy Tediousness as a trophy of Wit's victory. Again particular symbols enhance the dramatic spectacle and accentuate the allegorical meaning.

However, it is the marriage of Wit and Science that marks the climax of the dramatic action and the capstone of the allegory. Science, who observed Wit's victory from Mount Parnassus, is welcomed with her entourage (Experience, Reason, and Confidence) to the main playing area by Wit and his supporters (Instruction, Study, and Diligence) in song. This third song in the performance is sung in parts as Wit's group of four and Science's group of four respond to each other. This musical number concludes the scene of combat and sets the ceremonial tone for the celebration of the marriage. However, before an exchange of vows, Science warns Wit that she may be a clog rather than a key to joy if she is not properly used. Combining her roles as both woman and knowledge, she explains:

> my presence bryngyth you acologg no naye
> not in the kepynge of me onelye
> but in the vse of science cheeflye
> for I science am in this degree
> as all or most part of woomen bee
> yf ye use me well in good sorte
> then shall I be youre Ioy & comfort
> but yf ye use me not well then dowt me
> for sure ye were better then wyth out me. (1056–64)

Wit, who has earned Science by demonstrating the proper use of knowledge, promises to continue to honor Science and understands that if he misuses her, "father reson" will "correct" him (1069–70). Experience reinforces her daughter's warning as she threatens,

> yf you use her contrary wyse
> to her good nature & so devyse
> to evyll effecte to wrest & to wry her
> ye & cast her of & set nowght by her
> ... thys talent from you shal be taken
> & you ponysht for your gayne forsaken. (1085–92)

Redford emphasizes that the winning of Science and the receiving of the academic gown are but the beginning of a lifetime of employing knowledge. The youthful Wit must make a commitment, to which he will be strictly held if he is to find joy.

The play illustrates the contemporary schoolboy's struggle for a sound education and the pitfalls he encounters along the way, but the final message addressed to the adult audience, including the king, the queen, and "ther honorable cowncell" (1121–22), declares the need to use knowledge appropriately throughout one's life. Knowledge rather than divine grace is Wit's goal, and though he like the hero of the morality play must overcome sin, here perceived as sloth, reason rather than truth is his guide. *Wit and Science* may be "one of the purest allegories that have come down to us," as F. P. Wilson claims (43–44), but its message is secular rather than religious, as it integrates features of the morality play with the traditions of intellectual allegorical romance, folk drama, and court pageantry. The dramatic spectacle of Wit's progress toward knowledge brilliantly illustrates the fusion of actor and symbol that instructs as it entertains.

A generation later, in 1567–68, an adaptation of Redford's play was produced by the Children of Paul's, apparently at court (Craik, *Tudor Interlude* 15–16). Entitled *The Marriage of Wit and Science*, this version, probably created by Sebastian Westcott, Redford's successor at St. Paul's, was entered in the Stationer's Register in 1569 and published in 1569–70, which indicates its contemporary appeal. Though retaining the principal characters and the outline of the plot from Redford's original, this adaptation imposes a five-act structure on the action as it extends the length by some 440 lines, or approximately a half-hour of playing time.

Even more important are the internal alterations. The most significant change is in the elaboration of the romantic elements of the wooing and of the quest as the allegorical aspect is reduced, which curiously results in a more prosaic dimension. For example, at the beginning of *The Marriage of Wit and Science*, Wit expresses the manifestations of his love for Science, but at the end of his long speech he declares that he is "too young to shewe her sport in bed, / Yet are there many in thys lande that at my yeares doe wedde" (I.i.45–46), though later Wit is said to be about seventeen (II.ii.471).⁵ The fact that the adapter felt it necessary to justify the "adult" love represented by the child actor suggests a self-conscious concern with the dramatic illusion and the verisimilitude on which it depends. Developed in the manner of the Petrarchan lover, as portrayed in contemporary sonnets and prose romance, Wit gushes on first meeting Science:

> O pearle of passing price, sent downe from god on hye!
> The swetest beauty to entise, that hath bene sene with eye:
> . . . .
> What wordes shal me suffice to utter my desyre?
> What heate of talke shal I devise for to expresse my fyer?
> I burne and yet I frese; I flame and coole as fast.
> In hope to wyn and for to lese, my pensiveness doth last.
> (III.ii.609–18)

The suffering and paradoxes of the Petrarchan lover expressed by a boy may appear inappropriate on the surface, but this image is in keeping with the prevailing image of Wit, who is more a lover than a scholar.

Also expanded is the family context for Science, who is cast in the role of a daughter being pressured to marry. Unlike the passive symbol of Science in Redford's play, Science in *The Marriage of Wit and Science* is reluctant to admit suitors; but when urged by her father, Reason, and by her mother, Experience, to marry for the advancement of the "common wealth" (II.ii.402), she accepts Wit's suit, though she lays down the conditions upon which she will be won. Describing Tediousness as her personal enemy, she assigns Wit the task of overcoming him (III.ii.700–721). A more realistic dimension is also added when Wit is initially defeated by Tediousness, for upon being revived by Recreation and her companions, Wit angrily sends a message to Science cursing the day and hour he was given the mission that nearly destroyed him. Wit's resuscitation is followed by an invitation to dance, which he does until out of breath, and this realistically makes him more vulnerable to Idleness who lulls Wit to sleep with a song. However, this second fall and subsequent repentance, though retaining the form of the morality convention, is reduced in length and significance from Redford's version as the last act focuses on the romantic climax, the triumph over Tediousness.

The final victory over Science's enemy is staged as if it were a tournament, and it is observed by Science from her "closet." Tediousness is beheaded in full view of the audience, unlike Redford's version where the beheading occurs off stage, and the remarkably brief celebration lacks the didactic message of the original. Instead Science announces that the "mariage may forthwith procede" (V.vi.1554), and a self-satisfied Wit reminds the audience that he has passed his test; he ends the play with the romantic sentiment that henceforth he and Science are "one soule in bodyes twayne" (V.vi.1562).

This is a fitting conclusion to the play dominated by features drawn from the romance tradition. The allegorical meaning of the original is generally sacrificed to a later generation's taste for romance but leavened by a new dimension in realism. The only moral element that may be strengthened in this later version is the introduction of Will as Wit's page. Replacing Confidence in the original, Will promises as Wit's adviser and emissary of love to provide an allegorical role as a vicelike misleader of youth, but Will serves that function only briefly, when he urges Wit to dismiss Study and Instruction before first encountering Tediousness. Otherwise Will, identified as a child "Betwene eleven and twelve" (II.ii.466), serves essentially as a functionary in his role as page to the older Wit. As in all the other aspects of *The Marriage of Wit and Science*, the romantic perspective prevails over the moral.

A few years later another version of the Wit and Science plot appeared under a new title, *The Marriage Between Wit and Wisdom*. Composed by Francis Merbury, apparently in the 1570s, this interlude adapts the school play action for performance by a professional troupe and adds several new comic characters and farcical elements. The shortest of the three Wit plays at 770 lines, Merbury's version not only reduces the central plot, Wit's encounters with Tediousness (renamed Irksomeness) and Idleness before winning Science (renamed Wisdom), to just 460 lines, but Merbury also restructures it. Adding parents for Wit introduces a domestic context in the first scene, but because the father, Severity, and the mother, Indulgence, offer contrasting advice, the play begins in the manner of the popular "spare the rod" or parental-direction plays (see chapter 10). However, in the second scene, Merbury falls back on morality play conventions by introducing Idleness in the role of the vice. Posing as Honest Recreation, Idleness is a male, unlike his namesakes in the previous Wit interludes, but he introduces as a female counterpart, Wantonness posing as Honesty, to assist him in tempting Wit, who falls asleep in her lap. By presenting Wit's encounter with Idleness before his meeting with Tediousness (Irksomeness) and omitting the academic implications of Redford's play, Merbury casts Wit in the role of the traditional morality play youth. Good Nurture rather than Reason leads Wit to recognize his error, but not before Idleness has stolen his purse. From this point on the vice Idleness becomes the dominant character of the play, and assuming various disguises, Idleness is both a victim and a victimizer in a series of farcical scenes related by the motif of stealing but unrelated to the skeletal Wit plot.

Wit, led by Idleness to the den of his brother Irksomeness, quickly falls, is quickly revived by his future bride, Wisdom, and then quickly drives the monster off the stage and returns with his head. The two encounters with Tediousness in the previous Wit plays are reduced to one, and the implications of neither the romance nor the intellectual allegory are developed here. This climactic event ends the first part of the play, but after an apparent interval the play continues for another three hundred lines of comic sequences performed by a new array of characters. Wit suffers a third fall when he is tricked by Fancy and then bound fast, but as in his first encounter with Idleness and Wantonness, Wit is restored by Good Nurture. However, part 2 largely belongs to Idleness, who appears as a rat catcher, a beggar, and a priest; in his final speech he describes his "chameleon" role and the pervasiveness of his vice. In the penultimate scene, after identifying himself as "the purveyor here in earth for the devil," he invites all those "that list not to work" to follow him (ix.681–705) and disappears from the play.[6] Only then does Wit regain center stage, and he and Wisdom celebrate their impending marriage in song. The play ends like the previous versions with Wit winning his bride, but neither its allegorical meaning nor its romantic climax is apparent. Rather it is only one more disjointed scene in the entertainment.

Though Tucker Brooke found what he termed the "irrelevant farce and melodramatic interest . . . tolerable reading" and considered Merbury's version "the most engaging of the three related plays, and at the same time the least faithful example of the interlude" (*Tudor Drama* 77), the lack of a controlling design and the failure to integrate the disparate morality motifs and popular comic devices with the skeletal plot make *The Marriage Between Wit and Wisdom* the least artistically satisfying of the group. Its purpose was clearly to entertain, and all of the elements of the play are directed to that end. Redford's carefully crafted educational interlude is reduced to coarse popular entertainment.

CHAPTER TWELVE

SKELTON'S *MAGNIFICENCE*

*T*HE educational morality takes on another significance and dimension when the youth represented is a prince: A political context is introduced that not only invites an identification with contemporary figures and events but also extends the significance of the action to the affairs of a nation. That is, it made the drama more immediate at the same time that it made it more important, for what the head of the government did in Tudor England affected those governed. At the same time the action demonstrated the influence of others on the judgment of the prince, which emphasized the importance of the monarch's advisers. As a result, the morality became political as it addressed both the king and his counselors. The play may have sought to instill particular values, as in other educational moralities, but it also sought to define the roles of the monarch and his advisers, and occasionally other groups in society as well.

These didactic aims were, of course, embodied in several other literary traditions in the Tudor period. A half-century before Henry VII established the Tudor line, Lydgate had written *The Fall of Princes* (1431–38) in the wake of Boccaccio's *De casibus virorum illustrium* and Chaucer's *Monk's Tale*. Republished in two new editions early in Queen Mary's reign, it taught that princes were especially vulnerable to error and the vicissitudes of fortune; Christian doctrine in Lydgate's view afforded the best means to escape the fall. These catalogs of cautionary exempla were followed in the sixteenth century by the *Mirror for Magistrates*, apparently intended as a modern addition to Lydgate's work in the mid-fifties but stayed from publication by Mary's counselors. The work, finally printed in 1559, includes counselors, such as the Duke of Buckingham, Richard III's partner in crime, and Cardinal Wolsey, as well as kings.

Instructions to political leaders took a more theoretical form in the books advising a prince on matters of government and personal conduct. Perhaps the best-known text of this type was the pseudo-Aristotelian *Secretum Secretorum*, found in about 500 manuscripts dating from the twelfth century onward. Purporting to be Aristotle's advice to Alexander, this popular medieval Latin translation of the Arabic *Kitab sirr al asrār* was further translated into the vernacular, including French and English. Several English versions in manuscript form, particularly from the fifteenth century, are extant, as well as a translation entitled *The Secrete of Secretes* directed to Henry VIII and printed by Robert Copland in 1528, and a version in rhyme royal by William Forest addressed to the Protector Edward Seymour, Duke of Somerset, and the young Edward VI in 1548.[1] Machiavelli's *The Prince* (1514) is, of course, the most famous sixteenth-century progeny of this advisory tradition. A variation on these works intended to influence the government of a kingdom were books describing a princely education. Deriving from Cicero's *De Officiis*, widely used in Renaissance grammar schools, these texts explain how certain virtues are inculcated and desired qualities are cultivated (W. Harris 152–53). The best-known example is Erasmus's *Education of a Christian Prince* (1516), but it is significant that this instruction is extended from the prince to society's leaders in Elyot's *The book named The governor* (1531). Again we see in Tudor England the concern with the group that holds power, not just its major symbol, the king.

Efforts to advise and influence the court took dramatic form in the masques, disguisings, pageants, and plays that were performed on both state and social occasions. Though designed to compliment the monarch, these entertainments were occasionally critical and offered judgments that at times proved to be controversial. Hall's *Chronicle* describes many entertainments in Henry VIII's reign that have political implications, but a Christmas disguising at Gray's Inn in 1527 was particularly bold. Hall reports that "the effecte of the plaie was, that lord governance was ruled by dissipacion and negligence, by whose misgoverance and evill order, Lady Publicke wele was put from governance: which caused Rumor Populi, Inward grudge and disdain of wanton souereigntie, to rise with a great multitude, to expell negligence and dissipacion, and to restore Public welth again to her estate, which was so done" (719). Cardinal Wolsey interpreted the play as directed at himself, and claiming that Henry VIII was displeased, had its author, John Roo, sent to prison. This well-known incident illustrates the potential danger in instructing the powerful. It was safer to flatter those in high places, as was apparently done a year later in a play representing the pope's recent release from the control of Charles V. The performance before Henry VIII and Francis I, according to Hall, portrayed a cardinal freeing the pope from captivity and making intercession between the kings of France and England. Hall comments, "At this play wisemen smiled & thought that it sounded more glorious to the Cardinal [Wolsey] then true to the matter in dede" (735).

The political morality that emerged in the early sixteenth century carried on the didactic nature of traditional court entertainment, but it also incorporated the aims of the "mirror" tradition and the works of princely instruction. As a result, both its purpose and its audience were specific, but its form was highly flexible. Though it retained the allegorical mode of the early morality play, the political morality adapted the pattern of sin and redemption as well as the roles of the vices and virtues, and readily accommodated features of other dramatic and nondramatic forms. It proved to be so adaptable that it quickly became one of the major types of morality play; five of the twelve identified morality plays from the first three decades of the sixteenth century are perceived as political. After the Reformation the numbers increase. In the period from 1530 to 1558, twenty-one of the forty-four identified moralities and interludes are linked to the political and religious controversy; fourteen were written or performed between 1533 and 1540 (ten by John Bale), and seven were produced between 1548 and 1553. None appeared during the last eight years of Henry VIII's reign or during the last five years of Mary's reign because of governmental restrictions.[2] The morality became an important vehicle for promoting political and religious reform during Cromwell's leadership in the 1530s and during the reign of Edward VI. Only a few political moralities have survived, but they illustrate a wide variety of adaptations.

Magnificence, the first extant political morality play, was written, significantly, by Henry VIII's tutor, John Skelton, sometime between the end of the fifteenth century and 1522. Most scholars believe the play was composed between 1515 and 1518.[3] Others have suggested that it was written before 1502, when Skelton's official duties as tutor ended after the death of Prince Arthur (Winser, "Skelton's *Magnyfycence*" 14–25), and as late as 1520–22, during Skelton's poetic attacks on Cardinal Wolsey (Skelton, *Magnificence*, ed. Neuss 15–17). The play survives in only one complete printed copy, and the publication date is unknown; however, it is generally believed to have been printed by John Rastell about 1530–33. We also have no specific evidence about the place and date of its initial performance; scholars speculate that the play was presented at court or at a great hall in London. Whether the king was a member of the original audience is unclear, but evidently the play was designed for presentation before the men who directed the affairs of the kingdom, if not for Henry VIII himself.

Skelton on at least one other occasion sought formally to instruct the king. In *Speculum Principis*, a short Latin treatise dated August 28, 1501, Skelton advised the young Henry and his brother Arthur to pursue a moral, responsible life and to beware of the traditional temptations awaiting princes. Citing examples from the Bible and classical literature, he urged the princes to avoid the vices of gluttony, lechery, and anger and to embrace public virtues: "Scis cum ratione munificus, largus, benignus, et dapsilis"—"Know with reason to be munificent, liberal, kind, and magnificent"—(Salter, "Skelton's *Speculum Principis*" 35). After Henry became king in 1509, Skelton apparently dusted off this earlier advice and formally presented it to His Majesty. *Magnificence* seems to be designed for the same purpose, though it is presented in a form that is more palatable than the series of commonplaces that make up *Speculum Principis*.

Identified as a "comoediam" by John Bale in his *Scriptorum Illustrium* (651), *Magnificence* in fact adopts the morality framework for its didactic purpose, but because its theme is worldly prosperity rather than heavenly salvation and its central figure a prince rather than generic man, the morality design is altered. The morality pattern of temptation, sin, repentance, and redemption is conceived in the context of the court, and as a result the emphasis shifts from the personal to the political. Ramsay identifies the order of development as I. Prosperity, II. Conspiracy, III. Delusion, IV. Overthrow, and V. Restoration (Skelton, *Magnifycence* xxvi), and though we may quibble with the labels he attaches to the stages of development, we must recognize that society rather than the individual is the major concern of the play. The prince, Magnificence, is represented in his role as governor, and his actions are perceived in terms of their implications for the kingdom. The play illustrates the consequences of a ruler being misled by evil counselors, and this serves as a warning to the young Henry VIII to choose his advisers and companions carefully if he is to avoid the fate of the titular hero of Skelton's political interlude.

Because the characters and pattern of action are presented in a general rather than a specific context, the exact date of composition cannot be determined from internal evidence and the identification of dramatic characters with contemporary figures remains elusive. Ramsay and other modern scholars identify the character Magnificence with Henry VIII and interpret the manipulation of the titular hero as an expression of the growing power of Wolsey, who became both a cardinal and Henry VIII's chancellor in 1515. The play is perceived as Skelton's first salvo in his campaign against the cardinal that culminated in the satiric poem *Why Come Ye Nat to Court* in 1522 (Skelton, *Magnifycence*, ed. Ramsay cx–cxxv; Bevington, *Tudor Drama and Politics* 54–63).

No evidence has been discovered to corroborate Skelton's opposition to Wolsey before about 1520 (W. Harris 12ff.), which may have led Paula Neuss, a recent editor of the play, to date the composition between 1520 and 1522, during Skelton's anti-Wolsey period, and to reconsider the figure of Magnificence as a possible characterization of Wolsey (Skelton,

Magnificence, ed. Neuss 31–42). This argument, like previous attempts to make the play an explicit topical allegory, remains tenuous. Skelton appears purposely to have avoided direct contemporary allusions or specific representations of contemporaries, perhaps to safeguard his position as *orator regius*, to which he had been appointed in 1512, an official status in the court that entailed his composition of occasional poems to celebrate such events as the English victory over the Scots at Flodden in 1513.

Skelton's fear of offending the king or his principal counselors may have led him to tread warily in expressing his advice, but if *Magnificence* was written between 1517 and 1519, the threat of the king being misled by corrupt courtiers must have been rather pointed. As G. R. Elton explains, by 1517 Henry VIII had added to the Privy Chamber "a group of very lively and very fashionable young men, younger than himself, who seemed to be able to do everything with him. Known familiarly as the King's minions, they caused raised eyebrows at court and worse in Wolsey's mind." They became even "more ominous" in the fall of 1518, when the Privy Chamber was reorganized and the "minions gained a formal and powerful place at court." The threat finally passed in May 1519, when Wolsey had four leaders of the young men expelled and exiled (*Reform and Reformation* 79). If the action of the play is viewed in the perspective of this political context, the play is not an attack on Wolsey or a warning against Wolsey's influence, as previous scholars have argued; rather it casts Wolsey more in the role of Redress, who helps Magnificence to regain his position after Adversity has struck. Whether Skelton had the king's minions of 1517–18 in mind or not, the threat is perceived as a group who encourage the prince to pursue his desires and lavish his favors on a select few.

To place the threat of evil counsel in perspective, Skelton begins the play with an examination of the conflicting demands of Liberty and Felicity, associated with Wealth and Prosperity. Cast in the traditional mode of a rhetorical debate, in which the opposing characters vie for supremacy, the dialogue highlights a contentious Liberty seeking unrestricted freedom. Like Will in the traditional morality scheme, Liberty rejects all appeals to reason made by Felicity, but Measure appears to resolve the argument as the opponents recognize that neither Felicity nor Liberty can be maintained unless he is guided by Measure: "Wealth without measure would bear himself too bold; / Liberty without measure prove a thing of nought" (Skelton, *Magnificence,* ed. Neuss 116–17).[4] Identifying Horace as his source, Measure applies the doctrine of the mean to the government of the state. Though Ramsay perceived Skelton's philosophical position as Aristotelian (*Magnifycence* lxxi–lxxvii) and William Harris linked it with the cardinal virtue tradition (46–70), its more immediate source may be the pseudo-Aristotelian *Secretum Secretorum*. In the mid-fifteenth-century Ashmole manuscript, an English version of this popular advice on kingly rule, Alexander is directed to "shvnne superfluous habundant expenses, and lette temperaunce rewle largesse" (*Secretum* 33–34). This expresses Skelton's general principle — "Where measure is ruler there is nothing amiss. / Measure is treasure" (124–25) — which is stated at the beginning of the play and then applied more particularly to largess as the drama unfolds.

When Magnificence appears for the first time, he reinforces Measure's philosophy by putting Liberty under the control of Measure. However, Fancy posing as Largess calls the doctrine of the mean into question as he, in the role of the principal vice, begins his assault on the ruler of the state. Unlike the typical morality, *Magnificence* does not represent the temptation of the titular hero; rather he leaves the stage with Fancy, and while he is absent nearly a thousand lines are devoted to the individual exhibition of the courtly vices — Counterfeit Countenance, Cloaked Collusion, Crafty Conveyance, and Courtly Abusion. Though these vices adopt names of virtues to hide their true natures, in typical morality play fashion, their static descriptions of their activities are reminiscent in both form and substance of Skelton's satiric poems, such as *The Bowge of Court*.[5] Counterfeit Countenance may be particularly associated with the court, but he declares that he is known throughout the world. At the end of thirteen formally patterned seven-line stanzas listing the manifestations of counterfeiting (including kindness, language, maidenhood, preaching, conscience, holiness, reason, and wisdom), he concludes with a description of the counterfeiting practiced by friars, nuns, and canons, though he ironically excludes monks (487–93). This indictment of the church by Skelton, who took holy orders in 1498 and served as rector at Diss from 1504 onward, seems almost playful when compared to the savage attack on the religious orders later expressed by Bale and Lindsay.

The second vice, Cloaked Collusion, is represented as more serious in his expression of the evil ends for which deception is used. Delighting in mischief, he hinders "wealth and prosperity," meddles "among these great estates," and sows "seditious seeds of discords and debates" (734–37). Though less sinister than Cloaked Collusion, the third vice, Crafty Coveyance, also puts dishonesty into practice by advocating theft and bribery, and he takes credit for bringing "Unto Magnificence a full ungracious sort" (1374), apparently alluding to his fellow vices who lead Magnificence astray. Of the four vices particularly associated with the court, Courtly Abusion is the most entertaining as well as the most superficial, for he is preoccupied with fashions of dress and manners. Depicting in doggerel rhyme the extravagance of the court society who waste their wealth on appearances, Courtly Abusion also demonstrates his basic nature by his attire and his gestures. He brags:

> What now? Let see
> Who looketh on me
> Well round about.
> How gay and how stout
> That I can wear
> Courtly my gear.
> My hair busheth
> So pleasantly,
> My robe rusheth
> So ruttingly;
> Meseem I fly,
> I am so light;
> To dance delight. (828–40)

Courtly Abusion adds a comic dimension as he makes courtly fashions ridiculous; of the courtly vices he is least threatening, but like his compatriots he significantly contributes to misleading the prince.

Fancy, who had drawn Magnificence aside in the first place and thus provided the opportunity for the courtly vices to flourish, offers the greatest danger to Magnificence. With a disarming wit and a bullying manner, Fancy resembles the archetypal seducer in the prodigal plays. However, because he poses as Largess, he here epitomizes the misdirection in the court. Like the morality-play tempter, he seeks to distract Magnificence with pleasure; but rather than developing this conventional motif, Skelton focuses on Fancy's influence on Magnificence in removing Liberty from Measure's control, which results in the loss of Felicity. Folly, the generic fool, provides comic diversion among the courtly vices. His exchange of his dog for Fancy's hawk emphasizes their close association. Posing as Conceit, Folly not only supports Fancy's design to mislead Magnificence, but his presence in the court symbolizes Magnificence's folly.

The seduction of Magnificence incorporates conventional elements from contemporary drama, but they are adapted to the political message of the play. After falling under the influence of Fancy (False Largess) and giving him kingly authority (1457), Magnificence demonstrates his internal change by expressing in soliloquy the classic hubris of the tyrant. Earlier critics see this action as mirroring Henry VIII's elevation of and dependence on Wolsey (*Magnifycence*, ed. Ramsay cxxi–cxxv; Bevington, *Tudor Drama and Politics* 54–63), but as noted above, this identification is unconvincing. Magnificence congratulates himself on being "like as a prince should be" in having "wealth at will, largesse and liberty" (1458–59). Then like Herod in the Corpus Christi plays and Tamburlaine and Sejanus in later Renaissance drama, Magnificence declares that he will rule Fortune. Comparing himself to Cyrus, Cato, Hercules, Charlemagne, and other past worthies, he claims to be greater than all of them. This expression of pride marks Magnificence's fall, and it is immediately followed by the welcoming of Courtly Abusion and Cloaked Collusion, who instruct Magnficence in the ways of the tyrant. After offering to buy a lusty lass for the king's pleasure, Abusion urges Magnificence, "By wayward wilfulness let each thing be conveyed; / Whatsoever ye do, follow your own will" (1595–96); telling the king to put his own desires before concerns for his subjects, Abusion cries, "Let your lust and liking stand for a law" (1608).

When Cloaked Collusion enters with Measure, Magnificence proves his corruption by dismissing Measure completely. The form the misleading of the king takes becomes more politically specific as Collusion advises the king to lavish his largess on a few favorites: "Chose out two, three of such as you love best, / And let all your fancies upon them rest" (1770–71). He reiterates, "Pluck from an hundred and give it to three" (1776). This counsel epitomizes the methods of the tyrant as it inverts the advice of *Secretum Secretorum* to dispense largess with temperance. Further, it betrays the highest role of the king, to practice justice in emulation of God, as described in Book Seven of *Secretum*.[6] Shortly after promising to reward Collusion, Magnificence welcomes Folly and delights in his absurdity, which indicates the king's unawareness of the consequences of his action and suggests his affinity with the fool.

When Fancy returns to report the destruction in the kingdom that results from Magnificence's ineffectual government, Folly departs and Adversity enters. In a symbolic action meant to represent the plight of the king and kingdom when False Largess and the court vices hold sway, Magnificence *"is beaten down and spoiled from all his goods and raiment"* (s.d. 1876). Adversity, like the court vices before him, describes at length the various forms he takes, but most significantly he identifies himself as "The stroke of God" sent to "pluck down king, prince, lord, and knight" (1883–84). Emphasizing the punishment that must follow transgression, Adversity welcomes Poverty as his natural companion. Skelton relies on a series of conventional motifs in illustrating Magnificence's response to his changed condition. Poverty evokes the image of Fortune's wheel to emphasize the mutability of this world, a recurring theme for the remainder of the play. Magnificence, recalling the *Ubi sunt* complaints of medieval poetry, bemoans the loss of his lands, rents, and servants; then following the generic pattern of man in the morality plays, Magnificence regrets his folly and his wanton will (2,063). This exercise in self-pity is, however, interrupted by unrestrained Liberty, who reminds Magnificence and the audience that the king's failure to recognize the nature of liberty and his failure to maintain control have been his undoing. Liberty says:

> I am a virtue if I be well used,
> And I am a vice where I am abused.
> . . . if measure had ruled liberty as he began,
> This lurdan that here lieth had been a noble man. (2102–13)

The political context of the drama makes Magnificence's plight especially significant, but the despair that leads him to the brink of suicide offers a glimpse of the man beneath the symbol.

Succumbing to Despair, Magnificence is prompted by Mischief to kill himself, a stock response of the sinner who recognizes the consequences of his errors.[7] Magnificence's attempted suicide reflects his self-absorption, another face of pride, for this manifestation of his hopelessness ignores the promise of mercy and redemption. The cleric Skelton steps in at this point to offer the desperate monarch another chance. Good Hope snatches the sword from Magnificence and, like Una in the *Faerie Queene*, reminds the fallen sinner of the "grace of God" (2350). Developing the metaphor of God as physician and himself as a "potecary," Good Hope explains the cure that Magnificence must undergo before his redemption can be realized. Emphasizing adversity as the punishment for error and poverty as painful purgation, Good Hope indicates what is further required of Magnificence: He must experience the "rhubarb of repentance" and in "drams of devotion" must his "diet . . . be dressed." Further, he must change his behavior: "Put fro your presumption and admit humility." God may then mend Magnificence's mood and restore prosperity, Good Hope promises (2350–68). But only after Magnificence repents his "wilfulness" and asks God's "mercy" for his "negligence" (2380–81) does Redress enter and clothe the penitent in a new garment signifying Magnificence's regeneration.

The king's personal responsibility for the government of the kingdom is emphasized by his spiritual crisis.

At the end of the play Redress, Circumspection, and Perseverance reiterate the moral lesson for the king and his counselors. After Redress reminds Magnificence that "of nobleness the chief point is to be liberal, / So that your largesse be not too prodigal" (2484–85), repeating the central message, the emphasis shifts once again to the theme of mutability. Circumspection, identifying the play with the "mirror" tradition, stresses the inconstancy of this life:

> A mirror enclered is this interlude,
> This life inconstant for to behold and see:
> Suddenly advanced, and suddenly subdued;
> Suddenly riches, and suddenly poverty;
> Suddenly comfort, and suddenly adversity;
> Suddenly thus Fortune can both smile and frown,
> Suddenly set up, and suddenly cast down. (2520–26)

The moral perceived from the dramatic example just witnessed has a general application rather than an expressly political one, and Perseverance links the uncertainty of life to the *de contemptu mundi* motif, as each stanza concludes with the refrain "Thus in this world there is no earthly trust" (2540, 2547). The morality framework prevails in the final movement of the play as the political implications for the king and his counselors remain unexplained.

The didactic allegory imposes a political context on the morality framework, and in so doing shifts the emphasis from heavenly salvation to worldly prosperity, but at the end Skelton repudiates the wealth and glory that can be acquired in this world. Yet he does not direct his audience to seek divine aid. In the final line he provides a rather negative blessing: "Jesus preserve you from endless woe and shame" (2568). It would seem that Skelton was wary of making his political judgment too plain; the political vices represented are more generic than personal, and the political warning to the monarch and his counselors more general than specific. Whether Skelton suffered a failure of nerve in expressing his political message, or whether he changed his intention in the course of the play, his lively satiric sketches give way to an abstract pattern and pronouncement. The poet is replaced by the priest and the schoolmaster, while the dramatist is only fleetingly perceived.

CHAPTER THIRTEEN

BALE'S *KING JOHN*

WITHIN a year or two of his conversion to the Protestant cause, the Carmelite friar John Bale appears to have taken a wife, "the faithful Dorothy," and embarked upon his mission as a propagandist for the Reformation. By 1536 he had, according to his *Anglorum Heliades*, completed several antipapal plays as well as two plays dealing with historical conflicts between secular and clerical authority in England: *Pro Rege Ioanne* and *De Traditione Thome Becketi*. Bale repeats references to these two historical plays in subsequent lists of his works, his *Summarium* (1548) and *Catalogus* (1557), though under slightly altered titles: *Pro Ioanne Anglorum rege* and *De Thomae Becketi imposturis*.[1] The play on Becket has not come down to us, but the revised title and Bale's references to the popular English saint in his other works suggest the play must have supported the king, Henry II, and represented Becket as traitorous and the miracles associated with him as fraudulent.

The play on King John has survived in a single manuscript (now at the Huntington Library) that indicates extensive revision by Bale, apparently for a later performance of the play. The first version (A-text) in a scribal hand is generally believed to represent the version of the play that was performed at Archbishop Cranmer's house on January 2, 1539, and the revised version with a new ending (B-text) is thought to have been prepared for presentation to Queen Elizabeth, probably at Ipswich in August 1561.[2] The revision essentially clarifies and updates the message of the play: to warn the monarch and his or her counselors of the dangers the Catholic Church poses to the rule and order of the state. Apparently like Bale's play on Becket, *King John* presents a historical analogue designed to reflect the contemporary situation. As the Interpretour added by Bale in the revision points out at the end of act I,

> In thys presant acte we have to yow declared
> As in a myrrour the begynnynge of Kynge Johan,
> How he was of God a magistrate appoynted
> To the governaunce of thys same noble regyon,
> To see maynteyned the true faythe and relygyon.
> But Satan the Devyll, whych that tyme was at large,
> Had so great a swaye that he coulde it not discharge.
> (1086–92)³

The conventional image of the mirror may have been given particular significance by Baldwin's publication of *The Mirror for Magistrates* in 1559, but the concept of instructing the ruler and his counselors had a long and venerable tradition, as Bale's audience would have recognized (see chapter 12). The interpretation of historical examples and their application to current circumstances are determined, of course, by the perspective of the instructor, and for Bale the perspective on King John had already been established by fellow reformers. His task was to dramatize the interpretation and clarify its application to the contemporary scene.

Tyndale's view in *The Obedience of a Christian Man* (1528) of King John as a royal martyr destroyed by unwarranted papal power may have provided the impetus for Bale's play, but Simon Fish in his *Supplicacyon for the Beggers*, addressed to Henry VIII and published perhaps as early as 1524 in Antwerp, points to the "nobill predecessour king John," victimized by a papal conspiracy with the French king, for which "your most nobill realme wrongfully (alas for shame) hath stod tributary (not unto any kind temporall prince but unto a cruell devilisshe bloudsupper dronken in the bloud of the sayntes and marters of Christ) eversins" (quoted in Bale, *Complete Plays* 1:150). Robert Barnes, some ten years later in his *Supplicacion unto the most gracyous prince H. the viii* (1534), reiterates the perception that King John had been destroyed for resisting the pope's incursion into domestic affairs and for taxing the monasteries to support his war against the Irish (see Bale, *Complete Plays* 1:149–50).

In his first version of his play on King John, written between 1534 and 1536, Bale may have been aware of the reformist positions of Barnes and Fish, as well as Tyndale's, but Bale was also endorsing legislation of the Reformist Parliament adopted between 1532 and 1534: the Act of Supremacy, making the King "Supreme Head of the Church of England"; acts restraining the payment of "Peter's pence" to Rome and annexing the annates (or first fruits) and tenths to the crown; and acts governing the submission of the clergy and the consecration of bishops. However, as he prepared the play for presentation at Archbishop Cranmer's residence in January 1539, he must have been responding to more recent events as well, particularly the adoption of the Ten Articles in 1536, the dissolution of the monasteries beginning in 1536, the northern rebellions in 1536 and 1537, and the completion and revision of *The Bishops' Book* in 1537 and 1538. This is demonstrated by the many allusions in the A-text to events and circumstances that occurred between 1536 and 1538. Apparently the A-text represents a revision of Bale's initial composition, and the B-text a later revision adapted to the new monarch, Elizabeth, crowned twenty years later.[4] That an intermediate version designed for performance during Edward VI's reign was prepared has been suggested but not substantiated.[5]

The text presented to Archbishop Cranmer and friends at the beginning of 1539 takes into account recent events, but it also addresses the changing atmosphere at court as Chancellor Cromwell's influence was being threatened by the more conservative faction led by the Duke of Norfolk and Bishop Stephen Gardiner. Henry VIII's growing reluctance to endorse the reformist position was signaled by his unwillingness to accept the exposition of doctrine in *The Bishops' Book* and by his own participation in its revision in 1538. His return to a more orthodox position was confirmed by his submission in the spring of 1539 of the Six Articles reaffirming traditional beliefs, which were passed by both Houses of Parliament on June 16. John Bale appears to be warning his fellow reformers and policymakers of the dangers of the new conservatism.

How fully Cromwell was involved in the message of Bale's *King John* we may never know, but the Chancellor appears to have taken an interest in Bale as a promoter of the Reformation at least two years before the performance at Cranmer's house. On January 25, 1537, John Leland wrote to Cromwell asking for his help in getting Bale released from prison at Greenwich (Bale, *Complete Plays* 1:4), and later. in the autobiography included in his *Catalogus* (1557), Bale relates that he was "dragged from the pulpit to the courts of justice, first under Lee at York, and then under Stokesley at London: but the pious Cromwell who was in the confidence of King Henry always set me free on account of the comedies I had published" (quoted in Bale, *Complete Plays* 1:147). Records indicate that Cromwell paid "Balle and his ffelowes" for "playing before my lorde," forty shillings in September 1538 and thirty shillings in January 1539 (quoted in Bale, *King John*, ed. Pafford and Greg xvii). What play or plays were performed is not identified, but since these payments were made both before and after the performance for Cranmer on January 2, 1539, we can assume that Bale had Cromwell's support during this period. It is possible that Bale and a troupe of players were being used in a propaganda campaign to support the Reformation cause, and *King John* may have been performed on more occasions than the one reported at Cranmer's house. Whether or not Bale's portrayal of King John had the official endorsement of the Reformation leaders, both Cranmer and Cromwell probably witnessed its performance, and neither was likely to object to its interpretation of this historical example and its application to the contemporary situation.

King John introduces himself at the beginning of Bale's play in the conventional manner of the civic and morality drama, and he declares, on the authority of Peter and Paul, "that all pepell shuld shew there trew alegyauns / To ther lawfull kyng Christ Jesu dothe consent, / Whych to the hygh powres was evere obedyent" (5–7). The reformist Act of Supremacy (1534) is endorsed by scriptural proof and the example of Christ. The position of the king is given even greater significance a hundred lines later by the allegorical character, England, who expresses the Tudor and Stuart doctrine of rule by divine right: Be the king "good or bade he is of Godes apoyntyng; / The good for the good, the badde ys for yll doyng" (103–4). A good king is perceived as a reward for virtue and a bad king the punishment for evil.

There is no question about the category into which John is placed, for he concludes his initial speech in the play by expressing his purpose "by practyse and by stodye / To reforme the lawes and sett men in good order, / That trew justyce may be had in every border" (19–21). John is identified as a reformer king bent on improving society. Like his namesake, John the Baptist, the archetypal reformer to whom Bale apparently devoted a cycle of fourteen plays (now lost)[6] as well as the extant *John Baptist's Preaching*, King John finds his reformation thwarted by enemies in league with the devil and suffers a martyr's death. In the new ending that Bale provided for performance during Elizabeth's reign, he reiterates the independent and supreme authority of the king through the character of Veritas, who states that "in hys owne realme a kynge is judge over all / By Gods appoyntment, and none maye hym judge agayne / But the Lorde hymself" (2347–49). Endorsing Elizabeth's new Act of Supremacy (1559), Bale underlines the view of kingship that informs the play from its inception.

Drawing especially upon the traditions of the morality and saints' play, Bale represents the conflict between the king and the church as an allegorical battle between good and evil with historical characters and events subordinated to the abstract conception. In the first 900 lines of the play, or most of what in his Elizabethan revision he designated as act 1, Bale creates an image of a corrupt clergy exploiting the state of England, represented as a weak widow who appeals to the king for relief, thus providing the motivation for the reformation the king had promised at the beginning. The king's major adversary, the church, is portrayed by various allegorical characters who merge with historical figures as the play progresses, but the leader of the opposition is Sedition, developed in the manner of the morality play vice. He identifies himself as "Sedycyon playne: / In every relygyon and munkysh secte I rayne" (186–87), and he explains that he is by turns a monk, a nun, a canon, a cardinal, and a pope; later in the play he is identified with the historical

Stephen Langton, who as the pope's candidate for Archbishop of Canterbury tests the king's authority. In his role as tempter, he leads Nobility to desert the king, but his major function is to expose the evils of the church that demand correction.

Typical of the morality vice in his liveliness and his boldness, Sedition offers comic diversion in his mockery of Catholic practices and doctrine. John vows to destroy all the monasteries Sedition inhabits (259) as Bale endorses the dissolution of the monasteries, begun in 1536. Sedition reveals that auricular confession, strongly opposed by the English reformers but retained in the Ten Articles of 1536 and reinforced in the Six Articles passed in 1539, is used to gain information for treasonous purposes (266–73), and later he demonstrates this tactic by leading Nobility during the act of confession to desert the king and follow the bidding of the pope (1150–86). Sedition also parodies the Litany of the Saints (636–56) and the Vespers for the Dead (764–69), ridiculing the celebrations of saints and the orthodox belief in purgatory (Miller, "The Roman Rite" 802–22). Sedition suggests that Usurped Power (dressed as a cardinal and later identified with Cardinal Pandulphus) kiss Dissimulation's arse, "for that is holy . . . yt hath an hole evyn fitt for the nose of yow" (893–95), reducing Catholic ceremony to coarse humor.

Satire on the veneration of holy relics also takes a comic turn when Sedition offers in the act of absolution "a bone of the blyssyd Trynyte, / A dram of the tord of swete Seynt Barnabe," and "a feddere of good Seynt Myhelles wyng" (1215–17). Expanding his catalog of relics in his revision, Bale adds "a lowse of Seynt Fraunces," "a scabbe of Saynt Job," "a maggot of Moyses, " and "a fart of Saynt Fandigo" (1220–22). Sedition's mockery of the church's representatives and practices provides a bit of humor in Bale's rather heavy-handed exposure of clerical hypocrisy and exploitation, but it obviously has much more to do with contemporary Reformation perceptions than with the reign of King John.

Only in the second part, act 2 in the Elizabethan revision, does Bale develop the pattern of the analogue by blending the allegory with historical events as the abstract vices become identified with individuals in the reign of King John. The first two-thirds of the second part focus on the appointment of the Archbishop of Canterbury, the excommunication of John for his defiance of the church, his subsequent resignation of his crown, his recoronation, and his poisoning. His conflict with the barons, which resulted in the Magna Charta, his relationship with young Prince Arthur, and other aspects of John's reign that might reflect negatively on his character are ignored; only his conflict with the church and his martyrdom appear to be relevant. By casting the allegorical characters in the roles of historic figures, Bale makes their actions toward John more reprehensible and at the same time indicative of their natures. Sedition's manifestation as Stephen Langton and Dissimulation's identification as Simon of Swinsett, the poisoner of King John, objectify the Catholic Church's evil. With Private Wealth appearing as a cardinal, first perhaps suggesting Wolsey and then more specifically identified with the historical Cardinal Pandulphus, and with Usurped Power's portrayal as the pope, the abstract threats of the church in act 1 are more fully realized.

The implicit application of the historical analogue to the contemporary scene in the late 1530s is reinforced by parallels and allusions to current actions and concerns. Sedition's temptation of Nobility to desert the king and support the pope recalls the northern rebellions of 1536 and 1537. The Lincolnshire rebellion during the first twelve days of October 1536 was accompanied on October ninth by the more extensive Pilgrimage of Grace, led by Robert Aske, which involved Yorkshire, Lancashire, and the northeast counties. This was put down on the fifth of December, but in January 1537 a revolt in Cumberland and Westmorland was succeeded by renewed uprisings in Yorkshire and again Cumberland. Though these rebellions may have had strong economic motivation, they appear to have exploited anti-Reformist sentiment in the North, and such noble families as the historically powerful Percies supported Catholic orthodoxy and opposed the reform faction led by Cromwell (Dickens 122-28).

From Bale's perspective, the alignment of the Nobility with the old church led by the pope against the king was most ominous for Henry VIII's rule and for the reformist cause. By recreating the excommunication of John, accompanied by the external threat from France and other

Catholic monarchies, Bale is reminding Henry VIII and his ministers of the pope's action following Henry's divorce from Catherine of Aragon and his assumption of the leadership of the English Church. John, enfeebled by Nobility's desertion, gives up his crown to the papal legate, but he explains in Bale's Elizabethan revision that he does so not out "of cowardnesse / But [out] of compassyon" (1719–20) as he contemplates the destruction that would ensue in a religious war: "The burnynge of townes, . . . Destructyon of corne and cattell, . . . Defylynge of maydes, and shedynge of Christen blood" (1707–9). The treachery of the church is demonstrated by restoring the crown to John with the exaction of his promise that he will "Nomore . . . meddle with the Churches reformacyon" (1969) and then almost immediately plotting his death. This is Bale's warning to Henry VIII and his ministers of the king's fate should he make peace with the Catholic Church as suggested by the conservative faction led by Norfolk and Gardiner at the end of 1538.

Likened to Christ, betrayed by a "false Judas kysse" (2144), John explains that he provoked the hatred of the church by "doynge justice" and that "synne and wyckednesse / In thys wretched worlde, like as Christe prophecyed, / Have the overhande" (2160–71). John follows the paradigm of saints overwhelmed by evil forces, but in this instance they are masquerading as Christians. This perception is emphasized by the Widow England's tragic lament:

> O horryble case that ever so noble a kynge
> Shoulde thus be destroyed and lost for righteouse doynge
> By a cruell sort of disguysed bloud soupper,
> Unmercyfull murtherers all dronke in the bloude of marters.
>   (2186–90)

Echoing Fish's *Supplicacyon for the Beggers*, John is described as dying for his righteousness, while his poisoner, Simon of Swinsett (alias Dissimulation), claims to be dying for the church like Thomas Becket and looks forward to sainthood: "I do not doubte it but I shall be a saynt; . . . No doubt but I shall do myracles in a whyle, / And therfor let me by shryned in the north yle" (2130–32). This Elizabethan revision continues Bale's scorn of Becket's sainthood, an old theme as indicated by his earlier play *De Thomae Becketi imposturis*. Bale may also be alluding to the demolishing of Thomas Becket's shrine at Canterbury in 1538 and the burning of his bones, the ashes of which were mixed with earth and shot from the mouth of a cannon. In Bale's revised Elizabethan ending for the play, Sedition expresses a similar expectation while awaiting hanging, but the choric Imperial Majesty comments that Becket was "exalted without reason / Because that he dyed for the Churches wanton lyberte" (2597–98). Clearly Bale is contrasting England's most famous martyr, now denounced and removed from church calendars by royal decree in 1538, as an example of false godliness and the epitome of treason, with the proto-Reformation King John, a true martyr who gave up his life like Christ in the real service of God.[7]

John is overwhelmed in Bale's view because the nobility allows itself to be coerced by the church. Had the nobility stood firm with the king and had the clergy recognized the legitimate power of the king in his kingdom, the tragic end of John and the sorry plight of the commonwealth would have been averted. The political message of the play is direct and immediate, and in his new Elizabethan ending Bale devotes 500 lines to its application to contemporary England. Whether the version that was performed before Cranmer in January 1539 included Imperial Majesty, an idealized image of Henry VIII, is not known, but his lengthy epilogue spells out the proper relationship between the church, the king, and the estates of the realm, which underlies the conception of the play. Emphasizing the divine right of kings, Bale endorses Tudor absolutism. As King John insists earlier when he defies the pope:

> The powre of princys ys gevyn from God above,
> And, as sayth Salomon, ther hartes the Lord doth move.
> God spekyth in ther lyppes whan they geve jugement. (1342–44)

John's tragedy is that he cannot sustain this belief. Bale in his final plea reiterates that biblical precepts and examples support the primacy of the king's power. Solomon, the book of Ecclesiastes, Joseph, and Mary all acknowledge civil authority, and even Saint Jerome is hailed as a defender of secular power (2231–32). A chastened Nobility recalls the punishment meted out to the rebels who have opposed civic authority—Brutus, Cassius, Catiline, and Absalom (2605–10)—but the most explicit statement of the king's role and the subject's duty of obedience is made by Veritas after Imperial Majesty forgives Nobility's and Clergy's error in putting the pope before their king. Veritas says:

> For Gods sake obeye lyke as doth yow befall,
> For in hys owne realme a kynge is judge over all
> By Gods appoyntment, and none maye hym judge agayne
> But the Lorde himself. . . .
> I charge yow therfore as God hath charge me
> To gyve to your kynge hys due supremyte
> And exyle the Pope thys realme for evermore. (2346–60)

Bale ensures that there is no mistaking his message. He advocates a strong king supported by both the nobility and the clergy, and he would ban the pope from England "for evermore." But Bale goes even farther in spelling out the reformation program. Private Wealth's expulsion from monasteries endorses their dissolution, and Sedition's hanging by Civil Order may recall the execution of Robert Aske, leader of the rebellious Pilgrimage of Grace, but it also approves the Reformation action that makes the clergy subject to civil law. The church, rather than being an agency of foreign power, is to be made an arm of the state.

Bale exploits the anti-Catholic attitude that was manifested in the iconoclasm encouraged by Cromwell in the late 1530s (see Aston 1:222–28) and was intensified in the wake of Mary's reign by her Spanish marriage and intolerance. But he also indicates the philosophical basis for his religious and political position. Though he is more a purveyor of others' ideas than an original thinker, Bale is adept at infusing his historical analogue with contemporary implications. This often involves the subordination of his drama to his political purpose, but he clearly regarded his roles as reformer and propagandist as more important than that of entertainer. He sought not just to instruct but to persuade his audience of political leaders at the end of 1538 to complete the reformation that had begun. They appear not to have acted on his advice, as a return to orthodoxy soon swamped the reformation cause and led to the deaths of several of its leaders, including Cromwell, and to the exile of Bale and other Protestant proponents. By 1560–61, when Bale adapted the play to Elizabeth and her court, the times had changed and his message may have been more fully appreciated.[8]

CHAPTER FOURTEEN

RESPUBLICA

*R**ESPUBLICA*, the most effective dramatically of the extant political moralities, if not the most entertaining, was according to its manuscript a "Christmas devise" performed in 1553, the first year of Queen Mary's reign.¹ The play was acted by boys, but the auspices of its production are not identified. However, since the prologue begins with a new year's greeting to "this moste noble presence heare" and entreats "Gentle Sufferaunce" (2–3), the performance appears to have been designed for an aristocratic audience in London. Whether the play was performed at court or before the new queen is not clear, but it was certainly addressed to the political leaders of the realm.² After indicating a fear that its message may be misconstrued, the prologue explains:

> oure meaninge ys (I saie not, as by plaine storye,
> but as yt were in figure by an allegorye)
> To shewe that all Commen weales Ruin *and* decaye
> from tyme to tyme hath been, ys, and shalbe alwaie,
> whan Insolence, Flaterie, Opression,
> and Avarice have the Rewle in theire possession. (17–22)

The prologue, spoken by "a poet" according to the dramatis personae, goes on to express the hope that the new sovereign will restore "goode Englande . . . from hir late decaye" and "reforme thabuses which hithertoo hath been" (45–50). Like Lindsay's *Satire of the Three Estates*, performed a year earlier at Cupar in Fife and repeated a year later at

Edinburgh, *Respublica* seeks to expose past and present ills, and suggests the cure rests in the hands of those who govern the realm. However, unlike Lindsay, who was a prominent member of the aristocracy and had a recognized court appointment, the author of *Respublica* is not identified.

Perhaps the anonymity of the author stems from his caution in instructing the new court being formed after some six years of rule by the Protectors of Edward VI. The role of drama as a vehicle for political persuasion had been severely curtailed in the last seven years of Henry VIII's reign, silencing the propagandistic Bale; then after some loosening of the restrictions under Edward, Mary's ministers proclaimed on August 18, 1553, only a month after her accession, that all books printed and all interludes played required "her graces speciall license in writynge" because of the danger of sedition (quoted in Wickham, *Early English Stages* 2.1:71–72). Since *Respublica* appears to have been publicly performed a few months later, it must have received the permission of the new government. The wariness of the author and his support of Mary's correction of past abuses reflect the political realities of late 1553, yet in his portrayal of the immediate past and the present, the playwright had to exercise extreme care, for half of the Privy Council formed by the Duke of Northumberland continued under Mary (G. R. Elton, *Reform and Reformation* 376–77). Allegorizing the image of the Protectorates of Northumberland and his predecessor, the Duke of Somerset, avoided specificity and possible offense to members of the old regime.

By adopting the morality structure previously used by Bale and Skelton as a vehicle for political instruction, the anonymous author of *Respublica* could distance contemporary circumstances and at the same time emphasize a pattern of abuse.[3] Selected vices from the morality tradition are so generalized as to make identification with historical individuals difficult if not impossible; they represent prevailing forces in society. Avarice, Insolence, Adulation, and Oppression are not courtly vices like Skelton's or vices particularly associated with the church like Bale's and Lindsay's; rather they are social vices manifested by governmental leaders. Eschewing the conventional morality warning to resist temptation,

Respublica focuses instead on the dangers of giving authority to self-serving officials. The play combines classical dramatic form, with division into acts and scenes (one of the first English plays so organized), with the morality pattern of the growth and subsequent exposure of the vices.

In contrast to the previous political moralities, the monarch is not the central character of *Respublica*. Instead the focus is on the country, as is indicated by the title. Further, the play does not develop moral choices as is customary for moralities, but rather emphasizes the sufferings that follow misjudgment. Of the principal figures in the play, the title character is least fully formed. More a condition than a person, Respublica serves as a passive victim of the exploiting vices. Her complaints are reminiscent of the Widow England's in Bale's *King John*, but mostly Respublica functions as a choric voice. At the beginning of act 2 she makes her first appearance, and in soliloquy, after observing that the falls of Troy, Babylon, Athens, and Corinth derive from pomp and pride, she concludes:

> in Comon weales while goode governors have been
> All thing hath prospered, and where suche men dooe lacke
> Comon weales decaye, and all thinges do goe backe.
> (II.i.454–56)

She looks to "good governemente att ons [to] recover all" (460) after her decay, but in the next scene she puts herself "whollye into [Avarice's] handes, / Metall, graine, cataill, treasure, good*es and* land*es*" (II.ii.499–500). Respublica does not examine Avarice's offer of his services; she simply accepts that he is Policy, as he says he is, and that he will serve her interests and not his own. The drama of the scene comes not from Respublica's decision-making nor from the vice's skill in deception; rather it comes from Avarice's asides, in which he reveals his true nature and his true motives to the audience with comic effect. In response to Respublica's speech placing herself in Avarice's hands, Avarice says, "Well I will take some paine but this to youe be knowen, / I will doe ytt, not for your sake, but for myne owne." Respublica may have heard the last line, though it may have been spoken as an aside, for she asks, "Howe saie ye *that* policie?" Avarice then rephrases his comment, "I will doe all for y*our* sake, and not for myne owen" (II.ii.501–4).

The role of Respublica as a victim is extended by the introduction of the rustic People, who provides details of the political abuse and corruption as he extends the comedy. Representing "the poore Commontie," People enters calling for "Rice puddingcake," his first of many malapropisms; and in his country dialect he complains of the falling prices of corn and cattle and the rising costs of goods he must purchase. Though he says the last forty years, which would include most of Henry VIII's reign, have been bad (III.iii.721–22), he finds the last five or six years (the period of the Protectorate) to have been the worst:

> vive or zixe yeare ago chad vowre kine to my paile
> *and* att this p*rez*ent houre cham scarce woorthe a good cowe taile
> ... Nowe Iscan geate nothing my zelfe and my wife to kepe.
> (IV.iii.1021–24)

He blames the problem on "coumpacing" or the enclosing of land, which forced the peasants from their livings as their small holdings were turned into great sheep pastures. Though People sees "the sugar mowthed howrecop" Flattery, Oppression, Insolence, and Covetise as responsible for his plight (III.iii.677–96), his complaints are essentially economic. People is angry but ineffectual, and his appeal to Respublica earns him only the intimidation of the vices, who continue to exploit the country and its people. The vices hold sway without tangible opposition through the first four acts of the play. People represents serious concerns, yet he is treated comically; thus the criticism of the immediate past and present is somewhat muted. His personal helplessness emphasizes the dependence of the common people on its governors.

As is typical of the sixteenth-century morality play, the major dramatic interest is provided by the vices. They occupy the stage exclusively in act 1, and for the next three acts they control the plot. T. W. Baldwin notes that the play follows the five-act formula and three-part structure associated with classical drama (*Shakspere's Five-Act Structure* 412–13).

However, after the *protasis*, which introduces the vices and their plan of action in acts 1 and 2, the responses of the well-intentioned Respublica and the boorish People are so feeble that the *epitasis* in acts 3 and 4 depends for its dramatic interest more on the comic byplay of the vices than on conflict. The vices are the most fully developed characters in the play and they provide much of the comedy, but their most important function is to manifest the social vices that have prevailed in the commonweal.

Avarice, the chief vice and called by the others their "founder," is both the source of the conspiracy against Respublica and an archetypal miser. He combines characteristics of the morality play manipulator and the comic hero of Plautus's *Aulularia*.[4] Conceived as an old man with purses hanging at his back, purses that are filled during the course of the play, Avarice resembles an emblematic device, but he is given dimensions unusual for a morality type. He manifests a bad temper when he believes knaves are waiting to rob him, and he is impatient at the ignorance of Adulation when he tries to remember the counterfeit names of his fellow vices. His allegorical representation of greed under the guise of policy symbolizes the corruption in the Commonweal during the previous reign, and since he is officially commissioned by Respublica at the beginning of act 2 to take charge, he must be generally identified with the principal ministers of the Protectorate, if not the Dukes of Somerset and Northumberland (formerly Earl of Warwick) themselves. This identification is made when Avarice is exposed in the last act, for he confesses:

> I woulde have browght haulfe kent into Northumberlande
> *and* Somersett shiere should have raught to Cumberlande,
> Than woulde I have stretche[d] the countie of warwicke
> vppon tainter hook*es*, and made ytt reache to Barwicke.
> A pece of the Bisshoprique shoulde have come southwarde.
>   (V.vi.1547–51)

This is the most specific the author of *Respublica* becomes in charging particular individuals with abusing their positions, but since both of the former Protectors were disgraced and executed, it was safe in this case to name names.

Insolence, described in the dramatis personae as "the chief galaunt," is declared the leader of the vices by Avarice (I.iii.272–83), and he assumes the role of Authority in the government of Respublica. Insolence becomes the means by which avarice is accomplished, and he is officially given the place of command. In the action of the play, however, his role remains secondary as he quarrels with the other vices for a share in the pickings and fills out the chorus when the vices occasionally burst into song. His position is more symbolic than real, and his character remains indistinct.

The most entertaining character, also identified as a "gallaunt," is Adulation, who combines aspects of the classical parasite (*Revels* 2:217–18) with the court fool. Adulation's difficulty in mastering the newly adopted names of the vices before meeting Respublica (I.iv.378–412) turns the conventional morality disguise motif into lively comedy. He contributes most among the vices to keeping the tone light. He seeks to prevent People from presenting his suit to Respublica (III.i), and threatens to have him "on the hyppe" after People has made his case, but the words are spoken only after People has left the stage. Adulation is the least effectual of the vices; his exploitation is so paltry that Avarice declares that he shames their "fraternitee" (III.v.788). The little danger that Adulation poses in society is indicated by his being pardoned at the end after promising to mend his ways.

Significantly, the least important of the vices is Oppression, who adopts the name "Reformation," which the comic Adulation mistakes as "dyffamacion" and "deformation" (I.iv.405–7). Oppression later reports on his and Authority's exploitation of church lands:

> I almoste leaft them never a ferme nor graunge.
> ... We lefte the best of them a threde bare bisshop:
> to some we left one howse, to some we left none,
> The beste had but his see place, that he might kepe home.
> we enfourmed them / *and* we defourmed theym,
> we confourmed them, *and* we refourmed theym. (III.v.798–806)

This appears to refer to the dissolution of the chantries in 1547, but the subject is not explored in detail. Avarice later alludes to the farming of benefices (III.vi.955–64), and Oppression subsequently discusses with Respublica and People the changes in the church. When Oppression announces that "youre priestes *and* bisshops have not as thei have had," Respublica responds, "[whan they] had theire lyvinge*s* men were bothe fedde and cladde." In response to Oppression's statement that the clergy "were prowde and covetous / *and* tooke muche vppon theim," People sarcastically replies, "but they were not covetous that tooke all from theym" (IV.iv.1069–74). The defense of the old church is not vigorous, and the implicit criticism of the reformers concentrates on their economic exploitation. Nothing is said here or later in the play about restoring church lands. Instead the conversation turns to the problems resulting from the debasing of the coinage, a more immediate and a more pervasive economic crisis. Compared to the indictments of the Catholic Church by both Bale and Lindsay, the author of *Respublica* is mild in the extreme in his criticism of the Reformation.

As in the conventional morality, *Respublica* ends with the exposure of the vices and the promise of a better world. However, the triumph of virtue does not come about because People is successful in convincing Respublica she has made a misjudgment in naming her ministers; People's efforts fail. The vices are defeated only through the grace of God, as Misericordia announces when she appears at the beginning of act 5. In a providential conception of history, Mercy, Peace, and Justice come from Heaven, and Truth, the daughter of Time, comes from Earth to effect a restoration of the commonweal. Obviously reflecting the end of the Protectorate with the death of Edward VI, Respublica is rescued through divine intervention, and the correction of past abuses is to be accomplished through Nemesis, whose role is identified in the prologue with Queen Mary (48–52). Though resembling in part the ending of classical comedy, in which the deceptions are revealed and the problems resolved, the conclusion is much longer than the traditional comic *catastrophe* or the conventional redemption of the morality play: 769 lines, or 39.7 percent of the play, is devoted to the restoration of the commonweal in act 5.

The restoration begins with the arrival of Lady Misericordia, who declares that God "all comonweales hath protected" and "Compassion he hath quickelye directed / to revive *and* recover theym everie one" (V.i.1197–200). It is significant that Misericordia is the first of the four virtues to appear, for the emphasis throughout act 5 is on mercy rather than on punishment. Misericordia directs the resolution as she and the other female virtues—Veritas, Justicia, and Pax—expose the male vices and remove them from their positions as ministers of Respublica. The feminine nature of the virtues is seen by Avarice, the leader of the masculine vices, to make them vulnerable: "thei bee weemen and perchaunce maye bee faced owte" (V.v.1462). But like the four daughters of God in the morality tradition, the virtues are divine and invulnerable. Justice arrests the vices, and each is exposed by Truth: All must put off their false robes hiding their true identities. The morality motif of the disguise is again turned to humor as the multitude of Avarice's purses are discovered, and the seriousness of the deception is lightened by People, who tells Respublica the vices "have ofte made youe beeleve the moone was a grene chese" (V.ix.1779).

It is Nemesis's role to provide the correction, as she embodies the functions of the female virtues in an obvious compliment to Mary, England's first ruling queen. Veritee explains Nemesis's role as "the goddess of correccion" just before she appears:

Cleare of conscience *and* voide of affeccion
she hath powre from a bove, *and* is newlie sent downe
T[o] redresse all owtrages in cite *and* in Towne
(she hathe powre from godde all practise to repeale
which might bring Annoyaunce to ladie comonweale.
To hir office belongeth the prowde toverthrowe
and suche to restore as iniurie hath browght lowe.
tys hir powre to forbidde *and* punishe in all eastates
all presumptuous immoderate attemptates. (V.ix.1783–91)

Redress, punishment, and restoration are the key aspects of her role, and after Avarice admits the abuses he and his fellows have committed, Nemesis, responding to the debate between Justice and Mercy, promises that the vices will "receyve oure mercie or *our* Ire, / As the wealthe of Respublica shall best require" (V.ix.1876–77).

What best serves the commonweal is the basis for the dispensing of justice. She pardons Adulation on his promise of amendment, requires Avarice to make restitution, and places Insolence and Oppression in custody until "tyme maie serve / texamine and trie their cause" (V.x.1918). The treatment of Adulation and Avarice is very mild, and judgment of the vices posing as Authority and Reformation is postponed. Punishment of past offenders is virtually ignored as the correction concentrates on recovery. No clear expression of the restoration of Catholicism is made, and no details about restitution are indicated. No mention is made of the organization or doctrine of the church. The author deals only with principles largely of an economic nature; he presents no program of social or religious change.

Perhaps the fact that the play was presented as a "Christmas devise" encouraged a positive ending, though it is also appropriate to the comic tone that prevails throughout the play. The festive spirit of this lively political morality must have been appreciated by many members of its first audience, but the message for the new queen's ministers is quite clear. The author is not writing from a militant Catholic position; he is advocating gentle correction, not radical purgation. The focus throughout the play, as the title suggests and the prologue emphasizes, is on the commonweal, not the church. The avoidance of religious polemics suggests that the author was not a Catholic advocate as previous critics have assumed, but rather a Protestant who has accommodated to the change in government.[5]

In addition to probably being a Protestant, the author was also an entertaining and effective playwright with not only a knowledge of the popular morality conventions but also a grounding in Latin drama. He adapted the native and the classical dramatic traditions with the practiced hand of a professional. The spirit and skill with which the play was written point toward the most popular candidate for the authorship of the play, Nicholas Udall, schoolmaster, poet, playwright, and translator, who on several other occasions offered advice to his monarch.[6] In a biblical drama entitled *Ezechias* (ca. 1546) Udall apparently commended Henry VIII for following Hezekiah's example of purging religion of idolatry and purifying it after a period of corruption and contempt of God's laws; though this play was revived for a performance before Queen Elizabeth in 1564, it is no longer extant. However, in his dedicatory letters to Queen Catherine Parr and later to Edward VI that preface his translations of parts of Erasmus's *Paraphrase upon the New Testament*, published in 1548, Udall again applies Hezekiah's role to Henry VIII (1:fols. iii and vii–viii) and instructs the young King Edward to avoid the example of Hezekiah's son, Manasse, who became king at twelve years old and who, enticed by sensuality, became the easy prey of false prophets and covetous priests. Rather Edward should emulate Hezekiah's grandson, Josias, who though even younger than Manasse, steadfastly returned the kingdom to Hezekiah's virtuous path.[7] Udall in these letters also compares David to Henry VIII, who slew the Papist Goliath, and calls Edward "our young Solomon" (fols. vi and viii–ix). Praise joined with biblical example appears to have been the Protestant Udall's favorite method of instructing his monarchs, and he also compliments young Edward's "good counsellors," particularly the Duke of Somerset and his brother Sir Thomas Seymour (fols. ix–x). This praise, published in 1548, may have been prompted by a desire to curry favor with the powers of the realm, but with the fall of Thomas Seymour and Somerset and the subsequent death of Edward, Udall must have found himself in a vulnerable position.

Udall had already established a respectful relationship with Mary, for he had involved her in the translation of Erasmus's *Paraphrase*. In his dedicatory letter to Queen Catherine prefacing the translation of the paraphrase of John, Udall commends Princess Mary "for takyng suche great studie, peine and travaill, in translatyng" the work "emiddes the enticementes of worldly vanities." Udall reveals in the letter that one Doctor Malet "finished and made complete" the translation, but the praise of Mary is effusive (fol. ii). Perhaps Udall drew upon this old connection to secure the position of royal entertainer for the new queen by the Christmas season of 1554, for the revel accounts indicate he was paid for plays performed at court between December 13, 1554, and January 5, 1555 (*Roister Doister*, ed. Scheurweghs xlix). Clearly by this time the Protestant Udall had accommodated to the new reign.[8] A year earlier, when *Respublica* was first performed, Udall may not yet have found acceptance at court, but his old friendship with the reinstated Bishop Gardiner and his past tutoring of the released Edward Courtenay (*Roister Doister*, ed. Scheurweghs xxxix) might have given him access to the new political leadership. Perhaps *Respublica* was a part of Udall's campaign to gain favor with Mary's court, but if so, his effort proved more than his loyalty to the new queen. It urged that the commonweal be restored by gentle correction not by radical purgation. By adapting aspects of classical comedy to the morality tradition, this lively mirror for the monarch achieves a higher level of dramatic art than any of its predecessors, for in avoiding a doctrinaire Catholic position, it rises above propaganda. As F. P. Wilson says, "As drama it is worth all that Bale and his successors wrote" (40).[9]

CHAPTER FIFTEEN

LINDSAY'S *SATIRE OF THE THREE ESTATES*

O F ALL the writers of political moralities in the sixteenth century, David Lindsay was probably most directly knowledgeable about the circumstances he addressed, and he may also have had the greatest influence on his monarch if not on his country's governance. Named an usher to the infant James V, Lindsay went on to assume an important place at the Scottish court that involved him in diplomatic missions as well as artistic endeavors, and early in James's reign Lindsay adopted the role of instructor to the youthful king. In his first extant poem, *The Dreme of Schir David Lyndesay*, written in 1528 shortly after the sixteen-year-old James had freed himself from the domination of the Douglases and had assumed personal rule of Scotland, Lindsay establishes the major themes that inform his work, as he declares that "Sensuale plesour hes baneist Chaistitie" (983), and the lords of religion, blinded by ambition, exploit the kingdom for their own personal gain; he urges the king to be just to all and "From Lychorie . . . keip thy body clene. / Taist neuer that Intoxicat poysoun" (1092–93).[1] James appears not to have heeded this last advice, for by 1534 he had fathered four illegitimate sons.

In 1529–30, in *The Complaynt of Schir David Lindesay*, Lindsay elaborates his role as a reformer by representing the banishment of Chastity by Sensuality in a moral allegory; but it is in *The Testament and Complaynt of Papyngo* in 1530 that Lindsay becomes more explicit about the moral decay in the court and kingdom, which he links to the corrupt church. After blaming fools, flatterers, and panders at court for leading princes into harlotry, Lindsay describes the development of the church that engendered Riches and Sensuality, who "tuke hole the gouernance / Off the moste part of the stait spirituall" (851–52). Elaborating on the expulsion of Chastity by nuns and friars and the births of prelates' bastards, Lindsay blames the "Wantyng of Wyffi's" for the priests' lechery (870). In Lindsay's view, subjection to sensuality leads the clergy to forget their duties "to study, praye, and preche" (857), and the church's avarice, to which the Pope gives license, weakens the state.

After this concerted attack on clerical exploitation, Lindsay remains silent for a half-dozen years, but in his *Answer to the King's Flyting* in 1535–36, he boldly reprimands James:

> lyke ane boisteous Bull, ʒe rin and ryde
> Royatouslie lyke ane rude Rubeatour,
> Ay fukkand lyke ane furious Fornicatour. (47–49)

Lindsay appears not to have been banished for his impudence, but the fragmentary nature of the poem may suggest that more sensitive lines were excised. Lindsay's position at court seems not to have suffered, for he was a member of the Scottish delegation to arrange James's marriage with Madeleine on January 1, 1537, and he wrote a poem deploring the queen's death, which occurred just six months later. Lindsay extended his role of court poet to court entertainer by composing a masque to welcome James's second bride, Mary of Guise, to Scotland on June 10, 1538; and as his kinsman Robert Lindsay of Pitscottie noted, the poet took this opportunity to instruct the queen "to serue her god, obey hir husband, and keep hir body clene according to godis will and commandement" (Lindesay 1:379). Significantly David Lindsay adds to the conventional advice about religious piety and wifely obedience a concern for the marital fidelity of the bride.

Lindsay's special place in James's court was demonstrated again by his contribution in 1540 to the celebration of the Feast of Epiphany at the Palace of Linlithgow. In a letter to Cromwell in Henry VIII's court, the English ambassador, Sir William Eure, writes that Lindsay's "enterlude" was played before the king and queen "and the hoole counsaile sprit*u*all and temporall" and "concluded vpon the Declaration of the noughtines in Religion / the presumpcion of busshops / The collucion of the sprituall Courts . . . and mysusing of preists." A more detailed summary of the performance by a Scotsman sympathetic to the reformers, enclosed with Eure's letter, establishes beyond question that Lindsay's "enterlude" is an early version of *An Satire of the Three Estates*. Eure notes that "after the said enterluyd fynished the King of scotts Dide call vpon the busshope of Glascoe being Chauncelour and diuerse other busshops / exorting thaym to reforme thair facions and maners of lyving / saying that oneles thay soe did / he wold sende sex of the proudeste of thayme vnto his vncle of england." Eure adds that James "is fully mynded to expell all spirtuall men frome having any auctoritie by office vnder his grace / either in household or elles where within the Realme" (quoted in *Works* 2:2–3).

The king's response to the exposure of the corrupt Church and the call for reformation must have pleased Lindsay; however, the king's initial gesture was not supported by governmental action. Unfortunately only this summary of Lindsay's first version of *An Satire of the Three Estates* survived, but the audacity of indicting the church in a royal performance attended by church and temporal leaders is remarkable. Lindsay must have felt secure in James's favor to challenge one of the most powerful groups in the realm and to publicly advocate reformation. Lindsay's role at court appears not to have altered as a result of his advice that the king reform the Scottish Church, and in addition to his *Supplicatioun to the Kingis Grace in Contemptioun of Syde Tailes*, a satire on long dresses written in 1542, he published, though anonymously, a satire on auricular confession in *Kitteis Confessioun* in the same year. This was also the year that Lindsay received the distinguished title Lyon King of Arms before James's defeat at Solway Moss and subsequent death.

The king's demise clearly changed Lindsay's status. Whether the David Lindsay that served in Parliament for Cupar from 1541 to 1546 was the poet or his younger brother is not clear, but the power struggle that ensued over the rule of the kingdom and the governing of the church thrust the poet-courtier from center stage. The reform movement with which Lindsay had identified himself was seriously threatened by Cardinal Beaton's growing influence, which Lindsay later, in his poem *The Tragedie of the Umquhle Maist Reuerend Father Dauid* (1547), bitterly declared was the cause of James's failure to meet Henry VIII, of his defeat at Solway Moss, and of his subsequent death. Beaton, in league with the King of France and the pope, posed the most serious threat to the survival of Scotland as an independent state, according to Lindsay. The pressure on heretics, symbolized by the execution of the reformer George Wishart, provoked Beaton's assassination, which Lindsay interprets as retributive justice. In his poem the spirit of the late cardinal confesses his manipulation of the late King James, his plots against the Earl of Angus, and his exploitation of his place as head of the Scottish Church and as royal counselor. He concludes his monologue with warnings to prelates and princes to note his example and reform the policies that allowed men of his ilk to flourish. A few months later, when Beaton's assassins, including John Knox, were captured by the French at the Castle of St. Andrews, Lindsay's spirits along with those of other performers must have flagged. Still he did not give up the fight. In the late 1540s and early 1550s he composed the most ambitious works of his career: *Ane Dialogue betuix Experience and ane Courteour, Off the Miserabyll Estait of the Warld* (generally known as *The Monarche*), a 6,338-line poem in four books, and his later version of *An Satire of the Three Estates*, a 4,630-line drama in two parts.

In the "Epistil to the Redar" that prefaces *The Monarche* (1548–53), Lyndsay mourns the absence of a king in Scotland and worries about young Queen Mary's residence in France (10–18), but in the aged Experience's instruction of a desolate courtier in the poem, the current rule of Scotland is addressed more obliquely. Recounting biblical and church history in a litany of cautionary examples, Experience tells the story of Semiramis, Queen of Babylon, who performed many great deeds but was brought to a shameful end through insatiable lust. She is described as taking one young gentleman after another to serve her appetite and then having them killed. Incest with her son ultimately leads him to kill her, but the moral of the story drawn by Experience shifts the focus from lust to woman's proper role and has a particular relevance for the Queen Mother, Mary of Guise, who was engaged in a struggle for the governance of the kingdom, and for her daughter, Mary Queen of Scots, eleven years old in 1553 when the poem was completed. Experience says:

> no way I can commend
> Wemen for tyll be to manlye.
> For quhy, It bene the Lordis mynde
> All creature tyll vse thare kynde;
> Men for tyll haue preheminens
> And women vnder obediens,
> Thocht all wemen inclynit be
> Tyll haif the Soueranite. (3234–42)

Experience then reminds his audience that Semiramis was permitted to share the rule by her husband but would not rest until she had full sovereignty; then she imprisoned her husband and had him killed as she embarked on a forty-two-year reign that ended in disaster after her abuse of her power. It is significant that Mary of Guise's appointment as governor, which began in 1544 when the Earl of Arran was suspended, was rescinded in 1552 and Arran was restored to the governorship; but in 1553 Arran was again deposed and Mary once more achieved command, which was formally recognized in 1554. Clearly Lindsay is suspicious of female rulers, but he is also critical of effeminate men in his treatment of King Sardanapulus of Nineveh, a male ruler with "sensuall luste intoxicate" (3294) who dressed in feminine attire and was led by women. Again the dominance of women is abhorred, but the most vitriolic criticism in *The Monarche* is directed toward the papal monarchy.

In a 728-line diatribe Lindsay elaborates on the charges he had brought against the church in several of his earlier poems as well as in *An Satire of the Three Estates*, where there are many verbal echoes. Once more, Sensuality and Avarice are represented as the major clerical vices. "Lady Sensuality," says Lindsay, has become the "lady Souerane" (4422) of Rome, later described in typical reformation language as Babylon, where every kind of vice flourishes, including lechery, covetise, simony, and sodomy (4946–52). In more immediate terms priests are charged with exploiting their positions in the local parishes for sexual pleasure and personal gain. Not daring to marry, they cultivate concubines and cuckold husbands (4583–85, 4695, 4707); wishing to be called "sir" like a knight and adopting the title "dean," they grow rich with their rents; and they ignore their duties of preaching and teaching (4439–41). The critique ends with a prayer for reformation (4960–73).

In his revised *Satire of the Three Estates*, performed a year before *The Monarche* was completed, Lindsay presents his most memorable and most devastating attack on the Scottish Church. This performance, at Cupar on June 7, 1552, must have been before a sympathetic audience, for not only was East Fifeshire Lindsay's home region, it was also a center of reformist activity. Lindsay may have been preaching to the converted, but his exposure of clerical abuses is designed to rouse his audience to action, as he had roused the king a dozen years earlier in his first version of the play. However, his realization of the demands of a popular audience probably led him to incorporate more comic material in the work. The proclamation of the banns for the Cupar production provides a preview of comic entertainment along with the announcement of the subject, time, and place of performance. By introducing stock characters and stock situations from Roman comedy, folk drama, and the fabliaux, Lindsay may be guilty of misleading advertising, since none of the preview characters appears in the play, but the shrewish cotter's wife anticipates the tailor's and sowtar's wives in the drama to come; the cuckolding of the old man by the young wife and the fool initiates the theme of sensuality; and the braggart coward sets the mode of burlesque that pervades the later performance. The comic spirit that dominates this invitation may mask the serious intent of the play itself; however, in the performance, comedy keeps the audience's attention and makes the message more palatable.

The success of the Cupar production must have led to a repeat performance two years later at Edinburgh, though this time for a more aristocratic audience. Henrie Charteris's preface to the *Warkis* of Lindsay, published in 1568, claims that this performance was attended by the

Queen Regent, Mary of Guise, "and ane greit part of the Nobilitie, with ane exceding greit nowmer of pepill" (quoted in *Works* 4:139). No reference is made to members of the clergy in the audience, as was noted at the first royal performance, but one wonders how many of the spectators at Edinburgh in 1554 besides Mary of Guise had witnessed the original version at Linlithgow in 1540.

What differences existed between the texts used for the three known performances will probably never be fully known, but clearly the productions in 1552 and 1554 were considerably longer and were presented outdoors to larger audiences than the court performance in 1540. Comic material and the seduction of Rex Humanitas must have been added, as well as passages alluding to events that occurred after 1540. I think Hamer is right in suggesting that a thorough reworking of the original version was done before the 1552 performance (*Works* 4:127–29), but the changes in the text between the Cupar and Edinburgh productions are more problematic. The Cupar banns announce the play will be performed between the hours of seven and eleven, indicating a four-hour production, but Charteris in 1568 says the performance before the Queen Regent lasted "fra .ix. houris afoir none, till .vi. houris at euin" (quoted in *Works* 4:139). Allowing an hour's break for refreshment between the two parts would suggest an eight-hour performance, twice the length of the Cupar production. However, the longest text that has survived is 4,630 lines, and given the usual estimate of roughly 1,000 lines of text for each hour of performance, the play could have been performed in less than five hours. Perhaps the Cupar performance for the popular audience was a little shorter and included only a brief intermission, while the Edinburgh command performance may have developed some points more fully for the Queen Regent and her ministers. Also there may have been a longer interruption between the parts for a royal banquet.

The Bannatyne manuscript, dated 1568 and thought to represent the Cupar performance, omits several passages attacking the clergy as well as the discussion of the reforms and the reading of the acts of reformation at the end of the play that appear in the other surviving text. Altogether it is nearly 1,600 lines shorter than the printed edition published in 1602, which includes the Cupar banns and is thought to represent the Edinburgh performance. Most of the omissions in the Bannatyne manuscript may, as Hamer argues, have been made by the transcriber because he regarded the sermons, some of the satiric attacks, and the reading of the reformist acts as unnecessarily prolix (*Works* 4:134–36). The printed edition most closely represents the version performed for the royal audience and the nobility, and it also appears to have been Lindsay's last version of the play. It, therefore, is the fullest as well as the most authoritative text.[2]

At the beginning of *An Satire of the Three Estates*, Diligence announces that Rex Humanitas "hes bene absent this monie ʒeir" (17) and while he "lang tyme hes bene sleipand, . . . misreull hes rung thir monie ʒeiris" (24–25). But Diligence promises that the king will soon appear and will bring reformation. Then after summarizing the two parts of the play to follow, Diligence begs the audience:

Tak na man greif in speciall:
For wee sall speik in generall,
For pastyme and for play. (71–73)

Lindsay thus sets the context for the action by emphasizing the chaotic state of the kingdom, which has long lacked a ruler, and by assuring the audience that reformation is coming. The seduction of the king by Sensuality and false counselors, the subject of part 1, represents the past and present, while part 2, demonstrating the exposure, correction, and reformation of the three estates — Temporality, Merchant, Spirituality — presents a scenario of the future. Wary about giving offense to the governors and royal counselors in the audience, Lindsay disclaims a particular allegorical identification of persons and events as he plays down his serious purpose. His conventional apology is not completely disingenuous, for although Lindsay may be attempting to protect himself from courtly displeasure, he is emphasizing that the meaning is in the general pattern of action not in the exposure of particular individuals.

The seduction of Rex Humanitas appears to be a new element in the versions of *An Satire of the Three Estates* performed in the 1550s, for no mention is made of it in Eure's letter or the accompanying notes on the production of 1540. The exposure of royal dalliance and errors in judgment might have seemed too daring or inappropriate to present before James and his new bride. Whether this part had been in Lindsay's original conception and had been omitted from the performance before James V for political reasons, or whether it had been written as a separate interlude for another occasion is not known, but it clearly is in the spirit of Lindsay's princely instruction beginning in 1528 with *The Dreme* and continuing in the 1530s, as discussed above. Why it was included in the versions performed a decade after James's death is a bit puzzling. Perhaps it was intended as a warning to the Earl of Arran in the 1552 performance, as Kantrowitz argues (30), for Arran was restored to the governorship in that year, or it could have served as a cautionary exemplum for the Queen Regent and her youthful charge, Mary Stuart, twelve years old in 1554 and at the threshold of puberty. In light of Mary's later pursuit of amorous pleasure, which cost her the crown, Lindsay may have worried about the family penchant for sensuality, for under the veil of allegory he represents the history of James V's reign, except for its end. Rather than meeting death as a result of being misled, as was James's fate, Rex Humanitas is personally reformed in order to bring about a reformation of the kingdom. Lindsay imposes the old morality play paradigm on his allegorical king as Skelton does in *Magnificence*, but the emphases are different in the manner of the misleading as well as in the nature of the reformation.

In succumbing to Sensuality, Rex Humanitas follows the conventional pattern of the youth-oriented moralities, particularly the prodigal plays, for lechery is the traditional sin of youth; however, in James's case, as Lindsay indicates in his poems, this sin was pursued with particular enthusiasm. The Douglases have been charged with introducing the teenage king to lechery (Kantrowitz 32), but the pander, Wantonnes, is not sufficiently individualized to make a specific identification. Wantonnes, like Placebo and Solace, appears to be a generic toady who appeals to the king's basest instincts in contrast to responsible courtiers, such as Diligence and Gude Counsall, who, as Lindsay himself had done, strive to guide the impressionable youth. James apparently found several accommodating courtiers to feed his appetites long after he had broken with the Douglases; Lindsay here appears to be characterizing the king's vulnerability to sensual delights. Sensuality introduces her sisters, Hameliness and Danger, suggested perhaps by *The Romance of the Rose* (cf. Kantrowitz 64–65), and in the paradigm of the morality play, the king after falling to a sin of the flesh is vulnerable to other vices.

These vices appear in the form of a second group of misleaders who offer a much more serious threat to the king and the kingdom. First to appear is Flattery, *"new landit owt of france"* (s.d. 602).[3] This suggests the French influence at court that promoted Catholicism and sought to keep Scotland from a peaceful alliance with England in James's reign and, following his death, grew even more powerful under the chancellorship of Cardinal Beaton and the regency of Mary of Guise. Flattery considers taking on the guise of a friar in order to become the king's confessor (739–43), thus implicating the church in the misleading of the king, but he is persuaded by his companion vices to impersonate virtues as they are doing. Flattery pretends to be Devotion, Dissait Discretion, and Falset Sapience. Like Magnificence's courtiers in Skelton's play, these vices follow the conventional motif of deception in the morality; in gaining the king's favor, they demonstrate the misrule of the kingdom. After thrusting out Gude Counsall, they abuse their power by putting Verity and Chastity in the stocks. In the stifling of truth and chastity, Flattery, Deceit, and Falsehood show they are in league with the church's corruption of the king and kingdom.

Wantonnes, before introducing Sensuality to the king near the beginning of the play, links her to the church, the "lemand lamp of lechery" (237), which rejects Chastity's appeals for protection. A comic note is struck when Chastity is welcomed by the Tailor and Sowtar, only to be chased away by their wives, who complain about their husbands' impotence. The Sowtar sardonically comments: "Bischops ar blist howbeit that they be waryit, / For thay may fuck thair fill and be unmaryit" (1362–63). Clerical lechery, a recurrent complaint in Lindsay's earlier poetry, is here directly tied to the church's oppressive power. As Chastity is put into the stocks, she declares:

> I wyte the Empreour Constantine,
> That I am put to sic ruine,
>   And baneist from the Kirk:
> For sen he maid the Pape ane King,
> In Rome I could get na ludging. (1450–54)

Chastity for Lindsay is symbolic of purity and self-discipline, and he is incensed not only by the church's flagrant disregard of its own moral code but also by its sexual exploitation of its parishoners. To further emphasize clerical corruption, Sensuality requests "licence to pas again to Rome" when she is separated from Rex Humanitas, and is warmly welcomed by Spirituality. Lindsay focuses in this first part of his play on the pervasiveness of lechery within the church as well as the danger of Sensuality for the monarch because it leads the king to ignore his responsibilities and to allow false counselors to stifle virtue and promote vice.

James V's historical example appears to underline Lindsay's portrayal. Robert Lindesay of Pitscottie, in his final judgment of James, provides the reformist perspective mirrored in David Lindsay's dramatic action:

> This nobill prince, gif he had ressawit goode consall, of wyse and godlie men and spetiallie of his great lordis and keipit his body frome harlotrie and had left the evill consall of his papistis bischopis and gredie courteouris, he had ben the most nobilist prince that ever rang in the realme of Scottland. Ffor he was full of pollacie and honestie in his beginning and did money goode actis in his realme.... Bot fre tyme he was abussit wihth papistrie and wald nocht suffer the worde of god to haue frie passage.... The great profeit that the bischops gaif to him to be the popis man and to defend his autoritie and the kirkmens libertie that he, abussit throw covettousnes, consentit to thair wickit and evill consall aganis the evangell of Jesus Christ quhilk was the principall caus of his ewill succes in his latter dayis. Ffor the bischopis and priestis and freiris

seand that they could not haue him better nor be flatterie [they wnderstude] that he might tak his plesour throw all Scottland [and they him cheise any] of quhat gentillwoman he pleissit, quhither they war marieit or unmarieit and sa to spend his body wpoun thame as he pleissit contrair the command of God.... So they gart him both wse idolatrie and adulltierie, idolatrie in stopping of Christis evangell, adulltierie in using of uther mens wyffis. So they abusit this nobill prince that he tint the favour of god and the nobillis of his realme, quhairthrow he tuik great displesour and melancolie, quhairby he was constranit and stranglit to the deid. (Lindesay 1:408–9)

This estimate of James's good nature being overcome by his misleaders, the corrupt clergy who stifle truth and feed the king's sexual appetite, summarizes the first 1,580 lines of *An Satire of the Three Estates*, but David Lindsay provides a new conclusion to the historical example in his allegory. Lindesay of Pitscottie had interpreted James's tragic death to be a result of his despair following his defeat at Solway Moss through the evil counsel of his clerical advisers, who feared peace with England would lead to a reformation of the church (1:402–4). In David Lindsay's play Divine Correction offers Rex Humanitas the opportunity for reformation rather than death; Verity and Chastity are freed and together with Gude Counsall are brought to the king, while Sensuality, banished from the king's presence, finds refuge with the clergy. Correction moralizes on the examples of Sardanapulus (1697–1700), also noted in *The Monarche*, and the Roman Tarquin (1761–66), who lost their respective crowns by pursuing sensual pleasure.

The king's personal reformation is accompanied by Gude Counsall's comment on the king's responsibility to God and his country. Reminding Rex Humanitas that he is "bot ane moral instrument, / To that great God and King Omnipotent," Gude Counsall declares:

The principall point Sir of ane kings office,
Is for to do euerilk man iustice,
And for to mix his iustice with mercie
But rigour. (1878–85)

Again Robert Lindesay of Pitscottie expresses a similar view, as he elaborates on the king's obligation at the end of his consideration of James V: "to minister iustice equallie to great and small, puire and riche and revaird thame that dois good and punische them that dois ewill and treit and honour the trew lordis of the realme quhilk is godlie and honest, and wse thair counsall and in lyke maner punische and correct the gredie and covetous lordis and barrouns quho is oppressouris of thair nichtbouris and dissobedient baith to god and to thair prince" (Lindesay 1:410).[4]

The association of the historian's judgment with Lindsay's is further indicated in one version of *The Historie and Chronicles of Scotland* by the insertion of "Ane deploration of King James" taken from Lindsay's *Testament and Complaynt of Papyngo*, to which are added two stanzas that conclude with the expression of the king's duty:

> To serwe zour god and lord omnipotent
> his law and will to vtter and expres
> in doing of justice both to moir and les. (1:414)

The king's responsibility to administer justice to all in his kingdom in emulation of God himself is accomplished in part 2 of Lindsay's play, as the king calls the three estates to court and extends the reform he has personally experienced to the kingdom.

However, before embarking on the formal examination of the ills of the kingdom in part 2, Lindsay offers a comic respite that centers on the chief cause of injustice in the kingdom, the clergy. Pauper complains of the church's avarice, which has reduced him to poverty. Preying on Pauper's misfortunes of losing a father, mother, and wife, the vicar has claimed Pauper's land and livestock for payment of death duties; this material exploitation is linked by Pauper to the sexual exploitation of prelates who "swyfe Ladies, Madinis and vther mens wyfis, / And sa thair cunts thay haue in consuetude" (2026–27). After providing a glimpse of clerical abuse from a victim's perspective, Lindsay introduces a favorite target of religious satire in the Pardoner, who curses the reformers Martin Luther, Black Bullinger, and Melanchthon, because they threaten his trade. Like Sedition in Bale's *King John*, the Pardoner advertises ludicrous holy relics: "The culum [anus] of Sanct Brydis kow, / The gruntil [snout] of Sanct Antonis sow" (2107–8). His abuse of his office takes an even more vulgar turn when for a fee he divorces the Sowtar and his shrewish wife by mutual arse-kissing. This symbol of clerical avarice is humorously ridiculed and finally repudiated by Pauper, who casts the false relics and pardons into the water. Shifting the attention away from the king and toward the country, this comic interlude emphasizes the other clerical vice, avarice, that is more fully developed in part 2.

The essential design of part 2 is evident in the 1540 version of the play presented before King James and his bride, Mary of Guise, as is indicated by Eure's letter and his accompanying notes, though the text has apparently been expanded and updated for the 1552 and 1554 performances. This is clearly the part of the play that prompted the title, *An Satire of the Three Estates,* for each estate is examined before the king. When the estates are introduced, each is led by the vice or vices linked to his calling. Temporality is led by Public Oppression, Merchant by Falset and Dissait, and Spirituality by Sensuality, the major vice of part 1, and by Covetise, emphasized in the interlude between parts 1 and 2. The arraignment of all three estates suggests that all are guilty of wrongdoing and in need of amendment. Their principal accuser, John the Commonweal, is joined by Pauper, the complainant of the interlude, and together they represent the common people of the kingdom. The testimony against Temporality for oppression and against Merchant for deceit remains quite general, and the representatives of these two estates readily accept the judgment of Correction. Repenting their errors before the king, they embrace John the Commonweal, and their vices are separated from them and placed in the stocks to demonstrate their reformation. Temporality and Merchant are not only exonerated, they join the accusers of Spirituality, who refuses to recognize his errors or to accept correction. The play once again focuses on clerical abuses, which are represented here by individual members of the church, including an abbot, a prioress, and a parson. The charges are numerous and detailed, and they are made by various represetatives of society who form a chorus of condemnation.

The levying of death duties by local clergy, which reduces surviving kin to poverty as Pauper had earlier complained, is deplored by John the Commonweal and reinforced by Pauper, who describes prelates cavorting with the wives of the parish and bishops living luxuriously (2723–66). Charging that the land is "clein denudit / Of gould and silver quhilk daylie gais to Rome," John the Commonweal declares that were he king "never ane penny sould go to Rome at all" (2837–43). This typical reformer's complaint, which Bale also expresses in *King John*, is seconded by Merchant, who accuses priests of simony. Temporality claims the priests consume the country's wealth without contributing anything, and Gude Counsall decries the priests' failure to perform their duties to preach and teach (2901–13), a recurring complaint in Lindsay's earlier poetry. Here, however, the failure is compounded by clerical arrogance and ignorance as Spirituality admits: "I red never the New testament nor auld . . . I heir freiris say that reiding dois na gude" (2920–22).

The litany of charges continues as John the Commonweal accuses the abbesses and their nunneries of "publick huirdomes and . . . harlotries" (2957), and Temporality requests a reform in the consistory laws to keep the clergy from interfering in temporal matters. Demands for reformation grow as Chastity complains of her rejection and Verity calls for more "cunning Clerks" and more "prudent pastours" (3125–26). Saying that "Sowtars and tailʒeours . . . ar far mair expert / In thair pure craft and in thair handie art, / Nor ar our Prelatis in thair vocatioun" (3149–51), Gude Counsall too calls for reformation. Temporality objects to the prelates marrying off their daughters to noblemen with a two-thousand-pound dowry from church funds while the temporal lords' daughters remain at home unwed because they cannot provide so handsome a settlement. This accusation was addressed in 1549 by the church council, which not only prohibited the illegitimate sons of clergy from receiving church preferment but also prohibited the custom of clergy providing dowries for their illegitimate daughters out of church funds (Murison 127–28). Apparently the practice had not, however, stopped by 1554, for Spirituality admits to giving his sons rich rewards and marrying his daughters to "lairds." He also incriminates himself by justifying concubines because clergy cannot marry and by condoning bribery because the favor of temporal lords must be won (3360–71).

Other representatives of the spiritual estate also testify to clerical abuse. The abbot brags of his "fat and fair" paramours, of his sons sent to Paris, and of his daughters being well provided for (3404–9). The parson burlesques clerical morality by defending the seven deadly sins:

> I say pryde is bot honestie.
> And Covetice of warldlie win
> Is bot wisdome, I say for me.
> Ire, hardines and gluttonie,
> Is nathing ellis but lyfis fude:
> The naturall sin of lecherie
> Is bot trew luife. All thir ar gude. (3534–40)

These admissions and rationalizations corroborate the accusations brought by John the Commonweal, Pauper, Temporality, and Merchant as they demonstrate the pressing need for reformation. When Flattery is exposed under a Friar's cowl and the prioress betrays the dress of a whore under her habit, Correction, with the approval of the king and the aid of Diligence and Gude Counsall, strips the prelates of their glorious gowns, banishes the corrupt members of the spiritual estate, and places the religious robes on John the Commonweal to symbolize the repudiation of Roman Catholicism and the installation of a native, reformed clergy.

Then in the most explicit appeal for action of any of the extant political moralities, Lindsay proclaims fifteen parliamentary acts of ecclesiastical reform. Intended to correct the abuses demonstrated in the play, these acts may have been revised after the 1540 performance to support the actions taken by the Church Councils of 1549 and 1552 to reduce the clergy's exploitation of their offices and to improve the quality of preaching and teaching (Donaldson 81–82), but Lindsay goes even further by endorsing the reformist doctrines of a married clergy and of independence from Rome. Advocating such particular changes as the elimination of nuns and the appointment to benefices of men of "gude eruditioun" only (3865–66), the acts demand that each bishop remain in his diocese and each parson in his parish. The concluding act is addressed to both the temporal and spiritual estates:

> From this day forth our Barrouns temporall
> Sall na mair mix thair nobil ancient blude
> With bastard bairns of Stait Sprituall: . . .
> Gif Nobils marie with the Sprituality,
> From thyne subiect thay salbe, and all
> Sal be degraithit of thair Nobilitie,
> And from amang the Nobils cancellit. (3929–36)

The punishment of the nobility for consorting with priests' bastards is harsh because it extends the moral corruption of the clergy to the temporal estate. The thrust of the acts is to create a new church nationally independent and morally purified; to accomplish this the nobility must participate in the reform. This may have been where the 1540 performance ended, but the later versions offer a final demonstration of retributive justice as well as comic diversion.

The execution of Theft, Dissait, and Falset redirects the action from the reformation of Spirituality to the dramatic purpose expressed by the title, *An Satire of the Three Estates*, for in their final speeches before hanging, these vices indicate their presence among various classes and occupations in the realm. Theft, who has appeared only briefly in the previous action, identifies a number of families who have helped him in his mischiefs; many of these names — Nickson, Robson, Armstrong — have been traced to border families who were famous for their thievery (*Works* 4:231–32), but others may be jesting allusions to Lindsay's neighbors around Cupar. Theft's attempt to evade hanging by claiming an urgent need to make water introduces a comic note to the administration of justice. Dissait, who had misled the king under the guise of Discretion in part 1 and had also drawn Merchant into the court at the beginning of part 2, confesses that he had taught merchants many tricks to beguile "Vpalands wyfis," on market day (4041–42); and like Theft, Dissait identifies particular families as his pupils — the Clan Jameson, Andersons, Patersons, and Williamsons. Falset, a companion of Dissait in misleading the king and the merchant, is given more time to describe his activities, which are pervasive. He declares he has given lessons to men of craft — Websters, Walkers, Millers, Tailours, Brewsters, Sowtars, Wrights, Masons, Cordiners, Goldsmiths — as well as shepherds, but his most sardonic references are to prelates "that hes ma benefeits nor thrie, / And will nocht teich nor preiche the veritie" (4212–13) and to priests who corrupt citizens' wives. He claims that priests made him "nine tymes cuckald on ane nicht" (4239). When Falset is hanged, a "Craw or ane Ke" is cast out of his body, "as it war his saull" (s.d. 4241), apparently to demonstrate his demonic possession. The executions of Theft, Dissait, and Falset symbolize Divine Correction's purgation of vice from the kingdom; however, this cleansing of society remains incomplete as Flattery and Folly escape punishment.

Flattery, the king's misleader in part 1 who had adopted the guise of Devotion in the form of a friar, admits to beguiling all three estates, yet expects to find safe harbor with Spirituality. Although Flattery may go undercover to emerge again later, Folly maintains his irrepressible and ubiquitous public role. In a lengthy comic routine Folly, repeating several earlier motifs, provides the final satiric voice of the drama. Recalling the unfaithful Cotter's wife of the Cupar banns, the shrewish Sowtar's and Tailor's wives in part 1, and the wicked Sowtar's wife who prompts a diatribe against wives in the interlude between parts 1 and 2, Folly takes anti-feminist satire to new depths by describing his wife's inability to control her bowels. The theme of lechery, introduced by the fool in the Cupar banns, pursued by the king in part 1, and repeatedly associated with the religious community, is graphically demonstrated by the fool with his exaggerated phallus; like his counterpart in the Cupar banns, he echoes the wooing play of folk drama. The concern with justice, identified as the king's major duty at the end of part 1 and the dominating force of part 2, is burlesqued by Folly's demand that the sow who had caused him to fall in the mud receive correction; but it is in Folly's comic sermon that Lindsay offers his final satiric vision.

As in Erasmus's *Praise of Folly*, which no doubt served as Lindsay's model for this oration, Folly declares that fools are infinite in number and ubiquitous; he further claims that wisdom in the world is folly in the sight of God. Both judgments are, of course, proverbial, but Lindsay's application of them to his contemporary society is revealing. Once again returning to the old man with the young wife motif that he had introduced in the Cupar Banns, Folly says the "auld and cald" man of fourscore who marries a girl of fourteen deserves the fool's hat (4515–26), and Folly reserves his "holy hude" for the "Sprituall fuillis" who

> For gredines of warldlie pelfe,
> ... can nocht iustlie gyde them selfe.
> Vthers sauls to saife it settis them weill,
> Syne sell thair awin saullis to the Deuil. (4530–36)

After taking a final swipe at the spiritual estate, Folly turns at the end to the lords imperial. Noting the conflicts among the princes of Germany, Spain, Flanders, and Italy, as well as the pope's dispatch of his army into battle, Folly concludes: "I think it folie be Gods mother, / Ilk Christian Prince to ding doun vther" (4586–87). This appears to be directed at the Regent Mary of Guise and her noble entourage at the Edinburgh performance; the aging courtier Lindsay emphasizes the folly of war as he appeals for a peaceful resolution of the problems facing Scotland.

Lindsay gives Diligence rather than Folly the last word. Addressing the "Famous peopil" present, Diligence asks that they "This lytill sport ... tak in patience" and in a traditional modesty topos apologizes for the tediousness and lack of eloquence of the play; he then significantly adds that perhaps to some it may be "odious" (4614–20). Lindsay recognizes that not all members of his audience would be sympathetic to his message, but he clearly counts on the humor with which he seasons his satire to make it more palatable, as he once again seeks to influence the magistrates of the commonwealth to effect the reformation spelled out in the fifteen acts of his mock parliament. The Regent Mary's response is not recorded, as James V's was after the 1540 performance, but unlike James's useless threat to his bishops, the reformation of the church, begun in the councils of 1549 and 1552, was finally legislated in 1559, five years after the Edinburgh performance of *An Satire of the Three Estates* and four years after David Lindsay's death.

PART FOUR

THE DEVELOPMENT OF COMEDY

CHAPTER SIXTEEN

MEDWALL'S *FULGENS AND LUCRES*

*F*ULGENS *and Lucres*, generally recognized as "the first purely secular English play that has survived" (F. P. Wilson 7), appears to have been a Christmas entertainment at Lambeth, Cardinal Morton's residence, in the 1490s. Boas and Reed (Medwall, *Fulgens* xix–xx) and Baskervill ("Conventional Features" 419) suggest the first performance was before the Flemish and Spanish ambassadors in 1497, though Alan Nelson believes the play may have been performed in the early nineties (Medwall, *Plays* 17). Whatever the particular occasion, the play, written by Henry Medwall, chaplain to Morton, was designed for an aristocratic audience. Morton, after serving both Henry VI and Edward IV, and joining the Duke of Buckingham in a conspiracy against Richard III, became Henry VII's chancellor on March 6, 1486 — less than a year after Henry was crowned — and Archbishop of Canterbury on December 6, 1486. He was created a cardinal in 1493, and until his death in 1500 is said to have been "preeminent among the councillors and Henry VII's most trusted adviser" (Chrimes 106; see also Alexander 64). That Cardinal Morton enjoyed entertaining his guests with dramatic performances is attested by Thomas More, who as a youth in Morton's household took the part of a player on more than one occasion (Roper 5). Medwall's other extant play, the morality *Nature*, also performed at Lambeth, expresses the religious calling of both Morton and Medwall as it instructs its audience about the dangers of sin, particularly sensuality and covetousness, and conventionally promises redemption through repentance. *Fulgens and Lucres* by contrast reflects the political position of Morton in the form of secular entertainment.

The political implications are suggested in the description of the play in its first printed edition (ca. 1512): "Here is conteyned a godely interlude of Fulgens cenatoure of Rome, Lucres his doughter, Gayus Flaminius, and Publius Cornelius, of the Disputacyon of Noblenes." (Medwall, *Plays* 32).[1] The disputation of nobility, identified as the central issue of the play, was not a new topic — many literary antecedents existed, including such well-known examples as *Le Roman de la Rose* (18,589–896) and Chaucer's Wife of Bath's consideration of *gentillesse* in her tale (1109–64).[2] But it was the first time, so far as we know, that the nature of nobility was discussed in a dramatic presentation. Medwall used as his source Buonaccorso's *De Vera Nobilitate* (ca. 1428), written in imitation of the classical *controversia*.[3] The work was translated into English by John Tiptoft and printed in 1481 by William Caxton. But the question of whether nobility depends upon birth and wealth or upon honor achieved by merit was especially relevant to Henry VII's court, for Henry had selected as the bulwark of his government men who could not trace their heritage to old noble families. Justices of the peace, the key to Henry VII's control in the counties, were chosen from the local gentry, which effectively reduced the powers of the aristocratic sheriffs. Moreover, Henry rewarded his loyal supporters with knighthoods and other titles.[4] Although Henry retained a considerable number of councillors who had served his Yorkist predecessors, his new appointments were chiefly men who earned their positions by their intelligence and their deeds rather than by their pedigrees.[5]

The epitome of the men who had emerged in Henry VII's court was his chief minister, Cardinal Morton, who began his career as a lawyer. By championing honor achieved by merit rather than by birth in the disputation of nobleness, Medwall is complimenting his master, Morton, and other "new" men such as Thomas Lovell, Chancellor of the Exchequer, who was descended from a line of country gentlemen, and Dudley, Poynings, and Empson, all men from the gentry or bourgeoisie who reached high positions in Henry VII's government. But Medwall was also sensitive to offending the old aristocracy, some of whom were no doubt present at the first performance.⁶

To make the political message more palatable, therefore, Medwall designs an elaborate comic context that mitigates his potentially radical position without undercutting the value system upon which it is based. Two comic characters, identified only as A and B, serve as presenters of the serious action, but both disclaim responsibility for it and deny their association with the players who perform it. However, each at different times indicates a knowledge of what is to follow, and both enter into the serious plot by taking the roles of servants to the principal contenders, who represent the new men and the old aristocracy. Most importantly, A and B serve as a chorus, and they claim an identification with the audience while they comment on the words and actions of the other dramatic characters. They constantly remind the audience that they are watching only an illusion of life, and though they deny that they are part of that illusion, they are in fact caught up in it.

On the one hand, they remind us that the dispute about nobility is set in ancient Rome, thus distancing the matter; but on the other hand, they emphasize the relevance of the pattern of action by anticipating the response of the contemporary audience. At the beginning of the play after B has summarized the circumstances of the disputation and revealed its outcome — that the baseborn Gayus Flaminius, whose honor was achieved by merit, wins the hand of Lucres — A advises the players to "change that conclusion":

> What? Wyll they afferme that a chorles son
> Sholde be more noble than a gentilman born?
> Nay, beware, for men wyll have therof grete scorn —
> It may not be spoken in no maner of case.
>   (Medwall, *Fulgens* I, 129–33)

B answers that no "reasonable man" will take offense and, speaking now for the author, explains the nature of dramatic entertainment and the purpose of the play that is to follow:

> I love to beholde suche myrthes alway,
> For y have sene byfore this day
> Of suche maner thingis in many a gode place
> Both gode examples and right honest solace.
> This play in like wyse I am sure
> Is made for the same entent a[n]d purpose
> To do every man both myrth and pleasure. (I, 150–56)

Although B mentions the "gode examples and right honest solace" to be perceived in drama, he speaks only of mirth and pleasure in *Fulgens and Lucres*. A remains unconvinced, and after abhorring flattery B compliments the audience by assuring A that "these folke" will not object to the "playne trouth" and facetiously notes that no man present is a "kyn or sede / Of either partie" in ancient Rome (I, 175–80). By registering the possible charges of the audience and defusing them with humor, A and B maintain the tone of good fellowship appropriate to the festive banquet to which the play is an accompaniment.

After the intermission, during which the dining had resumed, A summarizes the competition for Lucres's hand and then adds:

> there was
> Dyvers toyes mengled yn the same
> To styre folke to myrthe and game
> And to do them solace. (II, 21–24)

Like B earlier, A emphasizes the entertainment value of the play and explains this is done to "content" all members of the audience, even "The leste that stondyth here" (II, 43–44), though he adds that solace also will be provided.

A superficial examination of the play reveals that much more of the play is devoted to "game" than to the serious issue of "true nobility." The disputation of nobleness does not begin until 1,836 lines have been delivered, and compared to Buonaccorso's *controversia* upon which it is based, the debate is much abbreviated. Tiptoft's translation, from which Medwall worked, covers both sides of nineteen folio sheets, while Medwall's debate occupies just 367 lines; if Lucres's judgment, for which there is no precedent in Buonaccorso, is added, the issue is completed in 404 lines. If all the lines exchanged by the rival wooers, the lady wooed, and her father are added together, they number but 667 of the 2,353 lines in the play, or 28.3 percent of the total. The choric comic servants, A and B, and Lucres's maid, Jone, dominate more than 70 percent of the play. Though the relationship of the comic action to the serious plot is described by David Bevington as "a compilation of humorous skits added in the manner of a popular entertainment" to the debate on nobility (*From "Mankind" to Marlowe* 44), the "Dyvers toyes mengled" are perceived by Robert Merrix to be "equally significant" to the serious action. In his view the serious and the comic structures "together illustrate two important facts, both aesthetic and moral: the artistic basis of successful drama — 'mirth and care'; and the paradoxical nature of man — comic and serious, lowly and elevated, flawed and flaw-less" (Merrix 23). A close analysis of the commentary and sport that A and B provide reveals that their primary purpose is to guide the audience's response to the characters and themes of the serious action.

B assures A when they determine to serve the principal contenders for Lucres's hand that they will not "Distroy the play"; rather, B says, "The play began never till now" (I, 363–65). Their first involvement in the Lucres plot occurs after the exposition of the situation and the introduction of the principal characters, when A, ingratiating himself with his prospective employer, Gayus, reports a conversation he had observed between Lucres and Cornelius (I, 582–602). Lucres's virtue, earlier manifested in her respectful deference to her father when Gayus plies his suit, is called into question as A accuses her of dissembling, and suspense about her true character is introduced. A short time later B describes Cornelius's prodigality and his preoccupation with extravagant dress: He follows the "fascyons ... new and straunge ... non of [his gowns] passith the mydde thy" (I, 738–39). This exposure of the superficial and wasteful Cornelius identifies him with the vice of the morality play, thus making him an unworthy suitor if Lucres's virtue is true.

However, it is in their own view of marriage and their wooing of Jone that A and B most fully reflect on the issues of the serious plot. Commenting on the contention for Lucres, A says:

> I wene veryly he shall sped best
> That must her forsake!
> He is well at ease that hath a wyf,
> Yet he is better that hath none, be my lyf! (I, 783–86)

A justifies his cynical view of marriage by revealing that after wedding a shrew and losing her, he had "marryed two or thre" whose "chef meane of ther levynge / Is lechery" (I, 792–802). Yet this critical judgment of wives as either shrews or whores, which contrasts with the virtuous image of Lucres, does not prevent A from competing with B for the favors of the maid Jone.

The competition for Jone reduces wooing to a series of contests to prove "maystry," but before the contests get underway, Jone establishes the mercenary concerns of marriage. She declares that any prospective husband must first assure her of "twenty pound londe in joyncture" (I, 927), and she then mocks B's suit, before allowing him a kiss. The competition for "maystry" required by Jone to determine which of her suitors is more worthy compares, of course, to the competition set by Lucres to determine which of her wooers is the more noble, but for Jone the mastery can be demonstrated "in cokery or in pastry" as well as "fettis of warre or dedys of chevalry" (I, 1096–97). In fact the contests involve singing, wrestling, and finally a "just at farte pryke in cule" (I, 1169), in which the opponents, apparently in a squatting position with a stick under the bends of their knees and in the crooks of their elbows and with their hands tied together, jab at each other with their sticks as they try to knock each other down.[7] This low-life game ends with A being thrust in the arse, which prompts B to accuse A of having unclean linen and giving off a bad smell. For all their attempts to determine "maystry," A and B are told by Jone that neither will have her because she is promised to another, and she rewards both with a beating before flouncing off the stage. This comic parody of wooing may owe something to contemporary folk drama as Baskervill suggests ("Conventional Features" 424–25), but its effect in this play is to make the suitors ridiculous and to emphasize the independence and control of the woman wooed, even if they are manifested in shrewishness.

After mirroring their masters' competition in their ludicrous fashion, A and B discuss whether Cornelius or Gayus is "most noble." B, who at the beginning of the play had summarized the action and identified the less wealthy and lowborn Gayus as the victor, now reduces the question to materialistic concerns:

> He that hathe moste nobles in store,
> Hym call I the most noble ever more,
>   For he is most sett by. (I, 1377–79)

This ironic thrust at public opinion leads A to promise "a reyal disputacyon" after the intermission to answer the question (I, 1410). The roles of A and B are virtually interchangeable as they alternate as *raisonneurs* of the author and ironic spokesmen for the audience.

Following the intermission A and B both serve as messengers for their masters to Lucres, and both prove their incompetence, but in different ways. Turning an innocent reminiscence into a scatological insult, B, when sent to remind Lucres of a stroll she took with his master Cornelius, tells her:

>   ther satt a byrde,
> And than ye delyveryd hym your muskball
> For to throw at the byrd with all,
> And than as he sayd, ye dyd no wors
> But evyn fayr kyst hym on the noke of the ars.

When Lucres declares that false, B corrects himself, "Trouth, it was on the hole of thars I shulde say," and when Lucres denies it, B continues, "By my fayth, ye kyst hym or he kyst you / On the hole of thars, chose you now" (II, 279–89). Lucres finally sets matters straight when she patiently explains that Cornelius *cast* the muskball in the hole of an *ash*.[8] This counterproductive message makes both master and messenger appear ridiculous, yet it does not detract from Lucres's dignity. In fact it demonstrates a poise and intelligence that characterize her throughout the drama. When the other messenger, A, arrives to deliver his message, he discovers that he has lost his master's letter and has forgotten his master's name as well as his own. He appeals to the audience for assistance but to no avail. Again the comedy is at the messenger's expense, but unlike B's garbled message, it does not implicate the master, Gayus. Again Lucres patiently maintains her composure. The final participation of the comic servants in the wooing of Lucres is B's announcement of the minstrels and dancers who represent Cornelius's final attempt to influence Lucres's decision before the disputation.

By the time the climactic debate comes, thanks to the commentary and participation of A and B, the members of the audience are prepared for the judgment. Ever sensitive to offending the aristocracy by the potentially radical position Lucres takes, Medwall has Lucres insist before the disputants present their cases that her decision "may not be notyde for a generall precedent, / All be it that for your partis ye do therto assent" (II, 432–33). Gayus agrees, but Cornelius remains silent on this point. As in Buonaccorso's *controversia*, Cornelius is the first to speak, but because of B's earlier description of his vicelike prodigality and his previously demonstrated arrogance, the audience is not sympathetic to his position. Cornelius's emphasis on his ancestors' fame and his inherited wealth is punctuated by his scorn of the lowborn Gayus, for which he is reproached by Lucres; he then offers Lucres "ease and plesaunt idelnesse" as well as an unlimited supply of apparel, hunting, hawking, dancing, and "mynstralsy" both day and night. Again Cornelius sounds like a morality vice. He concludes his speech by sneering at how little Gayus could offer.

Gayus, whose address in Buonaccorso is nearly twice the length of Cornelius's, is here given twenty lines fewer than his rival; but he takes full advantage of his position as second speaker by refuting his rival's charges and then elaborating on Cornelius's "voluptuouse" and "bestiall" life (II, 630) which falls so far short of his ancestors' noble example. Unlike his counterpart in Buonaccorso, Gayus does not catalog historical precedents of men like himself who have won fame by merit — including Socrates, Euripides, Demosthenes, Cato, and Marius — but he reminds his audience that both Cornelius and he "cam of Adam and Eve" and insists:

There is no difference that I can tell
Whiche makith oon man an other to excell
So moche as doth vertue and godely maner. (II, 665–68)

Comparing his victories and awards with Cornelius's idleness, Gayus promises Lucres "moderate richesse" (II, 696) as he confirms, in his eloquent and dignified address, the nobility that his earlier appearances had led the audience to expect in spite of A's and B's contemptuous references to him as a churl's son.

Lucres also proves the good judgment the audience had expected of her after her father had confidently placed the choice of a husband entirely in her hands, unlike Buonaccorso's version, where the decision is to be made by the senate. Lucres's independence and intelligence make her a well-qualified and diplomatic judge, for she is careful not to demean Cornelius's blood, though she explains that "unto the blode I wyll have lytyl respect / Where the condicyons be synfull and abject" (II, 764–65). She epitomizes the meaning of the play when she declares: "For vertue excellent I will honoure a man / Rather than for hys blode" (II, 777–78).

Together A and B discuss Lucres's decision and reestablish a comic tone as they ask the audience for their opinion. Though A registers the possible objections of some that "this matter sholde have procede / To som other conclusion" (II, 879–80), B, again serving as the *raisonneur* of the author, expresses the play's intended effect:

Not onely to make folke myrth and game,
But that suche as be gentilmen of name
   May be somewhat movyd
By this example for to eschew
The wey of vyce and favour vertue;
   For syn is to be reprovyd
More in them, for the degre,
Than in other parsons such as be
   Of pour kyn and birth. (II, 890–98)

Mirth and game, emphasized earlier in the commentary, are now subordinated to the didactic end. Although Medwall has written a secular rather than a religious play, his purpose is ultimately the same as in his morality *Nature*: He means to instruct his audience to embrace virtue, which is exemplified here in the "new" man. As he makes clear, the gentlemen of "degre" have an even greater responsibility to reprove sin than the poor, for their positions of authority and their roles as models in society increase their influence. Yet fearful that he has overstepped the mark, Medwall ends the play with the conventional apology that "if ther be ony offence. . . It is onely for lacke of connynge" (II, 909–12). By equating the lowborn achiever with virtue and the proud aristocrat with vice, Medwall has imposed the dichotomy of the morality play on the issue of true nobility. To make this construct more acceptable, he diverts his audience by mirth and game as he leads them to endorse the concept of the new men. Although he never acknowledges Horace to be his critical guide, Medwall subtly combines profit with delight, or as he puts it, "solace" with "mirth."

By integrating the classical *controversia* with the wooing motif of folk drama, the *débat* of medieval poetry, and elements from the morality play, Medwall creates a new and distinctive dramatic form. The pattern of action that results involves characters of high social status striving to win a desirable bride, which is parodied by characters on a lower social plane. This is exactly the formula of romantic comedy explored by Lyly in *Endymion* and elaborated by Shakespeare, notably in *As You Like It* and *Twelfth Night*. This peculiarly English form of comedy antedates by nearly a half-century the adaptation of the classical comic structure by Udall in *Roister Doister*, generally regarded as the first "regular" English comedy (see chapter 19). The success of Medwall's drama largely depends on his ubiquitous and entertaining guides, A and B. Though the medieval *garcio*, the impudent, saucy servants of the Corpus Christi cycles, and the presenters of the folk play may anticipate the roles of A and B in *Fulgens and Lucres*, Medwall has developed their characters and functions far beyond their predecessors'. Their roles as presenters, choric commentators, and participants in the action provide wit and coarse humor as they direct the audience's response. Though they may not have been the direct models for the witty servants of Lyly and the household fools of Shakespeare, A and B point the direction for such choric comic successors as Touchstone and Feste.

Whether *Fulgens and Lucres* directly influenced or only anticipated the course of development that comedy took in Tudor England it is difficult to determine, but the play was not immediately forgotten after its presentation at Lambeth Palace in the 1490s. Printed by John Rastell in about 1512, it has the distinction of being "the first vernacular play to issue from an English press" (Medwall, *Plays* 1). However, it was not reprinted in the sixteenth century, and it disappeared from view until 1919, when a copy of the play was rediscovered among books purchased by the Huntington Library. Though *Fulgens and Lucres* had a close brush with oblivion, its recovery provides a better understanding of dramatic innovation and the emergence of formal comedy in early Tudor England.

CHAPTER SEVENTEEN

CALISTO AND MELEBEA

CALISTO *and Melebea*, published by John Rastell in the late 1520s, was identified on the title page as "A New Commodye in Englysh in Maner of an Enterlude." This designation as a comedy, the first play composed in English to be so identified, may derive from the original title of Fernando de Rojas's novel in dialogue, *Comedia de Calisto y Melibea* (1499), upon which the interlude was based.[1] In the revised edition, published in 1502, the novel was retitled *La Tragicomedia de Calisto y Melibea*, because, as Rojas explains in his new prologue, his work falls between the extremes of tragedy and comedy. Since this prologue provides the comment on strife used in the first speech of the English adaptation, the 1502 edition of the novel, which became popularly known as *Celestina*, must have been the source for the play, and the play's designation as a comedy probably results from the happy ending adopted for the dramatic production. The change in the ending may be the most striking aspect of the transformation of the novel into a moral interlude, but the English adapter alters the characters and spirit of the original as well as the structure by imposing a new set of social and aesthetic values for his particular audience.

Neither the auspices of the dramatic performance nor the identity of the adapter has been determined, though addresses in the text to "lords" (310 and 465) and "sirs" (612) and the moral application of the play at the end to maidens (1039), fathers, mothers, "Rulers of yong folkis" (1046–47) and "all governours" (1083) imply an aristocratic if not a courtly audience.[2] That the play was performed for a social wedding, as has been argued, seems unlikely, though its appeal to Catherine of Aragon and her Spanish entourage at court is obvious.[3] Rojas's novel had met with immediate popular success, and by the end of the third decade had gone through more than a score of editions as well as translations into Italian, German, and French. Though Vives, the Spanish humanist who had spent much time at Catherine's court and at Oxford between 1523 and 1528, had decried the novel as unfit for girls in his *De institutione feminae Christianae* (1523), addressed to the Princess Mary, he later allowed in *De disciplinis* (1531) that the work was a moral exemplum demonstrating the punishment of death for illicit passion (see chapter 7). There is no indication that Vives had a hand in transforming the earthy Spanish novel into an English interlude, in spite of efforts to link him with the production (Ungerer 17; Hogrefe 344–45), but he probably would not have objected to the chastened morality that the English version offered. The major candidates for the authorship of the English interlude are Richard Morison, who translated Vives's *Introductio ad sapientiam*, and John Rastell, who printed the play. Recent critics have favored the printer John Rastell, though the evidence for his composition is inconclusive.[4]

Whoever was responsible appears to have worked directly from the Spanish text (Rojas, *Celestina*, ed. Allen 342–44), and in spite of a few serious mistranslations he (or she) appears to have had quite a good command of the Spanish language. Alterations from the dialogue of the original appear to have been largely governed by practical considerations of staging as well as by a desire to purify the didactic implications of the original. Allen's claim that 800 of the 1,088 lines in the play were "translated more or less literally" from the Spanish novel (Rojas, *Celestina* 332) has been generally accepted, and if the introductory monologue of 42 lines and the new ending of 168 lines are deducted from the adapter's original 288 lines, only 78 new lines were added to the body of the text (Geritz 19). However, these figures are most deceiving if one considers the selectivity of the translated lines as well as the omissions and reductions entailed in the adaptation.

As previous critics have noted, the English interlude adapts the first four acts of Rojas's novel, though in fact only act 1 and part of act 4 are rendered dramatically. Act 1, dealing with the first meeting between Calisto and Melebea and the enlistment of Celestina's aid in the seduction of Melebea, is most fully presented, occupying nearly 550 lines (43–590), or approximately half of the play. Forty-one lines of the play (591–632), representing Parmeno's decision to join Celestina and Sempronio in Calisto's design on Melebea's virtue, are drawn from act 2 of the novel, though in a significantly adapted form, as we shall see. Act 3 and the first part of act 4 are ignored by the English adapter, as he focuses on Celestina's temptation of Melebea from the latter part of Rojas's act 4; this scene of some 270 lines (634–905), which provides the crisis of the plot, is followed by a 14-line soliloquy (906–19) delivered by Celestina that is made up of lines based on isolated passages from acts 5 and 6 (Purcell 3–5). The English adapter ignores the remaining fifteen acts of Rojas's novel, and in the final 168 lines provides a completely new moral conclusion and epilogue. The adaptation is much more subtle and complex than earlier commentators have indicated. A careful analysis of the parts of the novel that are selected and altered by the English adapter reveals that his formative guide was the moral interlude and his didactic intent was to present a positive model of feminine virtue rather than a titillating and sensational tale demonstrating the destructive effects of passion.

Following the novel, the play begins with a scene between the young lovers; but before Calisto enters, Melebea, as in Rojas's prologue, comments on the universality of strife and then decries the "dotage" of Calisto and his "carnall desyre" (1–42). The English adapter, by adding Melebea's introductory monologue, emphasizes the role of the woman and establishes a moral stance for dealing with the impending attempted seduction. Melebea, though sorry for Calisto's "troble," abhors his "voluptuous appetyte" (29–35). Presented without the domestic support of her mother or the maid Lucrezia from the novel, Melebea in the interlude may be more vulnerable, but she is also more independent and more pious than her Spanish counterpart. Cast in the morality-play role conventionally portrayed by a male protagonist who undergoes temptation, Melebea expresses the self-assurance and the traditional religious values associated with the allegorical figure of Reason, who in the traditional morality warns the protagonist of the dangers of sin. When confronted with Calisto's adoration of her above God and all the saints, Melebea in Rojas's text rejects Calisto's wicked intent to "have [her] virtue," but the English Melebea responds less shrilly as she perceives the danger of becoming his "thrall" (71–72).

The role of Calisto is diminished as Melebea's is heightened, and though he expresses the symptoms of the suffering Petrarchan lover, as in the original, his complaint is reduced both in length and in dimension. After using his lute to express his internal disharmony, Calisto points to his contradictory emotions, which are manifested in physical suffering:

> I fele sharp nedyls within my brest,
> Peas, warr, truth, haterad, and injury,
> Hope and suspect, and all in one chest. (116–18)

However, it is the image of fire that the English adapter particularly emphasizes to express Calisto's passion. Following the original, Calisto in the interlude regards his fire as greater than that which destroyed Nero's Rome and declares that "yf the fyre of purgatory bren in such wyse," he would rather his spirit were in brute beasts so that he would avoid the pain (133–35). This image of the fire of love is reintroduced by the adapter at the end of the first scene, as Calisto prays that his servant, Sempronio, aid him in quenching "the leme / Of this fyre which my hart doth wast and spende" (301–2); later Celestina alludes to "the hote fyre of love" (348), and Sempronio reiterates that "Calisto in the love of fayre Melebea / Burynth" (381–82). Calisto epitomizes in the English interlude the carnal lover who, led by his burning passion, perverts his Christian values in his worship of a woman in place of God and heretically suggests, in anticipation of Dr. Faustus, that his soul descend to brutish beasts to escape divine punishment. However, the English adapter does not include Sempronio's blasphemous jest about sodomy among the angels that provokes Calisto's laughter in Rojas's version.

Calisto's moral degeneration is emphasized by his servants, the conniving Sempronio and the loyal Parmeno. Again reducing the complexity of the original, Sempronio in the interlude warns Calisto against the wiles, inconstancy, and lust of women and, appealing to Calisto's rationality or "clere wyt" (207), declares women's inferiority to men. Calisto's response is to reaffirm his belief that woman is a goddess, and in a catalog of Melebea's beauty, Calisto focuses on her physical attributes as he demonstrates his besotted state. Only after this exchange does Sempronio, having been given a gold chain, seek out Celestina. Parmeno warns Calisto about the dangers of pursuing his passion by enlisting the aid of Celestina, whom he characterizes as a bawd, a witch, and a "false hore" (411). In a departure from the original, the English adapter places Celestina and Sempronio on stage to overhear and interrupt Parmeno's warning. Calisto registers his moral blindness by welcoming Celestina as an "auncyent vertew," and, applying religious terms to the old bawd, he makes her his savior:

> O gloryous hope of my desyryd intent!
> ... My regeneracion to this lyfe present,
> Resurreccon from deth. (431–34)

This response is a close translation of the original, but the English adapter emphasizes Calisto's delusion by the gift of his cloak to Celestina in payment for her future service; in the original, Calisto, alluding to the keys to his treasure, only promises a reward. In addition, after Calisto leaves the stage, the English adapter has Parmeno, moralizing on Calisto's folly and the deceitfulness of servants, conclude, "Nothyng but for lucre is all theyr bawdry" (471).

In the scene between Parmeno and Celestina that follows, not only does the English adapter reduce the length, he also makes Parmeno a spokesman for virtue and loyalty as he vows not to follow Sempronio's false example in spite of Celestina's claims of intimacy through Parmeno's mother. Only after Calisto dispenses another hundred pieces of gold to Celestina and ignores a further warning from Parmeno does Parmeno determine to "chaunge [his] copy" (623) and become a flatterer. In contrast with Rojas's original, where Celestina convinces Parmeno to join forces, the English adaptation provides a twenty-line soliloquy addressed to the audience that expresses Parmeno's moral decision after observing the rewards of dishonesty. That speech thus becomes a complaint about the corrupt world as Parmeno ironically concludes his role as a moral chorus, but he does not reappear in the interlude so does not demonstrate his acceptance of the ways of the world. This focus on Parmeno as a moral voice in the interlude is one of the most significant departures from Rojas's novel.

Another significant change in the interlude is the role of Celestina, whose vibrant dialogue and comic dimension so dominate the novel that her name quickly became its popular title. The English adapter retains her central position as the instrument for Calisto's lust, but focuses her character on her role as a temptress. Stripped of her earthiness and much of her proverbial wisdom, Celestina resembles a morality play vice as her cunning and hypocrisy become her major characteristics. Her altered role is indicated by her introduction. After Sempronio has been sent by Calisto to enlist her aid, Celestina appears alone on stage at the beginning of the second scene (311) and introduces herself to the audience in a typical morality play manner.[5] What is unusual is her narration of a dialogue that in the novel takes place between Sempronio and Elicea, one of her whores. The narration, which captures the comic tone as it concisely summarizes the conversation of the original, illustrates Celestina's cunning "craft of bawdery," as she characterizes it (329). Her account further demonstrates the deceptiveness of women and the gullibility of men, as Elicea with Celestina's help fools the conniving Sempronio. The narration concludes with a reference to a friar who is reported to have sent a wench to Celestina; a gap in the text at this point may result either from excising an allusion to a local brother, or it may suggest that the actors were to supply a name appropriate to the fat friar described. Most significantly, Celestina clearly establishes her evil and cunning character before she begins to interact with the other figures in the play.

Celestina's part in the remainder of the play is to corrupt the virtuous. She first seeks to enlist in her cause Parmeno, who, familiar with her wicked past, had warned Calisto. This dialogue follows Rojas in general, but the English adapter makes some significant alterations. Celestina in the original first speaks of love to draw Parmeno in, but in the interlude she adjusts her line to Parmeno's moralizing by demonstrating her hypocrisy:

> vertew warnyth me
> To fle temptacyon and folow charyte,
> To do good agayns yll, and so I rede the. (475–77)

Then to put Parmeno into a more malleable mood, she gets him to join her in a song, a motif the English adapter has added to the original. Celestina proceeds, in a shorter version than in the novel, to discredit Parmeno's morality by declaring that his mother was a whore and that all masters are selfish. She concludes her temptation with an expression of her priority of values, as she places wealth over truth and honesty and makes delight the "chefe maistres" in accord with nature (541–84). Again the English adapter calls for music to further the temptation as Celestina cries: "Stryke up, mynstryl, with sawes of love, the old problem! / Syng swete songes" (574–75). Celestina's temptation ends in the novel with Parmeno agreeing to join with her, but in the English interlude he leaves the stage uncommitted, and only after Parmeno's final warning to Calisto goes unheeded does Celestina's temptation bear fruit as Parmeno declares: "syth these bawdys get good provokyng lechery, / I trust flatery shall spede as well as bawdery" (631–32).

However, it is Celestina's temptation of Melebea that demonstrates her major function in the play. Again the English adapter follows the form of the original, though he makes adjustments for his dramatic audience. No mother or maid is on hand to warn or intercede as Melebea receives the satanic Celestina. Beginning as in the novel with a celebration of youth and a complaint about the miseries of old age, though somewhat reduced in the interlude, Celestina deftly proceeds to flatter Melebea's beauty as she stresses its ephemerality. Appealing next to Melebea's sense of pity and charity, Celestina demonstrates her hypocrisy without reference to magical powers or appeals for devilish assistance as in the novel. Melebea's moral indignation upon recognizing Celestina's part in Calisto's scheme of seduction is quickly softened by

Celestina's humility and a renewed appeal for pity and charity, which the English adapter strengthens by adding a year to Calisto's age—making him twenty-four—a day to his declared agony, and six years to the length of his metaphoric suffering—"he semyth he had leyn this seven yere" (865–71). Again Celestina's hypocrisy is emphasized: The English adapter introduces a comparison of Calisto's welcome of Celestina bearing Melebea's girdle to Gabriel coming to "our lady with *Ave Maria*" (887), in what may be a Reformist poke at Mariolatry (R. Axton, "Folk play" 21). In another departure from the original, Celestina's last words to Melebea are a prayer for Christ's comfort, but then, left alone on stage, Celestina congratulates herself on her skill in accomplishing her design; in the novel Celestina expresses relief in escaping a dangerous situation. Once more the morality play vice appears to have influenced the dramatic handling of Celestina as a panderess.

In the conclusion the morality-play form eclipses the design of Rojas's novel. Eschewing the titillating consummation of the young lovers' passion and the sensational destruction of Celestina and the servants who had abetted the clandestine relationship, as well as the deaths of the lovers, the English adapter demonstrates the positive power of divine providence rather than the fickleness of fortune or the force of divine retribution perceived in the original. Rojas's honor-bound father, Pleberio, is reshaped into a morality-play God, or his lieutenant Reason, as he calls the sinner to account and moralizes on the example. Rechristened Danio, he indicates the living presence of the divine in a dream warning of his daughter Melebea's danger. In an allegory presenting life as a moral choice between good, represented as a wholesome hot bath, and evil, "a pyt of foule stynkyng water" (946), the dream features temptation in the form of "a foule rough bych . . . strakyng her body along on the gras" (951–52), who by fawning distracts and misleads the unwary Melebea. Though no direct source for the allegory has been discovered, the motif of the weeping bitch has been linked to the medieval story of Dame Sirith, who convinces a lady that her daughter has been transformed into a bitch by a clerk when she refused his love. Pepper placed in the bitch's eyes enhance the reality of the daughter's supposed grief (R. Axton, "Folk play" 16–17). The reduction of Celestina to a foul, fawning bitch epitomizes the moral perspective of the English interlude, which ignores the vibrant realism of her character and the attraction of her moral ambiguity.

Melebea's moral awakening is registered by her interpretation of Danio's allegorical dream, and she begs forgiveness both from her father and from God. However, she emphasizes that "though I dyd consent / In mynd, yet had he never hys intent" (1009–10); thus her fall is regarded as mental rather than physical, and she triumphs over temptation. She explains that she has "kept trew" because of her morning habit of praying to God "for grace all vyce to eschew" (1006), as recommended by her father. Her preservation of her chastity demonstrates the "verteu" or power of prayer, according to Danio (1011–12), yet because it was her intent to offend, Melebea is chastened and repentant. The conclusion emphasizes the positive model of feminine virtue in Melebea as it manifests the providential role of God, who protects the innocent believer from the snares of sin.

The title page promises an interlude "wherein is shewd and dyscrybyd . . . the bewte and good propertes of women, as theyr vycys and evyll condicions, with a morall conclusion and exhortacyon to vertew"; both the positive image of women and "theyr vycys and evyll condicions," presumably as depicted by Sempronio in his diatribe against women and by Celestina in her attack on female virtue, are emphasized. However, the bawdiness, the blasphemy, and the witchcraft that characterize Celestina in Rojas's novel are largely avoided in the purified English version, as the vibrant realism and philosophical dimension of the panderess are sacrificed to her hypocritical cunning. Her proverbial wisdom and understanding of human nature are barely glimpsed behind the imposed facade of the morality-play vice. The power of passion, expanded by Rojas in his revised edition of the novel, is reduced in the English interlude to a satire on romantic love as the flame of desire consumes the Petrarchan Calisto, yet his role as the motivator of the plot is all but forgotten as the last half of the play focuses on the dichotomy of womanhood in the figures of Celestina and Melebea. The erotic development of the lovers' clandestine relationship and the sensational violence of the novel's end are precluded by the didactic perspective of the English moral interlude.

The final "exhortacyon to vertew" is first addressed to "vyrgyns and fayre maydens all," which calls attention to the play's special orientation to young women. One wonders if the Princess Mary or the daughters of Thomas More, nieces to the printer John Rastell, were in the audience when the play was first performed. That young women were a significant component of the intended reading audience cannot be overlooked. The message, however, goes beyond a warning to the potential sinners to "Serve God dayly" and "withstand all evyll temptacions" (1041–44) in the manner of the morality play, for Danio exhorts:

> ye faders, moders, and other which be
> Rulers of yong folkis . . .
> To bryng them up verteously . . .
> . . . to teche them some art, craft, or lernyng,
> Whereby to be able to get theyr lyffyng. (1046–52)

This appeal to parents and teachers to look to their children's education in both virtue and learning recalls the aims of education advocated by the humanists Erasmus, Vives, and More (see chapters 6–8), as well as by Rastell in his earlier youth-morality, *The Nature of the Four Elements*.

Finally the play indicts society's governors for "theyr neglygens" in "Not puttyng [youth] to lernyng nor occapacyons" (1054–55) and calls for

> The hedys and rulers . . .
> To make good lawes, and execute them straytely,
> Upon suche maystres that be neclygent. (1061–63)

Extending the exhortation to the makers of the laws suggests that the adults present for the first performance were aristocratic if not courtly. Though the monarch is not addressed, education is perceived to be the concern of his ministers and the parliament, and the portrayal of feminine virtue withstanding temptation through the power of prayer would have especially pleased the pious Queen Catherine of Aragon. This first designated comedy in English proves the strength of the didactic impulse and the influence of the morality play form; but in its emphasis on the importance of education it anticipates the educational interludes that emerged a decade later (see chapters 10–11), and in its focus on the good and evil in women it indicates the growing interest in the role of women in drama and in society.

CHAPTER EIGHTEEN

JOHAN JOHAN

*A*LTHOUGH Noah's wife and Mak with his "sothren tothe" may possibly provide examples of farcical action in the Towneley cycle, *Johan Johan*, published by William Rastell in 1533, is the first play printed in England to represent farce as a dramatic form. Attributed to John Heywood by the bookseller Francis Kirkman in 1671, *Johan Johan* has long been recognized as vastly different in form and style from Heywood's known plays or those of his contemporaries. Karl Young in 1904 sought to explain these differences by suggesting that Heywood was influenced by French farce in several of his plays and that *Johan Johan* was drawn from the *Farce de Pernet qui au vin* ("Influence of French Farce" 97–104). Later scholars elaborated this argument, and in 1946 Ian Maxwell published what was thought to be the definitive work on this matter: *French Farce and John Heywood*. However, with the appearance of Gustave Cohen's *Recueil de farces françaises inédites du XVe siècle* in 1949, William Elton and T. W. Craik almost simultaneously noted that *Johan Johan* was in fact a translation of *Farce nouvelle très bonne et fort joyeuse du Pasté* (XIX in Cohen's *Recueil de farces*). Elton describes *Johan Johan* as "a fairly literal translation, with some minor differences" ("Note on *Johan Johan*" 128), and Craik, claiming that the translator "has taken very few liberties with his real source," says that "*Johan Johan* is a close (though none the less spirited) translation" ("True Source" 290). Both accept the traditional view that the translator is Heywood, though neither supplies evidence on this point. Craik discusses some variations in the French and English versions, most notably the priest's accounts of the three miracles and the endings of the two plays; but neither Elton nor Craik investigates the hundreds of variants in details or considers the implications of these changes. What a close examination of the two texts reveals is that *Johan Johan* is in fact a very careful adaptation of the French farce to the English cultural and dramatic context.

A few gallicisms appear in the English play, such as Johan Johan's threat to "traine [his wife] by the here" (14) for "la trainer par les cheveulx" (23)[1] and his later comment that "I almost enrage that I ne can / Se the behav[i]our of our gentilwoman" (89–90) for "J'enrage presque je ne puis / Veoir le tour de nostre bourgeoise" (91–92); but generally the language is attuned to the English setting. Not only are references to place changed — "Nostre-Dame" (154) becomes "the Church of Poules" (153) and "Romme" (166) becomes "Coventre" (164) — but also allusions to the saints are altered as "saincte Me[s]aise" (148) is changed to "swete Saint Diri[c]k" and invocations to "Sainct Julien" (209), "Saint Pol et Saint Remy" (218), "Saint Anthonie" (227), and "Saincte Marie" (229, 231) are dropped from the English version altogether. Local customs are taken into account as ale (287, 387, 618) is substituted for *vin* (300, 397, 698). Even more significant, colloquial oaths and proverbs are introduced into the English text, occasionally to fill out the metrical line but more often to provide a homely touch. "By Gogges" or "cokkes blood" (9, 30), "cokkes bones" (72), "Gogges body" (74, 83), "cokkes soule" (127), and "Kokkes lily woundes" (163) sprinkle the speech of Johan Johan throughout the play. Johan Johan adds the proverb "He must nedes go that the divell driveth" (313) when he is sent by Tib to invite Sir Johan; later, after Sir Johan and Tib have eaten the pie, Johan Johan emphasizes Sir Johan's arrogance by adding, "nowe I se well the olde proverbe is trew: 'The parisshe preest forgetteth that ever he was clarke'" (594–95). The translator provides a more specific sense of place as well as expanding the colorful language of the play.

The translator occasionally reduces the details of a passage in French. For example, in *Farce du Pasté*, there are a daughter of a neighbor, a nephew, an uncle, and two cousins who are involved in the preparation of the pasty in addition to the wife, the priest, and the woman friend (157–65), but only the "neybours yongest daughter, An" aids Tib, Sir Johan, and the gossip Margery in the English version (158–56, 400–404). Some passages from the French are summarized, and some are omitted altogether; more often, however, the French lines are expanded in the English version as new details are added. These expansions may involve the addition of a few words, of a line or two, or of several lines, but the usual effect is to make the passage more concrete. At times the expansion is redundant, as in the line "Ma femme n'a eu nulz enfans" 102), translated as "My wife had never child," to which the words "doughter nor son" are added (100). More frequently the addition extends the meaning or makes the expression more colorful, such as the end of Johan Johan's initial monologue, just before Tib enters. The speech in *Farce du Pasté* ends:

> Or brief, par le sacrament de l'autel,
> Elle en aura son payement,
> Car je l'ordiray tellement
> Que l'allée luy sera dure. (115–18)[2]

This rather general statement is transformed in *Johan Johan* as follows:

> But, in faith, all these wordes be in wast,
> For I thinke the matter is done and past.
> And whan she cometh home she will begin to chide,
> But she shall have her payment-sti[c]k by her side!
> For I shall order her, for all her brawling,
> That she shall repent to go a catter-wawling. (105–10)

The vague concern of the French husband becomes for Johan Johan an anticipation of his wife's behavior and an expression of his response, which he fails to carry out. Earlier in this same monologue some twenty lines are added to reiterate Johan Johan's determination to give Tib a sound beating when she returns, but her offensiveness is emphasized as her body odor becomes a comic motif. Here is a short sample:

> And I shall beate her, by Cokkes bones,
> That she shall stinke like a pole-kat,
> But yet, by Gogges body, that nede not,
> For she will stinke without any beting;
> For every night, ones she giveth me an heting,
> From her issueth such a stinking smoke
> That the savour thereof almost doth me choke. (72–78)

This addition not only contributes concrete images and humor to Johan Johan's monologue, but also serves to reveal his character and his wife's.

Many of the additions provide insight to the characters or express another dimension to their portrayals than is represented in the French version. The translator's interest in characterization is suggested by the change of title from *Farce nouvelle très bonne et fort joyeuse du Pasté*, which emphasizes the motivating force for the action, the *pasté*, to *A mery play betwene Iohan Iohan the husbande / Tib his wyfe / & syr Ihan the preest*, which stresses the persons of the play. Although Johan Johan is an anglicization of Jehan-Jehan, or Jehan-Jehannin, in the French text Jehan-Jehan is identified in the dramatis personae simply as L'Homme, and he retains this designation in the speech prefixes throughout the play. The wife in the French version is never named; she is simply La Femme. The priest too is consistently called Le Curé, though his name is revealed to be Guillaume in the dialogue. In the English version, not only is the wife called Tib, but the priest is given the same name as the husband, perhaps to emphasize the priest's assumption of the husband's role. The translator's interest in character led him to develop the individual figures in greater depth as aspects of the French originals are extended and new dimensions are added.

Tib retains in the English version most of the characteristics of the stereotypical promiscuous and cunning shrew encountered in both the French fabliaux and the French farces, but she is bolder and more cynical than her French counterpart. Tib directly expresses her awareness of her husband's suspicions about her visits to the priest (169–70) shortly after arriving on stage, unlike La Femme, and rather than resorting to tears when confronted by her husband as La Femme does, Tib calmly out-faces her husband's jealousy and then insists Johan Johan invite the priest to share the pie. After calling Johan Johan back several times for various tasks before fetching the priest, Tib physically threatens her husband for taking so long, but Tib's impatience is emphasized by a longer speech than La Femme's and by Johan Johan's extended response, which adds the proverb noted above likening his wife to the devil. The boldness and cynicism of Tib is even more apparent during the priest's visit. Though no stage direction in the English text indicates that the wife embraces the priest when he arrives, as in the French text, Tib clearly greets Sir Johan as a lover in front of her husband. La Femme addresses Le Curé, "Vous, soyez le tresbien venu! / A'vous celle que vous aymez" (441–42; You are very welcome! Here's the one you love). Tib is more specific: "Welcome, min[e] owne sweetharte! / We shall make some chere or [ere] we depart" (427–28), which stresses the special endearment as well as promising pleasure. Later when Tib and Sir Johan are eating the pie while Johan Johan chafes the wax to mend the pail, Tib says, "Loke how the kokold chafith the wax that is hard, / And, for his life, darith not loke hetherward" (505–6). The French text provides no equivalent lines; nor is Jehan-Jehannin so directly called a cuckold by his wife, though the name Jehannin is traditionally associated with the cuckold. Moments later La Femme calls attention to her husband's folly—"Par mon serment, c'est bien pour rire / D'ung homme qui folie maine" (557–58; By my oath it is good to laugh at a man who is foolish)—but the sentiment is shifted in Tib's lines to the wife's role in making the husband a comic butt. Tib says, "Now, by my trouth, it is a pretty jape / For a wife to make her husband her ape" (513–14).

Just as the wife is bolder and more cynical in the English version, so also is the priest. Shortly after receiving Johan Johan's invitation, Sir Johan alludes to his relationship with Tib. He tells Johan Johan, "Yet thou thinkist amis, peradventure, / That of her body she should not be a good woman," which loosely translates the French text, but then Sir Johan adds:

But I shall till the[e] what I have done, Johan,
For that matter: she and I be sometime aloft,

> And I do lie uppon her many a time and oft
> To prove her; yet could I never espy
> That ever any did wors with her than I. (346–52)

No precedent for this admission of adultery exists in the French version. Even though these lines may appear to be interpreted more innocently by Johan Johan, who blithely replies, "Sir, that is the lest care I have of nine, / Thankyd be God and your good doctrine" (353–54), the priest is most blatantly testing the intelligence or the spinelessness of Johan Johan. Sir Johan's part in the mockery of Johan Johan as the priest and wife greedily eat the pie while the husband chafes the wax follows the French original quite closely, but given his earlier admissions, Sir Johan appears more cynical than Guillaume. This cynicism is stressed at the end of the play; when Johan Johan confronts the pair and calls Tib a "prestes whore," Sir Johan answers, "Thou liest, [w]horson kokold, evyn to thy face!" (656–57). By directly calling Johan Johan a cuckold, the priest reaffirms his earlier admission at the same time that he appears to contradict himself. Again the translator departs from the French version.

The extension of the boldness and cynicism of both the wife and priest in the English version makes Johan Johan more victimized, but it also makes him appear more cowardly and/or more stupid than his French counterpart. Further, his own speeches develop his humiliation and the discrepancy between what he promises to do and what he does. The twenty lines added to the opening monologue in the English version justify Johan Johan's beating of Tib and whet his appetite for the encounter, but because he answers so mildly when she appears, the emptiness of his threats is stressed. Even more significant, Johan Johan's recognition that he is being cuckolded by the priest is made more graphic than in the French text. Tib complains of being sick when she arrives home, a detail not included in *Farce du Pasté*, which leads Johan Johan to say apparently as an aside:

> By Cokkes soule, nowe, I dare lay a swan
> That she comes nowe streyght fro Sir Johan.

> For, ever when she hath fatched of him a lyk,
> Than she comes home and saith she is syk. (127–30)

A few lines later Johan Johan refers to the priest giving Tib "absolution upon a bed" (141), another detail the English translator adds.

Shortly after this point in the French version, the husband *à part* (aside) expresses a rather subtle image of the priest and wife in amorous play:

> tout à l'entour du lit,
> Voire entre vous deux et non plus
> Et à la fin montez dessus
> Pour la processio parfaire. (175–78)

These lines are translated quite literally in the English text,[3] and then another line is added: "He lepeth up, and thou liest down" (178). Again the added detail emphasizes Johan Johan's awareness of his plight, which makes his cooperation with Tib and Sir Johan while they mock him in the pie-eating episode appear even more spineless.

Johan Johan's position as a comic butt and the irony of his role are most fully expressed in the ending of the English play. In *Farce du Pasté*, L'Homme at the end finally turns on La Femme and Le Curé, accuses them of lying, threatens them, and beats them with a sack full of bread. The final lines are assigned to Le Curé, but in fact they indicate an altercation punctuated by the cries of all three characters:

> LE CURÉ
>   Par delà!
> Je vous pry, suyvons-le de près.
>   *L'Homme revient par derrière*
>   *atout ung sac plain de pain.*
> Après curé, après, après.
> A! vous me gastés le pasté,
> Après, curé, après, curé,
> A ly! à ly! à ly! à ly!
> Or, Messeigneurs, adieu vous dy!
>   EXPLICIT. (761–67)[4]

Gustave Cohen appears to be in error in his note that the husband and wife join together to beat the priest, for there is nothing in the lines to indicate the wife's change in loyalties.[5] It is possible that the extant text is corrupt, but the French farce unquestionably ends with the dispute unresolved. By contrast the English Johan Johan, after complaining about what he has suffered, throws the pail to the floor where it breaks, and then threatens Tib and Sir Johan with a shovel full of coals. Neither the breaking of the pail nor the shovel full of coals is indicated in the French text, but the most significant change is in the outcome of the row. The stage direction in the English version reads: "Here they fight by the e[a]rys a while, and than the preest and the wife go out of the place" (664). This leaves Johan Johan alone on stage as he was at the beginning of the play. He first boasts that he has "paid some of them even as I list" (665), but his triumph evaporates as he fears Tib and Sir Johan "Will make me kokold, evyn to anger me" (674). The plot has come full circle as Johan Johan finds himself back where he started. The English ending is not only more subtle than the French version, but also it focuses much more fully on the ironic dimension of the central comic character.

The change in the ending may be the most remarkable alteration of the French source, but another significant adaptation occurs in the handling of the religious element in the play. The English translator generally drops the allusions to saints, and he alters the wife's reference to the priest as a "vray Catholicque" (242; true Catholic) to a description of him as "vertuouse and full of charité" (232). Perhaps these changes were dictated by religious trends in England before the play was printed in 1533. Fear of possible censure may also have led to the omission of lines from the French text that could be considered blasphemous. After Le Curé's account of a woman who "miraculously" gave birth to a fully developed child only seven months after marriage, La Femme compares this to their cat bearing kittens after seven weeks. L'Homme then comments:

> Dea! m'amye,
> Dieu doit de tout estre loue,
> Mais qui cet s'elle evoit voué
> Son fruit au Glorieux Corps saint? (664–67)[6]

This jesting implication that the Holy Spirit has impregnated the cat does not appear in the English text, but the "miracles" that prompt the joke are made even more "miraculous" in the translation. The fully developed infant is born only five months after the mother's marriage rather than seven, and Puss the cat is described as having eighteen kittens in a year (588–89) rather than a litter in seven weeks.

The accounts of the other two miracles are also altered in the English version. The identification of Arnoul as the source of the miracles is dropped; instead Sir Johan personally attests to knowledge of these events. In his reference to knowing a woman who bore a fully developed child after only five months, he may be implying that he has fathered the child as Bevington suggests (*Medieval Drama* 577n.); however, in his account of the first miracle, which in the French describes a woman who had fourteen children without benefit of her husband, Sir Johan reduces the number to seven but adds, "Yet had she not had so many by thre / If she had not had the help of me" (547–48). Sir Johan's personal involvement in these miracles, which is absent from the French text, reinforces the abuse of his clerical role that informs his relationship with Tib as it emphasizes the clerical satire in the play.

One miracle described in the English version has no basis in the French text at all. This miracle, the second in the series, describes a woman who had been married "many a day" but had no child:

> Wherefore to Saint Modwin she went on pilgrimage,
> And offered there a live pig, as is the usage
> Of the wives that in London dwell. (561–63)

Within a month she is said to have had a child. This does not point to clerical abuse as the other miracles do, but instead apparently ridicules a current superstitious practice. The translator treats traditional objects of clerical satire with increased vehemence as the priest is perceived more negatively than in the French version, and at the same time the religious perspective is adjusted to the contemporary English context.

The translator also adapts the staging of the play to current dramatic practice. As G. R. Proudfoot indicates, the "English text . . . makes more precise reference to an indoor location for the performance than its original" (*Johan Johan* vi). This is especially evident at the end of the play, where Tib threatens Johan Johan with her "distaf" and "clipping-she[a]rys" and Johan Johan takes up a shovel full of coals. This appears to support the traditional association of the English play with Heywood and the More circle and initial production in a great hall or at court (Reed, *Early Tudor Drama* 146–47; Bevington, *Medieval Drama* 970). In the French farce the staging is less definite. Even more important, the involvement of the audience in production, which is characteristic of the popular French dramatic tradition (Aubailly 182–83, passim), not only is retained by the English translator, but is also expanded. At the beginning of *Farce du Pasté*, L'Homme comes on stage and enquires about his wife, but in *Johan Johan*, the husband first greets the audience—"God spede you, maysters, everychone!"—and then directly asks, "Wote ye not whither my wife is gone?" (1–2). The twenty-line addition the English translator makes to this initial monologue is also introduced with a direct address to the audience: "But, masters, for Goddes sake, do not entrete / For her whan she shall be bete!" (65–66). The entire monologue in both the French and English versions is, of course, obviously played to those assembled, but the English text more directly acknowledges their presence.

In *Farce du Pasté* the husband, as Cohen's edition indicates, clearly speaks a number of his lines *à part*, or as asides, when the wife and the priest share the stage with him; but a greater number of Johan Johan's speeches appear to be asides.[7] Tib is also given an occasional aside not found in the French text (e.g., 35–38, 226). The asides, by revealing the real thoughts of a character in addition to what is spoken for the benefit of the other characters on stage, imply a bond with the audience, and as in Roman comedy the device frequently is used for humorous effect. By expanding the number of asides from the French text, the English translator extends the relationship with the audience as he seeks at the same time to heighten the comedy.

Audience involvement for humorous effect is carried a step further when a member of the audience is asked to hold a cloak while the husband fetches the priest. In *Farce du Pasté* La Femme asks a spectator to hold her husband's cloak, but then, realizing the man asked is near the door and could run away with the cloak, she gives it to another. In *Johan Johan* the French lines are translated quite literally, including the comic details of not putting the cloak down where a dog has urinated and asking the person holding the cloak to scrape off the dirt; however, the wife's part in this action is eliminated as her speeches are given to Johan Johan. Both Pollard and Sultan, unaware that *Farce du Pasté* was the true source of *Johan Johan*, suspected Rastell was in error in assigning the entire sequence (242–59) to the husband, and both scholars suggested emendation (Gayley 1:72–73 and Sultan 491–97). Modern editors, however, have generally followed Rastell's text, for it appears that the translator has purposely reassigned the lines from the wife to Johan Johan. The first of La Femme's speeches—"Sire, mettez-la dessoubz vous / Ou entre vous et la boutte, / Mais venez cà!" (261–63; Sir, put it on you / Or between you and your arse / But come here!)—is adapted to Johan Johan by introducing the first person pronoun: "Therefore I pray you take ye the paine / To kepe *my* gowne till *I* come again." That it is Johan Johan and not the wife as in the French version who has second thoughts is suggested by the repetition of "But yet" that signals his change of mind: "But yet I am afraid to lay it down" (243) and "But yet he shall not have it, by my fay" (252). The effect is to enhance Johan Johan's comic role and to reinforce his bond with the audience.

Both the French and English versions of the farce end with a farewell to the audience, but the French text, "Or, Messeigneurs, adieu vous dy" (767; And so, masters, I bid you farewell), follows a physical row, and it is not clear in the text who speaks the line. In the English text Johan Johan remains alone on the stage after his fight with Sir Johan and Tib and brags of his triumph to the audience, but then he asks, "But yet, can ye tell / Whether they be go?" (668–69). Johan Johan varies the question with which the play began, "Wote ye not whither my wife is gone?" (2). He is again appealing for help in seeking his wife, but now he knows she is with the priest. His decision to go to the priest's chamber "To se if they do me any vilany" (677) provides motivation for his exit lacking in the

French original, which ends with the altercation unresolved. Before exiting Johan Johan says, "fare well this noble company" (678), which may imply an aristocratic audience, though "noble" could be a general compliment. "Company" does not specify men; however, this speech begins with an address to "Sirs," and the play itself begins with a greeting to "maysters." Whatever the composition of the audience, Johan Johan's relationship to them remains close throughout the play as he asks them questions, confides in them, and even involves them in disposing of his cloak.

Johan Johan extends the relationship between actor and audience beyond its source, *Farce du Pasté*, in addition to developing the characters, adapting the clerical satire, and refining the conclusion of the original. In most every respect the English version is more artistically sophisticated and more dramatic than the French text. Whether the translator was John Heywood, as has been traditionally assumed though neither external nor internal evidence has been discovered to prove his authorship, or whether it was William Cornish, as C. W. Wallace argues (51–52), or even Thomas More as Reed would like to believe (*Early Tudor Drama* 146–47), the translator demonstrates uncommon literary talent and practical knowledge of dramatic production. *Johan Johan* serves as a creative precedent for the incorporation of French farce into English Renaissance comedy.

CHAPTER NINETEEN

UDALL'S *ROISTER DOISTER*

*R*OISTER *Doister* is traditionally considered to be "the first regular English comedy."[1] This designation seems to result primarily from the play's observance of the five-act structure and its perceived imitation of Latin comedy. It is not, of course, the first English comedy; England's first extant secular play, Medwall's *Fulgens and Lucres*, performed more than fifty years earlier, has a better claim to that title (see chapter 16). And it is not the first play in England to use the five-act structure; Grimald's *Archipropheta*, composed in 1546–47, adopted that form (see chapter 23). It may also not be the first English play to imitate Latin comedy; *Jacke Juggeler*, which announces in its prologue its indebtedness to Plautus's "first commedie," *Amphitruo*, may precede *Roister Doister* by a year or two. *Roister Doister* may be the most fully developed comedy to be produced in England before the reign of Elizabeth; however, it is not as "regular" a comedy nor as "English" as previous critics believed.

Though some earlier scholars thought the play was written during Nicholas Udall's tenure as headmaster of Eton, between 1534 and 1541, it is now generally accepted that the play was completed between 1551 and 1553.[2] This is based on the fact that Roister Doister's mispunctuated letter is included in Thomas Wilson's third edition of *Rule of Reason* in 1553 as an example of ambiguity, but the letter is not included in the editions of 1551 and 1552 (Reed, "Nicholas Udall" 282). It is also in this reference to the play that Udall, Wilson's former schoolmaster, is identified as the author of *Roister Doister*. The question still remains as to whether the play was performed before the end of Edward VI's reign or after Mary came to the throne. Scheurweghs and Edgerton argue that the play was presented to young Edward in late 1552; Edgerton specifically sets the first performance in September 1552 at Windsor Castle (Scheurweghs ed. lv–lx; Edgerton, "The Date" 555–60). However, Baldwin (*Shakspere's Five-Act Structure* 381) and Bevington (*Tudor Drama and Politics* 121) believe the play was performed after Mary's coronation, perhaps as a part of the Christmas festivities in 1553. Harbage's *Annals of English Drama* simply notes that the auspices of the play are unknown (30), but recent scholars generally assume the play was produced by choristers, perhaps from Bishop Gardiner's school, because of the five songs and mock-requiem in the play (Baldwin, *Shakspere's Five-Act Structure* 381; Edgerton, "The Date" 559; Bevington, *Tudor Drama and Politics* 121). The music and mirth, emphasized in the prologue and manifested throughout the play, point to a festive occasion, if not the celebration of the Lord of Misrule, perhaps a presentation at court.

The subject of the play, Roister Doister's wooing of Christian Custance, would be especially appropriate for Mary, whose marriage with Philip of Spain was negotiated in the fall of 1553. The attentions of unwelcome suitors, which Mary must have inevitably faced as an unmarried princess and queen, are here dispelled with laughter. This is not to suggest that Udall is singling out Edward Courtenay, whom Udall tutored in the Tower, or any other contemporary candidate for Mary's hand. Udall, who also apparently wrote *Respublica* for Mary's court at about the same time, was much too adept at making his way in the new reign to create unnecessary enemies.[3] Rather the wooer is created from literary precedents; the wooing is reduced to burlesque; and in the resolution, as at the end of *Respublica*, reconciliation prevails. Perhaps the humorous treatment of wooing led to the licensing of the play in 1566–67 and a possible revival for Elizabeth, the object of many suits during her earlier years as queen.

Whatever the particular occasion for composition or performance, the prologue indicates a self-conscious design for the play as it reveals its author's critical perspective. In the first fourteen lines the word *mirth* appears eight times, in a defense of mirth as the appropriate effect of comedy because it lifts spirits and promotes good fellowship; but the prologue also emphasizes that the mirth the audience is about to witness is without abuse and is "vsed in an honest fashion" (8), for it is "mixed with vertue in decent comlynesse" (13).[4] Assuring spectators that the play will not offend, the prologue expresses a moral aim. This joining of profit with pleasure is to be expected from the old schoolmaster Udall, well versed in Horace's principle of *utile et dulce*. Udall, also a translator of Terence, a standard school author taught in the second through the fourth forms at Eton (Baldwin, *Shakspere's Small Latine* 1:641), expresses in the third stanza of the prologue his orientation toward classical comedy:

The wyse Poets long time heretofore
   Vnder merrie Comedies secretes did declare,
Wherein was contained very vertuous lore,
   With mysteries and forewarnings very rare.
Suche to write neither *Plautus* nor *Terence* dyd spare,
Whiche among the learned at this day beares the bell.
These with such other therein dyd excell. (16–22)

This stress on the didactic message of Latin comedy reflects Udall's grounding in the commentaries on Terence by Donatus and Renaissance humanists published with the texts of the plays in sixteenth-century editions. Melanchthon especially emphasized the moral implications in his commentaries, first published in 1525 and reprinted in many later editions, including the influential De Roigny edition published in Paris in 1552 (see chapter 5).[5] The identification of "secretes," "mysteries," and "fore-warnings very rare" in the "vertuous lore" could refer to the intrigue upon which many of Plautus's and Terence's plots depend, but Udall adds that these two authors "with such other therein dyd excell." He does not identify what other authors he has in mind, but in the context of ancient comedy that Udall is considering, the only other extant classical comic dramatists were Menander, whose works were known only in fragments, and Aristophanes, who was recommended by Erasmus to be read before Homer (*Collected Works* 24:669) and who was identified as a model of comedy by Vives (*Opera* 6:364). However, because the earlier part of the prologue had repudiated "scurilitie" (5), a quality particularly associated with Aristophanes, Udall may have deliberately avoided naming the Greek dramatist. Certainly the didactic purpose of the "Comedie . . . Which against the vayne glorious doth inuey" (25), as explained in the last stanza of the prologue, resembles Aristophanic satire more than the intrigue comedies of Plautus and Terence. The identification of Roister Doister's "humour," which "the roysting sort continually doth feede" (26), suggests the dramatic emphasis is on comic exposure rather than the knot of errors characteristic of Latin comedy.[6]

Udall's adoption of the classical five-act, three-part structure, explained by Donatus in his commentary on Terence, has long been recognized by scholars of early Tudor drama. Acts 1 and 2 introduce the principal characters and the principal action, the wooing of Custance, in accordance with the functions of the *protasis*. The division between acts 1 and 2 appears arbitrary, with the first act being approximately twice the length of the second. Act 3 begins the *epitasis*, "the business of the play" according to Ben Jonson, as Roister Doister's suit to Christian Custance and her response are dramatically portrayed.[7] Acts 3 and 4, which are nearly equal in length, are clearly divided at the beginning of the fourth act by the complication that Custance's fidelity may be misperceived. Act 4 ends with Roister Doister's ludicrous attempt to get revenge because Custance spurned him, a climax to the wooing plot that compares to Renaissance commentators' designation of the *summa epitasis* or *catastasis* in Terentian comedy (see Herrick 119–22). Act 5 resolves the complication regarding Custance's virtue and provides reconciliation for the opposing parties, which is the function of the *catastrophe* in Donatus's structural analysis. Latin comedy, as interpreted by Donatus and Renaissance humanists, clearly served as the external model for *Roister Doister*, though as Udall's old schoolmaster at Oxford, Vives, believed, the classics should be regarded not as masters but as guides (*Opera* 6:7). Udall took as his guides in adapting classical materials to a contemporary context not only Plautus and Terence, as has long been recognized, but also Aristophanes, whose influence has been overlooked.

Plautus's *Miles Gloriosus* and Terence's *Eunuchus* have traditionally been perceived to be the sources of *Roister Doister*, yet as Maulsby pointed out at the beginning of this century, Udall's indebtedness to Roman drama has been exaggerated (251–77). Hinton may be right in seeing *Eunuchus* as the essential source of the play *Roister Doister* (273–78), but Terence's popular comedy was more a source of inspiration than a model of imitation for Udall. The motif of an unwanted lover threatening violence after being spurned may owe something to Thraso's response to Thais in *Eunuchus*, but the differences in the circumstances of the two plays are very great. Thais is, of course, a wily prostitute who had entertained the braggart soldier on many occasions, and she rejects him only to protect the girl given her by Thraso after she realizes the girl is in fact freeborn and the sister of a Roman gentleman. When Thraso prepares his attack, he means to recover the girl and punish Thais. Thais's counterpart in *Roister Doister* is an exemplar of feminine virtue whose "courage, charity, and firm materialism" were, Bevington believes, meant to please the newly crowned Mary (*Tudor Drama and Politics* 121–24). Christian Custance, whose name suggests piety and constancy, engages in battle only for sport as she helps to create the liveliest comic scene of the play. In *Eunuchus* the threatened battle does not in fact occur.

The character of Roister Doister may have been suggested by Thraso and may owe something to Plautus's *Miles Gloriosus*, but the braggart soldier was so well-known a comic type that "Thraso" had become an insulting epithet traded by religious polemicists, including Luther and Thomas More (see chapter 8). This familiar stock character of Roman comedy may have merged as early as the sixteenth century with the swaggering heroes of folk drama. Certainly the exploits recounted by St. George and his rivals in the hero-combat texts savor of the type, and in the wooing folk plays the braggart is cast as a wooer, as in *Roister Doister*.[8] Udall may have observed contemporary representations of the bragging suitor before his creation of Roister Doister, and if he is responsible for the short interlude *Thersites*, as some scholars believe (see M. Axton, *Three Tudor Classical Interludes* 2, 5–10), he had previously drawn a caricature of the cowardly braggart. However, the most distinctive aspect of Roister Doister's character is his image as a mock-hero of chivalric romance who is compared to "Sir *Launcelot du lake*" and "greate *Guy* of Warwike" (I.ii.188–89) as well as to classical and biblical heroes. In his role as the lovesick knight, he recalls Chaucer's Troilus, as Plumstead notes ("Satirical Parody" 142), but the parody also pokes fun at contemporary sonneteers who had rediscovered Petrarch's love poems. Roister Doister is a complex portrait created from both ancient and contemporary sources.

Matthew Merrygreek has traditionally been linked to Gnatho, the parasite in *Eunuchus*, whose name like Thraso's had become generic for his character type. In his introductory soliloquy, Merrygreek identifies himself as a parasite who lives off "Lewis Loytrer," "Watkin Waster," "Dauy Diceplayer, " and other such idlers, but his "chiefe banker, / Both for meate and money, and [his] chiefe shootanker" (I.i.19–30) is Roister Doister. He thus establishes his relationship with his host as a parasitical one. Yet as the play proceeds, his manipulation of Roister Doister more closely resembles the role of the witty slave of Roman comedy than the parasite. His energy and propensity for mischief may suggest the vice of the morality, but he lacks sinister intent. His motivation is sport, and like the comic servants of the cycle plays he promotes laughter at the expense of fools. His essential relationship to Roister Doister is that of guller to gull, and the effect of his words and actions is to expose the folly of his host. In the words of the prologue, he "feeds" the "humour" of Roister Doister, thus fulfilling the play's purpose: "against the vayne glorious [to] inuey" (25). This role as an instrument of satire may be inspired by Aristophanes, whose works along with Terence's were popular sellers in Oxford in 1520, when Udall was an undergraduate there, according to sales records of John Dorne (Lancashire, *Dramatic Texts and Records* xxiv). The name Merrygreek, usually glossed simply as "merry fellow" though "a Greek" also meant a "cheat" or "sharper" (OED), may allude to the Aristophanic connection, for Merrygreek is indeed more Greek than Roman.

An examination of the action of the play reveals that Aristophanic comic exaggeration in fact prevails over Terentian intrigue. The precedent for misinterpreting Christian Custance's loyalty may be found in Terence, where misunderstandings of actions and characters' identities are often the foundations of the plots, but in *Roister Doister* this misapprehension is introduced only at the beginning of act 4 and is quickly resolved in act 5. It becomes hardly more than a momentary consideration as the play focuses on Roister Doister's gulling.[9] Gulling is, of course, a motif in Roman comedy, as the witty slave in aiding his young master misleads and diverts the hard fathers, grasping pimps, and foolish rivals. However, when Syrus misdirects Demea and ironically praises his "well-beloved" son, Ctesipho, in *The Brothers*, or when Gnatho flatters Thraso in *Eunuchus*, these actions are but means to an end, which is the triumph of youthful desire over constraining or blocking forces. Gulling is, however, often a primary action in folk tales and folk drama as well as in farce. Perusal of Chaucer's *Canterbury Tales*, the chapbooks of "merry tales" associated with Tarlton, and farces such as *Johan Johan* (see chapter 18), reveals how pervasive and how central gulling as a comic motif is in popular entertainment in late medieval and early Renaissance England. Many native literary and dramatic precedents of gulling plots were available to Udall, but most were more comic than satiric. Aristophanes, on the other hand, offered a model of a satiric structure that often depended on gulling and that also employed the mode of burlesque. Aristophanes's fools—Strepsiades, justifiably beaten by his son with his newly learned logic in *The Clouds*, or Cinesias, teased by his sex-striking wife in *Lysistrata*—are comic butts, but, most important, they demonstrate the satiric point of the action. The satiric design coupled with the burlesque mode, which distinguishes Udall's gulling plot from both Roman and contemporary precedents, could have been found in Aristophanes.

The didactic purpose—inveighing against the vainglorious—expressed in the prologue to *Roister Doister* determines the design of the play. The character of Roister Doister is described by Merrygreek in his opening monologue as the image of vainglory in the realms of both combat and love, for not only is Roister Doister a cowardly boaster as a swordsman, but also he believes that any woman who looks at him must love him. Merrygreek then explains how easily he can manipulate Roister Doister. The play thus opens with an exposition of the roles of Roister Doister as an object of ridicule and Merrygreek as the ridiculer.

However, Roister Doister's first words indicate another dimension as he declares, "Come death when thou wilt, I am weary of my life" (I.ii.71). This melancholic association of death with love, anticipated in Merrygreek's description of Roister Doister's despair if his love is not returned, introduces the burlesque treatment of the lover that prevails throughout the play. Merrygreek's later identification of Roister Doister with "Sir *Launcelot du lake*" and the "tenth Worthie" (I.ii.188, 196) is extended into a parody of the hero of the popular romances. After purposely mistaking the old toothless Madge Mumblecrust as Roister Doister's new love, Merrygreek contends that Roister Doister

> killed the blewe Spider in Blanchepouder lande.
> . . . .
> ... he bet the king of Crickets on Christmasse day,
> . . . .
> he wrong a club
> Once in a fray out of the hande of Belzebub.
> . . . .
> ... He conquered in one day from *Rome*, to *Naples*.
> (I.iv.471–88)

This iteration of Roister Doister's imaginary feats is significantly similar to the boasts of St. George and other combatants in the folk drama texts collected in the last two centuries.[10] Whether the sixteenth century versions of the folk plays burlesqued popular romance and provided a model for Udall is not known.

The burlesque spirit becomes more fully developed in *Roister Doister* as the action proceeds. After Roister Doister's tokens of love are refused by Christian Custance, Merrygreek reports that she has called Roister Doister "such a calfe, such an asse, such a blocke" (III.iii.900) that Roister Doister determines to "go home and die" (931). This prompts the most extensive parody of the play, as Merrygreek takes Roister Doister at his word and proceeds with the death service. Scholars have suggested several possible sources for the mock funeral here, including Skelton's *Philip Sparrow* and the poem "On the Death of the Duke of Suffolk, May 3, 1450," in which parts of the service are put in the mouths of Henry VI's courtiers (*Udall's Roister Doister*, ed. Scheurweghs lxx); but it appears that once again the precedent in Aristophanes has been overlooked. At the end of the *agon* in *Lysistrata*, Lysistrata, furious with the Magistrate whom she has been debating, tells him " 'tis time [you] were dead . . . an urn shall be bought," and she will bake him a funeral cake. Her attendant women offer fillets to wear and a chaplet for his hair, and the metaphor continues with Lysistrata shouting, "What are you waiting for? / Charon is staying, delaying his crew, / Charon is calling and bawling for you" (Aristophanes, *Works*, 3:63). This does not, of course, reenact a funeral service in detail, but it employs in parodic form several elements associated with the rites of death in the ancient Greek world.

The death service is elaborated in *Roister Doister*, but the comic exaggeration is Aristophanic. The mock requiem printed at the end of the extant text of the play appears to have been inserted at different points in the dialogue in performance so that the lines of the Catholic rites, accompanied by Merrygreek's sermonizing, are occasionally interrupted by conversations between Merrygreek and Roister Doister for comic effect. Following Merrygreek's recitation of the *Psalmodie*, praying for Christ's mercy and expressing woman's cruelty, Roister Doister moans, "Heigh how, alas, the pangs of death my hearte do breake." Merrygreek rebukes him, "Holde your peace for shame sir, a dead man may not speake," and then continues, "*Nequando*: What mourners and what torches shall we haue?" (III.iii.938–40). The service proceeds with an alternation of solemn ritual and impromptu intrusions that break the illusion of the funeral.[11] When Roister Doister responds, "None," to the above question, Merrygreek intones:

> *Dirige*: He will go darklyng to his graue, —
> *Neque lux, neque crux, neque* mourners, *neque* clinke,
> He will steale to heauen, vnknowing to God I thinke.
> *A porta inferi*, who shall your goodes possesse?
> (III.iii.941–44)

The effect of this elaborate burlesque, which concludes with the peal of bells, is to satirize the lover, whose metaphor of "dying for love" is acted out literally. The Catholic rites are not themselves satirized, as E. S. Miller notes ("Roister Doister's 'Funeralls' " 56–57); Udall merely uses them as a means to ridicule the posturing lover, further elaborated in Roister Doister's mispunctuated letter.

This letter, an example of ambiguity in Wilson's *Rule of Reason* and a precedent for the mechanicals' mispunctuated prologue to their Pyramus and Thisbe play in *Midsummer Night's Dream*, inverts a well-established convention of love. Dependence on a scrivener to provide an expression of love indicates not only Roister Doister's vacuous mind but also the emptiness of the convention. Whether Roister Doister is responsible for mispunctuating the love letter as he copied it or whether Merrygreek purposely misreads it—and evidence in the play supports both interpretations[12]—the letter when read to Custance turns compliment into insult and promises misery rather than joy in marriage:

> If ye mynde to bee my wyfe,
> Ye shall be assured for the tyme of my lyfe,
> I will keepe ye ryght well, from good rayment and fare,
> Ye shall not be kepte but in sorowe and care.
> Ye shall in no wyse lyue at your owne libertie,
> Doe and say what ye lust, ye shall neuer please me,
> But when ye are mery, I will be all sadde,
> When ye are sory, I will be very gladde.
> When ye seeke your heartes ease, I will be vnkinde,
> At no tyme, in me shall ye muche gentlenesse finde.
> (III.iv.1080–98)

The lover's honey-tongued promises of marital bliss become a warning against marriage. The mockery of the letter is interpreted by Custance to be directed against her, though in the context it is the wooer Roister Doister rather than the wooed who is mocked, as well as the love convention he is representing. Roister Doister's response to Custance's angry dismissal of his suit is to weep, and another convention — that of the unrequited lover — is ridiculed, but it is Roister Doister's secondary response, revenge prompted by Merrygreek, that provides the burlesque climax for the vainglorious lover.

Dame Custance and the audience are prepared for the burlesque battle by Merrygreek, who insists that all is done in "mockage" for "pastance" and "sport" (IV.vi.1573–89), and as a result Custance joins with Merrygreek in Roister Doister's final exposure. She initially flees in supposed terror when Roister Doister approaches in battle array, which prompts a manifestation of hubris, but when she returns with her household of women ready for the fight, Roister Doister's true colors are shown. The scene quickly turns into a battle of the sexes as Roister Doister, decked out with a cooking pot for a helmet, is urged on by Merrygreek, who purposely misdirects his blows on Roister Doister's head. Roister Doister and his men ignominiously flee before the courageous women in a farcical display of male cowardice. Now this resembles more the confrontation of old men and old women in Aristophanes's *Lysistratra* than the defeat of Thraso in Terence's *Eunuchus*, for Thraso leaves the field without doing battle. In *Lysistrata* the boasting chorus of old men threaten the old women with torches, but they are quickly dispersed when the women extinguish the men's phallic torches as well as their courage. This confrontation between the male and female halves of the chorus reduces the conflict between the sexes to absurdity and foreshadows the feminine victory at the end of the play. In *Roister Doister* the burlesque battle makes the vainglorious lover even more ludicrous, as it demonstrates the independence and courage of Christian Custance. As in *Lysistrata*, the burlesque action compliments women at the expense of the men, a judgment not to be missed by the newly crowned Mary, England's first ruling queen, or by her sister Elizabeth, if indeed the licensing of the play in 1566–67 signaled a royal revival.

The reconciliation that follows Roister Doister's comic exposure may be comparable to the typical endings of Terence's comedies, but in spirit it is more like the conclusion of *Respublica. Eunuchus*, Udall's supposed source, ends with a cynical accommodation of Thraso's fleshly appetites as Phaedria agrees to share Thais's favors with his rival. However, in Udall's play the chastened but not changed Roister Doister seeks to salvage his honor in a Falstaffian manner, as he pleads courtesy rather than instinct as the source of his cowardice: "By the aunciently lawe of armes, a man / Hath no honour to foile his handes on a woman" (V.vi.1974–75). He is then invited to sup by his rival Gawin Goodluck, and he joins his new-made friends in song. The serious threat to Custance's reputation is quickly dismissed as forgiveness and good fellowship prevail in the spirit of Misericordia, who directs the resolution of *Respublica*, and in the spirit most appropriate for the festive occasion on which *Roister Doister* was first performed. The prayer for the queen and the "commontie" with which the play ends may indicate the presence of the queen at the performance, and the appeal that "God graunt hir as she doth, the Gospell to protect, / Learning and vertue to aduaunce, and vice to correct" (V.vi.1999–2000) echoes the role of Nemesis (symbolizing Queen Mary) at the end of *Respublica*.

Regardless of how one might feel about the militant Protestant Udall's accommodation to the new Catholic reign, one must remember Mary's role in translating Erasmus's *Paraphrase* of the gospel John under the direction of Udall in the late 1540s. This may be a gentle reminder by Udall of their earlier association as well as an appeal to be prudent and judicious, which is also the message of *Respublica* (see chapter 14). If the play were revived for Elizabeth, the advice would be appropriate to her as well, for like Mary she was perceived as "the protector of the faith," though that faith had changed, and the other royal missions to advance learning and virtue and to correct vice would be as much her responsibility as queen as it was Mary's.

In either case the play provides a message along with the entertainment as the prologue promises, but in merging profit and delight in accord with Horace's advice, Udall developed a structural satire "against the vayne glorious" that may owe more to Aristophanes than was earlier realized. Udall's adoption of the burlesque mode in his integration of native elements with classical models anticipated the major traditions of Elizabethan comedy, for both Shakespeare's romantic parody and Jonson's humour comedies developed motifs explored by Udall. *Roister Doister* is a more innovative experiment in comic form than its conventional designation as "the first regular English comedy" suggests.

CHAPTER TWENTY

GAMMER GURTON'S NEEDLE

*G*AMMER *Gurton's Needle*, traditionally identified like *Roister Doister* as one of the first "regular" comedies in English, apparently because of its five-act structure, is also an early example of vernacular college comedy.[1] Published by Thomas Colwell in 1575, his last year as a London printer, the play is identified on the title page as "A Ryght Pithy, Pleasaunt and merie Comedie . . . played on Stage, not longe ago in Christes Colledge in Cambridge." However, because the border on the title page is the same as that for Thomas Ingelend's *Disobedient Child*, printed by Colwell in 1560 in his first year as an independent printer (McKerrow 74), and because the border does not appear on any extant printings by Colwell in the latter years of his career, it appears likely that at least the title page of the play was set in print much earlier than its publication date of 1575. An entry in the Stationers Register in 1562–63 licensing Colwell to print a play entitled *DYCCON of Bedlam &c* may indicate Colwell's intent to publish the play under an earlier title. The title "*Gammer gur / tons Nedle*" is in a smaller italic typeface than the words preceding and following it on the title page, suggesting, as Henry Bradley argues, the change in title after the page had been set. "Dyccon of / Bedlam" would have fit more neatly into the space, and the division of the line would have been less awkward than the later title (Gayley 1:199). In the same smaller italic type, the lines "Colledge in Cambridge / Made by Mr. S. Mr. of Art" appear directly after "Christes," indicating that these lines were added at the same time as the revised title. The implication is that the original printing was delayed and the identification of the author was purposely avoided.

The first allusion to the author of the play appears in the first of the "Martin Marprelate" tracts in 1588, addressed to John Bridges, a student at Pembroke College, Cambridge, in the 1550s who had become Dean of Salisbury in 1577. The pamphleteer alludes to the interlude as Bridges's "first book" but then disputes the authorship because of Bridges's lack of "witte and invention." Two further allusions in the second Marprelate pamphlet imply Bridges's association with the play, but neither confirms his authorship (Gayley 1:200). Joseph Hunter in 1848 first noted the attribution to Bridges, and his argument is endorsed by F. S. Boas (*University Drama* 82–87). However, Bridges had no connection with Christ's College, where the title page indicates the play was performed, and his name does not begin with "S." Bishop John Still, a Master of Arts from Christ's, was put forward as the author in 1782 by Isaac Reed, but no modern scholars have accepted this attribution.

The candidate favored by most critics in the twentieth century is William Stevenson, who matriculated at Christ's in 1546, proceeded to the B.A. in 1549–50, to the M.A. in 1553, and the B.D. in 1560. A fellow in the college from 1551 to 1554 and reinstated in 1559–60, apparently after his fellowship was withdrawn during Mary's reign (Gayley 1:198–99), Stevenson is identified in the Christ's College accounts as being involved with the production of plays during his fellowship. The first reference, in 1550–51, is to "Sir Stephenson . . . his play," and in 1551–52 "S. Stephenson play" appears.[2] Also according to the college accounts for 1551–52, a carpenter was paid for removing the tables in the hall and "setting y^{em} vp agein. Wth ye houses & other things," in connection with the "S. Stephenson play" (Moore Smith 28), which suggests a playing area was prepared with a somewhat representational set. Accounts for Trinity and Corpus Christi indicate "makyng houses" for other productions, so the practice appears not to be unusual. References to "Sir Stephenson . . . his plaie" or "plaies" recur in 1552–53 and Christmas 1553; then after a lapse of six years, in 1559–60 a final reference is made to "Mr. Stevensonnes play" in Christ's College accounts. It is not clear whether the references are to a single play that is repeated in successive years or whether the references are to different plays. The one reference to "plaies" in 1552–53 may indicate more than one play associated with Stevenson was performed that year, or the final "*s*" may be a scribal error.

Further, it is not clear whether Stevenson was the author of the play or plays with which he is identified or merely responsible for the production in his role as a fellow. A few entries in the accounts list authors and the titles of their plays, such as "N. Udall's *Ezechias*" at King's August 8, 1564; but productions of other plays, particularly classical ones, are often listed with names of members of the colleges, suggesting their responsibility for production. Most entries simply list individuals' names with generic terms such as play, ludus, comedy, or show; titles of plays except for Latin and Greek productions are generally omitted. Neither the title *Gammer Gurton's Needle* nor the possible earlier title *Dyccon of Bedlam* appears in the college records, and there are no contemporary associations of William Stevenson with the play. Stevenson, however, is the only name beginning with *S* that appears in Christ's College accounts related to drama for some twenty-five years before the play's publication in 1575; he may, therefore, be the most likely candidate even though there is no irrefutable evidence of his composition of any plays during his lifetime.[3] Curiously the play appeared in print in the same year that Stevenson died. If Stevenson were the author the delay in publication after entry in the Stationers' Register might be explained by the potential embarrassment to Stevenson who was appointed as prebendary of Durham in January 1560–61. His death would remove the impediment, though respect for his memory might dictate avoiding a clear identification.

The circumstances of the composition and performance of *Gammer Gurton's Needle* remain a mystery. That the play was presented "on Stage, not longe ago in Christes Colledge in Cambridge," as the title page indicates, appears reasonable, but just how "longe ago" and how many times before publication in 1575 we do not know. That this play, from among the vernacular comedies being produced at the universities during the third quarter of the sixteenth century, was selected for publication attests to its success in performance, and the many references to the play in the years that followed indicate its appeal to a larger reading public.

Written for and performed by boys in their late teens, *Gammer Gurton's Needle* adapts the conventions of classical Latin drama to the contemporary world as it exploits the perennial undergraduate interests in drinking, scatalogy, name-calling, mischief, and horseplay. Compared to *Roister Doister*, which, grounded in the Latin comedies of Plautus and Terence, parodies conventions of the romance in the manner of Aristophanes (see chapter 19), *Gammer Gurton's Needle* depends far less on classical models, as it draws on the popular traditions of the farce, the jestbook, and the morality play. More concerned with entertainment than the moral instruction offered by the paradigm of the prodigal or the allegory of the contemporary educational interludes, *Gammer* provides critical insight into human nature as well as a barbed thrust at the corrupt cleric. That theme was represented as well in the Cambridge prodigal play *Misogonus*, which survives in a manuscript dated 1577, but, like *Gammer Gurton's Needle*, it may have been written and performed several years earlier (see chapter 10).

Set in a rural village similar to many that surrounded Cambridge in the sixteenth century, the play may be linked to the nearby village of Girton, as John Robinson suggests ("Art and Meaning" 50–51). The atmosphere of the village created in the play may result from the author's direct observation, but it also recalls images of village life represented in the popular jestbooks of the time. Generic types rather than individualized characters are portrayed from the perspective of a bemused outsider, who appeals to the superiority of his audience observing the antics of the rural folk. The mood remains good-humored and the laughter unmalicious in its treatment of the rustics; only the physical abuse of the self-important cleric smacks of sadistic delight.

Diccon the Bedlam provides an introduction to the village and a controlling perspective for judging its characters. Functioning as a presenter of the play as well as the engineer of the plot, he takes the audience into his confidence as he self-consciously identifies his role. After demonstrating his ability as a con man by exposing Hodges's superstition and cowardice in "conjuring up" the devil, Diccon indicates he will extend his activity as he challenges the audience to approve his sport:

> A man I thyncke myght make a playe
> And nede no worde to this they saye
> Being but halfe a Clark.
> Softe, let me alone, I will take the charge
> This matter further to enlarge
> Within a tyme shorte,
> If ye will marke my toyes, and note
> I will geue ye leaue to cut my throte
> If I make not good sporte. (II.ii.10–18)[4]

Diccon then begins the series of lies that provokes the conflict between Gammer Gurton and Dame Chat, upon which the plot depends. Like the jestbook Skelton or Skogan, Diccon practices deceit not simply for personal gain but also for the joy of the game as he appeals to his victims' baser instincts as well as their naiveté.

Compared to Matthew Merrygreek, who combines the roles of parasite, guller, and vice as he focuses on exposing the manifestations of Roister Doister's vainglory, Diccon demonstrates a parasitical nature and vicelike mischievousness, made more immediate by his identification as a bedlam, as he gulls most of the characters in the play. A former inmate of Bethlehem Hospital for the mentally ill, Diccon is a wandering beggar who supplements the charity of others by stealing and deception. A contemporary type, and like the jestbook trickster a perennial outsider, he has developed his insight into human nature through observation. Diccon indicates his extensive experience when he first appears on stage:

> Many a mile have I walked, divers and sundry waies
> And many a good mans house haue I bin at in my daies
> Many a gossips cup in my tyme have I tasted. (I.i.1–3)

His subsequent description of the "howlynge and scowlyng," "whewling and pewling," and "Syghing and sobbing" in Gammer's household leads him to conclude that "the folkes be not well in theyr wyts" (11–18). This judgement—from a certified zany who may wear the badge of the madman on his cloak[5]—is the first of several ironic truths that he utters, and like Henry VIII's wise fool, Will Summer, whom the parasite-vice Cacurgus in the contemporary *Misogonus* recalls (II.3), Diccon proves to be mentally superior to those regarded as sane. Edgar adopts a similar role when he becomes Tom o' Bedlam in *King Lear*. Diccon's parasitical nature is thus overlaid with native and contemporary associations that complicate and extend his role.

Another dimension to his part in the play is the particular form Diccon's manipulation of others takes. When Diccon takes charge of the plot, he promises "good sporte" (II.ii.18), and after setting up Gammer and Chat for a confrontation, he reiterates his promise of sport before directing the musicians to "pype upp [their] fiddles" (II.v.8–11). The sport results from reported accusations of neighbors in the manner of the *badin* in the French *Farce du raporteur*. As B. J. Whiting pointed out some forty years ago, the *badin* typically foments trouble between characters, like Diccon, setting several people at odds by reporting false accusations out of a supposed sense of friendship before being exposed in the end (31–40).[6] The deception in *Gammer* is however essentially free of sexual innuendo, unlike the farce, and it is more elaborate as well; the character of Diccon is more fully developed than his French counterpart. Nevertheless, Diccon's action smacks of the kind of situation out of which French farces were made; contemporary French farce may have offered some inspiration if not the plot of *Gammer Gurton's Needle*. Yet any French influence, like the Roman influence of the manipulating parasite, is rather thoroughly anglicized, and the action goes beyond the promised sport as a satiric edge emerges in the course of the play.

Diccon's exploitation of human weakness and pretension may provoke the promised mirth, but it also leads the audience to look down in scorn at the victims of Diccon's deception. Hodge, the first and the simplest object of derisive laughter in the play, introduces the satiric modus operandi. Appearing first as a simple rustic, Hodge functions as the expositor of the source of the "howlynge and scowlyng" that Diccon had earlier described. He also establishes the mock-serious tone upon which the comedy depends. Perceiving Tome Tannkard's cow "flynging about his halfe aker fysking with her taile, / As though there had ben in her ars a swarme of Bees," to be a portent of some dire event, such as the robbery of Gammer's poultry or the gelding of her cat (I.ii.32–38), Hodge prepares for Gammer's exaggerated reaction to the loss of her needle: "She is vndone she sayth (alas,) her ioye and life is gone / If shee here not of some comfort, she is sayth but dead" (I.iii.16–17). The subsequent narration of Hodge mistaking the cat's eyes for sparks and his fearful warning that Gyb will burn down the house with the fire in her tail confirm his rustic simplicity, and he quickly becomes the butt of the scatalogical comedy that pervades the play. After examining a stinking cat turd in his search for the needle, Hodge soils his breeches in fear when he believes Diccon is conjuring up the devil. Playing on Hodge's earlier expressed superstitious nature, Diccon exposes Hodge's cowardice as well. Hodge's role as a country fool appears to be taken from contemporary popular traditions, though qualities of the classical *miles gloriosus* are demonstrated in his confrontation with Dame Chat. Even more cowardly than Roister Doister's rout at the house of Christian Custance, Hodge's fearful failure to come to Gammer's aid makes his pretensions to bravery particularly ignominious as his comic role moves into the realm of satire.

The women, Gammer Gurton and Dame Chat, have no antecedents in Roman drama, though French farce and fabliaux as well as native popular traditions abound in such independent comic figures as the Wakefield Noah's wife or Chaucer's Wife of Bath. The characters of Gammer and Dame Chat are not very fully developed, but their comic dimensions would have been enhanced by boys playing their parts. Gammer is little more than a foolish housewife who places a ridiculously high value on a tiny household tool, and Dame Chat is an alehouse keeper quick to protect her name and her property. Both are gullible victims of Diccon's manipulation because of their basic mistrust of each other. They are an even match in name-calling, but the younger Dame Chat has the advantage in the physical bout. This farcical confrontation of middle-aged matrons is punctuated by Hodge shouting encouragement as he cowers on the sidelines. Like the comic altercation of Mrs. Gogan and Bessie Burgess in O'Casey's *The Plough and the Stars*, Gammer's and Dame Chat's exchange of verbal and physical abuse intensifies their conflict as it demonstrates their foolishness. Though Diccon is not on hand to witness it, his exploitation of human weakness produces the mirth he had promised.

However, it is in the final trick, on Dr. Rat, the Curate, that the comedy becomes most savagely satiric. The lazy, boozing cleric, long an object of satire in Continental and English literary and popular traditions, is incidentally castigated in the character of the drunken priest who ignores his duties to join the prodigal in lechery and gambling in the contemporary *Misogonus*. The anticlerical attitude of both plays smacks of the Reformation zeal of Edward VI's reign, and the allusion in *Gammer* to the "kings name" (V.ii.236) supports a composition date before the reigns of either Elizabeth or Mary (Gayley 1:198n; Tydeman 211–12). Dr. Rat's image of the self-serving local priest provokes the harshest treatment of all of Diccon's victims. Though introduced as a means of resolving the conflict between Gammer Gurton and Dame Chat and described initially as "a man estemed wise" (III.iii.59), he is found at "hob filchers house" with "A cup of ale . . . in his hand" (III.iv.26–27); and when he appears, he complains that he has been called away before he had time to finish his two pots of ale. Dr. Rat's preoccupation with ale is further emphasized by his promise to give Diccon a pot of the "best ale in the towne" if he finds the lost needle (IV.ii.133) and by his agreement at the end to share a pot of ale with Diccon as a mark of their amity (V.ii.274–77).

Dr. Rat's name may be derived from his office, with *rat* a pun on *curate* (Kozikowski 16), but it may also hint of a French source for the incident. *Rat* is the same word in both French and English, but *chat*, of course, is the French word for cat, and it is Dame Chat who catches Dr. Rat creeping through the hole to her house. Though the priest is angry at the affront to his dignity and to his head, Master Baily declares he deserved the beating as well as "the stockes" for his ignorance: "To come in on the backe side, when ye might go about, / I know non such, vnles they long to haue their braines knockt out" (V.i.28–30). The religious authority first thought to be wise proves to be a fool; rather than resolving the problem, he is as readily deceived as the other villagers, and he must appeal to Master Baily, the secular power, to discover the source of the confusion.

Master Baily, like his namesake, Chaucer's Host in *The Canterbury Tales*, serves as a peacemaker, but his position more closely resembles that of the morality-play God by revealing the truth and dispensing justice. Because he steps in when the religious authority fails and because he imposes his judgment on the priest as well as the people, his role undercuts that of the clergy. He resolves the plot by uncovering Diccon's deceptions, which exposes the gullibility of his victims; but he does not recover the lost needle that initiated Diccon's lies. Refusing to be a conventional moral arbiter, Baily ignores the cleric's demands that Diccon be placed in fetters and sent to the gallows; instead Baily reminds Rat that he should "teach vs to forgeve" (V.ii.256). The impudent Diccon, after admitting his manipulations, is forgiven and is directed to swear a comic oath on Hodge's breeches, which fortuitously turns up the lost needle. Master Baily thus reconciles the gulls and guller and prompts the conclusion of the action. This secularizing of the resolving force, which operates ironically rather than moralistically, is a major departure from the didactic dramas of the time and anticipates the roles of Justice Clement in Jonson's *Every Man in His Humour* and Lovewit in *The Alchemist*.

This transformation of a religious function to the secular realm is one of the most subtle aspects of *Gammer Gurton's Needle*, but perhaps even more significant is the adaptation of the ancient Roman comic structure to the contemporary English world of the play. Observing the classical unities of time, place, and action, the play is divided into the five-act, three-part Donatian structure that was perceived by commentators in Terence's comedies and that by the middle of the sixteenth century had begun to be emulated in plays produced at court and in schools, such as *Respublica* and *Roister Doister* (see chapters 14 and 19). The *protasis* is clearly divided into two parts: Act 1 expresses the reactions to the loss of Gammer's needle, from which the action in the play develops, and introduces three of the principal characters, Diccon, Hodge, and Gammer; in act 2, after a break marked by a song celebrating ale, a fourth member of the cast, Dame Chat, appears, and the plot is launched by Diccon, who, after gulling Hodge, sows dissension among the neighbors. Again after a musical interlude, the second part of the Donatian division, the *epitasis*, gets underway in act 3. The altercation between Gammer Gurton and Dame Chat climaxes Diccon's plot, and a possible solution is signaled by the introduction of the curate as a potential arbiter. Act 4, which begins without a musical interruption, represents a second climax as Dr. Rat rather than resolving the problem becomes involved in it. Renaissance commentators on Terence regarded this kind of further complication to be the *catastasis* or *summa epitasis* of the play (Herrick 119–22). Ben Jonson follows a similar pattern with Bonario in *Volpone* and Surly in *The Alchemist*, characters who seek to reveal the games of the deceivers but are caught up in the deception as the exposure is postponed. Together acts 3 and 4, which number 347 lines, only 22 lines more than act 2 and 24 lines less than act 5, make up "the busie part of the play," as Ben Jonson later termed the *epitasis*.[7] Act 5 portrays the last major division, the *catastrophe*, where, as in Roman comedy, the errors are exposed and the truth is revealed. The resolution of the conflict as Diccon's part is uncovered is skillfully integrated with the discovery of the lost needle, which parodies the Roman comic ending in which a lost child is identified and reunited with a parent, a motif used also in the contemporary *Misogonus* (see chapter 10). The final invitation to drink, recalling the festive ending of contemporary court entertainment, is combined with the traditional Roman appeal for applause.

    The formal structure perceived in Terence's comedies by Donatus and Renaissance commentators and generally taught in the grammar schools from at least the 1520s onward (see chapter 5) must have been reinforced in the university. The record of classical productions at Cambridge, beginning in 1510–11 with a Terentian comedy, continues well beyond 1575, the publication date of *Gammer Gurton's Needle*, and includes a high proportion of Roman comedies, especially Terence, as well as *Acolastus* and other contemporary plays emulating classical structure (see Moore Smith 50–61). This inevitable reinforcement of earlier teachings about dramatic structure must have led Stevenson, or whoever was responsible for *Gammer*, to construct the comedy in the manner of the ancients not only in its external division but also in its internal relationship between parts. As Donatus notes in his commentaries, Terence's plots are typically based on a "knot of errors"; sometimes they result from misapprehension, sometimes from ignorance, but very often from deception perpetrated by a lusting son or a cunning slave, as in *Eunuchus* and *Adelphi*, where the errors are further complicated by a double plot. The cause-effect relationship between events in Terence's plays establishes a close continuity and an organic unity that was noted and admired by later commentators (see chapter 5). *Gammer* is constructed in a similar fashion as a knot of errors is perpetrated by Diccon, who first deceives Hodge about conjuring up the devil and then uses his false report of the devil's words as the basis for deceiving both Hodge and Gammer about the loss of the needle. The misapprehension implanted in the minds of both Dame Chat and Dr. Rat complicates the errors already evident, as Diccon presides over a continuity of deception. The plot is a model of organic unity as the machinations of Diccon exploit the mundane loss of the needle, which ironically is found by accident.

The pattern of deception may resemble the Terentian plot, but the motivation for it is significantly different. Diccon is not prompted by lust or avarice, the typical motives for error or deception in Roman comedy. Rather Diccon's delight in mischief, which recalls the morality-play vice and the French *badin* as well as the jestbook Skelton, is particularly adapted to the college audience who would delight in the knockabout farce that the errors provoke. Diccon's "good sporte," which exposes the superstition, cowardice, and gullibility of the rustics as well as the ignorant self-importance of the cleric, ends in laughter and good fellowship.

The final discovery of the lost needle pricking the arse of Hodge, followed by Gammer's invitation to go in and drink, fittingly concludes the scatalogical humor and bibulous spirit of this comedy singularly suited to undergraduate taste. Fortunately the printing of the play extended its life beyond that of the usual college entertainment.[8] Whether the play directly influenced the drama that followed is difficult to assess, but it clearly offered a model of the integration of classical form with contemporary popular motifs. Whether Ben Jonson found in Master Baily the model for his ironic resolvers or found in act 4 the pattern for his *catastases*, or whether Shakespeare was inspired by Diccon in his image of Tom o' Bedlam cannot be finally determined. More important, *Gammer Gurton's Needle* demonstrates for later generations of playwrights the domestication of formal comedy that ingeniously incorporates satire with entertainment.

PART FIVE

THE EMERGENCE OF TRAGEDY

CHAPTER TWENTY-ONE

WATSON'S *ABSALOM*

*T*RAGEDY as a dramatic form made its debut in England in an academic setting. Though given less attention in the schools than comedy, tragedy was recommended for study by Erasmus, Vives, and Melanchthon, for much the same reasons as comedy: to inculcate virtue and to promote eloquence. Melanchthon, succinctly expressing the humanists' view, declares, "The reading of tragedies is thoroughly beneficial to young persons, both for preparing their minds for the numerous duties that life brings and the control of immoderate desires and for giving them some training in eloquence" (quoted in McFarlane 200). On the other hand, Thomas Elyot, believing comedies to be more appropriate to youth, urged that tragedies be read "when a man is come to mature years" and "reason is confirmed with serious learning and long experience" (*The governor* 33). This view may explain why tragedy was more widely studied in the universities than in the secondary schools. The Latin plays of Seneca and the two plays of Euripides that were translated into Latin by Erasmus, *Iphigenia at Aulis* and *Hecuba*, appear to have been most widely read because they were the most accessible, though other plays by Euripides as well as plays by Sophocles are occasionally mentioned. Comedies were more frequently performed by students than were tragedies, but by the middle third of the sixteenth century references to tragedies begin to appear in performance accounts, and by the early 1540s the composition of tragedy had begun in England.

The first reference to the performance of a tragedy at Cambridge

University appears in the accounts for Christ's College in 1537–38 (Moore Smith 50), but no title is given and no indication is made as to whether the play was classical or contemporary. At about the same time at St. John's, Cambridge, according to Roger Ascham, Thomas Watson was writing a Latin tragedy about Absalom (139), and his student, John Christopherson, had by 1544 completed the tragedy of Jephthah in both Greek and Latin. Though *Absalom* and *Jephthah* appear to have been designed for performance by students, no proof of their production exists, and neither play was published until the twentieth century. Based on well-known stories from the Bible, these two academic tragedies reflect the growing popularity of scriptural drama after the Reformation. Between 1536 and 1556 more than sixty plays devoted to biblical subjects were composed in Latin and "scores of vernacular imitations" followed (Blackburn 79).

Martin Luther, who noted the makings of tragedy in the story of Judith, appeared to fellow reformers to have given approval to biblical drama (Roston 52), and such authors as John Bale and John Foxe dramatized scriptural subjects to promote the Protestant cause. Nicholas Grimald, though not as propagandistic as Bale or Foxe, also made drama the medium for conveying the Protestant interpretation in his plays on the resurrection of Christ and the martyrdom of John the Baptist; Martin Bucer, a leader of the reformers at Cambridge, recommended to the young King Edward that drama drawn from the Bible be developed to promote piety and the "amendment of character" (quoted in Wickham, *Early English Stages* 2.1:330). While biblical drama may be generally associated with the Protestant cause, the first biblical tragedies in England were written by avowed Catholics who were awarded bishoprics by Mary and imprisoned under Elizabeth for their refusal to endorse the Act of Uniformity. Their plays also remained in manuscript while those of their Protestant contemporaries were published. Whether the religious positions of their authors contributed to the neglect of *Absalom* and *Jephthah* in the sixteenth century may never be known, but these earliest extant tragedies to be composed in England differ markedly from the biblical dramas of the reformers.

More closely following the models established for tragedy—Seneca and Euripides—than did the English Protestant playwrights, Watson and Christopherson are comparable to the Scot George Buchanan, who in the early 1540s wrote neoclassical tragedies for his students at the College of Guyenne in Bordeaux. Linking Watson's *Absalom* with Buchanan's version of the Jephthah story, Ascham declares these are the only contemporary tragedies that "abyde the trew touch of *Aristotles* preceptes, and *Euripides* examples" (139). A colleague of Watson's at St. John's, Ascham also describes the "pleasant talks" with Master Cheke and Watson in which they applied Aristotelian and Horatian principles to the tragedies of Euripides, Sophocles, and Seneca. This implies a strong critical awareness at St. John's (where Christopherson was also educated) that we might expect to see reflected in Watson's and Christopherson's plays. However, in a disdainful comment on a contemporary writer of tragedy at Cambridge—"well liked of many, but best liked of him selfe," who began "the *Protasis*" with a verse form rarely found in tragedy and then used only in the "Epitasi whan the Tragedie is hiest and hotest and full of greatest troubles" (139–40)—Ascham reveals his structural terminology is from neither Aristotle nor Horace but from Donatus's commentaries on Terence. E. K. Chambers suggests that Christopherson, who is never named in *The Scolemaster*, may be the object of Ascham's criticism (*Medieval Stage* 2:195n), though the comment suggests more about Ascham's critical perspective than about the faulty tragedian. Watson and Christopherson may have been introduced to Aristotle, but like Ascham they were more fully grounded in the Donatian critical theory taught in the schools. Yet more important than critical theory for both Watson and Christopherson were the models they chose to emulate in their tragedies.

In spite of discussions with Ascham and Cheke about Aristotle, Euripides, and Sophocles, Watson chose Seneca as his guide in converting biblical story to dramatic form. Surviving in a single manuscript believed by its modern editor, John Hazel Smith, to be unquestionably in Watson's hand (T. Watson 3–16),[1] *Absalom* was not allowed "to go abroad," according to Ascham, "onlie, because, in *locis paribus, Anapestus* is twice or thrice vsed in stede of *Iambus*" (140). However, if Watson wrote the play before leaving Cambridge in 1545 to become chaplain to Stephen Gardiner, Bishop of Winchester, as most scholars believe, he may not have had the opportunity to bring the tragedy to the finished state that would satisfy his own critical standards or would not embarrass him in his public career. The holograph manuscript at the British Library, designated Stowe 957, shows signs of having been recopied; cancellations and revisions are frequent, yet some errors in the grammar and versification remain, as J. H. Smith points out (T. Watson 12–16). Even though Watson may have been unwilling to publish the tragedy, two addresses in the text to a youthful audience (I.iii.282 and II.iii.131) indicate his intention to have the play performed in an academic setting, where his adaptation of biblical material to classical tragic form would be appreciated.

The rebellion of Absalom against his father, David, described in 2 Samuel (2 Kings in Watson's Latin Bible) 14:32 to 19:8, would have had particular relevance to the student audience familiar with the prodigal son paradigm that dominated contemporary educational interludes. However, in accordance with the classical tradition of basing tragedy on historical or legendary material in contrast to the invented plots of comedy—a tradition codified by Evanthius in the standard prefatory essay published with Donatus's commentaries on Terence (Terence, *Comoediae* 39)—Watson accommodated the biblical narrative to his Senecan model. Beginning his tragedy after Absalom's murder of his brother, Amnon, in retaliation for the rape of their sister Tamar, Watson avoids evoking a prurient interest in incest in his youthful audience, but he also limits the action to the conflict between the father and son. In contrast *The Love of King David and Fair Bethsabe with the Tragedie of Absalon*, written by George Peele a half-century later (1593–94) for the popular theater, includes the rape of Tamar and the murder of Amnon along with the rebellion of Absalom and the relationship between David and Bathsheba. Peele, completely ignoring the classical unities, provides a variety of incidents and emotions, while Watson, dispensing with the minor unities of time and place, essentially maintains a unity of action by concentrating on the rebellion of Absalom. Perhaps the cursing of David by

Semei (I.iii) could be seen as extraneous, as J. H. Smith argues (T. Watson 63–64), but this scene dramatizes the personal threat to David that motivates his departure from Jerusalem. One result of the focus on the rebellion is the limitation of the cast to male figures, for though Tamar, Bathsheba, and the concubines of David are mentioned, none appears on stage, which avoids female impersonation by the boy actors.

The structure of the play, following the Senecan model, also abides by Horatian and Donatian critical theory. Divided into five acts, as recommended by Horace (*Ars poetica* 189–92) and represented in Renaissance editions of Seneca in all but one of his plays, *Absalom* proceeds through the three stages of development perceived by Donatus in the comedies of Terence.[2] Acts 1 and 2 function as the *protasis* by introducing the principal characters (Absalom, David, Joab, and Achitophel) and setting the plot of the rebellion in motion. Acts 3 and 4 traditionally serve as the *epitasis* or "busy part" of the plot, and in *Absalom* act 3 represents Absalom's concerted drive to usurp the throne and destroy his father, while act 4 deals with David's counteraction of undermining Absalom's strategy through the secret agent, Chusai (Hushai in the Bible). Act 5 in typical fashion provides the *catastrophe* as Absalom's death is narrated and mourned by David who is restored to his position as ruler of Israel.

In conjunction with this skeletal development is a rising and falling action particularly associated with the tradition of tragedy deriving from Boccaccio's *De casibus virorum illustrium* (*Concerning the Fall of Great Men*), which was later adopted by Shakespeare and his contemporaries. The first speech in the play introduces a troubled Absalom alienated from his father; in the course of acts 1 and 2 Absalom, supported by Achitophel, becomes increasingly angry and aggressive as he plots and executes his rebellion. In act 3, after debauching his father's concubines Absalom exhibits classic hubris in bragging of his achievement: "Who in the world rules as the equal of me? Now sated with prosperity I have fulfilled my vows: I now hold the high throne of my old father, and the crowd of servants begs my nod" (III.iii.1–3). Taken from Seneca, as J. H. Smith notes (T. Watson 181n), these lines mark the height of Absalom's rise, but like Shakespeare's Richard III and Macbeth, Absalom finds his glory ephemeral, for he quickly realizes the insecurity of his power while his father lives, and at the end of Absalom's speech, Chusai, David's secret agent, comes forward to begin undermining Absalom's position. The remainder of act 3 and act 4 demonstrate Absalom's fall as he succumbs to Chusai's deception and abandons Achitophel, who, disappointed and fearful of punishment, takes his own life. The deterioration and death of Absalom inevitably follow in acts 4 and 5.

Reinforcing the symmetry of the rising and falling action, which divides the play in almost equal halves, is the balance created by the principal characters. Though Absalom dominates the play by his physical presence and the number of lines he speaks, as well as by directing the course of action to the middle of act 3, acts 2 and 5 are given over to David; and it is David's counteraction that determines the pattern of events in the last half of the play. The counselors of Absalom and David, reminiscent of the vices and virtues of the morality play, further emphasize the dichotomy of the conflict. Joab, the true and faithful counselor at David's side, is opposed by Achitophel, who encourages Absalom's pursuit of his vicious plan. Chusai provides another comparison with Achitophel by betraying Absalom as Achitophel had earlier betrayed David. The structure of Watson's tragedy reveals an artistic design that makes Peele's sprawling *David and Bathsheba* appear inept by comparison. With Seneca providing the model, Watson pays little heed to the Greeks in spite of Ascham's claim. Neither the theory of Aristotle nor the examples of Euripides and Sophocles supply the guidance that Horace and Donatus do in Watson's imitation of Seneca, though contemporary paradigms of *de casibus* tragedy and the morality play supplement the Senecan pattern.

In characterization, as well, the major impetus comes from Seneca, whose types Watson modifies to the biblical context. Absalom, as he is portrayed in 2 Samuel, is alienated from his father after killing his brother in revenge, and he is subsequently carried along by ambition to conspire against King David. The motivations and emotions of the characters are not examined in the biblical narrative. George Peele in presenting Absalom does not go much beyond the scriptural portrait except in emphasizing Absalom's beauty and an abundance of hair, which Peele makes golden, in keeping with medieval and Renaissance tradition, and a major source of Absalom's vanity (Beicher 222–33). Watson provides a much more fully developed character than either the Bible or Peele. Introduced in the initial speech of the play, in Senecan fashion, Watson's Absalom explains that he is troubled because in redressing his sister's injury he has offended his father. But a short time later, in describing David's reconciliation as hypocritical, Absalom reveals an uncontrollable rage directed first at his father and then at all of Israel. Reminiscent of Atreus vengefully plotting against his brother Thyestes, Absalom cries: "My father's breast must be gouged with this sword, then the teeming race of Israel must be destroyed by treachery. Vengeful rage cannot easily be broken or bent: crime must be added to crime. My sorrow knows no bound" (I.iii.31–35). Absalom then engages in an internal dialogue in which he weighs the duty owing a father against his desire to become king.

Like the Senecan protagonist, Absalom is led by his passions, manifested by outbursts of anger, impatience, and cravings for violence. As Absalom moves toward his goal of usurpation, his threats against his father become more bloodthirsty. Like Shakespeare's Richard III and Macbeth, Absalom becomes increasingly evil as crime breeds crime. Symbolically defiling David's honor by debauching his concubines may be the most outrageous act that Absalom performs, but his fantasy of the miseries he would inflict upon his father indicates how monstrous Absalom becomes:

> Shall I bury my sword in his deadly breast? Or cut off his hateful head . . . ? Or shake his brains and crush them in a quick death? . . . Or shatter his carcass utterly with a huge iron plate and throw his mangled members to the savage wolves? . . . How if I bring him back here and lock him in an empty prison merely to be food for hairy worms? I shall refuse death to him though he repeatedly ask for it, and when he is dying I will cheat him of his deserved death. Scarcely any revenge is enough, and any revenge whatever is pleas-

ing. Never except when it surpasses its vows, can my furious mind be assuaged from its anger. (IV.ii.49–69)

This is Absalom's last speech in the play, and it registers the extent of his character deterioration. Like Seneca's tyrants, Absalom is possessed by a fury that cannot be contained, but unlike Senecan tragedy, Absalom's tragedy is set in a providential universe that exacts retribution.

The object of Absalom's hatred and his opposing force, David, is not created from the same model. He has no antecedents in Seneca but is instead formed according to his functional role as a father. In comparison with Peele's David, who is conceived as a lustful king who repents his sin only after God punishes him, Watson's David is a kindly *familias pater* concerned about his people and his wayward son. Seeking to protect the Ark of the Covenant, he avoids violence by retreating, and he interprets Absalom's rebellion as retributive justice for committing adultery with Bathsheba and arranging the death of her husband Urias. David explains to Joab, "This misfortune has been given by God the Father; this penalty has been invoked because of my wicked crime: now from my own home the heir of the father rises up against my head" (II.ii.132–35). He believes, "Nothing of God's proceeds without plan." Therefore, he endures his "punishment" with "equanimity" (II.ii.135–36). Many of David's speeches are drawn from Psalms, but the image of the king and father that Watson conveys is characterized by piety and love. So idealized is the portrait that David appears Godlike as he views with sadness the destruction wrought by Absalom. As Absalom becomes more monstrous, David becomes more admirable. Concern for his son undercuts his victory, and when he is told of his son's death, the famous biblical refrain, "O Absalom, my son, my son Absalom" is followed by David's elaboration of his sorrow, which concludes, "The end of my sorrow will be one with the end of my life. O Absalom, my son, my son Absalom! O death, the only companion of my everlasting sorrow!" (V.iii.146–48). David's grief is his most human feature, but the dominant image that Watson creates is a Godlike David burdened by a beastlike son.[3]

The other characters in the play are developed in terms of their functions. Joab, David's faithful counselor, first urges his king not to flee but to stay and fight Absalom at the beginning of the rebellion; and at the end Joab rouses David from his mourning and persuades him to reassume his leadership. Joab is presented as a man of action who leads his master to victory, but in Watson's play he is not personally responsible for Absalom's death, as he is in the Bible and in Peele's version. Watson keeps Joab's character free from personal malice and assigns responsibility for treachery to Chusai, David's secret agent in Absalom's camp. Chusai's character is determined by his mission to gain Absalom's confidence in order to betray his plans to David; Chusai's success in misleading Absalom and in supplanting Achitophel as Absalom's adviser attests to his abilities to deceive.

Achitophel is a much more fully developed misleader of the youthful Absalom. Though his function may resemble that of the vice in the morality play, Achitophel appears to be drawn from the *consigliere* of Seneca. In contrast with the rather insignificant role of Peele's Achitophel, Watson's portrayal of the evil counselor particularly recalls the Nurse in Seneca's *Phaedra*, as J. H. Smith notes (T. Watson 55). Following the biblical narrative, Watson shows Achitophel shifting his allegiance from David to Absalom. He adds a soliloquy in which Achitophel justifies his decision on altruistic grounds — "With Absalom ruling some peace is to be hoped for and as ruler he will establish the ancient laws of the country" — but Achitophel then admits to himself, "I shall serve my glory" (I.iii.197–203). Like the nurses of Phaedra and Medea or the attendant of Atreus, Achitophel, after urging Absalom not to embark on a criminal path, then endorses and abets Absalom's evil course. He advises Absalom to let his soldiers loot the temples: "Gratify their taste for plunder, the fruit of a recent victory . . . with these rewards you will arouse their hot desires. . . . By these arts you will induce them into any crime at all" (III.i.63–67). And it is Achitophel, in keeping with the biblical narrative, who presses Absalom to defile his father's bed by having sex with his concubines, though Watson adds the justification: to convince Absalom's soldiers that no reconciliation is possible between father and son.

The Bible states that after Absalom takes Hushai (Watson's Chusai) as his counselor, Achitophel went home "and put his household in order, and hanged himself, and died" (2 Samuel 17:23).[4] Watson elaborates Achitophel's disappointment in a 120-line soliloquy that begins by decrying the ingratitude of his master and his loss of reputation, and then in an exercise of contrition he realizes, "I destroyed myself by my own madness . . . sad blindness infatuated my powers of reason" (IV.iii.26, 49). He becomes an example of the self-justifying partner in crime who cannot accept the punishment he deserves. Rather than facing the king he betrayed, he chooses an ignoble death. Though very repetitious and self-pitying, Achitophel reaches a tragic perception that escapes the protagonist Absalom but that is later demonstrated by many of Shakespeare's tragic heroes.

The remainder of Watson's cast in *Absalom* provide a context for the action and comment on its significance. In addition to the attendants, soldiers, and people of Israel the biblical story includes, Watson adds Senecan messengers to narrate the action that he cannot conveniently stage or that according to the tenets of classical decorum he should not stage. A messenger at the beginning of act 2 reports the growing threat of Absalom's rebellion, and the battle scenes are, of course, narrated. David's final victory is described first by Achimaas and then in particularly graphic detail by Chusai, who also recounts Absalom's end. Again in contrast with Peele, who represents Absalom's death on stage, Watson follows his Senecan model by narrating the death in sensational terms. Building on the biblical description, Chusai explains that when Absalom sees his defeat is inevitable, he leaps on a war horse (not the biblical mule). Then adding the detail that in his flight Absalom's helmet falls from his head, Chusai expands on the physical aspect of Absalom's death:

> As Absalom is carried beneath this tree [carefully described earlier] by his fleeing horse suddenly his unlucky head becomes locked in a bent limb. It happens that, as he hangs from the limb, by his very weight he ties tight knots in his tangled hair. His mount slips out from his dangling knees, leaving his master hanging where the

master guided him. His fear disappears; his voice fails; he drags forth deep sighs from the depths of his breast; his eyes stare, fixed in his fast-held head; he looks upon his doom. Foul froth flows from his livid mouth through his drooping jaws. He cannot raise his lowered hands. Alas, terrible thing to look at, worse to speak of! His fine breast is pierced by three spears! With these eyes I saw him while his blood still dripped freely. (V.iii.113–29)

Like the description of Atreus's killing of the sons of Thyestes in Seneca's *Thyestes*, this account implies a morbid fascination with the physical suffering of death, which is in its way more shocking than Peele's actual portrayal of Absalom's end.

Another important Senecan element that Watson adds to the biblical story is the chorus. A traditional feature of Greek tragedy, the dramatic role of the chorus is limited by Seneca and in turn by Watson from its use by Sophocles and Euripides. Though Horace had advised that the chorus should take the role of an actor (*Ars poetica* 193–201), Watson, like Seneca, does not represent the chorus interacting with other dramatic characters; rather the chorus function essentially as commentators and narrative links between acts. Apparently remaining on stage throughout the play, the chorus of concerned citizens observe and then interpret for the audience the implications of what they have witnessed together. Moralistic in judgment, the choral interludes contain a plethora of *sententiae* and proverbial expressions gleaned from Seneca and other classical sources. The chorus thus underscore the meaning as they spell out the moral lessons to be learned by the youthful audience.

The choral speech at the end of act 1 illustrates Watson's practice. Responding to Absalom's conspiracy, which Achitophel has just joined, the chorus generalize about the pattern that is emerging — "Blind is sorrow when excited by anger: it allows no reins on passion and does not fear grim death" — then compare Absalom to a tigress rushing to kill his "holy parent" after killing a brother. They declare: "Let perish wretchedly whoever violates the pious laws of our mother nature" (I.iii.235–44). The fifty-eight line speech concludes with a direct address to the audience and a prayer for peace: "O all ye youths, be quick to learn what counsel is worth both pro and con. Otherwise evils befall many people. There is no using up of virtue. O God, Creator of the vast world, quickly remove these crimes, if Thou wilt, and restore desired peace" (I.iii.281–87).

The moral voice of the chorus articulates the message as the action unfolds, and its perspective emphasizes the providential nature of the universe. The final choral comment sums up this view: "Consuming ruin is often threatening, but splendid virtue is never overcome. It always endures into ripe old age. Blind ambition has never lacked a wicked end: it provokes crimes and heaps of evils. Any temptation yields easily to good. Evil always demands an evil end" (V.iv.48–55).

This series of aphorisms generalizes Watson's tragic vision, but more specifically the play as a whole endorses a particularly Christian interpretation of the Old Testament story. Absalom, the rebel, begins his criminal career by taking justice into his own hands. Killing his brother for raping his sister, Absalom breeches his relationship with his father. In Watson's view Absalom becomes drunk with vengeance and ambition, and his destructive course ultimately consumes his partners in crime and himself, but it does not destroy his virtuous father. David never becomes vengeful or hateful toward his threatening son. David suffers the punishment of the rebellion because of his sinful liaison with Bathsheba, but repentance earns him redemption. Absalom and David become the images of unrepentant and repentant sinners; both are subject to retributive justice, but one is damned while the other is saved by a gracious God who presides over the world. Divine providence insures that the good are rewarded and the evil punished. David assumes at the end of the play a role like God's in grieving for the lost son; David resembles the loving New Testament God whose promise of redemption has been ignored. The image of tragic loss of the prodigal who is not reconciled with his father is the moral lesson that Watson conveys to his youthful audience in this Christian tragedy modeled on Senecan form.

CHAPTER TWENTY-TWO

CHRISTOPHERSON'S *JEPHTHAH*

*T*HOMAS Watson's former student and colleague John Christopherson may have known *Absalom* (ca. 1536–44), but he never alluded to the play and he was not influenced by it in his own attempt to write a biblical tragedy. Choosing Euripides rather than Seneca as his guide, Christopherson adopted the language as well as the form of his Greek model. The sole extant example in England of academic drama written in Greek, *Jephthah* survives in two Greek manuscripts are separately dedicated to William Parr, Earl of Essex, and Cuthbert Tunstall, Bishop of Durham; the Latin version is addressed to King Henry VIII.
in 1929 by Bernard W. Wagner at the Bodleian.[1] The two Greek manuscripts are separately dedicated to William Parr, Earl ofsex, and Cuthbert Tunstall, Bishop of Durham; the Latin version is addressed to King Henry VIII.

Like Watson's *Absalom*, *Jephthah* must have been written for performance by students at Cambridge, but whether it was written or performed at Pembroke College or St. John's while Christopherson was a student or a fellow is not clear. It appears to have been completed by 1544 (Boas, *University Drama* 46–47), some two years before Christopherson was appointed one of the original fellows at Trinity College.[2] It is possible that the play was performed in 1554–55, after Christopherson was appointed Master of Trinity by Queen Mary, as suggested by Wilbur Sypherd (Christopherson 9n.); it also could have been the *Jephthes* performed at Trinity in 1566–67, as some scholars think, though the reference may be to Buchanan's tragedy on the same subject (Moore Smith 60, Christopherson 9, McFarland 385n.). Whether the play was performed or not, the three manuscripts accompanied by dedicatory letters to men in high places indicate the tragedy had reached a state of completion not evident in Watson's manuscript of *Absalom*, even though (thanks to Ascham) Watson's play was better known (see chapter 21).

The dedicatory letters and a *carmina* (short poem) prefacing the text, all written in Latin, shed light on Christopherson's dramatic design. In his epistle to Bishop Tunstall in the St. John's College manuscript, Christopherson explains the inspiration for writing the play: "As I was carefully going over the pages of Old Testament story, I came by a lucky chance upon the story of Jephthah's vow as it is related in Judges xi. This, so at least I thought, offered appropriate material for tragedy, for, as I examined the eloquent *Iphigenia* of Euripides, I saw clearly that the heroines were not dissimilar" (letter to Tunstall, 72–78).[3] The sacrifice of Agamemnon's daughter in *Iphigenia at Aulis*, well known as a result of Erasmus's Latin translation more than thirty years earlier, suggested an analogy to Jephthah's daughter and offered a model for Christopherson in transforming the biblical narrative to tragic form. At approximately the same time, the early 1540s, the Scots schoolmaster George Buchanan composed a tragedy on the same subject at the College of Guyenne in Bordeaux. Like Christopherson, Buchanan saw *Iphigenia at Aulis* as a tragic pattern to emulate, but his adaptation of classical form differed significantly from Christopherson's version.

Christopherson, a devoted Greek scholar, may have encountered Aristotle's *Poetics* at Cambridge, but he makes no allusion to the work, and he demonstrates no direct Aristotelian influence in either the form or content of his tragedy. Christopherson appears more concerned with the practical model Euripides offered than with inherited dramatic theory, and he was careful to distinguish in his own critical comments how his purpose differed from that of Euripides. Noting that his Greek model followed "the fictions of the poets of old, and, with perfect taste, produced a fictitious story," Christopherson declares, "I have sought the venerable springs of truth and have with truthfulness, as I hope, set forth a true history" (letter to Tunstall 85–90). His emphasis on the truth of scripture is repeated in the Latin verse preface to the play, where he writes that "the poets of old . . . fill their tragedy with lies. The substance is imaginary, the language magnificent, the style elegant. But the unadulterated truth is far removed" (*Carmina* 14–17). This leads Christopherson to reject "all monstrous portents" in his representation of "glorious examples for men's lives" (*Carmina* 18–22). Buchanan, on the other hand, uses a portentous dream described by Jephthes's wife, Storge, to establish the ominous mood at the beginning of his tragedy.

Christopherson intends that the biblical examples he has chosen will instruct his audience in God's truth. In his dedicatory letter to Essex, he explains the particular examples of conduct to be imitated and to be avoided:

> If a man be the victim of any injustice, he should learn from the example of Jephthah how to bear that injustice calmly. If a man's country be endangered, Jephthah will teach him to go to its aid gladly. If a man determine to make vows, he should learn from this story not to bind himself to God rashly. If children refuse to bow to the authority of their parents, they should set themselves to imitate Jephthah's daughter, who, from regard for her father's word, went to her death eagerly. Finally, if we are setting out to fight an enemy, we ought to trust not so much in our strength as in God. (Letter to Essex 66–75)

The moral lessons the tragedy teaches, upon which Christopherson also comments in his letter to Henry VIII, appear to justify its composition and performance; like the educational interludes intended to be an alternative to Terence, Christian tragedy was intended to offer instruction lacking in pagan drama. For Christopherson the didactic import determined his adaptation of Euripidean tragedic form.

Compared to Watson's *Absalom*, Christopherson's *Jephthah* is both more diverse and less fully developed. At 1,164 lines, *Jephthah* is some 200 lines shorter than Buchanan's *Jephthes* (and the average length of Euripides' tragedies) and 1,100 lines shorter than *Absalom*. In spite of its being only half the length of Watson's tragedy, the scope of *Jephthah* is larger, for it represents the entire narrative in Judges 11, from the banishment of Jephthah by his brothers to the sacrifice of his daughter. In contrast, Buchanan portrays only the homecoming of Jephthes and the fulfillment of his vow. Though Christopherson does not divide his play into acts and scenes, he separates the parts of the action by choral interludes as in Euripidean drama. Six divisions, not including the prologue, make up the tragedy, and each part deals with a separate episode in the biblical narrative. The classical unities of time and action are ignored as a chronological series of events occurring over a period of months, if not years, is presented. All of the scenes appear to be set in Gilead, for a chorus of Gileadites provide a perspective on the ensuing dialogue and respond to the action that occurs offstage; unity of place is thus maintained in a generalized permanent setting comparable to Greek drama. *Jephthah* has a beginning, a middle, and an end but not in the Aristotelian sense, because the play represents quite separate episodes dealing with the conflict between Jephthah and his brothers and with the recall of Jephthah before he leads the army against the Ammonites. Neither does the development of the tragedy correspond to the Donatian divisions of *protasis*, *epitasis*, and *catastrophe* in the manner of *Absalom*; rather the play proceeds episodically in the manner later adopted by Peele for *David and Bathsheba*. The relationship between the episodes in *Jephthah* is that of the biblical narrative, though the action is unified by the title character, who dominates every part of the drama, even when he is not physically present.

Christopherson's decision to dramatize each segment of the biblical narrative may stem from his conception of scriptural truth, but he nevertheless expands the individual parts by elaborating the human dimensions of the action. By introducing Jephthah speaking the prologue, Christopherson establishes not only the context for his protagonist but also a sympathetic bond between him and the audience, as Jephthah describes the injustice he suffers as a result of being a bastard. He also indicates his strength and prudence by representing himself as a man of peace, choosing exile rather than conflict, and as a man of God, expressing his strong faith. Unlike the developing Absalom, Jephthah's character is set at the beginning of the play; the dialogues that follow essentially elaborate the qualities he reveals in his prologue. In establishing Jephthah in the prologue as an exemplary man who has risen above his base birth, Christopherson considers the implications of the first verse of Judges 11 — "Now Jephthah the Gileadite was a mighty man of valour, and he was the son of an harlot" — and prepares the audience for the action to follow.

Verses two and three, describing the conflict between Jephthah and his brothers born within the bond of marriage, are rendered dramatically in the first dialogue of the tragedy. Reminiscent of Joseph being cast out by his brothers, this scene deepens audience sympathy for Jephthah as a victim of injustice but it also introduces the threat of death at the hands of a kinsman, which ironically reappears in Jephthah's vow of sacrifice. Fraternal rivalry over inheritance, recalling Jacob and Esau as well as the brothers in the parable of the prodigal son, harks back to the archetypal sin of Cain. In dramatizing the conflict between brothers, Christopherson creates an elder evil brother and a younger loving brother who argue about how to deal with Jephthah. Though evil appears to prevail as they force Jephthah's exile, tragedy is averted by the younger brother's love and Jephthah's faith in God's vengeance. Jephthah, avoiding violence, represents his base birth as a "blessing" (102) and depends upon God's mercy. As Christopherson says in his letter to Essex, Jephthah is presented as an example of a man bearing injustice calmly.

Jephthah's recall by the elders to Gilead in order to lead the army against the Ammonites, the second episode in the biblical narrative, is perhaps the least effective part of Christopherson's drama. In an attempt to particularize the situation, a First and a Second Elder discuss the people's need for Jephthah in their time of crisis and his probable response to their request to return. Fearing that the war initiated by the Ammonites is God's vengeance on behalf of Jephthah, the elders consider Jephthah's capacity for anger and for love. Again the exemplary aspect of Jephthah's character prevails as he places his love for his family and his duty to his country above personal malice. That Jephthah is a man of peace is emphasized by his attempts to settle the conflict with the enemy without battle. Only after a second appeal to the Ammonites is rejected does Jephthah determine to lead his soldiers into battle. Before setting off, Jephthah, as he had many times before, expresses his faith in God, and in prayer he vows that if God grants him victory,

> whoso from the door comes forth the first
> To meet me when I reach home again,
> Him will I slay as sacrifice to Thee. (585–88)

Occurring in almost the exact middle of the play, this vow becomes the focus of the remainder of the drama.

Jephthah's victory is recounted in typical classical fashion by a messenger who, employing epic similes, describes the battle in most sensational terms as he attempts to justify the bloody slaughter by making Jephthah and his army a Scourge of God to punish the offenders. The nature of the messenger's seventy-line narrative is illustrated by the following excerpts:

> In mass, with doughty blades, we hacked our way.
> The dead men's blood ran in a swollen stream;
> In God we had an ever-present help. . . .
> . . . .
> And as a lion, tough of hide, amidst
> The oxen plunges, his teeth dripping with gore,
> Drives them in panic flight, seizes the prey
> And breaks its neck and gulps its entrails down,
> So was the host of Ammon blood-besprent
> By Jephthah. . . .
> . . . .
> The battle-ground with corpses was piled high,
> With corpses and with stray, dismembered limbs.
> God from Olympus thundered loud. . . .
> Columns there were of wounded men, the one
> Wounded in mouth, another with his entrails

Dragging at feet, another armless ran, . . .
'Twas God's command to sack them utterly. . . .

. . . .
      Eternal God
Bade put them to the sword. The flower of youth
Was by the blade of ruthless bronze laid low. . . .

. . . .
"Ah! What a bane among mankind is war!
   . . . it is the scourge of God." (653–708)

This fascination with the gory details of suffering and death may resemble Seneca more than Euripides; its extended metaphors from the animal world make the slaughter appear even more horrific, yet it is demanded by God. Most important, this emphasis on human destruction emotionally sets the stage for the sacrifice Jephthah offers God in exchange for his victory.

It is in the homecoming of Jephthah and the fulfillment of his vow that Christopherson's particular Euripidean model comes into the foreground. Compared to Buchanan, who devotes his entire play to these events, Christopherson reserves only the final third of his play for the tragic climax. Christopherson creates a wife for Jephthah, though none is mentioned in the Bible, apparently to extend the emotional dimensions of Jephthah's dilemma. Clearly suggested by Clytemnestra in *Iphigenia at Aulis*, Jephthah's wife pleading for her daughter's life also recalls *Hecuba*, the other Euripidean tragedy that Erasmus had translated. Jephthah's wife, however, appears only in the final part, and her role is to question the legitimacy of Jephthah's vow. She argues in emotional terms that God "lusts not for human flesh" (999) and that because Jephthah's mind was distraught when making the vow, fulfillment is not required. As in the dialogues between the brothers and the elders earlier in the play, opposing points of view express the dramatic nature of the issue. Serving as a rhetorical device, the wife enhances the emotional dimension of Jephthah's dilemma and accentuates its cost by promising to follow her daughter in death.

In contrast, Jephthes's wife, Storge, playing a larger role in Buchanan's version, establishes the mood through her portentous dream at the beginning of the play; and at the end, after failing in her attempt to dissuade Jephthes from the sacrifice, she registers the final response to her daughter's death. Her emotional opposition to the sacrifice reinforces the rational arguments of Jephthes's friend, Symmachus, and the priest. Yet in spite of Buchanan's portrayal of Storge's scorn of her husband's perseverance in fulfilling the vow, which earns the rebuke of her daughter, and in spite of her expression of the pain of the consolation, her role is less emotionally intense than Christopherson's briefer image of the shattered mother yearning for death. Also because Christopherson does not develop the implications of the vow in a series of dialogues, as Buchanan does, Christopherson's representation of the vow remains more emotional and less intellectual than Buchanan's version.

The emotional quotient in the relationship between father and daughter is greater in Christopherson's tragedy than in Buchanan's. Buchanan's Jephthes defends his decision to sacrifice his daughter in separate dialogues with Symmachus and the priest as well as with his wife and daughter; his reiteration of his obligation to God over his love for his child makes him appear remarkably cold. Christopherson's Jephthah, on the other hand, is dominated by grief and plagued by doubt as he reluctantly fulfills his vow. In first meeting his daughter at his homecoming, the victorious Jephthah recognizes his personal defeat at his daughter's hands (747). The irony of Jephthah's position is extended through the daughter's ignorance, which resembles Isaac's at the moment of sacrifice in the civic religious drama. The comparison between Isaac and Jephthah's daughter is in fact directly made by the chorus, who see Jephthah like Abraham placing God above parental love (955–60). A marginal comment in the same hand as the text in the Latin version notes, "sic Augustinus in quaesti: De voto Jephte" (so Augustine on the question concerning Jephthah's vow), thus linking Christopherson's treatment of the vow with the pseudo-Augustinian *Quaestiones Veteris et Novi Testamenti*.

However, God does not exact the payment from Abraham that Jephthah feels obligated to make. It is this difference that draws Christopherson back to his classical model, *Iphigenia at Aulis*. Like Agamemnon,

Jephthah struggles with the contending demands of duty and love, and though he initially seeks to evade the reality of the sacrifice like Agamemnon, Jephthah does not purposely deceive, as Agamemnon does. Jephthah's lament at the prospect of losing his daughter and his perception of his act of sacrifice as unnatural lead him to tears on several occasions, and twice he is reproved by his daughter for unmanly weeping (757, 853–54). The image of the suffering father suggested by Euripides is developed by reducing the role of the mother to an extension of the father's grief. Jephthah's most poignant expression of loss comes after recounting the domestic bliss his daughter has provided:

> However much affairs abroad oppressed
> My mind, yet in the home my burden dropped
> At thy fair sight. In trouble thou didst cheer;
> Thou wert the staff of age, and thou didst guide
> My steps; thou wert a clear light to the blind.
> Mine only daughter! What am I now to do,
> Oh wretched that I am? To have no friend
> Is pitiable mischance; to have no child
> Cuts to the quick. O bitterness of fate!
> O bleeding heart! How happy is the man
> Blessed in his children! How disconsolate
> The childless! (826–36)

Apparently drawing upon quotations from his commonplace book to emphasize Jephthah's loss, Christopherson elaborates the pathos of the simple biblical statement that Jephthah's daughter "was his only child; beside her he had neither son nor daughter" (Judges 11:34).

This daughter, as Christopherson presents her, is calm and self-possessed like her dramatic model, Iphigenia. In keeping with the biblical source, the daughter in Christopherson's version accepts the necessity that Jephthah fulfill his vow but requests a postponement for two months that she "may go up and down upon the mountains, and bewail [her] virginity" (Judges 11:37). Buchanan, observing the classical unity of time, omits the delay. Both Buchanan and Christopherson follow

Euripides in emphasizing the nobility and bravery of the daughter before the sacrifice, but the two Christian playwrights add innocence and piety to the classical image as the daughter willingly embraces her sacrificial role. Buchanan's Iphis, whose name identifies her classical precedent, charitably seeks to reconcile her parents before offering herself as "expiation . . . to compensate for the slaughter of so many foes" (*Tragedies* 91),[4] but Christopherson, again emphasizing the human dimension, presents Jephthah's daughter first bewailing her virginity and then accepting God as a substitute for all she will miss. She prays:

> Husband art Thou
> To me, Thou art my children and my father;
> Thou art my light, my life; Thou art my all.
> In *Thy* hand am I: do Thou what Thou wilt. (926–29)

Demonstrating her faith by following God's will, the daughter is contrasted with her grieving mother who, unable to accept her daughter's fate, seeks death as an escape.

Both Buchanan and Christopherson conclude that the sacrifice is a righteous act, though Christopherson more closely follows the pseudo-Augustinian interpretation that Jephthah may have offended in vowing to sacrifice the "unsacrificeable" but did not sin in performing the vow because it was God's will and the daughter offered herself freely (Augustine [pseudo] 69–71). The daughter's sacrifice is described by both Buchanan and Christopherson in accordance with classical decorum, and both narrations include the dying words of the victim as well as a final response to her death. The perception of this climactic moment determines the final tragic effect of each play. Buchanan's Iphis offers herself to God as an atonement for the sins of her parents and fellow citizens in a manner and language that suggest the sacrifice of Christ, and instead of the "usual groaning" and "den of grief" expected after her death, the witnesses note the heights of blessedness as well as misery and emphasize the "great consolation" to be realized in the daughter's death (Buchanan, *Tragedies* 94).

Again the contrast with Christopherson is significant. In Christopherson's version the daughter "willingly" gives herself "to death for those who live, " but rather than addressing God she directs her words to her father, who, weeping, offers himself in her place. In the end he personally carries out the sacrifice in response to his daughter's plea, "Make haste! / Delay brings sour grief" (1125–44). In Buchanan's version the father is distanced from the sacrifice as the priest delivers the fatal blow. The gushing of blood and the writhing of the body are noted by Christopherson as well as the tears and lamentation of the audience, and we are told that "the dauntless deed / Filled them with wonderment." The daughter is not likened to Christ but is instead perceived as an exemplar of filial obedience. The vision of the messenger remains rooted in this life as he notes the meaning of her death:

> A paragon
> Was she of excellence to all the world.
> I envy him whose children will obey.
> She willingly obeyed her father's word;
> Hers is undying glory 'mongst mankind. (1152–55)

The positive instruction to be gained from the resignation and death of Jephthah's daughter does not lessen her tragic end, for the final words of the play are a warning from the chorus to be prudent in making vows. Though they conclude that Jephthah's sacrifice was "a righteous act," they declare "a vow at random made / Oft ends in ruin" (1161–64).

The chorus's concluding comment is indicative of their function throughout the play. As moral interpreters, the chorus of Gileadites respond to the action at intervals, both dividing and linking the parts of the play as in Senecan drama and the plays of Watson and Buchanan. Occasionally the chorus interact with Jephthah and serve as audience for messengers in the manner of Greek drama, but mostly they remain observers who express the didactic import and extend the emotional dimensions of the play. They generalize about the uncertainty of life after Jephthah's banishment by his brothers; they pray for Jephthah's return when the Ammonites threaten; they decry the horrors of war; they thank God for victory; they sympathize with the maid's untimely death; they reiterate their faith in God; and finally they warn their audience to be prudent in making vows. Their ultimate purpose is to provide a social context and moral resonance; like their classical counterparts they emphasize their author's tragic perspective. For Christopherson the chorus point out the positive and negative examples of conduct to be imitated and avoided that he had outlined in his dedicatory letter to Essex, and while confirming the righteousness of Jephthah's fulfillment of his vow, they stress the supreme human cost. Unlike Buchanan, who transcends tragedy by making Iphis a symbol of Christ, Christopherson demonstrates the irrevocability of one's commitment to God, implying his own unshaken Catholic faith. Jephthah is held to his bargain in spite of its tragic result. In adapting his Euripidean model to his biblical subject, Christopherson offers an example of biblical tragedy that rivals the drama of his better-known contemporaries George Buchanan and Thomas Watson.

CHAPTER TWENTY-THREE

GRIMALD'S *ARCHIPROPHETA*

WHEN Nicholas Grimald wrote *Archipropheta* at Oxford in 1546–47, biblical drama in Latin was at the peak of its popularity. Between 1536 and 1556, more than sixty plays devoted to biblical subjects were composed in Latin (Blackburn 79). Grimald had himself published *Christus Redivivus* some three years earlier and had probably also written the now lost *Christus Nascens*, which may have been a companion play to *Christus Redivivus*, as well as *Protomartyr*, thought to be about St. Stephen, traditionally regarded as the first Christian martyr.[1] Oxford seems to have encouraged the composition of neo-Latin drama, especially tragedy.[2] Its involvement with the reform movement may have led Grimald to write a tragedy about John the Baptist, a popular medieval saint who had emerged as a hero of the Reformation.

Though John the Baptist appears in all the extant cycles except Chester, his role is generally limited to his preparation for Christ. Only in the N-Town cycle is the miraculous conception of John the Baptist presented, and in that cycle John appears also as a prologue to Christ's passion and later in the harrowing of hell; but in none of the cycles is John the Baptist's confrontation with Herod or his beheading portrayed. Despite the nearly 500 ancient churches in England dedicated to John the Baptist (D. Farmer 215), there is no record of his being the subject of any of the saints' plays performed in pre-Reformation England. However, by the end of the 1530s John the Baptist is established as a model of the religious reformer. Bale lists among his own works fourteen books on John the Baptist, which are now lost but which, it has been suggested, may have been conceived as a cycle play (J. Harris 72–73).

Bale also makes John the Baptist the central figure in a series of three plays he wrote in 1538 and later described as being performed at Kilkenny in 1553, after his installation as Bishop of Ossory. In the first play in the series, *God's Promises*, John appears as the last of the prophets and is commissioned by God to prepare the way for Christ, his traditional role in the cycles. In the second play, *John Baptist's Preaching in the Wilderness*, John emerges as a Protestant hero contending with the Pharisees and Sadducees, who are to be identified with the Catholic Church. Called both a comedy and an enterlude in the text (Bale, *Complete Plays* 2:36), this play is essentially a vehicle for expressing Bale's polemical position. Christ, baptized by John in the second play, becomes the hero of the third, *Temptacyon of our Lorde*. As in the cycles, John the Baptist's beheading is not considered. Whether Bale influenced Grimald's decision to write a play on John the Baptist is not known; but the two reformist dramatists were friends by the end of the 1540s. Bale may have helped Grimald to find a publisher for his *Christus Redivivus* in 1543 in Cologne, as Merrill has conjectured (Grimald, *Life and Poems* 13), though Grimald does not draw upon Bale's extant dramatic work in his biblical plays.

Another reformer who had adapted the biblical story of John the Baptist to express a political message was George Buchanan. While teaching at the College of Guyenne in Bordeaux in the early 1540s, he wrote the play *Baptistes* apparently for production by his students (among them Montaigne) to provide practice in Latin pronunciation. Later when Buchanan was examined by the Inquisition in Lisbon, he declared that after escaping from Britain, "I recorded my opinion of the English in that tragedy which deals with John the Baptist, wherein so far as the likeness of the material would permit, I represented the death and accusation of Thomas More and set before the eyes an image of the tyranny of the time" (quoted in Aitken 24–25). Though modern scholars have sought to identify the characters in *Baptistes* with particular members of Henry VIII's court, such as Cromwell and Cranmer (Aitken

131–35), the play seems more generally to present "an image" of tyranny, and it is in these terms that the anonymous translator in 1642 perceived it, for he retitled the play *Tyrannicall-Government Anatomized, or A Discourse concerning Euil-Councellors, being the Life and Death of John, the Baptist* and presented it to Charles I. Buchanan, who had translated Euripides' *Alcestis* and *Medea*, adopts the crisis plot of classical tragedy, as he does in *Jephthes* (see chapter 22), and focuses upon the conflict that led to John the Baptist's beheading. Eschewing dramatic action, Buchanan depends heavily upon narration to present the political and spiritual issues. The play may have been the "Iohn babtiste" performed at Trinity College, Cambridge, in 1562–63, but it was not published until 1577, when Buchanan dedicated it to young James VI. It is highly unlikely that Grimald knew of Buchanan's play when he wrote *Archipropheta*, but the two versions provide interesting points of comparison in both form and substance.

It is also unlikely that Grimald knew *The Beheading of John the Baptist* written abut 1539–40 by James Wedderburn and performed at Dundee. This play, said to be a tragedy satirizing "the abuses of the Romish church" (*DNB* 60:136), is now lost, but it attests to the popularity of John the Baptist as a model of the religious reformer. The only dramatic version of the biblical story that Grimald probably knew was that of Jakob Schoepper entitled *Ectrachelistis, siue decollatus Ioannes*, published in Latin in Cologne in 1546 by Martin Gymnicus, who had published Grimald's *Christus Redivivus* in 1543 and who in 1548 published *Archipropheta*. Grimald's dramatic version of John the Baptist includes a number of elements also found in the Schoepper play — most notably the romantic treatment of Herod and Herodias, a court fool, and a banquet scene as the context for John's beheading — but to regard Grimald's play as an adaptation of Schoepper's (Harbage, *Annals* 30–31) misrepresents Grimald's handling of his material. Grimald clearly appears to have been influenced by Schoepper's version, but there are no verbal echoes (Boas, *University Drama* 35), and, more important, the elements that Grimald may have found in Schoepper are fully transformed. Grimald appears to be imitating (in the best Renaissance sense) a generic model rather than adapting a foreign import. That Grimald's play was regarded as independent of Schoepper's is indicated by the fact that Schoepper's and Grimald's versions were printed by the same publisher in Cologne within two years.

In many ways a more important precedent for *Archipropheta* is the youthful *Christus Redivivus*, Grimald's first experiment with biblical history in dramatic form. Whether he had witnessed a cycle production of the resurrection is not known, but one critic argues that Grimald drew upon the resurrection play in the N-Town cycle (Taylor 840–59). If he did find useful material in this civic pageantry, he reshaped it according to classical principles. In his dedicatory letter to Gilbert Smith, which prefaces the published play, Grimald calls his work both a sacred comedy and a tragicomedy and explains the decorum demanded by both his subject matter and his dramatic form. He regards it as "fitting" that he "had incorporated in the play no frivolous epigrams, no jokes about love, no silly talk, no mimes, no dialogue of the lowest types of men, no Atellan comedy, no tavern-plays, none of the strange tales of heathen dramas" because these elements associated with comedy "contribute nothing of profit toward the formation of character, to sound learning, or to the extension of divine praise," which are the subject of his drama (Grimald, *Life and Poems* 102–5).[3] He later explains that the meter of comedy "was preserved" and "propriety . . . observed," but he says his adoption of the term *tragicomedy* is appropriate because "the first act yields to tragic sorrow" and "the fifth and last adapts itself to delight and joy; likewise, in order that variety may be opposed to satiety, in all the other intermediate acts sad and cheerful incidents are inserted in turn" (108–9). His classical precedent for the movement from a "sad beginning to a happy ending" he finds in Plautus's *Captivi*, which like *Christus Redivivus*, he observes, does not hold strictly to the unity of time.

Grimald reiterates again and again that his teacher "Johannes Aerius" is the source of these judgments, but they clearly represent for Grimald a defense and explanation of his drama. What he reveals is a conscious adaptation of classical form for his religious subject. In the play itself he represents such central biblical figures as Mary Magdalene, Caiaphas, and the disciples of Christ just before and just after the resurrection, and thus focuses on the crisis of the resurrection in classical fashion. He also includes a choral narrator at the beginning of each act, as well as choruses of Galilean women and disciples, and he adds comic soldiers to divert the audience. Though *Christus Redivivus* may be lacking in dramatic action, Grimald conveys his didactic intent according to time-honored classical principles.

In *Archipropheta* he explains his critical perspective more fully, and achieves a more satisfying dramatic experience as well. Using the Bible and Josephus's *Antiquities of the Jews* as his major sources, Grimald once again seeks to render in dramatic form a major Christian event. He explains in his dedicatory letter to Richard Cox, Dean of Christ Church, Oxford, that "this history of John the Baptist" is intended "not only to delight the learned, but also to profit those of cruder intelligence" (232–33). He may be suggesting a wider appeal than to an academic audience, yet he is also indicating his dual concern for delight and profit, in accord with the oft-quoted Horatian maxim.[4] Grimald goes on to declare that the poet most proves his calling when "a deed is portrayed in adequate language, and characters are introduced as though living and breathing; when time, place, words, and deeds are vividly depicted; when the whole action is brought before your eyes and ears, so that it seems not so much to be told, to be narrated, as to be done, to be enacted" (232–35). Life-likeness in character and vividness in action are only fleetingly perceived in *Christus Redivivus*, but in *Archipropheta* they are established as desired dramatic qualities.

Grimald's emphasis on presentation rather than narration again echoes a Horatian principle.[5] It also suggests a change in dramatic method from *Christus Redivivus*, which depends heavily upon narration in typical classical fashion. This stress on action contrasts markedly with both Bale's and Buchanan's John the Baptist plays, both of which are essentially static dialogues devoid of action. Grimald concludes his explanation of his dramatic design by enumerating what the audience will gain from the play:

Here the reader or the spectator will learn true, genuine, unfeigned repentance, the way to approach Christ, and the lesson the first preacher of the Gospel so strongly impressed upon the ears and minds of men. He will learn, also, of the same man's wonderful birth, of his stainless life, of the power of baptism, of his zeal in propagating religion, his freedom of speech, devotion in prayer, earnest admonitions, and of his death at last, worthy of a Christian. He will also see how hypocrites delight in themselves, how blind they are in self-love, how eager for their own advantage, and how they either dissolutely neglect pure religion or attack it hostilely. He will observe, too, how so impious a monster as Herod is rejected of God. Nor will he be without an opportunity for noting the wantonness of women, regal luxury, the flattery of courtiers, and, on the other side, the constancy and fidelity of John the Baptist, and other things not unpleasing to learn and know. (Grimald, *Life and Poems* 234–35)

This catalog of positive and negative exempla emphasizes the didactic intent that informs the drama, as it expresses the religious experience the tragedy of John the Baptist offers.

The religious experience of witnessing the arch-prophet's commitment to Christ even unto death was essentially what the saints' plays had provided their audiences for some five centuries before the English reformation. "Scenes of real life, spectacular events, [and] conflicts of will," perceived by John M. Manley as features of the saints' or miracle play (140–41), describe the major ingredients of *Archipropheta*, and with Grimald's stress on lifelike characters and vivid action, the dramatic effect is made especially striking. The realistic portrayal of the sufferings of Christ in the Corpus Christi plays, particularly in the York cycle, must have obtained in the dramatization of the martyrdom of the saints as well, if *A Tretise of Miraclis Pleyinge* is to be believed. According to this late-fourteenth-century tract, "men and wymmen, seinge the passioun of Crist and of hise seintis, ben movyd to compassion and devocion, wepinge bitere teris" (39). The Wycliffite author decries such emotion as false because it is evoked by a mere illusion, but this attests to the power of dramatic performance. The mode of the popular saints' play may have been adopted by Grimald for his *Protomartyr*, and it is the natural choice for *Archipropheta*, which like the typical saints' plays represents the mission and martyrdom of a saint (see chapter 1).

However, the saints' plays, like the Corpus Christi cycles, are episodic and sprawling, and just as Grimald adopted classical form for *Christus Redivivus*, in *Archipropheta* he orders his dramatic material according to classical precedents. Again using a five-act structure and a crisis plot, Grimald focuses the drama on a single event, the beheading of John the Baptist, which provides a unity of action as well as restricting time and place. He extends his use of the chorus from *Christus Redivivus* by multiplying the number of choral units and by increasing their functions. A major difference between Grimald's earlier biblical drama and *Archipropheta* is generic. Whereas the Latin form of comedy had been altered by classical precedent to accommodate a tragicomic pattern that Christ's resurrection demanded, the pattern of classical tragedy prevails in the martyrdom of John the Baptist. Rather than following the essentially tragicomic pattern of both the native saints' play and his earlier biblical drama, Grimald composed what has been called "the first extant tragedy" written in England (Herford 84), though Watson's *Absalom* and Christopherson's *Jephthah* appear to precede it.

The tragic form that Grimald adopts for his John the Baptist play sets it apart from those of his contemporary British reformers. Bale's interlude is called a comedy, but its chief purpose seems to be polemical. Buchanan's tragicomic *Baptistes*, though imitative of Euripides and Seneca, emphasizes man's victory over fortune through faith; and like Bale, Buchanan makes his play a vehicle for a political message as well as a religious one. For both Bale and Buchanan their dramatis personae are primarily spokesmen for or objectifications of different political and religious views. Grimald, on the other hand, seeks to present his principal characters in human dimensions as he focuses on their relationships with one another. Political concerns are overshadowed by religious values, and motivations for action are examined in their psychological and social contexts. The result is that Grimald's play becomes a human tragedy, not a political statement or a religious lesson.

Grimald's emphasis on dramatic representation rather than narration has much to do with the greater depth and liveliness of his drama in comparison to those of his fellow reformers, but he does not eschew narration altogether. Because of the classical form's focus on a single crisis, it is necessary to narrate earlier events if they are relevant to the matter at hand. For instance, in *Oedipus the King* crucial incidents from the past are narrated as they relate to Oedipus's growing awareness of his identity. In *Archipropheta* narration is occasionally used in the interest of limiting time and place as well as of unifying the action, such as when John's disciples report the miracles of Jesus (IV.iii). The Syrian servants also provide narrative links between scenes, but usually these narrations are short and directly functional.

The one glaring exception is the very long narration of the miraculous conception and birth of John the Baptist (II.v.). This detailed account by the disciples of John follows the portrayal of these events in Play 13, "The Visit to Elizabeth," of the N-Town series, the only cycle to represent them. Grimald could have found the basic elements of the story in many places, but if he used the N-Town cycle in *Christus Redivivus*, as has been alleged, he may have turned to this source again. Whatever the source, the narration proceeds for several minutes without interruption, and though it is requested by Herod, who says at the conclusion of it that it gives him "the highest opinion" of John (274–75), the narration could readily become dull in performance. Grimald apparently wished to emphasize Herod's and Herodias's awareness of John's special mission that was heralded even before his birth. This narration is later remembered in the play as Herod is determining what action to take in regard to John (IV.vi, pp. 322–23). Its importance dramatically and didactically cannot be overlooked, even if it is not very skillfully incorporated into the tragedy.

For the most part Grimald achieves his aim of representing crucial events rather than narrating them. After an initial exposition provided by Jehovah and John in act 1, act 2 introduces the conflict between John and the old religion represented by the Pharisees — Philautus (meaning self-love) and Typhilus (meaning blind) — who indicate they mean to incite Herod against John. A comparable scene occurs in Schoepper's *Ectrachelistis* at exactly the same point (II.i), though Schoepper includes both Sadducees and Pharisees while Grimald only alludes to the Sadducees and to the Essenes, another Hebrew sect, later. Philautus and Typhilus reappear (II.vi and III.i) to mock John's message, but their role is minor as the conflict between the old law and the new religion signified by baptism fades into the background, and the conflict between John and Herodias, the incestuous wife of Herod, emerges as the central concern of the play and the ultimate cause of John's beheading. Unlike Bale, who focuses *John Baptist's Preaching* on the political and religious conflict in which John is an archetypal reformer, Grimald reduces the contemporary political context to a secondary interest.

Like Buchanan, who also concentrates in the manner of classical tragedy on the climax of the beheading, Grimald perceives the conflict with the secular ruler to be the determining factor in John's fate. Grimald emphasizes even more fully than Buchanan that the real culprit is Herodias, who by various means causes Herod to work her will. How she achieves her mastery over Herod and how she accomplishes her ends are the real drama for Grimald. Though Schoepper develops the relationship between Herod and Herodias and makes the incestuous marriage a major factor, Grimald extends and intensifies their relationship by elaborating their romantic love. Anticipating Enobarbus's portrayal of Antony's love for Cleopatra, to which Herod's and Herodias's relationship has been compared (Boas, *University Drama* 36; Blackburn 98), the Syrian slave describes the nature of Herodias's charm. Cataloging her beauty from her wanton eyes and dainty lips to her breasts "rounded like tender grapes," the Syrian reminds us of the Song of Solomon or the verbal portraits of the courtly love tradition. In addition to these physical features "the sweetness of [Herodias'] manners," "the grace of her speech," "the favor of great fortune," and "a certain wonderful joy of living" are noted (II.iii, pp. 262–63). In the following scene Herodias depicts their love in terms of the mutuality of their feelings and their essential compatibility. She says: "Truly I judge no addition could be made to our mutual love. One mind animates the bodies of us both. Our likes and dislikes are both the same. We are both of one mind . . . you alone give me the greatest pleasure, and I alone give you the greatest, as is evident from deeds and words" (II.iv, pp. 264–65).

Perhaps it is this portrayal that has prompted critics to call their love "modern" (Herford 117; Grimald, *Life and Poems* 225–26), though the "oneness" depicted here is celebrated also in the sonnets of Shakespeare and the love poems of Donne. This depiction of love prepares the audience for Herodias's hatred for John when he attacks her marriage with Herod as incestuous and impious. Her love when threatened "rages with a fury not to be borne" (II.ii, pp. 290–91), in the manner of Medea's, and when John insists that Herod "Reject the love of woman for the love of God" (III.vii, pp. 298–99), Herodias seeks John's death. The chorus at the end of the act compare the destructive power of love seen in Herod and Herodias to the "tender love" that "subdued the invincible Samson" and the "salaciousness" with which Solomon "was sprinkled beyond measure" (III.x, pp. 308–9). Grimald emphasizes that John the Baptist's downfall derives from his challenge of the morality of Herod's passion for Herodias, his brother's wife.

This emotional dimension of the tragedy is comically counterpointed by Gelasimus, the fool, and by the Syrian servants. Gelasimus may have been suggested by Schoepper's play, where a fool appears in three scenes with Herod and Herodias, but Schoepper's fool is neither as comic nor as functionally important as Grimald's. The comic counterpointing of the fool is significant in several scenes in *Archipropheta*. For example, after the Syrian girl has described Herodias's beauty, which has inspired Herod's love, Gelasimus offers the girl money if she will give him a kiss. Herod then appears with Herodias and begs a kiss, which prompts her description of their love noted above. Gelasimus may not be as witty or entertaining as Feste or Touchstone, but like them he uses parody and impudence to provoke laughter or annoyance as he makes his points. Commenting on the foulness of the world in the manner of a preacher, he declares: "Players abound in jokes, harlots in blandishments, games of chance in quarrels, the court in gossip, the marketplaces in lawsuits, feasts in whispering, and women in pride" (II.ix, pp. 280–81). He concludes his "sermon" by asking what is "the most difficult thing to know," and answers one's "own father." He then asks, "What is a woman?" and answers, "What, indeed, save a vain thing?"

The Syrian girl and a chorus of Herod's men find Gelasimus's performance entertaining, but its purpose is to comment on Herodias and John the Baptist, who enter with Herod at the end of the fool's speech. Gelasimus also serves as a comic foil at the banquet, where Herod is congratulated on his "wonderful fool, . . . who will inspire you with abundant laughter whenever you are so disposed" (IV.xii, pp. 334–35). But his boldest sally comes when Herodias is preparing her daughter for the banquet. The fool puts the ornaments meant for Tryphera on his own head, and when Herodias threateningly asks, "Do you not know me?" Gelasimus answers, "I know you better than I wish. You are Philip's wife [Herod's brother's wife]." Herodias strikes him for his impudence, and Gelasimus comments, "Alas, truth ever begets hatred, and blows as well! As long as I live I will never again speak the truth" (IV.ii, pp. 314–15). This exchange anticipates the Fool in *King Lear*, who functions in a similar way, as an unwelcome instrument of truth.

If Grimald borrowed the idea of the fool from Schoepper's *Ectrachelistis*, he nevertheless developed the figure much more fully and made him an integral part of the drama. Gelasimus and the Syrian servants, who have no counterparts in Schoepper's play, function as an informal chorus as they comment both directly and indirectly on the actions of the principal figures in the tragedy. Neither Bale nor Buchanan includes anything resembling this comic dimension in their John the Baptist plays.

Buchanan begins the last act of *Baptistes* with Herodias's daughter asking for John the Baptist's head, but the scene involves only Herod, Herodias, and the unnamed daughter, and the beheading itself is narrated by a messenger. Perhaps it was again Schoepper who inspired Grimald's more dramatic context for the beheading, for Schoepper in his fifth act represents a banquet attended by provincial governors, dukes, and ministers, as the occasion for the beheading. Grimald follows the same pattern in *Archipropheta* except that he moves the banquet scene forward to act 4 and develops it much more fully. Again if Grimald is imitating Schoepper, he outdoes his model as he elaborates the entertainment values and emphasizes the psychological and religious significance of the action.

Grimald prepares the audience for the banquet scene through Herodias's preparation of her daughter Tryphera (whose name means voluptuous) to enchant Herod. Herodias directs her daughter to "paint [her] little body with colors" (IV.ii, pp. 312–13) and then adds necklaces, bracelets, and rings resplendent with jewels. This ornamentation is interrupted briefly by the fool's impudence, as noted above, before Herodias instructs her daughter in the dance she is to perform for the king. The reason for this careful preparation is made apparent at the banquet as Tryphera's performance so fascinates Herod that he rashly offers her anything she asks, and she thus becomes the means by which Herodias can destroy the man who threatens her relationship with Herod. Grimald here emphasizes the calculating nature of Herodias as he looks toward the context of Herod's sentence on John the Baptist in the banquet scene itself.

The banquet scene is preceded by a series of scenes in which Herod and Herodias together and singly consider what is to be done about John, but up until the banquet begins, Herod resists Herodias's pressure. The banquet celebrating Herod's birthday is characterized by its extravagance. With a catalog of twenty-seven dishes ranging from pheasants, swans, and flamingoes to lamb, veal, pike, turbot, spelt, and brains of birds, the tables groan "with regal lavishness" (IV.xii, pp. 332–33). While the meal is being served and eaten, the guests are entertained with both instrumental and choral music. Finally Herodias and her daughter are invited to lead the fatal dance that ends with the request for John's head. This may be the most elaborately staged scene in English drama before Queen Elizabeth's reign, for it entails not only an extensive list of properties for the meal served on stage and a variety of music, but also it involves scores of entertainers and banqueters, including a chorus of Idumaeans, a chorus of Herod's men, and a chorus of banqueters, in addition to Herod, Herodias, Tryphera, the fool, the Syrian girl, and the Pharisees. Grimald appears to be imitating the reality of a royal reception. The festive atmosphere is occasionally punctured by the sardonic fool, which calls our attention to the indulgence and extravagance of the occasion. After the banqueters cheer Herod: "Io, io, io, io, uiuat Herodes (Long live Herod)," the fool adds, "Bo, bo, bo, bo: bibat Herodes (Long drink Herod)" (IV.xii, pp. 332–33). The Syrian servants also comment on the action, as do Herod and Herodias, so that we never lose sight of the implications of the entertainment. Greenwood claims that "as a combination of music and dialogue, [the banquet] is dramatically the most effective scene written by any English author up to that time" (322).

The climax of the scene is particularly effective. When Tryphera, prompted by her mother, asks for John's head as a reward for her enchanting dance, Herod replies, "I will give it, come what may, lest I should be thought either fickle or perjured" (IV.xii, pp. 344–45). After a brief musical interlude, the head is brought and the festivities abruptly cease. The amazement of the guests is registered by Tryphera, and the chorus, who speak at the end of each act, clarify what Grimald had sought to visualize in the scene itself. The chorus interpret John's beheading as madness resulting from the "frenzy of love, . . . feasting and dancing, . . . the lustful king violated all the law of the foremost and greatest compact, under the spur of so many pleasures" (IV.xii, pp. 346–47).

The elaborate context of John's beheading emphasizes the psychological motivation of Herod's sentence, but at the same time it contrasts the world of Herod with the simplicity and humility of John the Baptist. John is presented throughout the play as a simple man who dresses in the hides of animals rather than regal robes and prefers water to wine. Perceiving himself "unworthy to unloose the latchet" of Christ's sandals (I.ii, pp. 242–43), John is an unaffected symbol of truth. He sparks Herod's admiration, but the banquet scene manifests Herod's self-indulgence, pride, and weakness, which stand in opposition to John's virtues. The participation of scores of banqueters in Herod's pleasures implicates them in Herod's guilt. As the chorus at the end of the banquet scene conclude, "Out of so many guests, there was no friend of the king to advise him against committing so intolerable a crime. All, indeed, were either afraid, or else approved of the dreadful deed" (IV.xii, pp. 346–47). In the manner of Seneca the formal chorus delineate each act, but they also emphasize the social dimensions of the action, which are extended through the groups of banqueters and Herod's followers, who are also called choruses. John's disciples and a chorus of plebeians in other scenes serve a similar purpose in responding to the action and calling attention to its social implications.

The interpretative role of the chorus is especially important in the tragic conclusion, for it focuses the final dramatic effect. Unlike the popular saints' play that may have suggested Grimald's realistic portrayal of John the Baptist's conflict with tyrannical evil, *Archipropheta* does not end with the celebration of John being gathered to the communion of saints in heaven (see chapter 1). In his last speech on stage, when he appears alone just before the banquet scene, John thanks God that he has "spent [his] allotted time of life upon the earth," and he declares, "with unshaken faith and with untroubled conscience, I confidently await that day when I shall enter into the kingdom promised by Thee" (IV.xi, pp. 328–29). His readiness to die and his assurance of heavenly life are emphasized before his martyrdom, as one expects in a saints' play. And immediately after the banquet scene, which ends with John's head being brought onto the stage on a charger, Jehovah explains the "hidden victory" that "falls to him overcome by violence." Jehovah says that it is His design "to reveal heavenly wisdom by worldly folly, to make the Abels known by means of the Cains, to demonstrate our power by earthly weakness, to grant glory by means of the shame of the cross" (V.i, pp. 348–49). This generalizing statement that God's power is demonstrated in the context of evil actions interprets what the audience has just witnessed, as it alludes as well to the crucifixion of Christ that John's death anticipates. Again this appears to be in the spirit of the saints' play, and it is also similar to the response to John's death by the chorus in Buchanan's neoclassical *Baptistes*. However, unlike Buchanan's play, which concludes with the celebration of John as a defender of the truth "on behalf of religion and ancestral laws" and declares that we "in our prayers" should "ask for a similar end of life" (*Tragedies* 164), in Grimald's version our attention is drawn to other concerns.

Following Jehovah's departure, Herodias adopts a callous disregard for her guilt and for the hatred of others, and Herod reveals his stricken conscience and his personal suffering as he wishes what he had done could be undone. Herodias and Herod respond to their crime in a manner that foreshadows the Macbeths' initial reactions to their murder of Duncan, but unlike *Macbeth*, Grimald's tragedy does not end with retributive justice being visited upon this "butcher and his fiendlike queen." Instead the dramatic emphasis is placed on the tragic loss of John the Baptist as his disciples and the Syrian girl lament his unmerited death. John's beheading is narrated in gruesome detail, and the headless trunk is brought onto the stage. A chorus of plebeians question God's justice: "Is this the reward given to him who invokes what is right? Do they not expect the justice of God?" (V.iii, pp. 352–55). The play ends with John's disciples and the plebeians hovering over John's bloody body while in a repetitive lament they deplore the times. The reassuring words of Jehovah are forgotten as the audience is left not with the triumph of martyrdom, as in the saints' play and in Buchanan, but with a sense of tragic injustice and tragic loss.

This first published tragedy to be written in England fuses the native religious dramatic traditions manifested in the Corpus Christi and saints' plays with the language and form of classical tragedy. Though not the first to adapt the critical principles of ancient Rome to the religious instruction of Tudor England, Grimald created a remarkable example of biblical drama for the academic theater. In terms of characterization, structure, and staging, *Archipropheta* surpasses not only the three other extant plays written on John the Baptist in the same decade but also compares favorably with the tragedies of Watson and Christopherson, his Catholic contemporaries at Cambridge. Grimald's drama clearly must be counted among what Tucker Brooke calls those "Latin plays of

England that saved the day for the theatre and, so to speak, kept a door open for Marlowe and Shakespeare . . . when the courtly interlude had degenerated into unseemly and plebeian drivel" ("Latin Drama" 234). Grimald's largely ignored saint's tragedy may in fact have served as a model for the later adaptation of academic drama to the popular stage.

CONCLUSION

*D*RAMA at the beginning of Henry VII's reign was strongly influenced by local clerical and civic authorities. The content of the saints' plays and biblical civic drama no doubt depended on priestly learning, while the performance was the prerogative of local talent, drawn perhaps from the clergy as well as the parishioners. The economic support of the civic drama by the guilds gave them the final say on production, and the mayor and town councils determined which professional companies would perform and which plays would be presented before the citizenry. Only the folk plays appear to have escaped the manipulation of local religious and secular leaders, who seem to have tolerated if not always condoned the traditional mummings. Drama thus generally depended on the good will of the city fathers and the local clergy, and except for interludes provided by professional companies, staging of the plays demanded the involvement of the community.

Because all but the offerings of the itinerant players were associated with religious holidays and local traditions, the drama was for the most part periodic and repetitive as scripts of previous years' productions were reviewed and revised for the same occasions, the commemoration of the parish patron saint or the celebration of Shrovetide or Corpus Christi Day. The occasions for drama were festive and invited not only religious devotion but also liberal partaking of food and drink before or after fasting. Reenactment of the miracles and martyrdoms of saints or of the biblical stories that reflected on the redemption of man through Christ may have reminded audiences of their spiritual debts and induced them to offer thanks with both their voices and their purses, but the very familiarity of the dramatic renderings reinforced the didactic message. The purpose of the drama, like the visual art of the churches, was instruction, but in order to attract and retain the attention of the viewers, the religious lesson was fleshed out with emotion and humor. The dimension of entertainment or diversion necessary to reach the audience clearly became a major or perhaps the predominant concern of the professional actors, who depended on their popular appeal for their livelihood. The folk entertainers, who were rewarded with food and drink if not money, ignored the didactic dimension altogether, but the other popular dramatic traditions justified their existence in the community by their instruction in moral and religious values.

This general perception of drama as having a didactic purpose perhaps made the acceptance of classical drama in the schools easier. Because the comedies of Terence were considered to be an attractive and effective means of teaching Latin and the principles of rhetoric, they were incorporated into the standard school curriculum in spite of their representation of actions and attitudes that ran counter to the morals of early-sixteenth-century society. Erasmus dismissed moralists' objections as ignorant and petty, while Vives suggested that the works to be studied be carefully screened and that school texts omit offending passages. Melanchthon, on the other hand, ingeniously explained the plays as illustrating positive and negative examples of appropriate conduct. Whichever tack individual humanists took, as a whole they promoted the comedies of Terence, and to a lesser degree Plautus, as meriting careful study; and by bringing drama into the schools, they emphasized the details of the text that underlie performance. The commentaries of fourth-century grammarians and Renaissance humanists not only glossed difficult passages and identified rhetorical schemes and tropes but also explained Terence's dramatic structure and *oeconomia*. The effects were to improve the students' understanding of Latin, to develop their ability to manipulate language, and to enhance their perception of drama.

Because these classical comedies represented a totally secular image of life in which moral implications were not immediately obvious, they provided a strong contrast to the religious plays of the local communities. Civic and clerical authorities who exercised control over the popular traditions were displaced by schoolmasters who emphasized neither Christ's redemption nor the rewards of the soul's victory over the sinful self, but stressed instead the importance of knowledge and the cultivation of rhetorical skills. The performance of classical comedy provided practice in training the memory and in the pronunciation of Latin, and it also provided immediate involvement in dramatic production. When Seneca was introduced into the curriculum of the advanced students, they were already experienced in close textual study and in the recitation of rhetorical speeches. It is no wonder that when alternatives to classical drama were sought in an effort to offer more morally relevant or more edifying images of life, the school exemplars of comedy and tragedy, Terence and Seneca, were the models chosen to imitate. In giving biblical subject matter dramatic form, whether the parable of the prodigal or the rebellion of Absalom, the standard school authors provided guidance.

Terence and Seneca, as interpreted by classical and Renaissance commentators, illustrated for the future playwrights of the early sixteenth century the appropriate characters, action, and style for the genre they selected, techniques of characterization, and dramaturgical strategies as well as the conventional three-part (*protasis, epitasis,* and *castastrophe*), five-act structure. These aspects of dramatic composition were most influential on authors of both comedy and tragedy by the middle of the sixteenth century, such as Udall and Watson, though the concepts of the classical unities and of the crisis plot were not adopted. For students of Greek, the comedies of Aristophanes and the tragedies of Euripides supplemented the Latin exemplars. Departures from the classical models of comedy by Udall and the author of *Gammer Gurton's Needle*, or from classical models of tragedy by Watson, Christopherson, and Grimald, indicate considerable variation, but they are all indebted to their humanist instruction in classical drama. Humanism, with its emphasis on the study of ancient Greek and Roman authors, was clearly responsible for significant changes in the perception and direction of drama in the first half of the sixteenth century, and the changes can for the most part be regarded as positive.

The other major factor that altered the course of drama in early Tudor Britain, the Reformation, may be viewed more negatively. The Reformation came to Britain a generation after humanism, though it involved some of the same figures. Erasmus, Vives, More, and Melanchthon, the early champions of humanism, were caught up in the Reformation controversy, but they did not directly participate in changing the course of drama in Britain after the Reformation. A later generation, educated in the humanist curriculum, emerged in the 1530s, and though many, including Bale and Grimald, embraced the Reformation, others like Watson and Christopherson maintained their Catholic faith. These dramatic authors may demonstrate their humanism along with their different religious beliefs, but not all Catholics or reformers supported the humanist view of drama. Antitheatrical prejudice, manifested by the church fathers and by the earlier Lollard critic of miracle plays, surfaced in the moral concerns of Vives, but the most vociferous challenge came from the German Cornelius Agrippa, who attacked drama as well as poetry and other arts that he believed misled society. In England the reformers John Jewel, Thomas Becon, and Peter Martyr evidenced a similar distrust of drama, while the humanists Thomas Elyot and Thomas Wilson defended drama in the education of youth. Martin Bucer, following Martin Luther, advocated Christian drama drawn from biblical stories but cast in the traditional classical forms of comedy and tragedy as an alternative to the pagan plays of ancient Greece and Rome.

It was the reformers' recognition of the power of drama to influence behavior, especially of the youth, and to shape religious beliefs that made them suspicious of plays composed by both pagans and Catholics. The substitution of Christian comedies that demonstrate the perils of taverns and lusty women for Terence's images of youthful indulgence, or the introduction of biblical tragedies that illustrate sacred examples of piety and God's retributive justice as an alternative to Seneca's portrayals of tyranny and incest, sought to avoid potential moral ambiguities in classical drama. Likewise, Catholic religious plays were thought by the reformers to perpetuate the superstition and corruption of the old Church. Because reformers regarded the veneration of saints as idolatrous, the performance of saints' plays was banned. Fears of this, the longest and most pervasive tradition of religious drama in Tudor Britain, apparently led militant reformers to seize and destroy the texts of these plays, for in spite of their ubiquity throughout England and Wales into the early sixteenth century only a few have survived.

The biblical civic drama fared somewhat better, particularly in the North where the Reformation was long resisted, though accommodations to the new religion were made in some places. Revisions demanded by the new religion are particularly apparent in the Chester and N-Town cycles, and in York the Corpus Christi pageant was subjected to censorship. Though Queen Mary, who reinstalled Catholicism as the state religion in 1553, encouraged the old religious drama during her brief reign, in the later sixteenth century, as a result of governmental interference and waning local support, biblical civic drama faded from the scene.

As older medieval religious dramatic traditions were curtailed or outmoded by reformist sympathies, the more recent and more flexible morality play was adapted to the changing social conditions and religious beliefs. Not only was the paradigm of gaining salvation through repentance altered to a more worldly concern for education as the central figure of the morality became younger, but also the reformist emphases on faith rather than good works and on the need to purge clerical corruption became the subjects of post-Reformation morality drama. The new Protestants took up drama as a means of promulgating their religious beliefs and promoting reform. John Bale with his troupe of players and his repertoire of biblical and morality drama may be the most strident voice among the English reformers, but his dramatic exposition of Protestant doctrine was supported by influential men in both the church and the state, including Archbishop Cranmer and Lord Chancellor Cromwell. When Bale combined history with moral allegory in the play *King John*, he demonstrated the potential of drama as a vehicle for political as well as religious propaganda. In Scotland a short time later,

David Lindsay exercised his prerogative as a royal counselor to expose the license and corruption of the old church and to promote thorough-going religious reform in the political morality *An Satire of the Three Estates*. Only one example of what has long been thought to be a Catholic response to the reformers has survived, but this play, *Respublica*, dating from Mary's reign, is much less extreme as it calls for correction of abuses, not radical purgation.

These obvious political statements in dramatic form demonstrated the potential danger of drama to subvert government policy and authority and, no doubt, accelerated the growing concerns for censorship and the regulation of dramatic activity. Governmental acts and decrees determining *what* plays as well as *when* and *where* they could be performed developed as the Reformation proceeded. Beginning in 1543 with the Act for the Advancement of true Religion, which stifled scriptural drama used for polemical purposes, and continuing in the reigns of Edward VI and Mary, legislation was passed to exercise increasing control over drama, so that when Elizabeth came to the throne in 1558 the pattern of governmental regulation had been firmly established.

The involvement in political activity was not the only factor that incited regulation of drama when Elizabeth inherited the throne from her sister, Mary. By 1558 the control of drama by the church had virtually ceased; the tradition of the saints' plays had ended; and the religious civic drama was in decline. Town councils typically licensed the performances of itinerant players, but with the reduction in local amateur performances the wandering professionals apparently found an increased demand for their services, and their numbers grew. Though they had long found legal protection and some financial support from their aristocratic patronage, their extended activity may have prompted more centralized control. Their repertoires had also grown more varied and more secularized as they apparently adapted new texts from both court and academic venues, which had become their major competition by the middle of the sixteenth century. The growing interest in the composition and performance of drama at the schools and universities generated a proliferation of dramatic types and a renewal of the traditional classical genres of comedy and tragedy. The young men being educated in the humanist tradition developed a respect for the ancients, but they also learned by contemporary example to adapt elements from popular traditions when they created their own texts. In these circumstances it was natural that imitation and innovation characterized the drama as Elizabeth in 1558 claimed the throne won by her grandfather three-quarters of a century earlier.

NOTES

INTRODUCTION

1. For the identification of playing companies and their patrons in early Tudor Britain, see Lancashire, *Dramatic Texts and Records* 373–408.

2. This proclamation appears on the first leaf of British Library MS. Harley 2013.

CHAPTER 1, THE SAINTS' PLAYS

1. Lancashire, *Dramatic Texts and Records* offers a comprehensive list of sites of performances.

2. In addition to the Digby manuscript of *Mary Magdalene* and *The Conversion of St. Paul* and the Cornish manuscript of *Beaunans Meriasek* discussed below, Lancashire in *Dramatic Texts and Records* lists the following lost plays: St. Andrew (Braintree, Essex, 1525), St. Catherine (Coventry, 1491; Hereford, Herefordshire 1503; Shrewsbury, 1526–27), St. Christian (Coventry, 1505), St. Christina (Bethersden, Kent, ca. 1519–21), St. Eustace (Braintree, Essex, 1534), SS. Feliciana and Sabina (Shrewsbury, 1516), St. George (Bassingbourne, Cambridgeshire, 1511; Morebath, Devon, 1540; York, 1546–47), St. Martin (Colchester, 1527), Blessed Virgin Mary (New Romney, Kent, 1512–13), St. Swithin (Braintree, 1523), St. Thomas Becket (Mildenhall, Suffolk, 1505; Canterbury, 1504–5 to at least 1537–38; London, 1518–19; Bungay, Suffolk, 1539), and a "Mary Magdaleyn play" (Taunton, Somerset, 1504).

3. The most recent editors of the play — Donald C. Baker, John L. Murphy, and Louis B. Hall in *The Late Medieval Religious Plays of Bodleian MSS*

133 and e museo 160 — note the consistency of language throughout *Mary Magdalene*, which they believe indicates a single author, though they allow that "some scenes were probably drawn from other plays" (xlvii–viii). All subsequent references to the text are to this edition.

4. Charles Jones finds saints' lives to have been a "popular form of creative literature from the sixth to the tenth centuries" (52).

5. In London, Fitzstephen writes, one could see "representationes miraculorum quae sancti confessores operati sunt, seu representationes passionum quibus claruit constantia martyrorum" (representations of miracles that saintly believers have performed, or representations of the sufferings by which the steadfastness of martyrs is shown). Quoted in E. K. Chambers, *Medieval Stage* 2:379–80.

6. Clifford Davidson considers this art and its relationship to the saints' plays in "The Middle English Saint Play and Its Iconography" (31–122).

7. Stage direction. References are to line numbers in *The Digby Plays: Facsimilies*.

8. Jeffrey discusses the theme of recurrence in saints' plays (72–73).

9. *Beaunans Meriasek*, ed. and trans. Stokes, s.d. 510. All subsequent references to the text are to this edition. Markham Harris's more recent prose translation, *The Life of Meriasek*, offers a more colloquial version, but at the expense of poetic quality.

10. Markham Harris describes the structure as "antiphonal," but a number of the thematic correspondences he claims to perceive are not very convincing (*Life of Meriasek*, 11–12).

11. For a discussion of the adaptations of the saints' play in England after 1558, see Wasson, "The Secular Saint Plays" (241–60).

CHAPTER 2, THE CIVIC DRAMA

1. Exact dates of the manuscripts are difficult to determine. Earlier scholars suggested that the Towneley manuscript dates from 1475 to 1525, but Barbara Palmer argues that it appears to be clearly from the sixteenth century and may incorporate post-Reformation changes (318–48).

2. A number of the Towneley plays appear to be drawn from the earlier York cycle, while the N-Town cycle represents a compilation of plays from a

variety of sources; the Marian group of plays (numbers 8–11, 13) may have been "a separate and self-contained composite Mary play," as Meredith and Karhl suggest (*The N-Town Plays* vii).

3. This proclamation, written on the first leaf of Ms. Harley 2013 in the British Library, is printed in *The Chester Plays*, ed. Deimling 1:1. Subsequent quotations from the Chester plays are from *The Chester Mystery Cycle*, ed. Lumiansky and Mills.

4. All further quotations from the N-Town cycle are from this edition.

5. This and all further quotations from the Coventry pageants are from *Two Coventry Corpus Christi Plays*, ed. Craig.

6. This and all further quotations from the Towneley plays are from *The Towneley Plays*, ed. England and Pollard.

7. This and all further quotations from the York plays are from *York Plays*, ed. Toulmin Smith.

8. Roscoe E. Parker in his edition of *The Life of Saint Anne* claims that the anonymous work is a direct source of the Mary plays in the N-Town cycle (xxxviii–xl).

9. Teresa Coletti says, "The N-Town stage direction for the Incarnation suggests an awareness of the popular metaphor that compared the event to sunlight passing through glass" ("Devotional Iconography" 29–30).

10. See Meredith and Tailby, eds., *The Staging of Religious Drama* (244–45).

11. See Baird 161–69. Forrest declares "Joseph's Return" is "an interpolated comic interlude doing violence to the reverence of the other St. Anne's plays" and was prompted by "the playwright's obvious desire to entertain" (49). Gail M. Gibson sees this situation as "a comic parody of the Virgin's Divine Conception of Christ" ("'Porta haec clausa erit'" 142).

12. The trial of Joseph and Mary is found in the *Pseudo-Matthew*, but other than N-Town the only English literary text in which it appears is Lydgate's *Life of Our Lady*, which, Gail M. Gibson believes, links the cycle to Lydgate and Bury St. Edmunds ("Bury St. Edmunds" 56–90).

13. Kolve remarks: "The gynecological probing of the midwife is a terrifying action and so the audience would understand it" (*Play Called Corpus Christi* 139).

14. The Chelmsford records indicate a professional dimension in their productions, as Coldewey explains in "The Digby Plays" (103–21) and in "That Enterprising Property Player" (5–12). How extensive professional directing and acting became in civic productions remains questionable.

15. Martin Stevens counts 372 parts in the York cycle ("The York Cycle" 37–61).

16. Though the staging of the Towneley cycle is not expressly indicated in the manuscript, place-and-scaffolding staging seems to be required in the Cain and Abel play and in *The Second Shepherds' Play*, as Robinson demonstrates (*Studies in Fifteenth-Century Stagecraft* 113–43).

CHAPTER 3, THE MORALITY PLAY BEFORE THE REFORMATION

1. See, for example, Robert Potter, *The English Morality Play* (6). The first six chapters of Potter's book are designed to demonstrate this.

2. The figures cited are extrapolated from Harbage's *Annals* (9–37).

3. Potter declares that twenty-eight of the extant sixty-one plays from the period 1558–1586 have a morality connection (105), but he includes plays that are not primarily moralities, including biblical drama as well as comedy and tragedy.

4. See especially Owst, *Literature and Pulpit in Medieval England* (526–45), and Thompson, *The English Moral Plays* (293–312).

5. For a discussion of the history and form of the paternoster play, see Johnston 70–90.

6. For a discussion of the functioning of allegory in the morality play tradition, see Davidson, *Visualizing the Moral Life*.

7. *The Macro Plays*, ed. Eccles. All subsequent references to *Wisdom*, *The Castle of Perseverence*, and *Mankind* are to this edition.

CHAPTER 4, FOLK DRAMA

1. The text is reprinted in Wiles (72–79).

2. See chapter 10 of *The Golden Bough*. In addition to Ordish's "Folk-Drama," for the ritual interpretation see especially Baskervill, "Dramatic Aspects of Medieval Folk Festivals" 19–87; Dean-Smith, "Life-Cycle Play" 237–53; Brody, *The English Mummers and Their Plays*; and Helm, *The English*

Mummers' Play. For the revisionist perspectives, see especially Richard Axton, *European Drama of the Early Middle Ages* (37–42), and Pettit, "The Early English Mummers' Play."

3. Helm, *The English Mummers' Play* (2). All further references to this collection of folk drama texts will be cited in parentheses.

4. Note the references in the Churchwardens' Accounts listed by Wiles (64–66).

CHAPTER 5, THE TERENTIAN COMMENTARIES

1. The exact date of the translation or publication is not known. *The Short Title Catalog* places the date ca. 1520, while F. P. Wilson, in *The English Drama, 1485–1585*, estimates ca. 1530 (103).

2. See, for example, the St. Albans Terence at the Bodleian Library (MS. F. 2.13).

3. The rhetorical aspects of the commentary are considered by Marvin Herrick in *Comic Theory in the Sixteenth Century* and by Joel B. Altman, *The Tudor Play of Mind* (138–43). Bruce R. Smith in *Ancient Scripts and Modern Experience on the English Stage 1500–1700* argues that Cicero, Quintilian, and Horace directed later commentators and Renaissance readers to perceive "drama-as-rhetorical-event" (12–37).

4. All quotations from Donatus and Evanthius are taken from *Commentum Terenti*; references cite act, scene, and line number. Translations are from Michael Hilger's dissertation, "The Rhetoric of Comedy: Comic Theory in the Terentian Commentary of Aelius Donatus" (University of Nebraska, 1970), completed under my direction.

5. All quotations from Renaissance commentators except Badius are taken from Terence, *Comoediae* (Paris: Ioannem de Roigny, 1552). The translations are mine unless otherwise indicated.

6. Evanthius describes the parts of the drama as follows: "The *Protasis* is the first act and the beginning of dramatic action; the *epitasis* is the growth and movement of the complications or — one might say — the knot of error; the *catastrophe* is the resolution of the complications into a happy ending; the resolution is made clear to all by a revelation of past events" (Hilger 31).

7. *Summa epitasis* is the term adopted by several commentators. *Catastasis* is J. C. Scaliger's term in *Poetices libri septem* (I.ix.15; see Herrick 109).

8. This is the central thesis of Baldwin's *Shakspere's Five-Act Structure*.

9. Herrick notes that "virtually all the commentators from Donatus to Erasmus and Willichius agreed that the comic poet, who uses fictitious events and persons, may treat his characters as though they were individuals and therefore not always subject to the general rules of conduct" (141).

CHAPTER 6, ERASMUS

1. This letter addressed to a fictitious person provides Erasmus's own partial account of his early life.

2. Faludy claims the work went through 102 printings before Erasmus's death in 1536 (212), but Vander Haeghen lists 73 through 1536 and 119 for the century (35–37).

3. Vives, Erasmus's friend and protégé, identifies Euripides and Seneca as models of tragedy and Aristophanes and Terence as models for comedy (see chapter 7).

4. T. W. Baldwin contends that "the whole framework of the English grammar school was based upon the ideas and texts of Erasmus" (*Shakspere's Small Latine* 1:100).

CHAPTER 7, VIVES

1. Adolfo Bonilla y San Martín, *Luis Vives y la filosofía del Renacimiento*, 3 vols. (1901: repr. Madrid, 1929), and Marcel Bataillon, *Erasme et L'Espagne, Recherches sur l'histoire spirituelle du XVIᵉ siècle* (Paris: E. Droz, 1937), translated into Spanish by Antonio Altorre: *Erasmo y España, estudios sobre la historia espiritual del siglo XVI* (1950; repr. Mexico: Fondo de Cultura Económica, 1966).

2. *Opera omnia*, ed. Gregorio Mayáns y Siscar, 8 vols. (Valencia, 1782–90; repr. London: Gregg Press, 1964). All Latin quotations from Vives's work in the discussion that follows are from the 1782–90 edition.

3. T. W. Baldwin notes that Vives's *Ad sapientiam* was required at Eton, Westminster, and elsewhere as a "fit companion to Cato" (*Shakspere's Small Latine* 1:688).

4. Richard Hyrde in his English translation, *A very frutefull and pleasant boke called the Instruction of a Christen woman* (London, 1540), supplements

Vives's list of romances to be avoided by adding a group from England (sig. E). Bataillon contrasts Vives's moralistic view with the more tolerant view of Juan de Valdés toward the romance as a literary form (*Erasmo y España* 2:219–22).

5. This image of drama may echo St. Isidore's negative view of ancient theater conveyed by Spanish and French commentators into the sixteenth century (see Joseph R. Jones, "Isidore and the Theater" 26–48); however, more particularly it reflects contemporary criticism of Terence and Plautus addressed by Erasmus and later humanists.

6. Pearl Hogrefe raises the question of Vives's authorship of *Calisto and Melebea*, the Tudor interlude based on *Celestina*, and after rejecting that possibility suggests that the highly moralized adaptation was connected with Vives's visits to England in the 1520s (344–45). Also see chapter 17.

7. Note his earlier commendation of Donatus in his letter to Mountjoy outlining his plan of studies for boys (*Vives and the Renascence Education of Women* 247).

8. Atkins, in *English Literary Criticism: The Renascence*, finds it surprising that Vives "takes no cognizance of the new Aristotelian ideas" (50), but Vives's disinterest is in fact quite consistent with his critical attitude toward drama.

9. For a discussion of Jonson's use of the classics in *Catiline*, see my article "The Design of Ben Jonson's *Catiline*."

CHAPTER 8, MORE

1. Erasmus, in a letter to More prefacing the printed edition of *Moriae encomium*, writes: "They [critics] will loudly accuse me of imitating the Old Comedy or some kind of Lucianic satire, and of attacking the whole world with my teeth" (*Collected Works* 2:163).

2. Elizabethan abbreviations are spelled out here and in subsequent quotations.

3. More later refers to a stage sultan in his *Confutation of Tyndale's Answer*, as Sylvester points out (*Complete Works* 2:259).

4. Several scholars have commented on More's sensitivity to role-playing. See especially Greenblatt (11–73).

5. Gordon in "The Platonic Dramaturgy of Thomas More's *Dialogues*" argues that the Platonic dialogue is More's "most closely related paradigm" (198).

6. Also see chapter 7 and Foster Watson, "A Friend of Sir Thomas More" (540–52).

7. See also Sister Mary Thecla, "New Corn from an Old Field" (347).

8. For further discussion of More's design in his last dialogue, see my article "Comfort Through Dialogue: More's Response to Tribulation" (53–66).

CHAPTER 9, ATTITUDES OF REFORMERS AND HUMANISTS

1. *The Passetyme of Pleasure*, ed. Mead. All subsequent references are to line numbers from the text of this edition.

2. *Of the Vanitie and Vncertaintie of Artes and Sciences*, Englished by Ja. San. [James Sanford], 1569. All subsequent references are to folio numbers in the text of this edition.

3. Cf. Elyot's definition of tragedy in his *Dictionary*: "Tragoedia, a tragedye, whiche is an enterlude, wherin the personages do represent somme hystorie or fable lamentable, for the crueltie and myserye therin expressed" (sig. Dd).

4. See Thomas Wilson, *Arte of Rhetorique*, ed. Derrick (lxxxvii–xciv).

5. All subsequent references are to the text of this edition.

6. Though Jonas Barish largely ignores the attack on and defense of drama in the early Tudor period in *The Antitheatrical Prejudice*, his account of the Puritan opposition to the stage in the later sixteenth and seventeenth centuries is most instructive (see especially 80–131 and 155–90).

CHAPTER 10, THE PRODIGAL PLAYS

1. References to the text are to Wever, *An Enterlude Called Lusty Juventus*, ed. Thomas.

2. References to the text are to act, scene, and page number in de Volder, *The Comedy of Acolastus*, trans. Palsgrave.

3. Subsequent references to the text are to this edition.

4. See Bevington, "Misogonus and Laurentius Bariωna" 9–10, Kittredge

NOTES TO PAGES 157–184

335–41, and Tannenbaum 308–10. Anthony Rudd has been proposed as the possible author in Harbage's *Annals* (40), *REED: Cambridge* 2:911, and *Misogonus*, ed. Barber 11–25.

5. References to the text are to John S. Farmer, ed., *The Dramatic Writings of Richard Wever and Thomas Ingelend*.

6. Subsequent references to the text are to this edition.

CHAPTER 11, REDFORD'S *WIT AND SCIENCE*

1. All references to the text are to line numbers in the edition prepared by Arthur Brown for the Malone Society. Craik also interprets these lines as indicating a royal performance (*Tudor Interlude* 22).

2. Hanna Scolnicov applies the parable to Merbury's later adaptation of Redford's play, but the pattern appears first in Redford's version (1–11).

3. John W. Velz and Carl P. Daw, Jr., describe this scene as a "mirror" scene, which offers a "wry comment on Wit's intellectual shortcomings in the first half of the play" ("Tradition and Originality" 632–33).

4. Craik suggests that Wit probably puts on his original gown again (*Tudor Interlude* 85–86).

5. References to the text are to act, scene, and line number in Lennam's edition in *Sebastian Westcott*.

6. References to the text are to Wickham, ed., *English Moral Interludes*.

CHAPTER 12, SKELTON'S *MAGNIFICENCE*

1. For a more detailed discussion of the transmission of this text, see *Secretum Secretorum*, ed. Manzalaoui 1: ix–xlvi.

2. The figures cited are extrapolated from Harbage's *Annals* (9–37).

3. Skelton, *Magnifycence*, ed. Ramsay xxi–xxv; W. Harris 12–13; Happé, ed., *Four Morality Plays* 39.

4. All references to the text of *Magnificence* are to Paula Neuss's edition.

5. Heiserman describes *Magnificence* as "merely an ineptly dramatized *Bowge of Court*, a compound of indistinguishable characters and trite complaints against fortune and folly" (67).

6. Note particularly the mid-fifteenth-century Ashmole manuscript version of *Secretum* in the Manzalaoui edition (69–70).

351

7. See, for example, *Mankind* 792–807; the same pattern is represented, of course, in Spenser's *Faerie Queene* (I.ix.48–52) and Milton's *Paradise Lost* (X, 992–1009).

CHAPTER 13, BALE'S *KING JOHN*

1. In *Catalogus*, *Pro Ioanne* is changed to *De Ioanne*.

2. The last three scholarly editions of the play generally agree that the first version represents the play performed for Cranmer and the second was probably for Queen Elizabeth, though the editors vary in their views of the initial composition and the stages of the revision. See *King Johan by John Bale*, ed. Pafford and Greg (xiii–xvii), *John Bale's King John*, ed. Adams (20–24), and *The Complete Plays of John Bale*, ed. Happé 1:9–11.

3. This and all subsequent references to the text are to line numbers in *King John* in *The Complete Plays*, ed. Happé.

4. Happé would place the initial composition as early as 1533–34 (Bale, *Complete Plays* 1:4).

5. See Bale, *King Johan*, ed. Pafford and Greg, x–xxix; the argument for an Edwardian performance has generally not been accepted by subsequent scholars.

6. In his list of plays in *Anglorum Heliades* (1536) and in all of his subsequent lists, Bale includes "Vitam Diui Ioannes Baptiste Li. xiiii," but because *Li* is his abbreviation for *liber*, or book, which he uses to identify a play or an act, he appears to mean either that his *Life of John the Baptist* was a series of fourteen plays or a play of fourteen acts or parts. The effect in either case would be comparable to a dramatic cycle.

7. See Happé's discussion of Bale's adaptation of the saint play tradition in *King John* ("Protestant Adaptation" 207–26).

8. For a discussion of Bale's role in promoting the Protestant cause, see King, *English Reformation Literature* (56–75 and passim).

CHAPTER 14, *RESPUBLICA*

1. *Respublica*, ed. Greg, 1. All subsequent references to the text of the play are to this edition.

2. Neither Harbage's *Annals* (33) nor *Revels* (2:56) indicates a court performance, though both set the initial performance in London.

3. The author of *Respublica* in the prologue appears to allude to Skelton's principal vices in *Magnificence*, Cloaked Collusion and Courtly Abusion, as he explains his message: "Though these vices bycloked collusyon / And by counterfaicte Names, hidden theire abusion / Do reign for a while" (23–25), they will be exposed and the Commonwealth restored.

4. *Revels* notes Avarice's similarity to the "classical miser" (2:218).

5. Glynne Wickham comments that "at first glance the dialogue might be mistaken for that of a Protestant play," but then argues for a strong Catholic perspective (*Early English Stages*, 2.1:70–71).

6. Several arguments for Udall's authorship have been made on other grounds: Leicester Bradner finds metrical similarities between *Respublica* and Udall's *Roister Doister*, with "the unquestioned predominance of the twelve-syllable line" in both plays ("A Test for Udall's Authorship" 378–80); G. Scheurweghs discovers that "the uses of the relative pronouns and their frequencies are strikingly similar" in *Roister Doister* and *Respublica* ("The Relative Pronouns" 84–89); and W. W. Greg, on the basis of word choice, turns of phrase, motifs, and other aspects of style that *Respublica* and *Roister Doister* share, was so convinced Udall was the author of *Respublica* that he placed Udall's name on the title page of his edition of the play (*Roister Doister*, ed. Greg viii–xviii). Only W. L. Edgerton seriously questions Udall's authorship (*Nicholas Udall* 65).

7. John Foxe in his *Acts and Monuments of Martyrs* elaborates the comparison of Edward to Josias and declares that Edward followed Josias's example except that "he killed not, as *Josias* did, the Idolatrous Sacrificers, yet he put them to silence, and removed them out of their places" (2.9:2).

8. Udall's militant Protestantism and later accommodation to Mary's reinstatement of Catholicism have provoked various interpretations. See especially Peery 119–21 and 138–41, and Edgerton, "The Apostasy of Nicholas Udall" 223–26 and "Nicholas Udall in the Indexes of Prohibited Books" 247–52.

9. For my discussion of Udall's contemporary *Roister Doister*, see chapter 19.

CHAPTER 15, LINDSAY'S *SATIRE OF THE THREE ESTATES*

1. This and all subsequent references to the poetry and drama of Lindsay are to *The Works of Sir David Lindsay*, ed. Hamer. Lindsay's poetry is included in Volume 1.

2. This text, as edited by Hamer in *The Works*, vol. 2, is the basis for our examination of the play. The Bannatyne version is printed by Hamer on facing pages.

3. This identification with France in a stage direction appears only in the Bannatyne manuscript representing the Cupar production of 1552.

4. This is also similar to a king's responsibility for justice as expressed in *Secretum* (69–70).

CHAPTER 16, *FULGENS AND LUCRES*

1. Subsequent references to part and line numbers in the text of *Fulgens and Lucres* are to this edition.

2. See Baskervill, "Conventional Features" 421–23, for other examples in medieval love poetry.

3. The *controversia*, popular in Augustan Rome, was "the declamation *Par excellence*," as Eugene Waith explains (286–303).

4. For example, after the defeat of the Lancastrians at Stoke in 1487, Henry created thirteen bannerets and fifty-two new knights (Alexander 58).

5. See Lockyer (32–44) for a discussion of Henry's councils.

6. David Bevington considers the political context of the play and some of its political implications in *Tudor Drama and Politics* (44–51); see also his "Popular and Courtly Traditions" 100–101.

7. For a fuller explanation of the game, see Fletcher 134–39.

8. Colley sees B's garbled message as an ironic vision of Medwall's position as he strives to communicate with his audience (325).

CHAPTER 17, *CALISTO AND MELEBEA*

1. An English translation of Terence's *Andria*, which was also called a comedy on the title page, may have been published slightly earlier, but *Calisto and Melebea* is nevertheless the first play *composed* in English to be identified as a comedy.

2. References to the text are to lines in Richard Axton's edition in *Three Rastell Plays*.

3. Ungerer suggests the play was performed at the wedding of John More and Anne Cresacre in 1529 (26).

4. The arguments concerning the authorship are summarized by Lacalle in his edition of Rojas's *Celestine*, translated by Mabbe (4).

5. The stage is cleared before her entrance. Richard Axton suggests that the play is divided into "three almost equal 'acts' (1–309, 310–632, 633–919) and an epilogue (920–1087); the divisions fall when the acting place is empty and they may have intended as pauses in performance, perhaps for refreshment. Each 'act' begins with a solo entry" (*Three Rastell Plays* 17–18).

CHAPTER 18, *JOHAN JOHAN*

1. The edition of *Johan Johan* cited throughout is for convenience that of David Bevington in *Medieval Drama*, and the edition of *Farce du Pasté* is Cohen's included in *Recueil de farces*.

2. (Now shortly, by the sacrament of the altar, she will have her payment for it, because I will see to it in such a way that the path will be a hard one for her.)

3. "Yea, rounde about the bed doth he go,
   You two together, and no mo;
   And for to finisshe the procession." (Bevington 175–77).

4. (*The Priest:* Over there! I beg you, follow him closely. *The husband returns by the rear with a sack full of bread.* After priest, after, after. Ah! you spoiled the pasty for me, after, priest, after, priest, to him! to him! to him! And so, masters, I bid you farewell! THE END.)

5. Cohen says, "A la fin mari et femme se réconcilient sur le dos de leur hôte qu'ils battent" (*Recueil de farces* xiv; At the end the husband and wife are reconciled at the expense of their guest, whom they beat). Halina Lewicka also notes Cohen's error (108).

6. (Ye gods! my love, God deserves to be praised by all, but who knows if she had dedicated her fruit to the holy Glorious Body?)

7. Cohen's edition identifies twenty-five lines of L'Homme spoken *à part*, while Bevington suggests fifty-eight lines of Johan Johan are asides.

CHAPTER 19, UDALL'S *ROISTER DOISTER*

1. T. W. Baldwin, among others, makes this designation, in *Shakspere's Five-Act Structure* (380).

2. J. Q. Adams in a note to his edition of the play in *Chief Pre-Shakespearean Dramas* continues to favor Udall's Eton years as the period of composition (423).

3. Udall's adaptation to Mary's reign is the subject of considerable controversy (see chapter 14).

4. All references to the text are to lines in Udall, *Roister Doister*, ed. W. W. Greg.

5. De Roigny's variorium edition, Baldwin notes, would have incorporated most of the structural analysis of Terence (*Shakspere's Five-Act Structure* 398). It would have been available to Udall during his composition of *Roister Doister*, but as a veteran schoolmaster and former translator of Terence, he clearly knew earlier editions with their commentaries as well.

6. Donatus in his commentaries on Terence's plays emphasizes error as the basis of the comic-intrigue plots (see chapter 5).

7. See the summary of act 3 in Jonson's "Argument," prefacing *The New Inn*.

8. St. George, or King George, as he is sometimes called, typically introduces himself with an account of his exploits; other combatants and wooers often follow the same pattern (see chapter 4).

9. Robert F. Willson says the "testing of Custance [is] more of an occasion for rhetorical posturing than a crucial focus of the action" (20).

10. Beelzebub appears in several of the folk plays carrying a club or a frying pan (see chapter 4).

11. The text indicates the insertion of the *Psalmodie* printed at the end of the text with the note "*vt infra*" following line 937.

12. Note Merrygreek's admission that he read the letter "in a wrong sense for daliance" (IV.vi.1581). See also A. W. Plumstead, "Who Pointed Roister's Letter?" 329–31.

CHAPTER 20, *GAMMER GURTON'S NEEDLE*

1. Henry Bradley calls it the "sole surviving example of vernacular college comedies" (Gayley 1:202), but *Misogonus* is another example of the college play (see chapter 10).

2. For a chronological table of Cambridge plays prior to the publication of *Gammer Gurton's Needle* in 1575, see G. C. Moore Smith, *College Plays* (50–61).

3. Most recent scholars favor Stevenson as the author, including one of the most recent editors of the play, William Tydeman in *Four Tudor Comedies* (211–12), and Alan Nelson in *REED: Cambridge* (2:897).

4. All references to the text are to act, scene, and line numbers in *Gammer Gurtons Nedle*, ed. H. F. B. Brett-Smith, a reprinting of the most authoritative 1575 text.

5. Local authorities sometimes required this identification as a license to beg, as Robinson notes ("Art and Meaning" 55).

6. Karl Young ("The Influence of French Farce" 100) and Felix Schelling (1:92) also note a quality of French farce in the play.

7. See the summary of act 3 in Jonson's "Argument," prefacing *The New Inn*.

8. The fact that the play survives in eleven copies, an unusually high number, suggests its popularity in the sixteenth century (Whitworth xxiii).

CHAPTER 21, WATSON'S *ABSALOM*

1. All subsequent references to the text of *Absalom* are to this edition: *A Humanist's "Trew Imitation": Thomas Watson's Absalom*, ed. and trans. John Hazel Smith.

2. The exception to the five-act structure in Seneca's drama is *Oedipus*, which has only three rather than four choral interludes.

3. Watson emphasizes Absalom's beastliness by comparing him to a tigress (I.iii.240–41) and a lion (II.i.22).

4. The King James version of the Bible is the source of all biblical quotations.

CHAPTER 22, CHRISTOPHERSON'S *JEPHTHAH*

1. The Greek manuscripts at Cambridge are MS. 284, H. 19 at St. John's, and MS. O.I. 37 at Trinity. The Latin manuscript at the Bodleian is MS. Tanner 466, fols. 126–53, described by Bernard M. Wagner, "The Tragedy of Iephte," *TLS*, December 26, 1929, p. 1097; see also F. S. Boas, "The Tragedy of Iephte," *TLS*, January 30, 1930, p. 78.

2. See Christopherson, *Jephthah*, ed. and trans. Francis Howard Fobes with introduction by Wilbur Owen Sypherd (7–8). Subsequent references to the text are to this edition.

3. This and subsequent translations from Christopherson's dedicatory letters are from Christopherson, *Jephthah*, ed. Fobes 11–12n. Christopherson expresses a similar thought in his letter to Henry VIII prefacing his Latin version of the play.

4. All references to the text of *Jephthes* are to Buchanan, *Tragedies*, ed. P. Sharratt and P. G. Walsh.

CHAPTER 23, GRIMALD'S *ARCHIPROPHETA*

1. *Christus Nascens* is identified by John Bale as a comedy and *Protomartyr* as a tragedy in *Index Britanniae Scriptorum* (302). A number of scholars assume *Protomartyr* deals with St. Stephen; see, for example, Grimald, *The Life and Poems*, ed. Merrill (26).

2. Neo-Latin drama predominated over vernacular plays at both Oxford and Cambridge, but most of the extant tragedies were performed at Oxford (Greenwood 323).

3. All subsequent quotations from Grimald's plays are from this edition.

4. "Omne tulit punctum qui miscuit utile dulci, / lectorem delectando pariterque monendo" (*Ars poetica* 343–44; He has won every vote who has blended profit and pleasure, at once delighting and instructing the reader).

5. "Segnius irritant animos demissa per aurem / quam quae sunt oculis subiecta fidelibus et quae / ipse sibi tradit spectator" (*Ars poetica* 180–82; Less vividly is the mind stirred by what finds entrance through the ears than by what is brought before the trusty eyes, and what the spectator can see for himself).

WORKS CITED

Adams, J. Q., ed. *Chief Pre-Shakespearean Dramas*. Cambridge, Mass.: Houghton Mifflin, 1924.

Agrippa, Henrie Cornelius. *Of the Vanitie and Vncertaintie of Artes and Sciences*, Englished by Ja. San. (James Sanford). London: Henry Wypes, 1569.

Aitken, James M. *The Trial of George Buchanan Before the Lisbon Inquisition*. Edinburgh: Oliver and Boyd, 1939.

Alciati, Andreas. *Emblemata*. Padua, 1621.

Alexander, Michael. *The First of the Tudors, A Study of Henry VII and His Reign*. Totowa, N.J.: Rowman and Littlefield, 1980.

Altman, Joel B. *The Tudor Play of Mind, Rhetorical Inquiry and the Development of Elizabethan Drama*. Berkeley: University of California Press, 1978.

Anderson, M. D. *Drama and Imagery in English Medieval Churches*. Cambridge: Cambridge University Press, 1963.

Anglo, Sydney. "The Evolution of the Early Tudor Disguising, Pageant, and Mask." *RenD* n.s. 1 (1968): 3–44.

Aristophanes. *Works*, trans. B. B. Rogers. London: William Heinemann, 1924.

Ascham, Roger. *The Scholemaster*, ed. Edward Arber. London: Constable, 1935.

Aston, Margaret. *England's Iconoclasts*. Vol. 1. Oxford: Clarendon Press, 1988.

Atkins, J. W. H. *English Literary Criticism: The Renascence*. 2nd ed. London: Methuen, 1951.

Aubailly, Jean-Claude. *Le Monologue, le Dialogue et la Sotie*. Paris: Editions Honoré Champion, 1976.

Augustine (pseudo). *Quaestiones Veteris et Novi Testamenti CXXVII*, recensuit Alexander Souter. Vindobonae, Lipsiae, 1908.

Axton, Marie, ed. *Three Tudor Classical Interludes*. Cambridge: D. S. Brewer, 1982.

Axton, Richard. *European Drama of the Early Middle Ages*. London: Hutchinson University Library, 1974.

———. "Folk play in Tudor interludes," in *English Drama: Forms and Development, Essays in Honor of Muriel Clara Bradbrook*, ed. Marie Axton and Raymond Williams, 1–23. Cambridge: Cambridge University Press, 1977.

———, ed. *Three Rastell Plays: Four Elements, Calisto and Melebea, Gentleness and Nobility*. Cambridge: D. S. Brewer, 1979.

Baird, Joseph L., and Lorraine Y. Baird. "Fabliau Form and the Hegge *Joseph's Return*." *Chaucer Review* 8 (1974): 159–69.

Baker, Donald C., John L. Murphy, and Louis B. Hall, eds. *The Late Medieval Religious Plays of Bodleian MSS 133 and e museo 160*. Oxford: Oxford University Press, 1982.

Baldwin, T. W. *Shakspere's Five-Act Structure: Shakspere's Early Plays on the Background of Renaissance Theories of Five-Act Structure from 1470*. Urbana: University of Illinois Press, 1947.

———. *William Shakspere's Small Latine and Lesse Greeke*. 2 vols. Urbana: University of Illinois Press, 1944.

Bale, John. *The Complete Plays of John Bale*, ed. Peter Happé. 2 vols. Cambridge: D. S. Brewer, 1985–86.

———. *Index Britanniae Scriptorum*, ed. Reginald L. Poole. Oxford: Clarendon Press, 1902.

———. *John Bale's King Johan*, ed. Barry B. Adams. San Marino, Calif.: The Huntington Library, 1969.

———. *King Johan by John Bale*, ed. J. H. P. Pafford and W. W. Greg. [London]: Malone Society Reprints, 1931.

———. *Scriptorum Illustrium maioris Britannie*. Basel, 1557.

Barish, Jonas. *The Antitheatrical Prejudice*. Berkeley: University of California Press, 1981.

Baskervill, C. R. "Conventional Features of Medwall's *Fulgens and Lucres*," *MP* 24 (1927): 419–42.

———. "Dramatic Aspects of Medieval Folk Festivals in England," *SP* 17 (1920): 19–87.

———. "Mummers' Wooing Plays in England," *MP* 21 (1924): 225–72.

Bataillon, Marcel. *Erasme et L'Espagne, Recherches sur l'histoire spirituelle du XVIe siècle*. Paris: Librairie E. Droz, 1937.

———. *Erasmo y España, estudios sobre la historia espiritual del siglo XVI*, trans. Antonio Altorre. Mexico: Fondo de Cultura Económica, 1966 [1950].

Beaunans Meriasek, The Life of Saint Meriasek, Bishop and Confessor, A Cornish Drama, ed. and trans. Whitley Stokes. London: Trubner and Co., 1872.

Becon, Thomas. *A New Catechisme sette forth dialoge-wise in familiar talke betwene the father and the son* [1550], ed. John Ayre for the Parker Society. Cambridge: The University Press, 1844.

Beicher, Paul E. "Absolon's Hair." *Medieval Studies* 12 (1950): 222–33.

Bevington, David M. "Discontinuity of Medieval Acting Traditions." *The Elizabethan Theatre, V*, ed. George R. Hibbard. Toronto: Macmillan, 1975.

———. *From "Mankind" to Marlowe: Growth of Structure in the Popular Drama of Tudor England*. Cambridge, Mass.: Harvard University Press, 1962.

———. *Medieval Drama*. Boston: Houghton Mifflin, 1975.

———. "Misogonus and Laurentius Bariωna." *English Language Notes* 2 (1964–65): 9–10.

———. "Popular and Courtly Traditions on the Early Tudor Stage." In *Medieval Drama*, ed. Neville Denny, 91–107. Stratford-Upon-Avon Studies 16. London: Edward Arnold, 1973.

———. *Tudor Drama and Politics, A Critical Approach to Topical Meaning*. Cambridge, Mass.: Harvard University Press, 1968.

Billington, Sandra. "'Suffer Fools Gladly': The Fool in Medieval England and the Play *Mankind*." In *The Fool and the Trickster: Studies in Honour of Enid Welsford*, ed. Paul V. A. Williams, 36–54. Cambridge: D. S. Brewer, 1979.

Blackburn, Ruth H. *Biblical Drama Under the Tudors*. The Hague: Mouton, 1971.

Boas, Frederick S. *An Introduction to Tudor Drama*. Oxford: Clarendon Press, 1933.

———. "The Tragedy of Iephte." *TLS*, 30 January 1930, p. 78.

———. *University Drama in the Tudor Age*. Oxford: Clarendon Press, 1914.

Bonilla y San Martín, Adolfo. *Luis Vives y la filosofía del Renacimiento*. 3 vols. Madrid, 1929 [1901].

Bradner, Leicester. "A Test for Udall's Authorship." *MLN* 42 (1927): 378–80.

Brody, Alan. *The English Mummers and Their Plays*. Philadelphia: University of Pennsylvania Press, 1969.

Brooke, C. F. Tucker. "Latin Drama in Renaissance England." *English Literary History* 13 (1946): 233–240.

———. *The Tudor Drama*. Boston: Houghton Mifflin, 1911.

Buchanan, George. *Baptistes, sive Calumnia, Tragoedia*. London, 1577.

———. *Baptistes, sive Calumnia, Tragoedia*, trans. as *Tyrannicall-Government Anatomized, or a Discourse concerning Euil-Councellors, being the Life and Death of John, the Baptist* (London, 1642); attributed to John Milton. Reprinted in *George Buchanan: Glasgow Quatercentenary Studies 1906*. Glasgow: Jams Maclehose and Sons, 1907.

———. *Iephthes sive Votum Tragoedia*. Paris, 1554.

———. *Tragedies*, ed. P. Sharratt and P. G. Walsh. Edinburgh: Scottish Academic Press, 1983.

Buonaccorso da Montemagno. *De Vera Nobilitate* (ca. 1428), trans. John Tiptoft, Earl of Worcester (ca. 1460). London: William Caxton, 1481.

Calisto and Melebea. London: Rastell, ca. 1527–30.

The Cambridge History of English Literature. Vol. 3. Cambridge: The University Press, 1909.

Chambers, E. K. *The Elizabethan Stage*. 4 vols. Oxford: Clarendon Press, 1923.

———. *The Medieval Stage*. 2 vols. London: Oxford University Press, 1903.

Chambers, R. W. "The Continuity of English Prose from Alfred to More and His School." In Nicholas Harpsfield, *The Life and Death of Sir Thomas More*, ed. E. V. Hitchcock, xlv–clxxv. London: Oxford University Press, 1932.

———. *Thomas More*. Hammondsworth, Middlesex: Penguin Books, 1963 [1935].

The Chester Mystery Cycle, ed. Robert M. Lumiansky and David Mills. London: Oxford University Press, Vol. 1, 1974; Vol. 2, 1986.

The Chester Plays, Part 1, ed. Hermann Deimling. London: Kegan Paul, 1892.

Chrimes, S. B. *Henry VII*. Berkeley: University of California Press, 1972.

Christopherson, John. *Jephthah*, ed. and trans. Francis Howard Fobes. Newark, Del.: University of Delaware Press, 1928.

Clopper, Lawrence M. "Tyrants and Villains: Characterization in the Passion Sequences of the English Cycle Plays." *Modern Language Quarterly* 41 (1980): 3–20.

Cohen, Gustave, ed. *Recueil de farces françaises inédites du XVe siècle*. Cambridge, Mass.: Medieval Academy of America, 1949.

Coldewey, John C. "The Digby Plays and the Chelmsford Records." *Research Opportunities in Renaissance Drama* 18 (1975): 103–21.

———. "That Enterprising Property Player: Semi-Professional Drama in Sixteenth-Century England." *Theatre Notebook* 31 (1977): 5–12.

Coletti, Theresa. "The Design of the Digby Play of *Mary Magdalene*." *SP* 76 (1979): 313–33.

———. "Devotional Iconography in the N-Town Marian Plays." *CompD* 11 (1977): 22–44.

Colie, Rosalie L. *The Resources of Kind: Genre-Theory in the Renaissance*. Berkeley: University of California Press, 1973.

Colley, John S. "*Fulgens and Lucres*: Politics and Aesthetics." *Zeitschift für Anglistik and Amerikanistik* (East Berlin) 23 (1975): 322–30.

Cox, Leonard. *The Arte or Crafte of Rhetoryke*, ed. Frederick I. Carpenter. Chicago: University of Chicago Press, 1898.

Craig, Hardin. *English Religious Drama in the Middle Ages*. Oxford: Clarendon Press, 1955.

———, ed. *Two Coventry Corpus Christi Plays*. 2nd ed. London: Oxford University Press, 1957.

Craik, T. W. "The True Source of John Heywood's *Johan Johan*." *MLR* 45 (1950): 289–95.

——. *The Tudor Interlude: Stage, Costume, and Acting.* Leicester: University of Leicester Press, 1958.

Crossett, John. "More and Seneca." *PQ* 40 (1961): 577–80.

Davidson, Clifford. *Drama and Art: An Introduction to the Use of Evidence from the Visual Arts for the Study of Early Drama.* Early Drama, Art, and Music Monograph Series 1. Kalamazoo, Mich.: Medieval Institute, 1977.

——. "The Middle English Saint Play and Its Iconography." In *The Saint Play in Medieval Europe,* ed. Clifford Davidson, 31–122. Kalamazoo, Mich.: Medieval Institute, 1986.

——. *Visualizing the Moral Life, Medieval Iconography and the Macro Morality Plays.* New York: AMS Press, 1989.

Dean, Leonard F. "*The Praise of Folly* and Its Background." In *Twentieth Century Interpretations of 'The Praise of Folly,'* ed. Kathleen Williams. Englewood Cliffs, N.J.: Prentice-Hall, 1969.

Dean-Smith, Margaret. "Life-Cycle Play or Folk Play." *Folklore* 69 (1958): 237–53.

Dickens, A. G. *The English Reformation.* New York: Schocken Books, 1965.

The Digby Plays: Facsimiles of the Plays of Bodley MSS Digby 133 and e Museo 160, ed. Donald C. Baker and J. J. Murphy. LTM Medieval Drama Facsimiles 3. Leeds: University of Leeds, 1976.

Dobson, R. B. and Taylor, J., eds. *Rymes of Robin Hood: An Introduction to the English Outlaw.* London: William Heinemann, 1976.

Donaldson, Gordon. *Scotland: James V to James VII.* Edinburgh: Oliver and Boyd, 1971.

Donatus, Aelius. *Commentum Terenti,* recensvit Paulus Wessner. 3 vols. Lipsiae: B. G. Teubner, 1902–8.

Doran, Madeleine. *Endeavors of Art: A study of form in Elizabethan drama.* Madison: University of Wisconsin Press, 1954.

Duffy, R. A. "*Wit and Science* and Early Tudor Pageantry: A Note on Influences." *MP* 76 (1978): 184–89.

Dunn, Ellen Catherine. "The Origin of the Middle English Saints' Plays," in *The Medieval Drama and Claudelian Revival,* ed. F. Catherine Dunn et al., 1–15. Washington, D.C.: Catholic University of America Press, 1970.

Edgerton, William L. "The Apostasy of Nicholas Udall." *N&Q* 195 (1950): 223–26.

———. "The Date of *Roister Doister*." *PQ* 44 (1965): 555–60.
———. *Nicholas Udall*. New York: Twayne Publishers, 1965.
———. "Nicholas Udall in the Indexes of Prohibited Books." *JEGP* 55 (1956): 247–52.
Elizabethan Critical Essays, ed. G. Gregory Smith. 2 vols. London: Oxford University Press, 1959.
Elton, G. R. *Reform and Reformation, England 1509–1558*. London: Edward Arnold, 1977.
Elton, William. "Note on *Johan Johan*." *TLS*, February 24, 1950, p. 128.
Elyot, Thomas. *The book named The governor*, ed. S. E. Lehmberg. London: J. M. Dent and Sons, 1962.
———. *The Defence of Good Women*. London: Thomas Berthelet, 1545.
———. *Dictionary*. London, 1538.
The Enterlude of the iiii. Cardynal Vertues and the Vyces Contrary to Them, ed. W. W. Greg. *The Malone Society Collections*, IV (1956), 41–54.
An enterlude of Welth, and Helth, very mery and full of Pastyme, ed. W. W. Greg. [London, ca. 1557] Malone Society Reprints, 1907.
Erasmus, Desiderius. *Adages*. Basel: Froben, 1533.
———. *Ciceronianus, or A Dialogue on the Best Style of Speaking*, trans. Izora Scott. New York: Teachers College, Columbia University, 1908.
———. *The Collected Works of Erasmus*. Toronto: University of Toronto Press, 1974–.
———. *The Colloquies of Erasmus*, trans. Craig R. Thompson. Chicago: University of Chicago Press, 1965.
———. *On Copia of Words and Ideas* (*De Utraque Verborem ac Rerum Copia*), trans. Donald B. King and H. David Rix. Milwaukee: Marquette University Press, 1963.
———. *The Education of a Christian Prince*, trans. Lester K. Born. New York: W. W. Norton, 1968 [1936].
———. *The Enchiridion*, trans. and ed. Raymond Himelick. Bloomington: Indiana University Press, 1963.
———. *Erasmus Concerning Education*, ed. William Harrison Woodward. Cambridge, 1904. Reprinted in *Classics in Education* (No. 19). New York: Columbia University Teachers College, 1964.

———. *Opera omnia*. Basel, 1540.

———. *Opus Epistolarum Des Erasmi Roterodami*, ed. P. S. Allen, H. M. Allen, and H. W. Garrod. 12 vols. Oxford: Oxford University Press, 1906–58.

———. *The Praise of Folie. Moriae Encomium*, trans. Sir T. Chaloner. London, 1549.

———. *De Pueris statim ac liberaliter instituendis*, trans. Rychard Sherry under the title "A declamacion *That Chyldren even strayt fro' their infancie should be well and gently brought up in learnynge*" (ca. 1550).

———. *De ratione studii*. 1519.

Estelrich, Juan. *Vivès. Exposition organisée à la Bibliothèque nationale*. Paris, 1941.

Faludy, George. *Erasmus*. New York: Stein and Day, 1970.

Farmer, David Hugh. *The Oxford Dictionary of Saints*. Oxford: Clarendon Press, 1979.

Farmer, John S., ed. *The Dramatic Writings of Richard Wever and Thomas Ingelend*. New York: Barnes and Noble, 1966.

———, ed. *Six Anonymous Plays* (*Second Series*). New York: Barnes and Noble, 1966.

Ferrarius, Ioannes. *A Woorke of Ioannes Ferrarivs Montanus, touchynge the good orderynge of a Common weale . . .* Englished by William Bavande. London, 1559.

Fletcher, Alan J. "'Farte Prycke in Cule': A Late Elizabethan Analogue from Ireland." *Medieval English Theatre* 8 (1986): 134–39.

Forrest, Sister Mary Patricia, O.S.F. "Apocryphal Sources of St. Anne's Day Plays in the Hegge Cycle." *Medievalia et Humanistica* 17 (1966): 38–50.

Foxe, John. *Ecclesiastical History containing the Acts and Monuments of Martyrs*. London, 1684.

Frazer, James. *The Golden Bough*. 3rd ed. London: Macmillan, 1920.

Frye, Northop. *Anatomy of Criticism*. Princeton: Princeton University Press, 1957.

Gammer Gurtons Nedle, by Mr. S. Mr. of Art, ed. H. F. B. Brett-Smith. Oxford: Basil Blackwell, 1920.

Gardiner, Harold C., S. J. *Mysteries' End, An Investigation of the Last Days of the Medieval Religious Stage*. 1946. Hamden, Conn.: Archon Books, 1967.

Garth, Helen Meredith. *Saint Mary Magdalene in Mediaeval Literature.* Johns Hopkins University Studies in Historical and Political Science, Series 67, No. 3. Baltimore: Johns Hopkins University Press, 1950.
Gayley, C. M., ed. *Representative English Comedies.* New York: Macmillan Co., 1903.
Geritz, Albert J. "*Calisto and Melebea* (ca. 1530)." *Celestinesca* 4.1 (1980): 17–29.
Gibson, Gail McMurray. "Bury St. Edmunds, Lydgate, and the *N-Town Cycle.*" *Speculum* 56 (1981): 56–90.
———. "'Porta haec clausa erit': Comedy, Conception, and Ezekial's Closed Door in the *Ludus Conventriae* Play of 'Joseph's Return.'" *JMRS* 8 (1978): 137–56.
Gibson, R. W. and J. Max Patrick, eds. *St. Thomas More: A Preliminary Bibliography of His Works and of Moreana to the Year 1750.* New Haven: Yale University Press, 1961.
Glassie, Henry. *All Silver and No Brass.* Bloomington: Indiana University Press, 1975.
The Golden Legend or Lives of the Saints, as Englished by William Caxton, ed. F. S. Ellis. (Originally compiled by Jacobus de Voragine, Archbishop of Genoa ca. 1275.) 6 vols. London: J. M. Dent and Sons, 1922 [1900].
The Golden Legende, trans. William Caxton. London, 1483.
Gordon, Walter Martin. "Dramatic Elements in the Writings of Saint Thomas More." Diss. University of London, 1966.
———. "The Platonic Dramaturgy of Thomas More's *Dialogues.*" *JMRS* 8 (1978): 193–215.
Greg, W. W., ed. *Robin Hood Plays.* Malone Society Collections I:2. Oxford, 1908.
Greenblatt, Stephen J. *Renaissance Self-Fashioning, From More to Shakespeare.* Chicago: Chicago University Press, 1980.
Greenwood, David. "The Staging of Neo-Latin Plays in Sixteenth Century England." *Educational Theatre Journal* 16 (1964): 311–23.
Grimald, Nicholas. *Archipropheta Tragoedia.* Cologne: Martin Gymnicus, 1548.
———. *Christus Redivivus, Comedia Tragica, sacra et noua.* Cologne, 1543. Facsimile edition in *PMLA* 14 (1899): 371–448.

———. *The Life and Poems of Nicholas Grimald*, ed. L. R. Merrill. Yale Studies in English 69. New Haven: Yale University Press, 1925.

Hall, Edward. *Hall's Chronicle; Containing the History of England During the Reign of Henry Fourth . . . to the End of Reign of Henry VIII.* London, 1809.

———. *The Vnion of the two noble and illustre families of Lancastre and Yorke.* London: Grafton, 1548.

Hanham, Alison. *Richard III and His Early Historians 1483–1535.* Oxford: Clarendon Press, 1975.

Happé, Peter, ed. *Four Morality Plays.* Harmondsworth, Middlesex: Penguin Books, 1979.

———. "The Protestant Adaptation of the Saint Play." In *The Saint Play in Medieval Europe*, ed. Clifford Davidson, 205–40. Kalamazoo, Mich.: Medieval Institute, 1986.

Harbage, Alfred. *Annals of English Drama 975–1700*, rev. S. Schoenbaum. London: Methuen, 1964.

Harpsfield, Nicholas. *The Life and death of Sr. Thomas Moore, knight, sometymes Lord high Chancellor of England*, ed. E. V. Hitchcock. London: Oxford University Press, 1932.

Harris, Jesse W. *John Bale, A Study in the Minor Literature of the Reformation.* Urbana: University of Illinois Press, 1940.

Harris, William O. *Skelton's "Magnyfycence" and the Cardinal Virtue Tradition.* Chapel Hill: University of North Carolina Press, 1965.

Harsh, Philip. *Studies in Dramatic "Preparation" in Roman Comedy.* Chicago: University of Chicago Press, 1935.

Hawes, Stephen. *The Passetyme of Pleasure*, ed. William Edward Mead. London: Oxford University Press, 1928.

Heiserman, A. R. *Skelton and Satire.* Chicago: University of Chicago Press, 1961.

Helm, Alex. *The English Mummers' Play.* The Folklore Society Mistletoe Series, Vol. 14. Woodbridge, Suffolk: D. S. Brewer, 1980.

Herford, C. H. *Studies in the Literary Relations of England and Germany in the Sixteenth Century.* Cambridge: University Press, 1886.

Herrick, Marvin T. *Comic Theory in the Sixteenth Century.* Illinois Studies in Language and Literature, vol. 34, nos. 1–2. Urbana: University of Illinois Press, 1950.

Hilger, Michael J. "The Rhetoric of Comedy: Comic Theory in the Terentian Commentary of Aelius Donatus." Ph.D. dissertation, University of Nebraska, 1970.
Hinton, J. S. "The Source of *Roister Doister*." MP 11 (1913–14): 273–78.
Hogrefe, Pearl. *The Sir Thomas More Circle: A Program of Ideas and Their Impact on Secular Drama*. Urbana: University of Illinois Press, 1959.
Horace. *Satires, Epistles, and Ars Poetica*, trans. H. R. Fairclough. Cambridge, Mass.: Harvard University Press, 1961.
Hroswitha. *Opera*. Nuremberg, 1501.
———. *The Plays of Roswitha*, trans. Christopher St. John. New York: Cooper Square Publishers, 1966.
A Hundred Merry Tales. London: Rastell, 1525.
Jeffrey, David L. "English Saints' Plays." In *Medieval Drama*, ed. Neville Denny, 69–89. Stratford-Upon-Avon Studies 16. London: Edward Arnold, 1973.
Jewel, John. "Oratio Contra Rhetoricam." *The Works of John Jewel*, ed. J. Ayre for the Parker Society, Part 4, 1283–91. Cambridge: The University Press, 1850.
Johan Johan the Husband, ed. G. R. Proudfoot. London: Malone Society, 1972.
Johnson, Richard. *Historie of the Savern [sic] Champions of Christendom*. London: Part 1, 1596; Part 2, 1597; Part 3, 1686.
Johnston, Alexandra F. "The Plays of the Religious Guilds of York: the Creed Play and the Pater Noster Play." *Speculum* L (1975): 55–90.
Jones, Charles W. *Saints' Lives and Chronicles in Early England*. Ithaca: Cornell University Press, 1947.
Jones, Emrys. *The Origins of Shakespeare*. Oxford: Clarendon Press, 1977.
———. *Scenic Form in Shakespeare*. Oxford: Clarendon Press, 1971.
Jones, Joseph R. "Isidore and the Theater." *CompD* 16 (1982): 26–48.
Jonson, Ben. *Ben Jonson*, ed. C. H. Herford and Percy and Evelyn Simpson. 11 vols. Oxford: Clarendon Press, 1925–52.
Josephus. *The Works of Flavius Josephus*, ed. William Whiston. 2 vols. London, 1825.
Kahrl, Stanley J. *Traditions of Medieval English Drama*. London: Hutchinson University Library, 1974.

Kantrowitz, Joanne Spencer. *Dramatic Allegory: Lindsay's Ane Satyre of the Thrie Estaitis*. Lincoln: University of Nebraska Press, 1975.

Kelley, Michael R. *Flamboyant Drama, A Study of "The Castle of Perseverance," "Mankind," and "Wisdom."* Carbondale and Edwardsville: Southern Illinois University Press, 1979.

Kincaid, Arthur N. "The Dramatic Structure of Sir Thomas More's *History of King Richard III*." *Studies in English Literature* 12 (1972): 223–42.

King, John N. *English Reformation Literature: The Tudor Origins of the Protestant Tradition*. Princeton, N.J.: Princeton University Press, 1982.

Kirke, John. *The Seven Champions of Christendome*. London: 1638.

Kittredge, G. L. "The 'Misogonus' and Laurence Johnson." *JEGP* 3 (1901): 335–41.

Kolve, V. A. *The Play Called Corpus Christi*. Stanford: Stanford University Press, 1966.

Kozikowski, Stanley J. "Comedy Ecclesiastical and Otherwise in *Gammer Gurton's Needle*." *Greyfriar: Siena Studies in Literature* 18 (1977): 5–18.

Lancashire, Ian. *Dramatic Texts and Records of Britain: A Chronological Topography to 1558*. Toronto and Buffalo: University of Toronto Press, 1984.

———, ed. *Two Tudor Interludes: The Interlude of Youth, Hickscorner*. Manchester: Manchester University Press, 1980.

Lawton, H. W. *Contribution à l'histoire de l'humanisme en France: Terence en France au XVIe siècle, éditions et traductions*. Paris, 1926.

Lennam, Trevor. *Sebastian Westcott, the Children of Paul's and 'The Marriage of Wit and Science.'* Toronto and Buffalo: University of Toronto Press, 1975.

Lewicka, Halina. *Études sur l'ancienne farce française*. Warsaw: Éditions scientifiques de Pologne, 1974.

The Life of Meriasek. A Medieval Cornish Miracle Play, trans. Markham Harris. Washington, D.C.: Catholic University of America Press, 1977.

Life of Saint Anne, ed. Roscoe E. Parker. London: Oxford University Press, 1928.

Lindesay, Robert, of Pitscottie. *The Historie and Cronicles of Scotland from the Lauchter of James the First to the Ane thousande fyve hunerith thrie scoir fyftein 3eir*, ed. AE. J. G. Mackay. 3 vols. Edinburgh and London: William Blackwood & Sons, 1899–1911.

Lindsay, Sir David. *Ane Satyre of the Thrie Estaits*. Edinburgh, 1602 Facsimile. Amsterdam: Da Capo Press, 1969.

———. *The Works of Sir David Lindsay of the Mount 1490–1555*, ed. Douglas Hamer. 4 vols. Scottish Text Society. Edinburgh: William Blackwood and Sons, 1931–36.

Lockyer, Roger. *Henry VII*. London: Longmans, Green, 1968.

Lucian. *Works*. 8 vols. London: William Heinemann, 1913–61.

Ludus Coventriae or the Plaie Called Corpus Christi, ed. K. S. Block. London, 1922.

Lupset, Thomas. *An Exhortation to Young men perswadyng them to walke in the pathe waie that leadeth to honestee and goodness. The Life and Works of Thomas Lupset*, ed. John A. Gee. New Haven: Yale University Press, 1928.

The Macro Plays, ed. Mark Eccles. London: Oxford University Press, 1969.

Macropedius. *Two Comedies*, ed. and trans. Yehudi Lindeman. Nieuwkoop: B. DeGraaf, 1983.

Maltman, Sister Nicholas, O.P. "Light in and on the Digby *Mary Magdalene*." In *Saints, Scholars and Heroes: Studies in Medieval Culture in Honour of Charles W. Jones*, ed. Margot H. King and Wesley M. Stevens, Vol. 1, 257–80. Ann Arbor: University Microfilms International for St. John's Abbey and University, 1979.

Manley, John M. "The Miracle Play in Medieval England." In *Essays by Divers Hands*, ed. Margaret L. Woods. Transactions of the Royal Society of Literature of the United Kingdom, n.s. 7:133–53. London: Oxford University Press, 1927.

Marsh, David. *The Quattrocento Dialogue*. Cambridge, Mass.: Harvard University Press, 1980.

Marshall, Mary H. "Theatre in the Middle Ages: Evidence from Dictionaries and Glosses." *Symposium* 4 (1950): 1–39, 366–89.

Martyr, Peter (Vermigli, Pietro Martire). *A briefe Treatise, Concerning the vse and abuse of Daunting*, trans. I. K. (or T. K.?). London, 1580.

———. *Commentaries upon Judges*. London: John Day, 1564.

Mason, Harold Andrew. *Humanism and Poetry in the Early Tudor Period*. London: Routledge and Kegan Paul, 1959.

Maulsby, D. L. "The Relation Betwen Udall's *Roister Doister* and the Comedies of Plautus and Terence." *Englische Studien* 38 (1907): 251–77.

Maxwell, Ian. *French Farce and John Heywood*. Melbourne: University of Melbourne Press, 1946.
McFarlane, I. D. *Buchanan*. London: Duckworth, 1981.
McKerrow, R. B., ed. *Dictionary of Printers . . . 1557–1640*. London, 1910.
Medwall, Henry. *Fulgens and Lucres, A Fifteenth Century Secular Play*, ed. F. S. Boas and A. W. Reed. Oxford: Clarendon Press, 1926.
———. *The Plays of Henry Medwall*, ed. Alan H. Nelson. Cambridge: D. S. Brewer, 1980.
Melanchthon, Philip. *Epistolarum Philippi Melanchthonis*, ed. Caspar Peucereo. Wittenberg, 1570.
Meredith, Peter, and John. E. Tailby, eds. *The Staging of Religious Drama in the Later Middle Ages: Texts and Documents in English Translation*. Kalamazoo, Mich.: Medieval Institute, 1983.
Merrix, Robert P. "The Function of the Comic Plot in *Fulgens and Lucrece*." *Modern Language Studies* 7 (1977): 16–26.
A mery play betwene Johan Johan the husbande / Tyb his wyfe / and syr Jhan the preest. London: William Rastell, 1533.
Miller, Edwin Shepard. "Roister Doister's 'Funeralls.'" *SP* 43 (1946): 42–58.
———. "The Roman Rite in Bale's *King Johan*." *PMLA* 64 (1949): 802–22.
Mills, David. "Approaches to Medieval Drama." *Leeds Studies in English* n.s. 3 (1969): 47–61.
Misogonus, ed. Lester E. Barber. New York and London: Garland Publishing, 1979.
More, Thomas. *The Complete Works of St. Thomas More*. New Haven: Yale University Press, 1963–.
———. *The Correspondence of Sir Thomas More*, ed. Elizabeth F. Rogers. Princeton: Princeton University Press, 1947.
———. *The English Works of Sir Thomas More*, ed. W. E. Campbell and A. W. Reed. 2 vols. Facsimile of William Rastell's 1557 edition. London: Eyre and Spottiswoode, 1931.
———. *The Workes of Sir Thomas More Knyght, sometyme Lorde Chauncellor of England, wrytten by him in the Englysh tonge, 1557*, ed. William Rastell. 2 vols. London: Scolar Press, 1978.
Murison, W. *Sir David Lyndsay, Poet and Satirist of the Old Church in Scotland*. Cambridge: The University Press, 1938.

Myers, A. R. "The Character of Richard III." *History Today* 4 (1954): 511–21.

The N-Town Plays, A Facsimile of British Library MS Cotton Vespasian D VIII, ed. Peter Meredith and Stanley J. Kahrl. Leeds: University of Leeds, School of English, 1977.

Nashe, Thomas. *The Works of Thomas Nashe*, ed. Ronald B. McKerrow. Oxford: Basil Blackwell, 1958.

Nelson, Alan H. *The Medieval English Stage, Corpus Christi Pageants and Plays*. Chicago: University of Chicago Press, 1974.

Nelson, William, ed. *A Fifteenth Century Schoolbook*. Oxford: Clarendon Press, 1956.

Noreña, Carlos G. *Juan Luis Vives*. The Hague: Martinus Nijhoff, 1970.

Norland, Howard B. "Comfort Through Dialogue: More's Response to Tribulation." *Moreana XXIV*, 93 (1987): 53–66.

——. "The Design of Ben Jonson's *Catiline*." *The Sixteenth Century Journal* 9 (1978): 67–79.

Olin, John C., ed. *Christian Humanism and the Reformation, Selected Writings of Erasmus with the Life of Erasmus by Beatus Rhenanus*. New York: Fordham University Press, 1975.

Ordish, T. F. "English Folk-Drama." *Folk-Lore* 4 (1893): 149–75.

——. "Folk-Drama." *Folk-Lore* 2 (1891): 314–35.

Owst, G. R. *Literature and Pulpit in Medieval England*. Cambridge: Cambridge University Press, 1933.

Palmer, Barbara D. "'Towneley Plays' or 'Wakefield Cycle' Revisited." *CompD* 21 (1987–88): 318–48.

Parker, Roscoe E., ed. *The Life of Saint Anne* London: Oxford University Press, 1928.

Parmentier, Jacques. *Histoire de l'éducation en Angleterre*. Paris: Perrin et Cie, Libraires-Editeurs, 1896.

Partee, Morriss M. "Sir Thomas Elyot on Plato's Aesthetics." *Viator: Medieval and Renaissance Studies* 1 (1970): 327–35.

Peele, George. *The Life and Works of George Peele*, ed. C. T. Prouty. 3 vols. New Haven: Yale University Press, 1952–70.

Peery, William. "Udall as Timeserver." *N&Q* 194 (1949): 119–21, 138–41.

Pettit, Thomas. "The Early English Mummers' Play, A Contextual Reconstruction." *Pre-Publications of the English Department at Odense University* (Denmark), No. 31 (December 1984).

———. "English Folk Drama in the Eighteenth Century: A Defense of the *Revesby Sword Play*." *CompD* 15 (1981): 3–29.

———. "Ritual and Vaudeville: the Dramaturgy of the English Folk Plays." *Pre-Publications of the English Institute of Odense University* (Denmark), No. 19 (October 1981).

Phillips, Margaret Mann. *The "Adages" of Erasmus: a Study with Translations*. Cambridge: Cambridge University Press, 1964.

———. "Erasmus and the Classics." In *Erasmus*, ed. T. A. Dorey, 1–30. Albuquerque: University of New Mexico Press, 1970.

Pineas, Rainer. "Thomas More's Use of the Dialogue Form as a Weapon of Religious Controversy." *Studies in the Renaissance* 7 (1960): 193–206.

Plumstead, A. W. "Satirical Parody in *Roister Doister*: A Reinterpretation." *SP* 60 (1963): 141–54.

———. "Who Pointed Roister's Letter?" *N&Q* n.s. 10 (1963): 329–31.

Plutarch. *Moralia*. London: William Heinemann, 1927.

Pollard, A. F. "The Making of Sir Thomas More's *Richard III*." In *Historical Essays in Honour of James Tait*, ed. J. G. Edwards, V. H. Galbraith, and E. F. Jacob, 223–38. Manchester, 1933.

Potter, Robert. *The English Morality Play: Origins, History and Influence of a Dramatic Tradition*. London and Boston: Routledge and Kegan Paul, 1975.

Pra, Siboud. *Le Mystère de trois doms*, ed. Paul E. Girard and Ulysse Chevalier. Lyon: Librarie ancienne d'Auguste Brun, 1887.

Purcell, H. D. "*The Celestina* and the *Interlude of Calisto and Melebea*." *Bulletin of Hispanic Studies* 44 (1967): 1–15.

Quintilian. *Institutio oratoria*, trans. H. E. Butler. 4 vols. London: William Heinemann, 1961–66.

Rainolds, John. *Th'overthrow of Stage-Playes*. London, 1599.

Records of Early English Drama: Cambridge, ed. Alan H. Nelson. 2 vols. Toronto: University of Toronto Press, 1989.

Records of Early English Drama: Chester, ed. Lawrence M. Clopper. Toronto: University of Toronto Press, 1979.

Records of Early English Drama: Coventry, ed. R. W. Ingram. Toronto: University of Toronto Press, 1981.

Records of Early English Drama: Newcastle upon Tyne, ed. J. J. Anderson. Toronto: University of Toronto Press, 1982.

Redford, John. *Wit and Science*, ed. Arthur Brown for the Malone Society. Oxford: The University Press, 1951.

Reed, A. W. *Early Tudor Drama: Medwall, the Rastells, Heywood, and the More Circle*. London: Methuen and Co., 1926.

——. "Nicholas Udall and Thomas Wilson." *RES* 1 (1925): 275–83.

Rendall, Thomas. "Visual Typology in the Abraham and Isaac Plays." *MP* 81 (1983–84): 221–32.

Respublica, ed. W. W. Greg. London: Oxford University Press, 1952.

The Revels History of Drama. Vol. 1, *Medieval Drama*, ed. A. C. Cawley et al. London: Methuen, 1983.

The Revels History of Drama in English. Vol. 2, *1500–1576*, ed. Norman Sanders et al. London: Methuen, 1980.

Ringler, William. "The Source of Lodge's *Reply to Gosson*." *RES* 15 (1939): 164–71.

Ro: Ba:. *The Lyfe of Syr Thomas More, Sometymes Lord Chancellor of England*, ed. E. V. Hitchcock and P. E. Hallett. London: Oxford University Press, 1950.

Robbins, Edwin W. *Dramatic Characterization in Printed Commentaries on Terence 1473–1600*. Illinois Studies in Language and Literature 35, 4. Urbana: University of Illinois Press, 1951.

Robinson, John W. "The Art and Meaning of *Gammer Gurton's Needle*." *RenD* n.s. 14 (1983): 45–77.

——. *Studies in Fifteenth-Century Stagecraft*. Kalamazoo, Mich.: Medieval Institute, 1991.

Rojas, Fernando de. *Celestina; or the tragi-comedy of Calisto and Melibea*, trans. James Mabbe (1631), ed. H. Warner Allen. London: G. Routledge and Sons, 1923.

——. *Celestine or the Tragick-Comedie of Calisto and Melibea*, trans. James Mabbe, ed. Guadalupe Martinez Lacalle. London: Tamesis Books, 1972.

——. *Tragicomedia de Calisto y Melibea* . . . Venice, 1531.

———. *Tragicomedia di Calisto e Melibea de lingua hispana in idioma italico traduca... per Hieronymo claricio.* Milan, 1519.

Roper, William. *The Lyfe of Sir Thomas Moore, knighte,* ed. Elsie Vaughan Hitchcock. London: Oxford University Press, 1935.

Roston, Murray. *Biblical Drama in England from the Middle Ages to the Present Day.* Evanston, Ill.: Northwestern University Press, 1968.

Salter, Frederick M. *Medieval Drama in Chester.* Toronto: University of Toronto Press, 1955.

———. "Skelton's *Speculum Principis.*" *Speculum* 9 (1934): 25–37.

Scaliger, Julius Caesar. *Poetices libri septem.* Lyons, 1561.

Schelling, Felix E. *Elizabethan Drama, 1558–1642.* 2 vols. Boston: Houghton Mifflin, 1908.

Scheurweghs, G. "The Relative Pronouns in the XVIth [Century] Plays *Roister Doister* and *Respublica*: A Frequency Study." *English Studies* 45 (1964), Supp.: 84–89.

Schoeck, Richard J. "Sir Thomas More and Lincoln's Inn Revels." *PQ* 29 (1950): 426–30.

Schoepper, Jakob the Elder. *Ectrachelistis, sive Ioannes decollatus, Tragoedia Nova and Sacra.* Cologne: Martin Gymnicus, 1546.

Scolnicov, Hanna. "To Understand a Parable: the Mimetic Mode of *The Marriage of Wit and Wisdom.*" *Cahiers Elizabéthains* 29 (1986): 1–11.

Secretum Secretorum, Nine English Versions, ed. M. A. Manzalaoui. Vol. 1. Oxford: Oxford University Press, 1977.

Seneca. *Tragedies,* trans. F. J. Miller. 2 vols. London: William Heinemann, 1927–29.

Sidney, Sir Philip. *An Apology for Poetry,* ed. Forrest G. Robinson. Indianapolis: Bobbs-Merrill, 1970.

Simpson, Percy. "'Tanquam Explorator': Jonson's Method in the 'Discoveries.'" *MLR* 2 (1907): 201–10.

Skelton, John. *Magnificence,* ed. Paula Neuss. Baltimore: Johns Hopkins University Press, 1980.

———. *Magnifycence,* ed. Robert Lee Ramsay. London: Kegan Paul et al., 1906.

———. *Magnifycence, A Goodly Interlude and a Mery.* London: John Rastell?, ca. 1530.

———. *Speculum Principis*. British Library MS. Addit. 25, 787.
Slim, H. Colin. *The Prodigal Son at the Whores': Music, Art, and Drama*. University of California, Irvine, 1976.
Smart, W. K. "*Mankind* and the Mumming Plays." *MLN* 32 (1971): 21–25.
Smith, Bruce R. *Ancient Scripts and Modern Experience on the English Stage 1500–1700*. Princeton: Princeton University Press, 1988.
Smith, G. C. Moore. *College Plays Performed in the University of Cambridge*. Cambridge: Cambridge University Press, 1923.
Stevens, Martin. "The York Cycle: from Procession to Play." *Leeds Studies in English* n.s. 6 (1972): 37–61.
Stubbes, Philip. *The Anatomie of Abuses*. New York and London: Garland Publishing, 1973.
Sultan, Stanley. "The Audience-Participation Episode in *Johan Johan*." *JEGP* 52 (1953): 491–97.
Surtz, Edward L. *In Praise of Pleasure: Philosophy, Education, and Communism in More's Utopia*. Cambridge, Mass.: Harvard University Press, 1957.
Tannenbaum, Samuel A. "A Note on *Misogonus*." *MLN* 45 (1930): 308–10.
Taylor, G. C. "*Christus Redivivus* and the Hegge Resurrection Play." *PMLA* 41 (1926): 840–59.
Telle, Emil V. "Erasmus's *Ciceronianus*: A Comical Colloquy." In *Essays on the Works of Erasmus*. New Haven: Yale University Press, 1978.
Terence. *Comoediae sex, cum Aelii Donati interpretatione et expositione Joannis Calphurnii in Heutontimorumenum*. Venice, 1476.
———. *Comoediae sex*, per Phillipum Melanchthon restitutae. Cologne, 1527.
———. *Comoediae* (Melanchthon, Erasmus, Goveanus, Scaliger, Faustus, Bembo, Donatus, Calphurnius, Barlandus, Latomus, Marsus, Rivius, Doletus, Glareanus, Theodoricus, Willichius). Paris: Ioannem de Roigny, 1552.
———. *Comoedie*, ed. Juvenalis and Badius. Paris, 1504.
———. *Comedies*, trans. John Sargeaunt. 2 vols. London: William Heinemann, 1929.
———. *Terentius, in quem triplex edita est P. Antesignani Rapistagnensis commentatio*. Lyons, 1560.
Thecla, Sister Mary. "New Corn From an Old Field: St. Thomas More's 'Treatise upon the Passion.'" *Catholic World* 164 (1947): 344–50.

Theiner, Paul. "The Medieval Terence." In *The Learned and the Lewed: Studies in Chaucer and Medieval Literature*, ed. Larry D. Benson. Harvard English Studies 5, 231–47. Cambridge, Mass.: Harvard University Press, 1974.

Thompson, Elbert N.S. *The English Moral Plays*. Transactions of the Connecticut Academy of Art and Sciences, Vol. 14, 291–414. New Haven: Yale University Press, 1910.

Todorov, Tzevetan. *Mikhail Bakhtin: The Dialogical Principle*, trans. Wlad Godzich. Manchester: Manchester University Press, 1984.

The Towneley Cycle, ed. A. C. Cawley and Martin Stevens. Leeds: University of Leeds, School of English, 1976.

The Towneley Plays, ed. George England and A. W. Pollard. London: Kegan Paul, Trench, Trubner and Co., 1897 [repr. 1925].

A Tretise of Miraclis Pleyinge (A Middle English Treatise on the Playing of Miracles), ed. Clifford Davidson. Washington, D.C.: University Press of America, 1981.

Tydeman, William, ed. *Four Tudor Comedies*. Harmondsworth, Middlesex: Penguin Books, 1984.

Udall, Nicholas, trans. *Flovres for Latine Spekynge, selected and gathered oute of Terence*. London, 1533.

———. *Nicholas Udall's Roister Doister*, ed. G. Scheurweghs. Materials for the Study of the Old English Drama, vol. 16. Louvain: Librairie Universitaire, 1939.

———, ed. *The Paraphrase of Erasmus vpon the newe testament*. 2 vols. London, 1548–52.

———. *Roister Doister*, ed. W. W. Greg. Oxford: Malone Society Reprints, 1935.

Ungerer, Gustav. *Anglo-Spanish Relations in Tudor Literature*. Bern: Francke Verlag, 1956.

Vander Haeghen, Ferd. *Bibliotheca Erasmiana, Répertoire des Oeuvres D'Erasme*. Nieuwkoop: B. DeGraaf, 1961 [1893].

Velz, John W. "Sovereignty in the Digby *Mary Magdalene*." *CompD* 2 (1968): 32–43.

Velz, John W., and Carl P. Daw, Jr. "Tradition and Originality in *Wyt and Science*." *SP* 65 (1968): 631–46.

Vinter, Donna Smith. "Didactic Characterization: The Towneley Abraham." *CompD* 14 (1980): 117–36.

Vives, Juan Luis. *Of the Citie of God: with the learned Comments of J. L. Vives*, trans. John Healey. London, 1610.

———. *Fabula de homine*, trans. Nancy Lenkeith as *The Renaissance Philosophy of Man*, ed. Ernst Cassirer et al. Chicago: University of Chicago Press, 1948.

———. *De Institutione feminae Christianae*. Bruges, 1523.

———. *Introduction to Wisdom: A Renaissance Textbook*, ed. Marian L. Tobriner. New York: Columbia University Teachers College Press, 1968.

———. *An Introduction to Wysedome*, trans. Rycharde Morisyne. London, 1544.

———. *The office & dutie of an husband*, trans. Thomas Paynell. London, 1550.

———. *Opera Omnia*, ed. Gregorio Mayáns y Siscar. 8 vols. Valencia, 1782–90. Repr. London: Gregg Press, 1964.

———. *Tudor School-Boy Life, The Dialogues of Juan Luis Vives*, trans. Foster Watson. London: J. M. Dent and Co., 1908.

———. *A very frutefull and pleasant boke called the Instruction of a Christen woman*, trans. Richard Hyrde. London, 1540.

———. *Vives and the Renascence Education of Women (De Institutione feminae Christianae)*, ed. and trans. Foster Watson. London: Edward Arnold, 1912.

———. *Vives: On Education. A Translation of the De tradendis disciplinis of Juan Luis Vives*, ed. and trans. Foster Watson. Totowa, N.J.: Rowman and Littlefield, 1977 [1913].

de Volder, Willem. *The Comedy of Acolastus*, trans. John Palsgrave, ed. P. L. Carver. London: Oxford University Press, 1937.

Wagner, Bernard M. "The Tragedy of Iephte." *TLS*, 26 December 1929, p. 1,097.

Waith, Eugene. "*Controversia* in the English Drama: Medwall and Massinger." *PMLA* 68 (1953): 286–303.

The Wakefield Pageants in the Towneley Cycle, ed. A. C. Cawley. Manchester: Manchester University Press, 1958.

Wallace, Charles W. *The Evolution of the English Drama up to Shakespeare*. Berlin: Georg Reimer, 1912.

Wasson, John. "The Morality Play: Ancestor of Elizabethan Drama?" *CompD* 13 (1979): 210–21.

———. "The Secular Saint Plays of the Elizabethan Era." In *The Saint Play in Medieval Europe*, ed. Clifford Davidson, 241–60. Kalamazoo, Mich.: Medieval Institute, 1986.

Watson, Foster. "A Friend of Sir Thomas More." *Nineteenth Century And After* 83 (1918): 540–52.

———. *Les relacions de Joan Lluis Vives amb els Anglesos i amb L'Angeleterra*. Barcelona: Institut d'Estudis Catalans, 1918.

Watson, Thomas. *A Humanist's "Trew Imitation": Thomas Watson's Absalom*, ed. and trans. John Hazel Smith. Urbana: University of Illinois Press, 1964.

Weld, John S. *Meaning in Comedy: Studies in Elizabethan Romantic Comedy*. Albany: State University of New York Press, 1975.

Wever, R. *An Enterlude Called Lusty Juventus*, ed. Helen S. Thomas. London and New York: Garland Publishing, 1982.

Whiting, B. J. "Diccon's French Cousin." *SP* 42 (1945): 31–40.

Whitworth, Charles W., ed. *Three Sixteenth Century Comedies*. London: Ernest Benn, 1984.

Wickham, Glynne, *Early English Stages 1300 to 1600*. 3 vols. London: Routledge and Kegan Paul, 1959–79.

———. *The Medieval Theatre*. New York: St. Martin's Press, 1974.

———. "The Staging of Saint Plays in England." In *The Medieval Drama*, ed. Sandro Sicca. Albany: State University of New York Press, 1972.

———, ed. *English Moral Interludes*. London: J. M. Dent and Sons, 1976.

Wiles, David. *The Early Plays of Robin Hood*. Cambridge: D. S. Brewer, 1981.

Williams, Arnold. "The English Moral Play Before 1500." *Annuale Medieavale* 4 (1963): 5–22.

Williamson, George. "Sir Thomas More's View of Drama." *MLN* 43 (1928): 294–96.

Willson, Robert F. *"Their Form Confounded": Studies in the Burlesque Play from Udall to Sheridan*. The Hague: Mouton, 1975.

Wilson, F. P. *The English Drama, 1485–1585*. ed. G. K. Hunter. Oxford: Oxford University Press, 1969.

Wilson, Thomas. *The Arte of Rhetorique*. London, 1553.

———. *The Arte of Rhetorique*, ed. Thomas J. Derrick. New York and London: Garland Publishing, 1982.

Winser, Leigh. "*Magnyfycence* and the Characters of Sotie." *Sixteenth Century Journal* 12 (1981): 85–94.

———. "Skelton's *Magnyfycence*." *Renaissance Quarterly* 23 (1970): 14–25.

Wit and Science, ed. Arthur Brown. Oxford: University Press for the Malone Society, 1951.

Woolf, Rosemary. *The English Mystery Plays*. Berkeley and Los Angeles: University of California Press, 1972.

York Plays, The Plays Performed by the Crafts or Mysteries of York on the Day of Corpus Christi in the 14th, 15th, and 16th Centuries, ed. Lucy Toulmin Smith. Oxford: Clarendon Press, 1885.

The York Plays, ed. Richard Beadle. London: Edward Arnold, 1982.

Young, Karl. "The Influence of French Farce upon the Plays of John Heywood." *MP* 2 (1904): 97–124.

INDEX

Absalom (Watson): Absalom in, 298, 299–300, 301–2, 303–5, 306, 357 n.3; Achitophel in, 300, 303–4, 305; aphorisms in, 306; audience of, 298; characterization in, xxv, 300; chorus in, 305–6; Chusai in, 300, 303, 304–5; David in, 298–99, 300, 301–3, 304, 306; death in, 304–5; form of, xxv, 298, 299, 300; history of, 297–98; Joab in, 300, 303; messengers in, 304; morality play elements in, 300; rebellion in, 298–99, 302, 304–5; repentance and redemption in, 306; Semei in, 298–99; vices and virtues in, xxv, 300, 302

Acolastus (de Volder), 151–52

Act for the Advancement of true Religion (1543), 129, 340

Act of Supremacy (1534), 190

Act of Supremacy (1559), 192

Act of Uniformity (1559), 130

Acts and Monuments of Martyrs (Foxe), 353 n.7

Adelphi (Terence), 73–74

Agrippa, Henry Cornelius, xxi, 131–33, 338

Alchemist, The (Jonson), 59

allegories, xxiii–xxiv, 161–62. *See also* morality plays

Amphitruo (Plautus), 267

Andria (Terence), 72–73, 77

Anne of Cleves (queen of England), xviii

Answer to the King's Flyting (Lindsay), 211

Antibarbari (Erasmus), 87, 91

Archipropheta (Grimald): audience of, 323–24; banquet scene in, 321, 329–32; characterization in, 325–26; chorus in, 325, 329, 330, 332, 333; education in, 324; form of, 267, 325; Gelasimus in, 328–29, 330, 331; God in, 332; Herodias in, 321, 326, 327–28, 329, 330, 331, 333; Herod in, 321, 326, 327–28, 330, 331–32, 333; history of, 323; importance of, 325, 333–34; John the Baptist in, xxvi, 326–27, 328, 329, 330, 331–32, 333; love in, 327–28; narration in, 326; Philautus in, 326–27; politics in, 326, 327; purposes of, 323; religion in, 325; saints' play elements in, 325, 332, 334; Tryphera in, 330, 331; Typhilus in, 326–27

Aristophanes, 105–6

Aristotle, 105

art, defined, 141

Arte of Rhetorique (Wilson), 139–42

Arte or Crafte of Rhethoryke, The (Cox), 131

383

Arthur (prince of England), xviii
Aske, Robert, 194
Asotus (Macropedius), 150–52
Augustine, Saint, 81

Badius, Josse, 78–79
Bakhtin, Mikhail, ix
Baldwin, T. W., 96, 109, 348 n.4
Bale, John, 191, 198, 200, 320
Baptistes (Buchanan), 320–21, 329, 332
Beaton, David, 213
Beaunans Meriasek (Anonymous): Christ in, 11; Constantine in, 10; Harris on, 344 n.10; as hybrid play, 13; martyrdom in, 10; Meriasek in, 6, 8, 9–10, 11, 14; ministering in imitation of Christ in, 8, 9–10; miracles in, 6, 10; Silvester in, 10, 14; Teudar in, 10; unity in, 14, 344 n.10; Virgin Mary in, 10, 14
Beheading of John the Baptist, The (Wedderburn), 321
biblical drama. *See* civic drama
Bishops' Book, The (Anonymous), 190
Boas, Frederick S., 111
Boleyn, Anne, xviii
Book named The governor, The (Elyot), 135, 176
Briefe Tretise, A (Martyr), 135
Buchanan, George, 321

Calisto and Melebea (Anonymous): allegory in, 246–47, 251–52; audience of, 244–45, 253–54, 355 n.3; authorship of, 244, 245; Calisto in, 246, 247–48, 250–51, 252; Celestina in, xxiv, 248, 249, 250–52; and Dame Sirith, 251; Danio in, 251, 252, 253; education in, 246, 253, 254; form of, 355 n.5; God in, 252; history of, xxiv, 244, 251; importance of, 244, 354 n.1; Melebea in, 246–47, 250, 251, 252; morality play elements in, 246–47, 249, 251, 252–53, 254; Parmeno in, 247, 248–49, 250; purposes of, 246; satire in, 252; Sempronio in, 247–48, 252; and *Tragicomedia de Calisto y Melibea*, 244, 245–46, 247–51, 252–53; vices in, 249, 251, 252
Castle of Perseverance, The (Anonymous), 41, 44–45
catastrophe, defined, 75, 347 n.6
Catherine of Aragon (queen of England), xviii
Caxton, William, 344 n.4
Celestina (Rojas), 244, 245–46, 247–51, 252–53
Chambers, E. K., 61
Chester plays, 17–18, 25, 33, 339. *See also* civic drama; "proclamation for whitsone plays" (Anonymous)
Chinese opera, 55, 56
Christopherson, John, 307
Christus Nascens (Grimald), 319
Christus Redivivus (Grimald), 319, 322–23
Cicero, Marcus Tullius, 79, 105
Ciceronianus (Erasmus), 92–93
civic drama: allegory in, 32; anachronisms in, 35; audience of, 20; characteristics of, xx, 17, 335; Christ in, 22–23, 30–31; community involvement in, 18–19; and Corpus Christi, 22, 23; decline of, 18, 129, 339, 340; and education, 39; Frye on, 19; Gardiner on, 18; God in, 30; Herod in, 31; history of, 16–18; humor in, 24, 26; importance of, xxvi; Incarnation in, 24–26; Joseph in, 24–26, 31; justice in, 24; number of actors in, 33; pathos in, 24; performances of, 16, 17, 18, 335; pharaoh in, 31; popularity of, xix, 38;

384

presenters in, 20–21; and "proclamation for whitsone plays," 19; purposes of, xvii, 16, 19–21, 22, 35–36, 39; and Reformation, 129, 339; repetition in, 29–30; scriptural truth in, 23–24; staging of, 34–35; suppression of, 40; time and space in, 23; and *Tretise of Miraclis Pleyinge, A*, 19–20; types of, 16; typology in, 29–30; versions of, 33; Virgin Mary in, 22–23, 24–26, 31; Wickham on, 19; Woolf on, 18. *See also* drama; N-Town plays; Towneley plays; York plays
Cohen, Gustave, 262
Coletti, Teresa, 345 n.9
Colie, Rosalie, ix
Colloquia (Erasmus), 91–92, 93
Comedia de Calisto y Melibea (Rojas), 244. See also *Tragicomedia de Calisto y Melibea, La* (Rojas)
comedies: Cicero on, 79; defense of, 136–37, 141–43; defined, 70–71, 79, 81, 136, 143; Diomedes on, 71; Donatus on, 70–71, 74–75, 79; and education, 81, 337; Erasmus on, 72, 81, 85; error in, 356 n.6; Evanthius on, 71, 347 n.6; and humanists, 136–37, 141–43; and More, 113, 125–26; performances of, xxii; purposes of, 81, 269, 337; and Reformation, 338; Rivius on, 81; Vives on, 102, 103, 104, 349 n.6; Wagnerus on, 82; Willichius on, 72. *See also* drama
commedia dell'arte, 50
Commentaries upon Judges (Martyr), 134–35
Complaynt of Schir David Lindesay, The (Lindsay), 210
Conversion of St. Paul, The (Anonymous), 3, 8–9
Corpus Christi plays, 22, 23, 339
Coventry plays, 33

Craig, Hardin, 13
Craik, T. W., 255–56
Cromwell, Oliver, 191
Cromwell, Thomas, xix
cycles, xix–xx, 14. *See also* drama

Dame Sirith, 251
David and Bathsheba (Peele): Absalom in, 300–301, 304, 305; Achitophel in, 303; David in, 302; form of, 298, 310; Joab in, 303
Dean, Leonard, 90–91
Dean-Smith, Margaret, 56–57
De causis corruptarum artium (Vives), 98, 106
De copia (Erasmus), 94
Defence of Good Women, The (Elyot), 137–38
De incertitudine et vanitate (Agrippa), 132
De institutione feminae Christianae (Vives), 245
De Officiis (Cicero), 176
De officio mariti (Vives), 100–101
De ratione dicendi (Vives), 105, 107
De ratione studii (Erasmus), 88, 89, 93
De ratione studii puerilis (Vives), 99
De Regno Christi (Bucer), 142–43
De tradendis disciplinis (Vives), 97, 100, 101, 106–7
De Vera Nobilitate (Buonaccorso), 234, 236, 240, 241
Dialogue betuix Experience and ane Courteour, Ane (Lindsay), 213–15
Dialogue Concerning Heresies (More), 123
Dialogue of Comfort Against Tribulation, A (More), 126–27
didactics. *See* education
Digby plays, 6
Diomedes, 71
Disobedient Child, The (Ingelend), 156–58

Donatus, Aelius: on comedies, 70–71, 74–75, 79; on decorum, 77, 78; on form, 75–76; on morality, 79–80; on plot, 73; on Terence and Terence's comedies, 68, 69, 70, 72–73, 76, 77–78, 81, 356 n.6; Vives on, 104, 349 n.7

drama: and Agrippa, 132–33; and Anne of Cleves, xviii; and Arthur, xviii; and Bakhtin, ix; and Boleyn, xviii; and Catherine of Aragon, xviii; community involvement in, 335, 340; critical theory about, ix; and T. Cromwell, xix; defense of, 135, 143–44; and education, xxi, xxii–xxiii, 336, 340–41; and Edward VI, xviii; and Elizabeth of York, xviii; and Erasmus, xxii, 88–89, 92–93; and Fitzroy, xix; and Henry VIII, xviii, 200; and Howard, xix; and humanists, xxiii, 135, 143, 144, 337–38; and Mary I, xviii, 200; morality of, xxi–xxii, 128–30, 132–33, 135, 143–44; and More, xxi, 111–14, 124–25, 126, 127; and Northumberland, xviii–xix; and Parr, xviii; and Plantagenet, xix; purposes of, xix, 336; and Reformation, 132–34, 135, 338; and rhetoric, xxii–xxiii; and Richard III, xviii; and J. Seymour, xviii; and T. Seymour, xix; and Somerset, xviii–xix; suppression of, xix, xx, 130, 143–44; transition in, ix; ubiquity of, xvii, xxvi; and Vives, xxi, 99–100, 102, 105, 106–8, 109–10, 349 n.5 n.8. *See also* civic drama; comedies; cycles; folk drama; history plays; morality plays; paternoster plays; romances; saints' plays; tragedies

Dreme of Schir David Lyndesay, The (Lindsay), 210

Duke of Northumberland, xviii–xix

Duke of Somerset, xviii–xix

Dunn, E. Catherine, 4

Ectrachelistis (Schoepper), 321

education: and civic drama, 39; and comedies, 81, 337; and drama, xxi, xxii–xxiii, 336, 340–41; and Erasmus, xxi, xxii, 90, 92, 94, 348 n.4; and Lindsay, 210–12; and morality plays, 39–40, 149, 175, 177; and More, 123–24; and Plautus, xxiv; and saints' plays, 39; and Seneca, xxvii; and Terence and Terence's comedies, xxi, xxiv, xxvii, 65, 66–68, 69–70, 73, 80, 85, 89, 90, 94, 336; and tragedies, 295; and Udall, 207–8, 267, 268, 269, 356 n.5; and Vives, xxii, 95, 99, 101, 102–3, 104, 105, 106–7, 108–9

Education of a Christian Prince (Erasmus), 176

educational interludes, 129–30, 149. *See also* morality plays

Edward VI (king of England and Ireland), xviii, 3, 208

Elizabeth of York (queen of England), xviii

Elton, William, 255–56

Elyot, Thomas, 295

Enchiridion militis christiani (Erasmus), 87–88

epistles, farced, 4. *See also* saints' plays

epitasis, defined, 74–75, 347 n.6

Erasmus, Desiderius: Baldwin on, 348 n.4; on classical literature, 87–88; on comedies, 72, 81, 85; Dean on, 90–91; on decorum, 93–94; on dialogue, 91; on drama, xxii, 88–89, 92–93; on education, xxi, xxii, 90, 92, 94, 348 n.4; on Euripides, 86–87; on genres, 89; on irony, 90–91; Lodge on, 87; on meaning, 89–90; on morality, 90; and More, 90, 124; Phillipps on, 91; on

Plautus, 86; and Reformation, 338; on Seneca, 86; on Terence and Terence's comedies, xxi, 67, 71–72, 81, 84–85, 88, 89, 93, 94, 336; Thompson on, 91; as translator, xxi, 87, 90, 114
Estelrich, Juan, 108–9
Eunuchus (Terence), 271, 278
Euripides, 86–87, 105, 307
Evanthius: on comedies, 71, 347 n.6; on decorum, 77, 78; on Terence and Terence's comedies, 77, 78, 82–83
Everyman (Anonymous), 42, 45, 46
Exhortation to Young men, An (Lupset), 139
Ezechias (Udall), 208

fables, 134–35, 140
Fabula de homine (Vives), 96–97
Fall of Princes, The (Lydgate), 175
farced epistles, 4. *See also* saints' plays
Farce du Pasté (Anonymous): and *Johan Johan*, 255–66
Fitzroy, Henry, xix
Fitzstephen, William, 6, 344 n.5
folk drama: actors in, 52–53; adaptability of, 49–50; anachronisms in, 49–50; challenger's vaunt in, 50–51, 55, 56; Chambers on, 61; characteristics of, xx, 335; characterization in, 55; and Chinese opera and Kabuki, 55, 56; and commedia dell'arte, 50; contest and cure in, 56–57, 58–59; costumes in, 55–56; Dean-Smith on, 56–57; death and rebirth in, 49; decline of, 129; doctor in, 51–52, 58, 59; Frazer on, 49; heroism in, 49; history of, 48, 49; humor in, 59–60; importance of, xxvi, 60–61; improvisation in, 50, 51–52; legends in, 49; length of, 54–55; morality of, 54; as oral tradition, 50–52, 60; patriotism in, 49; payment for, 53; performances of, 335; popularity of, xx, 49, 55; purposes of, xvii; and Reformation, 129; staging of, 54; suppression of, 53–54; wooing in, 57–58. *See also* drama; St. George plays
Forrest, Mary Patricia, 345 n.11
Four Elements (Rastell), 44, 46
France, saints' plays in, 14
Frazer, James, 49
Frye, Northrop, 19
Fulgens and Lucres (Medwall): A and B in, 235–36, 237–40, 241, 242–43; apology in, 242; audience of, 233, 234–35, 236, 237, 240, 354 n.8; chorus in, 235; Cornelius in, 237, 239, 240, 241; debate in, 240; and *De Vera Nobilitate*, 234, 236, 240, 241; education in, 242; folk drama elements in, 58, 238, 242; form of, xxiv; Gayus in, 237, 239, 240–41; humor in, 112, 235–36, 237, 241–43; importance of, 267; irony in, 239; Jone in, 237, 238; length of, 236–37; Lucres in, 237–38, 239, 240, 241; marriage in, 238; morality play elements in, 240, 242; nobility in, 234, 235, 236, 241; politics in, 234, 235; purposes of, 235–36; secular nature of, 233, 234, 242; vices and virtues in, 240, 242; wooing play elements in, 242

Gammer Gurton's Needle (Anonymous): authorship of, 280–82, 357 n.3; Baily in, 288; as college comedy, 280, 283, 290–91, 356 n.1; Dame Chat in, 286–87, 290; Diccon in, 283–86, 287, 288, 290; farce in, xxv, 283, 285, 286, 290, 357 n.6; form of, 280, 288–90, 291; Gammer in, 286–87, 290, 291; generic nature of, 283; gulling in, 284, 286, 288; history of, 280–81, 282–83; Hodge in, 285–86, 287, 290, 291; im-

Gammer Gurton's Needle (cont.)
portance of, 280; irony in, 285, 288, 290; jestbook in, xxv, 283, 284, 290; "knot of errors" in, 290; morality play elements in, xxv, 283, 288, 290; popularity of, 291, 357 n.8; Rat in, 287–88, 290; religion in, 283, 287, 288; satire in, 285–86, 287, 291; Schelling on, 357 n.6; setting of, 283; vices in, 290; Young on, 357 n.6
Gardiner, H. C., 18
Gentlemen and Children of the Royal Chapel, xviii
Gibson, Gail M., 345 n.11 n.12
God's Promises (Bale), 320
Gorboduc (Sackville and Norton), xxvi
Grace, Pilgrimage of, 194
Grimald, Nicholas, 320, 322

Harris, Markham, 344 n.10
Henry VII (king of England), xvii, 233, 234, 354 n.4
Henry VIII (king of England): and Bale, 200; and drama, xviii, 200; and saints' plays, 3; and Six Articles, 190; and Udall, 208
Herrick, Marvin T., 94, 348 n.9
Hickscorner (Anonymous), 44, 46
history plays, 15. *See also* drama
Hock Tuesday plays, 53. *See also* folk drama
Hogrefe, Pearl, 109
Homer, 106
Horace, 78
Howard, Thomas, xix
Hroswitha, 4–5
humanists: characteristics of, xx–xxi; and comedies, 136–37, 141–43; and drama, xxiii, 135, 143, 144, 337–38; and fables, 140; and poetry, 135–38; and rhetoric, 139–40, 142; and tragedies, xxv

interludes, 129–30, 149. *See also* morality plays
Introductio ad sapientiam (Vives), 100

Jacke Juggler (Anonymous), 267
James V (king of Great Britain): death of, 212, 221; and Lindesay of Pitscottie, 220, 221, 222; and Lindsay, 210–11, 212; at Solway Moss, 212, 221
Jephthah (Christopherson): battle in, 312–13; chorus in, 310, 314, 317–18; daughter in, 314, 315–18; death in, 317–18; dialogue in, 311, 313; education in, 309, 317; elders in, 311; form of, 307, 310; history of, 307–8; Jephthah in, 310–12, 313, 314–15, 316, 317, 318; language of, 307; length of, 309–10; prologue in, 310; purposes of, 308–9; virtues in, xxv, 316–18; wife in, 313, 314, 316
Johan Johan (Anonymous): asides in, 264; audience of, 264–66; authorship of, 255, 266; Cohen on, 262; Craik on, 255–56; Elton on, 255–56; as farce, 255; and *Farce du Pasté*, 255–66; history of, xxiv, 255; humor in, 257–58, 261; irony in, 261, 262; Johan Johan in, 256, 257–62, 264–66; language of, 256; Proudfoot on, 263–64; religion in, 262–63, 266; satire in, 266; Sir Johan in, 259–62, 263; staging of, 263–64; Tib in, 257–62, 263, 264–65
John Baptist's Preaching in the Wilderness (Bale), 320
Jones, Charles, 344 n.4
Jonson, Ben, 110
"Joseph's Return" (Anonymous), 345 n.11

Kabuki, 55, 56
Kelley, Michael, 43

388

King John (Bale): allegory in, 191–92, 193, 194; analogue in, 193, 194, 197; biblical figures in, 196–97; civic drama elements in, 191; education in, 189; historical nature of, 189–90, 192–93, 194, 195–96, 197, 339; humor in, 193; John in, 189–90, 191–92, 194–95; ministering in imitation of Christ in, 196; mirror in, 189; morality play elements in, 191, 192–93; politics in, 191–92, 196–97, 339; purposes of, 188–89; religion in, 192–93, 194–95, 196; saints' play elements in, 192; satire in, 193; versions of, 188, 190, 192, 195–96, 198, 352 n.2; vices and virtues in, 192–93, 197
Kitteis Confessioun (Lindsay), 212
Kolve, V. A., 345 n.13

Last Four Things, The (More), 124–25
Latomus, 76
Life of Our Lady (Lydgate), 26, 28, 345 n.12
Life of Saint Anne (Anonymous), 26
Lindesay of Pitscottie, Robert, 220, 221, 222
Lindsay, David, 210–12, 229
Linguae latinae exercitatio (Vives), 108
Lodge, Thomas, 87
Love of King David, The (Peele). See *David and Bathsheba* (Peele)
Lusty Juventus (Wever), 149–50
Luther, Martin, 125, 126, 296

Macro morality plays (Anonymous), 38. See also morality plays
Magnificence (Skelton): allegory in, 186; criticism of, 351 n.5; *de contemptu mundi* motif in, 186; dialogue in, 180; doctrine of the mean in, 181; education in, 178–79, 186; form of, 179; Magnificence in, 45, 179–80, 183–86;

mirror in, 186; morality play elements in, 178–79, 180–81, 185, 186; politics in, 179, 184, 185, 186–87; repentance in, 185; rhetoric in, 180; vices and virtues in, 45, 181–84, 185–86
Mankind (Anonymous): costumes in, 41; death in, 46; symbolism in, 41; virtues and vices in, 43, 44, 45
Marriage Between Wit and Wisdom, The (Merbury), 172–74. See also *Wit and Science* (Redford)
Marriage of Wit and Science, The (Westcott), 170–72. See also *Wit and Science* (Redford)
Mary I (queen of England and Ireland): and drama, xviii, 200; and miracle plays, 129, 130; and Philip of Spain, 268; and Udall, 208–9, 278
Mary Magdalene (Anonymous): authorship of, 344 n.3; conversion in, 9; Craig on, 13; God in, 11, 13; as hybrid play, 12–14; king in, 9; light in, 13; Mary Magdalene in, 3, 8, 9, 11, 14; ministering in imitation of Christ in, 9, 13, 14; miracles in, 9; Paul in, 3; queen in, 9; sovereignty in, 13; unity in, 13–14; Wickham on, 13
Medwall, Henry, 233, 234
Melanchthon, Philipp, 80, 295, 336, 338
Menippus (Lucian), 114–15
Merry Wives of Windsor, The (Shakespeare), 59
"Mery jest, A" (More), 112–13
Miles Gloriosus (Plautus), 271
Minehead Mummers Play (Anonymous), 54, 60
miracle plays, 129, 130. See also drama
Mirror for Magistrates (Anonymous), 175–76
Misogonus (Anonymous), 59, 153–56, 356 n.1
Monarche, The (Lindsay), 213–15

monasteries, dissolution of, 190
moral interludes, 129–30, 149. *See also* morality plays
morality plays: abstract nature of, 43; adaptability of, xxiii, xxvi, 40, 46; ahistorical nature of, 7; allegory in, 39, 177; audience of, 7; cautionary nature of, 7; characteristics of, xvii; costumes in, 40–41, 42–43; death in, 46; decline of, 38, 46–47, 130, 177; and education, 39–40, 149, 175, 177; form of, 40, 47, 177; generic nature of, 7; history of, xxiii, 37–38, 44, 46, 47; ideology of, 40; importance of, xxvi; Kelley on, 43; mankind in, 41; mirror in, 177; monarchs in, 175; number of, 37–38, 346 n.3; and paternoster plays, 38; popularity of, xxiii, 177; and *psychomachia*, 38; purposes of, xx, 39, 45, 129, 149, 177–78; and Reformation, 129, 130, 339; repentance in, 45–46; and saints' plays, 7; secularization of, x, xxiii–xxiv, 38, 39–40, 47; symbolism in, 7, 40; tragicomedy in, 46; vices and virtues in, 43–45, 177; Wasson on, 37; Williams on, 38. *See also* drama; educational interludes; interludes; moral interludes; prodigal plays
More, Sir Thomas: Boas on, 111; and comedies, 113, 125–26; and dialogue, 126; and drama, xxi, 111–14, 124–25, 126, 127; and education, 123–24; and Erasmus, 90, 124; importance of, 111–12; on literature, 123; on Lucian, 115; on Luther, 125, 126; pageants by, 113; on poetry, 123; prose by, 115; and Reformation, 338; on role-playing, 118; as translator, 90, 114–15; on vices and virtues, 124; Vives on, 124
Moriae encomium (Erasmus), 90, 93

Morton, Cardinal John, 233, 234
mummings. *See* folk drama
Mundus and Infans (Anonymous), 46

Nature (Medwall), xxiii, 44–45, 233–34
Nature of the Four Elements (Rastell), xxiii
New Catechisme, A (Becon), 134
Nice Wanton (Anonymous), 158–60
Noreña, Carlos G., 96, 109
Northumberland, Duke of, xviii–xix
N-Town plays: allegory in, 32–33; Contemplacio in, 32; Death in, 32; and Grimald, 322; Herod in, 32; history of, 17–18, 344 n.2; humor in, 27–28, 29; Incarnation in, 26–28, 345 n.9 n.11; John the Baptist in, 319; Joseph in, 27–28, 345 n.12; and *Life of Our Lady*, 28, 345 n.12; midwives in, 29, 345 n.13; professionalism in, 33; and *Pseudo-Matthew*, 28, 345 n.12; realism in, 21; and Reformation, 339; scriptural truth in, 33; staging of, 33–34; Virgin Mary in, 26, 27–28, 31, 345 n.12; virtues in, 32. *See also* civic drama

oeconomia, defined, 76–77
Oedipus (Seneca), 357 n.2
Of the Citie of God (Vives), 97–98
opera, Chinese, 55, 56
"Oratio Contra Rhetoricam" (Jewel), 133–34
Oxford University, 319, 358 n.2

"Pageant of the Shearmen and Taylors" (Anonymous), 24, 25, 31
"Pageant of the Weavers" (Anonymous), 25
pageants, 113
Parmentier, Jacques, 109
Parr, Catherine Howard, xviii
Passetyme of Pleasure (Hawes), 130–31

paternoster plays, 38. *See also* drama
pedagogy. *See* education
Philip II (king of Spain), 268
Phillipps, Margaret Mann, 91
Pilgrimage of Grace, 194
Plantagenet, Arthur, xix
Plato, 98–99
Plautus, Titus Maccius, xxiv, 86, 104
Players of Lord Warden of Cinque Ports, xviii
Play of the Sacrament (Anonymous), 59
plays. *See* drama
Poetics (Aristotle), 105
poetry: Agrippa on, 131–32; criticism of, 131–32, 137–38; defense of, 130–31, 135–37, 138; Hawes on, 130–31; and humanists, 135–38; More on, 123; and Reformation, 130–32; Vives on, 98–99, 102, 104, 105, 107
political morality plays. *See* morality plays
Pollard, A. F., 115–16
Praise of Folly, The (Erasmus), 90
Pride of Life, The (Anonymous), 38, 46
Prince, The (Machiavelli), 176
Princess's Players, xviii
"Proci et puellae" (Erasmus), 92
"proclamation for whitsone plays" (Anonymous), xix, 19. *See also* Chester plays
prodigal plays, 150. *See also* morality plays
protasis, defined, 74, 347 n.6
Protomartyr (Grimald), 319, 325
Proudfoot, G. R., 263–64
Pseudo-Matthew (Anonymous), 26, 28, 345 n.12
psychomachia, 38, 41

Queen's Players, xviii

Rainolds, John, 103–4
Rebelles (Macropedius), 152–53
Records of Early English Drama (Nelson et al., eds.), ix–x
Reformation: and Agrippa, 338; and Chester plays, 339; and civic drama, 129, 339; and comedies, 338; and Corpus Christi plays, 339; and drama, 132–34, 135, 338; and Erasmus, 338; and fables, 134–35; and folk drama, 129; and interludes, 129–30; and Melanchthon, 338; and miracle plays, 129, 130; and morality plays, 129, 130, 339; and More, 338; and N-Town plays, 339; and poetry, 130–32; and rhetoric, 133–34; and saints' plays, 129, 339; and tragedies, 338; and Vives, 338
Reginald of Canterbury, 7
Renaissance, ix, xxvi
Republic (Plato), 119
Responsio ad Lutherum (More), 125
Respublica (Anonymous): allegory in, 200, 203–5; audience of, 199, 268; authorship of, 200, 207–8, 353 n.6; disguises in, 206; economics in, 205, 207; education in, 199–200, 209; form of, 201, 202–3; humor in, 202, 203, 204, 206, 207; morality play elements in, 200–202, 203, 205, 206, 207, 209; People in, 202–3, 205, 206; politics in, 203–5, 207; purposes of, 199–200; Reformation in, 205; religion in, 205, 207, 340, 353 n.5; Respublica in, 201–3, 205, 206; symbolism in, 204; vices and virtues in, 200–207, 353 n.3 n.4; Wickham on, 353 n.5
Revesby Sword Play (Anonymous), 53, 54
rhetoric: characteristics of, 141; criticism of, 133–34; defense of, 139–40; and drama, xxii–xxiii; and humanists, 139–40, 142; and Reformation, 133–34; Vives on, 106

Richard III (king of England), xviii
Richard III (More), 115–18
Rivius, 80–81
Robin Hood plays, 48–49, 53, 54. *See also* folk drama
Roister Doister (Udall): audience of, 268, 278; battle of the sexes in, 277, 278; burlesque in, xxiv–xxv, 60, 268, 273, 274–77, 279; Custance in, 271, 273, 274–75, 276–77, 356 n.9; education in, 269, 270, 273–74; exaggeration in, 273, 275; folk drama elements in, 60, 271, 274; form of, 267, 270; funeral in, 275–76; Goodluck in, 278; gulling in, 272, 273, 274, 356 n.9; history of, 267–68, 270–72, 273, 274, 275, 277, 278–79, 356 n.2; importance of, 267, 279; letter in, 276–77, 356 n.12; Merrygreek in, 272–73, 274, 275–76, 277, 356 n.12; morality play elements in, 272; parody in, 272, 274, 275; prologue of, 268–70, 273–74; purposes of, 270, 272, 273–74; reconciliation in, 278; Roister Doister in, 271–72, 274–75, 276–77, 278; satire in, xxiv–xxv, 272, 273, 276, 278–79; vices in, 272; wooing in, 268
romances, 15. *See also* drama
Roo, John, 176–77

saints' legends, 4, 344 n.4
saints' plays: celebratory nature of, 11–12; characteristics of, xx, 335; characterization in, 11–12; conversion in, 8; and cycles, 14; decline of, 15, 129; and education, 39; and Edward VI, 3; Fitzstephen on, 6, 344 n.5; in France, 14; generic nature of, 12; and Henry VIII, 3; historical nature of, 7, 12; history of, 14–15; and Hroswitha, 4–5; importance of, xxvi; martyrdom in, 5–6, 344 n.5; ministering in imitation of Christ in, 5, 7, 8, 39; miracles in, 6, 8, 14, 344 n.5; and morality plays, 7; performances of, 3, 335; popularity of, xix, 38; and *Protomartyr*, 325; purposes of, xvii, 39, 324; and Reformation, 129, 339; Reginald of Canterbury on, 7; and romances, 15; saints involved, 3; suppression of, 40, 339, 340; symbolism in, 12; and tragedies, 15; unity in, 13. *See also* drama; St. George plays
Satire of the Three Estates, An (Lindsay): allegory in, 217, 221; audience of, 211–12, 215–16; estates in, 223, 226; folk drama elements in, 58, 227; historical nature of, 221; humor in, 215, 216, 222, 225, 226, 228; morality play elements in, 218–19; nobility in, 228; politics in, 217, 218, 219, 221, 222; prodigal play elements in, 218; religion in, 212, 215, 216, 219–20, 221, 222–26, 227, 228, 339–40; satire in, 222–23, 227, 228; themes in, 215; versions of, 211–12, 213, 216–17, 223; vices and virtues in, 217–20, 221, 223–28; war in, 228; women in, 227; wooing play elements in, 227
Schelling, Felix, 357 n.6
schooling. *See* education
scriptural plays. *See* civic drama
Second Shepherds' Play, The (Anonymous), 32
Secretum Secretorum (Anonymous), 176, 181
Seneca, Lucius Annaeus: and education, xxvii; Erasmus on, 86; importance of, 337; Vives on, 105; Watson on, 297
sermons, 38
Seymour, Jane, xviii
Seymour, Thomas, xix
Sirith, Dame, 251
Six Articles (1539), 190, 193

Solway Moss, 212, 221
Somerset, Duke of, xviii–xix
Speculum Principis (Skelton), 178
Stevenson, William, 281–82, 357 n.3
St. George plays: contest and cure in, 57; and education, 65; history of, 48, 49; performances of, 53. *See also* folk drama; saints' plays
Supplicatioun to the Kingis Grace (Lindsay), 212

Temptacyon of our Lorde (Bale), 320
Ten Articles (1536), 190, 193
Terence and Terence's comedies: Agrippa on, xxi; Augustine on, 81; Badius on, 78–79; characterization in, 93; decorum in, 77–78, 93–94, 348 n.9; Donatus on, 68, 69, 70, 72–73, 76, 77–78, 81, 356 n.6; editions of, 65–66, 67; and education, xxi, xxiv, xxvii, 65, 66–68, 69–70, 73, 80, 85, 89, 90, 94, 336; Erasmus on, xxi, 67, 71–72, 81, 84–85, 88, 89, 93, 94, 336; Evanthius on, 77, 78, 82–83; foreshadowing in, 77; form of, 70, 76, 82–83, 84–85, 88; Herrick on, 348 n.9; and Hroswitha, 5; importance of, 337; as "knot of errors," 290; Latomus on, 76; Melanchthon on, 80, 336; morality in, 80; *oeconomia* of, 76–77; performances of, 69; Rivius on, 80–81; Theiner on, 67; Vives on, 81, 99, 104, 105, 336; Wagnerus on, 82; Wolsey on, 68–69
Testament and Complaynt of Papyngo (Lindsay), 210–11
textbooks. *See* education
Theiner, Paul, 67
Thersites (Anonymous), 272
Thompson, Craig, 91
Timber (Jonson), 110
Tobriner, Marian, 100

touring companies, xx
Towneley plays: Christ in, 24; history of, 17–18, 344 n.1 n.2; humor in, 24; Joseph in, 25; pathos in, 24; realism in, 21, 24; staging of, 346 n.16. *See also* civic drama
Tragedie of the Umquhle Maist Reuerent Father Dauid, The (Lindsay), 212–13
tragedies: defense of, 142–43; defined, 143, 350 n.3; and education, 295; Elyot on, 295; history of, xxv–xxvi; and humanists, xxv, 142–43; Luther on, 296; Melanchthon on, 295; and Oxford University, 319, 358 n.2; performances of, xxv; purposes of, 295; and Reformation, 338; and saints' plays, 15. *See also* drama
Tragicomedia de Calisto y Melibea, La (Rojas), 244, 245–46, 247–51, 252–53
traveling companies, xx
Treatise upon the Passion, A (More), 125
Tretise of Miraclis Pleyinge, A (Anonymous): audience of, 324–25; civic drama in, xix, 19–20; realism in, 21; saints' plays in, xix, 5

Udall, Nicholas: and education, 207–8, 267, 268, 269, 356 n.5; and Edward VI, 208; and Henry VIII, 208; history of, 207–8; and Mary I, 208–9, 278; on religion, 208, 353 n.8; as translator, 208, 269, 356 n.5
Utopia (More), 118–23

Vives, Juan Luis: on Aristophanes, 105–6; on Aristotle, 105; Baldwin on, 96, 109; on Cicero, 105; on comedies, 102, 103, 104, 349 n.6; on Donatus, 104, 349 n.7; on drama, xxi, 99–100, 102, 105, 106–8, 109–10, 349 n.5 n.8; and education, xxii, 95, 99, 101, 102–

Vives, Juan Luis (*cont.*)
    3, 104, 105, 106–7, 108–9; Estelrich on, 108–9; on Euripides, 105; Hogrefe on, 109; on Homer, 106; importance of, 108–10; Jonson on, 110; on More, 124; Noreña on, 96, 109; Parmentier on, 109; on Plato, 98–99; on Plautus, 104; on poetry, 98–99, 102, 104, 105, 107; Rainolds on, 103–4; and Reformation, 338; on rhetoric, 106; on Seneca, 105; on Terence and Terence's comedies, 81, 99, 104, 105, 336; Tobriner on, 100; on *Tragicomedia de Calisto y Melibea*, 245; on vices and virtues, 100, 102–3, 104–5, 107–8, 109; Watson on, 108, 109
Volpone (Jonson), 59

Wagnerus, 82
Wakefield plays. *See* Towneley plays
wandering players, xx
Wasson, John, 37
Watson, Foster, 108, 109
Watson, Thomas, 297, 298
Why Come Ye Nat to Court (Skelton), 179
Wickham, Glynne, 13, 19
Williams, Arnold, 38
Willichius, 72
Wisdom (Anonymous), 41–42

Wishart, George, 213
Wit and Science (Redford): allegory in, 161, 162, 163–64, 165, 166, 168–69, 170; audience of, 162, 170; costumes in, 166–67, 168, 351 n.4; education in, xxiii, 165, 169–70; folk drama elements in, 161, 165–66, 170; knowledge in, 169–70; mirror in, 164, 166, 167, 351 n.3; morality play elements in, 161, 166–68, 170; music in, 162, 169; pageant elements in, 170; portrait in, 164, 167; quest in, 161; repentance in, 168; romance in, 170; staging of, 162–63; symbolism in, 168. See also *Marriage Between Wit and Wisdom, The* (Merbury); *Marriage of Wit and Science, The* (Westcott)
Wolsey, Thomas, 68–69
wooing plays, 271, 356 n.8
Woolf, Rosemary, 18
Woorke of Ioannes Ferrarius Montanus, A (Ferrarius), 143–44

York plays: Christ in, 24; history of, 17–18; Joseph in, 25; number of actors in, 33, 346 n.15; pathos in, 24; realism in, 21, 24. *See also* civic drama
Young, Karl, 357 n.6
Youth (Anonymous), 44, 46